The Vulgar Tongue

Also by Jonathon Green

Green's Dictionary of Slang
Chambers Slang Dictionary
Chasing the Sun
Slang Down the Ages

The Vulgar Tongue
Green's History of Slang

Jonathon Green

OXFORD

UNIVERSITY PRESS

OXFORD
UNIVERSITY PRESS

Oxford University Press is a department of the
University of Oxford. It furthers the University's objective
of excellence in research, scholarship, and education
by publishing worldwide.

Oxford   New York
Auckland   Cape Town   Dar es Salaam   Hong Kong   Karachi
Kuala Lumpur   Madrid   Melbourne   Mexico City   Nairobi
New Delhi   Shanghai   Taipei   Toronto

With offices in
Argentina   Austria   Brazil   Chile   Czech Republic   France   Greece
Guatemala   Hungary   Italy   Japan   Poland   Portugal   Singapore
South Korea   Switzerland   Thailand   Turkey   Ukraine   Vietnam

Oxford is a registered trade mark of Oxford University Press
in the UK and certain other countries.

Published in the United States of America by
Oxford University Press
198 Madison Avenue, New York, NY 10016

Library of Congress Cataloging-in-Publication Data
Green, Jonathon, 1948- author.
The vulgar tongue : Green's history of slang / Jonathon Green.
   pages   cm
Includes bibliographical references and index.
ISBN 978-0-19-939814-0 (hardback)—ISBN 978-0-19-939816-4 (ebook)—
ISBN 978-0-19-939815-7 (ebook)   1. English language—Slang—History.
I. Title.   II. Title: Green's history of slang.   III. Title: History of slang.
PE3711.G745 2014
427—dc23   2014018521

9 8 7 6 5 4 3 2 1
Printed in the United States of America
on acid-free paper

For Richard Milbank, editor and friend

Contents

Preface

This is a history of slang, the city's language.

It is an under-discussed topic and with one exception[1] the last book-length attempt to tackle that history came in 1933: the slang lexicographer Eric Partridge's *Slang To-day and Yesterday*. In his case his researches were somewhat tentative, since he had yet to embark on the dictionaries that would make him the twentieth century's leading collector of the language. I can offer no such excuse: what follows is drawn from thirty years of slang study, and for much of the purely lexical research I have extracted material from the twenty years of work amassed by myself and others in making the multi-volume *Green's Dictionary of Slang* (2010) and on my continuing expansion and improvement of the database that underpins it.

Linguists have not, in general, paused to look that hard at slang. I am not one and I cannot pretend to remedy that omission. What I offer is very much the story of the language, its development and proliferation, those who have used it in plays, novels, journalism and other forms of story-telling and media, and, where necessary, those who have, especially in its early days, kept it alive by collecting it into glossaries and then dictionaries.

Thus this is a lexicographer's history, and in that I am following a tradition. Those few who have attempted to offer the history of the language have always been those who knew it first as practice, and collected the underlying history and devolved their theories afterwards. Without their dictionaries, in which such information appears as an introduction, we would know even less of the subject. What they and I offer is, one might say, a figurative 'etymology' of a whole lexis. The story not just of a single word or phrase, but of an entire vocabulary.

It is also the lexicographer-historian who has privileged access to the extent of slang, the sheer size of the lexis. As will be seen, that lexis is governed by a variety of dominant themes, and thus offers substantial areas of synonymy, but it cannot be made too clear that there is much more to the vocabulary than the misguided popular assumption that limits slang to a few dozen so-called obscenities and a page or two of rhyming slang. Standard English covers all the areas that does slang, but slang illumines them in unprecedentedly creative ways.

This is not the history of all slang – that is, every one of the near 120,000 words that make up a lexis that has been recorded for half a millennium, and from across the English-speaking world. Instead I have focused on certain strands that run through the word-list. If it can offer no other defining aspect, then slang offers a highly thematic vocabulary: sex both private and commercial; crime in all its aspects, bodily parts and functions, insults both person-to-person and racist/nationalist, drink and drugs ... One can see these themes in embryo when slang was originally recorded, and they remain its staples today. Reading such examples as I have included, one can see them in every instance of use and collection. There are local differences – typically the different styles and stimuli in America or Australia – but the over-riding themes will always emerge. Slang represents humanity at its most human, and that is not fettered by borders. Were I to have essayed non-anglophone slangs, I am certain that nothing would have changed.

The book is based roughly on chronological development, but after the eighteenth century, with the gradual accretion of the home-grown slangs of Australia and the United States, and the emergence of special slangs such as those of the campus, this must to an extent be abandoned, since developments are running in parallel. I have also chosen, among other subject-specific enquiries — among them slangs of students, teenagers, and of homosexuality — to approach the vastly important subject of African-American slang by itself. That anglophone slang is now dominated by America, and especially black America, might be thought to return everything to a central track, but as is the case throughout, niche vocabularies have ensured that there are now many slangs on offer.

If the early centuries of slang's recorded existence permit one to read most if not all of that limited roster of authors who allow its words into their work, initially as the criminal language *cant* and then expanding to include more general material, by the nineteenth century that aim has been defeated, and since then rendered a foolish dream. Even the long-term lexicographer can only hope to sample. And with the arrival of the on-line riches of the internet, even sampling becomes harder by the day. What I have attempted is to use literary and where pertinent social developments to give the slang vocabulary a backdrop. For that I have had to select, ever more so as time progresses. I have chosen exemplars and looked at them in detail, but I have no doubt that rivals could exist and that those rivals could be used to assert the same points. To me this persistent expansion is one of slang's glories. Like the Chinese trickster Monkey, it remains irrepressible.

Slang's trajectory has been social as well as linguistic. Beginning, at least in recorded terms, in the gutter and the thieves' tavern, and displayed only in a few criminological pamphlets, it has made its way up and out: across classes and into every medium. If the iceberg was once almost wholly submerged, some kind of sociolinguistic global melting has spread its waters throughout the sea of general speech. Even if at its creative core there remains an irreducible minimum of consciously developed incomprehensibility. Slang, after all, is not intended for unfettered understanding. But that secrecy has also eroded: modern communications are simply too fast and too omnivorous of all forms of available information. And slang, once despised, has become alluring, sexy, 'cool'. There is a need to know and thus to use. In language terms it remains a thing apart, but like cool itself, now wholly accessible.

For me slang represents in its preoccupations both the circus and the sewer, the unfettered pleasure principle and that which is consciously hidden and only shamefully revealed: the 'dirty words' as some would term them. Yet it remains as much a part of the English language as any other of its subsets. It is not standard, it has no wish to be, but it has a role to play and it is sustained and will continue to be used and to be invented. This is not its whole story – we have no concrete 'beginning' and while humanity thrives there is no reason for there to arrive an 'end' – but it is my hope that I have laid out a good representation of what we have.

Jonathon Green
London and Paris, 2013

1 Introduction:
Slang: A User's Manual

Slang: The Language That Says 'No'

Slang, widely seen as 'the language of streets', is far harder to define than it is to use. There have been dozens of definitions, whether lexicographical, linguistic, or simply from those who want to pin down something so hugely popular, yet so elusive. It seems sensible, then, to turn to the people who throng those streets for the current version. This is what we find in Wikipedia,[1] the distilled wisdom of the crowd:

> Slang [...] the use of informal words and expressions that are not considered standard in the speaker's dialect or language. Slang is often to be found in areas of the lexicon that refer to things considered taboo (see euphemism). It is often used to identify with one's peers and, although it may be common among young people, it is used by people of all ages and social groups.

There is nothing there to dispute. But there is much to add. The definitions found in works of reference are by their nature concise, pared to the bone. They do not deal in nuance. Let us, at the outset, add some suggestions.

Above all its functions, slang is a 'counter-language', the language that says no. Born in the street, it resists the niceties of the respectable. It is impertinent, mocking, unconvinced by rules, regulations and ideologies. It is a subset of language that since its earliest appearance has been linked to the lower depths, the criminal, the marginal, the unwanted or even persecuted members of society. It has been censored, ignored, shoved to one side and into the gutter from where it is widely believed to take its inspiration and in which it and its users have a home. It remains something apart, and for many that is where it should stay.

Yet slang is vibrant, creative, witty, and open to seemingly infinite re-invention. It is voyeuristic, amoral, libertarian and libertine. It is vicious. It is cruel. It is self-indulgent. It is funny. It is fun. Its dictionaries offer an oral history of marginality and rebellion, of dispossession and frustration. They list the words that have evolved to challenge those states. It is supremely human.

It subscribes to nothing but itself – no belief systems, no true believers, no faith, no religion, no politics, no party. It is the linguistic version of Freud's *id*, defined by him as 'the dark, inaccessible part of our personality [...] It is filled with energy reaching it from the instincts, but it has no organization, produces no collective will, but only a striving to bring about the satisfaction of the instinctual needs subject to the observance of the pleasure principle.'[2]

Slang is urban. The countryside has region-based dialect, or did, as dialect has been eroding since the industrial revolution began moving former peasants off the farm into the factory. The history of slang is also the history of the urbanization of modern life as reflected in this influential subset of the language. One may suggest a simple rule: no city, no slang.

One need only look at the dictionary definitions of slang to see what it is that links the city and its language: the over-riding suggestion is of speed, fluidity, movement. The words that recur are 'casual', 'playful', 'ephemeral', 'racy', 'humorous', 'irreverent'. The slang words themselves are twisted, turned, snapped off short, re-launched at a skewed angle. Some with their multiple, and often contrasting definitions seem infinitely malleable, shape-shifting: who knows what hides round their syllabic corners. It is a language that requires the city's hustle and bustle, its rush, lights, excitement and even its muted (sometimes far from muted) sense of impending threat. Then there are the value judgements: 'sub-standard', 'low', 'vulgar', 'unauthorized'. The word we are seeking is *street*. Street as noun, more recently street as adjective. The vulgar tongue. The gutter language.

Slang, it is often suggested, represents the users' innate inarticulacy. Their inability to use standard language. Not so. The reality is that slang remains in a state of constant reinvention. Even if that reinvention is not coming from elite sources. It is harder now to argue that slang is a secret language, as was once undoubtedly true. The speed of modern information transfer makes that level of secrecy almost impossible. Nonetheless the need for a level of perceived secrecy remains: when a slang word is coined it may well enjoy a period, however brief, of 'invisibility'. But once it has become 'revealed', then the immediate need is for re-coinage. A term may be ephemeral (though much slang is remarkably long-lived), but the imagery behind it, the great recurrent themes of the lexis remain the same.

Thus far an imagistic approach to a language, because if a means of communication is a language then slang is surely such, as much as any other subset – jargon, technicalities, regionalisms – a part of the over-arching *English language*. It is on equal terms with standard English, the language, traditionally, of the broadsheet press, the BBC news and other top-down communicators. Slang may be considered 'worse' than standard English and suffers such slipshod condemnations as 'bad' language or 'swear-words', but such dismissals spring from ignorance. Prejudice, not fact. In linguistic terms it is a cousin, a somewhat raffish and rackety one no doubt, but in no way a poor relation nor a black sheep. If it is scorned, the scorn is the product of fear and suspicion, and even, given slang's wonderful inventiveness, of jealousy.

At the same time, if slang is to be positioned as an innately oppositional language, it is necessary to identify the established version against which it is opposed. The concept of *standard English* is not recorded in print until 1836 but its development is generally accepted as starting in the fifteenth century. And according to the historian Alfred C. Baugh, this language was essentially that as used by the power centres that focused on contemporary London. 'It was the seat of the court, of the highest judicial tribunals, the focus of the social and intellectual activities of the country. To it were drawn in a constant stream those whose affairs took them beyond the limits of their provincial homes. They brought to it traits of their local speech, there to mingle with the London idiom and to survive or die as the silent forces of amalgamation and standardization determined. They took back with them the forms and usages of the great city by which their own speech had been modified.'[3]

It is now argued whether, as Baugh suggests, this development expanded via top-down osmosis, and encompassed both written and spoken language, or whether it was actively imposed through clerical and educational authorities using formal systems to spread a standard. In either case standard English became establishment English and literary English.

All this is widely and well attested. Such is not the case for slang. As will be seen in chapter 2, language that featured 'vulgar' themes – sex, parts of the body, defecation, commercial sex – existed and might already be found in the middle English (pre-1450) used by such as Chaucer, and must have continued on, but it cannot yet be listed as 'slang'. It is simply what Baugh terms 'vulgar or illiterate speech [...] the language of those who are ignorant of or indifferent to the ideals of correctness by which the educated are governed'.[4] It may well be that such words were in wide and popular use but they were rarely recorded and would certainly not have been included in standard speech or writing. Like the vocabularies of regional dialects, also excluded from the standard as London English took control, they were the losers, as it were, in the struggle. The difference, of course, is that slang was just as much a city speech; it was the source – the street rather than the court – that was then, and for centuries beyond, what mattered.

Slang may oppose standard English but it never abandons it. It rejects large areas of standard terms, notably those that move beyond concrete description to abstract conceptualizing, but it suborns a great deal. Like the mature poet, slang steals quite unashamedly and a breakdown of etymological roots shows that the majority of slang terms can be found in the standard dictionaries, but with their meanings turned, twisted and skewed, upside-down and inside-out, larded with a solid layer of irony or wit.

The Etymology of the Word 'Slang'

Where – as a word – does slang come from? Before looking, however constrainedly, at what comprises this particular subset, what about the word itself? Does it remain what my great predecessor Eric Partridge called it: 'that prize-problem word'?[5]

Although the currently accepted first use of the word in the context of language is dated to 1756, there is evidence through the 1740s of alternative senses, though all are underpinned by some idea of duplicity: a line of work (first found in 1741), nonsense (1747) and, as a verb, to cheat, to swindle, to defraud (1741) and to abuse or banter with (1749). There is also 'A Plan for a Hospital for Decayed Thief-Takers', a document attributed to the thief-taker and receiver Jonathan Wild, which contains the line: 'The master who teaches them should be a man well versed in the cant language, commonly called the Slang Patter, in which they should by all means excel.' Wild was hanged in 1725; the pamphlet is dated 1758. And while it was allegedly 'printed from a manuscript, said to be written by Jonathan Wild while under condemnation in Newgate', its signature 'Henry Humbug' almost certainly suggests a later, satirical author. (Though to what extent, given the paucity of citations, cant was 'commonly called the Slang Patter' even in 1758 remains debatable. The next such use is not until a ballad of the 1780s.)

The word was yet to reach the dictionary and no useful attempt at an etymology was proposed prior to that of the slang lexicographer John Camden Hotten in 1859. 'The word Slang is only mentioned by two lexicographers Webster and Ogilvie. Johnson, Walker, and the older compilers of dictionaries give "slang" as the preterite of "sling," but not a word about Slang in the sense of low, vulgar, or unrecognised language. The origin of the word has often been asked for in literary journals and books, but only one man, until recently, ever hazarded an etymology Jonathan Bee. With a recklessness peculiar to ignorance, Bee stated that Slang was derived from "the slangs or fetters worn by prisoners, having acquired that name from the manner in which they were worn, as they required a sling of string to keep them off the ground".'[6] Hotten's own belief was that 'Slang is not an English word; it is the Gipsy term for their secret language, and its synonym is Gibberish another word which was believed to have had no distinct origin.'[7]

Neither Barrère and Leland (1889–90) nor Farmer and Henley (1890–1904) took things any further in their slang dictionaries. It was left to the professionals at the on-going *OED*. Sir William Craigie, dealing with *slang* in its first edition, took that Dictionary's usual cautious view on such matters: it was 'a word of cant origin, the ultimate source of which is not apparent'; this refusal to hazard any further guess has not been modified since. Craigie compounded his rejection of possible origins with a further note: 'the date and early associations of the word make it unlikely that there is any connection with certain Norwegian forms in *sleng-* which exhibit some approximation in sense'. This flat declaration ran quite contrary to the views of another Oxford philologist, Walter Skeat, whose *Etymological Dictionary of the English Language* had appeared between 1879 and 1882. Skeat attributed *slang* unequivocally to the Scandinavian languages. Listing such terms as the Norwegian *sleng* ('a slinging, an invention, device, stratagem ... a little addition or burthen of a song, in verse and melody'), *ettersleng* (lit. afterslang, 'a burthen at the end of a verse or ballad'), *slengjenamn* (a nickname), *slengjeord* (an insulting word or allusion), the Icelandic *slyngr* and *slunginn* (well-versed in, cunning), and the Swedish *slanger* (to gossip), Skeat showed himself free of all doubt: 'that all the above Norwegian and Icelandic words are derivatives from "sling" is quite clear ... I see no objection to this explanation'. Contemporary etymologists tended to follow Skeat. More recently Eric Partridge, never one to let caution fetter his own deductive skills, modified the Norwegian thesis in his own etymological dictionary. For him *slang* is a dialect past participle of the verb *sling*, which has its roots in Old and Middle English and links to Old Norse, thus giving the concept of 'slung' or 'thrown' language. This conveniently encompasses the abusive side of slang, e.g. 'sling off at', and is duly bolstered by the Norwegian *slenga keften* (also cited by Skeat), lit. to 'sling the jaw', and thus, literally, to use slang, as well as Skeat's *slengjeord*. The current, on-line *OED* remains unconvinced.

Definitions

Thus the roots, or lack of them; what of the definition? Set firmly amid respectable language by the *OED*, *slang* as a word remains essentially unchanged as to its definitions and in its use, even if it continues to develop as a vocabulary. The philologists and lexicographers remain generally consistent in their opinions. Since the *OED* laid down lexicographical law they may have replaced simple definition by more complex explanation, but they differ only in the nuances.

'Slang is a poor man's poetry,'[8] suggested John Moore in *You English Words* (1962), a sentiment underpinning the title of the American academic Michael Adams's study *Slang: the People's Poetry* (2009). And like the poor, to whom must be attributed credit for the coinage, or at least the popularization of a major portion of its vocabulary, slang is always with us. Whether, as one observer suggests, it is the working man of language, doing the lexicon's 'dirty work' or, as Moore and Adams imply, it represents the lyrical creativity of the disenfranchised or, as its many critics still proclaim, it has nothing but the most deleterious effects on 'proper speech', slang remains a law unto itself.

As a linguistic phenomenon it surely predates the Christian era. The mid-nineteenth-century slang lexicographer John Camden Hotten, as keen as any other Victorian scholar to find antecedents in the classical and pre-classical worlds, offers the readers of his *Slang Dictionary* (1859) an alluring, if somewhat fantastical picture of this 'universal and ancient' species of language. 'If we are to believe implicitly the saying of the *wise man*, that "there is nothing new under the sun" the "fast" men of buried Nincvch, with their knotty and door-matty looking beards, may have cracked Slang jokes on the steps of Sennacherib's palace; and the stones of Ancient Egypt, and the bricks of venerable and used up Babylon, may, for aught we know, be covered with slang hieroglyphics unknown to modern antiquarians ...' As a word in itself, however, it only emerges into the (printed) language in the mid-eighteenth century. The *Oxford English Dictionary* (1933 and unrevised at the time of writing), which included primarily that slang terminology which occurred in literature and in the sixteenth- and seventeenth-century glossarists, defined the term as 'The special vocabulary used by any set of persons of a low or disreputable character; language of a low a vulgar type', and adds somewhat circuitously, 'Language of a highly colloquial type, considered as below the level of standard educated speech, and consisting either of new words or of current words employed in some special sense'. (*Colloquial* being defined as 'Belonging to common speech; characteristic of or proper to ordinary conversation, as distinguished from formal or elevated language'.) The word is so far first recorded in 1756, when in

Act I of William Toldervy's play *The History of the Two Orphans* one finds
'Thomas Throw had been upon the town, knew the slang well; [...] and
understood every word in the scoundrel's dictionary.' And immediately
one is faced by a possible question. Was Throw's 'slang' a reference to
his speech, or to a duplicitous and probably criminal way of conducting
himself? Given the final phrase, one may suppose that the reference is
indeed to his vocabulary. In which case the slang in question is no more
than a synonym for *cant*, or criminal jargon, and does not involve the
more general sense of today. (Toldervy himself 'knew the slang' as well.
Among the hundred-plus examples in his play are *dewbeaters*, shoes,
fribble, an impotent male, and *corner-cupboard*, the vagina.) By the turn
of the century the definitions had broadened.

As well as standing synonymous with cant, slang began to be used
as an alternative to jargon or 'professional slang' by such luminaries as
Charles Kingsley (in a letter of 1857). George Eliot (in *Middlemarch*, 1872)
referred not merely to the slang of shopkeepers (decrying 'superior' as
used of comestibles) but added that 'all choice of words is a slang [...]
correct English is the slang of prigs who write history and essays. And
the strongest slang of all is the slang of poets.'[9] G. A. Sala, in his 1856
essay for Dickens's *Household Words* (see Chapter 7), attacks slang, but
seems to be targeting the affectations and idiosyncrasies of various styles
of standard speech, rather than the lists of vulgar synonyms (for 'drunk',
etc.) which he appears despite his protestations to revel in itemizing.
More notably the word, if not the vocabulary, had been enlisted in
standard English by the mid-century and dignified by John Keble (in
1818), Thackeray (in *Vanity Fair*, 1848) and many other respectable users.
In 1858 Trollope, in *Dr Thorne*, a story featuring murder, seduction and
bastardy, speaks of 'fast, slang men, who were fast and slang and nothing
else', a citation that points up both their language and their rakehell,
buckish style.

Across the Channel, Balzac, writing of *argot*, the French equivalent to
cant, proclaimed that 'there is no more energetic or colourful language
than that of this subterranean world'.[10] Victor Hugo was less tolerant.
His 'condemned man' shrank from it as 'an odious phraseology grafted
on the general language, like a hideous excrescence'.[11] And in a whole
chapter devoted to argot in *Les Misérables*, Hugo saw it as 'a sort of

repellent animal intended to dwell in darkness which has been dragged out of its cloaca. One seems to see a horned and living creature viciously struggling to be restored to the place where it belongs. One word is like a claw, another like a sightless and bleeding eye; and there are phrases which clutch like the pincers of a crab. And all of it is alive with the hideous vitality of things that have organized themselves amid disorganization', and termed it 'a horrid murmur, resembling the human accent but nearer to growls than to words. That is argot. The words are misshapen, distorted by some kind of fantastic bestiality. We might be hearing the speech of hydras. It is the unintelligible immersed in shadow; it grunts and whispers, adding enigma to the encircling gloom. Misfortune is dark and crime is darker still, and it is of these two darknesses put together that argot is composed.'[12] Yet it was also Hugo who, in the *Hunchback of Notre-Dame*, evoked the 'kingdom of Argot' and all its supposed citizens, a tour de force of imaginative creation.

Zola, typically in *L'Assommoir* (1877), made it a cornerstone of literary realism, but Zola's use of argot and *langue populaire* elicited widespread criticism and in the UK such language was cited alongside his alleged 'immorality' as justification to ban his work and in 1889 to imprison Henry Vizetelly, the publisher who put it out in translation.

Francis Grose in his dictionary of 1785 defines it as 'cant language'. (Pierce Egan, in his revision of 1823, has dropped the entry.) But Grose does not expand, and the first 'proper' dictionary definition is to be found written by Noah Webster in 1828: 'low, vulgar, unmeaning language'. Webster's successors offered a variety of takes. Examples include the 1864 *Webster-Mahn*, which amended its definition to read: 'low, vulgar, unauthorized language; a colloquial mode of expression, especially such as is in vogue with some class in society'. Discussing 'The Rationale of Slang' (1870), the *Overland Monthly* defined it as the 'spontaneous outburst of the thought power become vocal' and noted that the lexis had no purpose 'other than emphasis or illustration'.[13] Webster's rival, Joseph Worcester (1879), called it 'vile, low, or vulgar language; the cant of sharpers or of the vulgar; gibberish'. Brander Matthews, writing in *Harper's* magazine on 'The Function of Slang' (1893),[14] defined it as 'A word or phrase used with a meaning not recognized in polite letters, either because it had just been invented, or because it had passed out of memory … A collection of colloquialisms gathered from all sources, and all bearing alike the bend sinister of illegitimacy.'

In 1913, the *New Standard Dictionary* explained slang as 'the speech or dialect of a special sect, profession, or class of persons' and added that slang is used for 'expressions that are either coarse and rude in themselves or chiefly current among the coarser and ruder parts of the community'. The *OED*'s somewhat circuitous definition has been noted above. The *New Encyclopedia Britannica* (1982), in a discursive entry written by the cant collector David Maurer, calls it 'unconventional words or phrases that express either something new or something old in a new way. It is flippant, irreverent, indecorous; it may be indecent or obscene. Its colourful metaphors are generally directed at respectability, and it is this succinct, sometimes witty, frequently impertinent social criticism that gives slang its characteristic flavour. Slang, then, includes not just words but words used in a special way in a certain social context.'

To turn to more recent definitions, John Simpson of the *OED* has explained that 'As a rule of thumb we classify a slang word as an alternative to a more formal word, typically used by a subset of the speech population, and a colloquial term as an informal term used widely in the speech community.'[15] The current on-line *Merriam-Webster* has 'an informal nonstandard vocabulary composed typically of coinages, arbitrarily changed words, and extravagant, forced, or facetious figures of speech' (http://www.merriamwebster.com/dictionary/slang). *Gale Cengage Learning* has 'A type of informal verbal communication that is generally unacceptable for formal writing. Slang words and phrases are often colorful exaggerations used to emphasize the speaker's point; they may also be shortened versions of an often-used word or phrase.'[16] Wikipedia's entry is cited above. The *Urban Dictionary*, in sway to lexicographic relativism, offers a choice of thirty-three variant definitions, of which the most popular is the self-congratulatory 'the only reason Urbandictionary.com exists'. The few more reasoned alternatives seem to be far less favoured by the users.

As Hugo's lines suggest, slang has also elicited a good many condemnations, rendering what should be scholarly assessment into mere value judgements. Even moral ones and certainly social assumptions. An unaccountable fear that the streets, even if suppressed economically, are somehow going to rise up linguistically.

Johnson was of course at pains to rid his dictionary of vulgarity, and his initial commission had been to prepare a lexicon of purified English. Slang rarely entered the standard dictionaries, although Elisha Coles allowed some cant in 1676 and Nathan Bailey offered an entire cant appendix in 1730. Critics pontificated *de haut en bas* on both sides of the Atlantic. Typically John F. Genung, who in 1893 announced that 'slang is to a people's language what an epidemic disease is to their bodily constitution; just as catching and just as inevitable in its turn [...] Like a disease, too, it is severest where the sanitary conditions are most neglected.'[17] The idea of slang as a 'disease'; or a 'perversion', not simply of language but of society at large, permeates such remarks. Few, however, could equal the editor James C. Fernald, who commenced his essay 'The Impoverishment of the Language: Cant, Slang, Etc.' in *Progressive English* (1918) thus: 'The touch of decay is upon all things earthly. Frost, rain, and wind are casting down the mountains, and the rivers are washing the rock-dust far out into the sea ... The Pyramids, stripped of the casing of hewn stone that once covered them are now but rude, though mighty towers in the lonely desert. The Parthenon [...] was desolated long ago ... The stately monuments of imperial Rome are dismantled from the top and dust-embedded from the base. Language shares the same tendency to decay.'[18] We may laugh: it would seem that Mr Fernald cried.

And continued: 'Slang, for the most part, comes up from the coarse and more ignorant portion of the community. [...] 'Slang ... saves the trouble – and the glory – of thinking. The same cheap word or phrase may be used for any one of a hundred ideas [...] Slang is the advertisement of mental poverty ... It so largely comes from the coarse and rude elements of our population, or even from the baser associations and pursuits.'[19]

Yay or nay, the reality remains that posited by Jonathan Lighter and Bethany K. Dumas in their 1978 essay 'Is Slang a Word for Linguists?':[20] 'Annoyance and frustration await anyone who searches the professional literature for a definition or even a conception of SLANG that can stand up to scrutiny. Instead one finds impressionism, much of it of a dismaying kind.'[21] And of all the definitions on offer there is much to be said for Lighter's own synthesis, in the *Cambridge History of the English Language*: 'So taking into account the various definitions in dictionaries as well as the more detailed treatments of such authors as Henry Bradley, Stuart Flexner [...] H. L. Mencken, and Eric Partridge, the following definition will be stipulated [...]: Slang denotes an informal, nonstandard, nontechnical vocabulary composed chiefly of novel-sounding synonyms (and near synonyms) for standard words and phrases; it is often associated with youthful, raffish, or undignified persons and groups; and it conveys often striking connotations of impertinence or irreverence, especially for established attitudes and values within the prevailing culture.'[22]

Etymology and definition aside, there is also the question of what is slang. And what is not. The dictionary and other definitions did not attempt this, until in 1933 Eric Partridge, writing his pioneering overview *Slang To-day and Yesterday*, offered some seventeen criteria which might make a word slang. Julie Coleman, in her history *The Story of Slang* (2012), has reduced the qualifications to eleven. Lighter and Dumas cut them down to four. In all cases these calculations would appear to be the product of reverse-engineering the vocabulary. Yet in answering their own question, Lighter and Dumas have made it clear that slang is not, ultimately, a word for linguists, that it cannot be shoehorned into twenty-one, let alone four sizes fit all.

The problem with the various sets of categories is that all assume a conscious will on behalf of the speaker. Mads Holmsgaard Eriksen, in a study on 'Translating the use of slang' prepared as a thesis for Aarhus University in 2010, offers a synthesis of what has come before and states that 'these elements shows us what the function of slang is: a social instrument of words and expressions employed in speech and informal settings in order to create group relations with people you identity with and to rebel against standard language, and to signal the speaker's attitude and the speaker's belief in the listener's ability to relate to and understand what is being said'.[23]

All of which may indeed be the case with slang as found in fiction: take for example the work of a superlative exponent of the style, P. G. Wodehouse, whose 100-plus novels are all saturated with slang, and who used the lexis for a reason. (Its humorous potential being, as story succeeds story, further intensified by the author's disregard for chronological accuracy: late-nineteenth-century terms cheerfully rubbing shoulders with those decades younger.) So too did the Restoration playwrights, the nineteenth-century Newgate novelists and the purveyors of modern *romans noirs*, movie scripts and graphic novels. Slang adds authenticity and atmosphere. Some users, those for whom slang is simply one more fashionable accessory, may use it consciously, but most do not. Their slang use is transparent. It is there, it is the way they talk. One may interrogate, say, an engineer and uncover the language that he uses for professional communications; fieldwork on the street is more difficult. 'What slang?' say the users. They may never use a standard word or phrase, but for them slang *is* the standard. This is not to deny a learning curve, as in any form of communication, and that may be dictated by the norms of the group with whom one wishes to be associated, but no one is thinking 'slang', simply 'that is what I/ we call ...' It is, as Eriksen, paraphrasing Michael Adams, puts it, 'a set of words and expressions in a given language used to create group dynamics'.[24] The problem for members of such groups begins when they move beyond their 'normal' environment and into the wider world. Slang fluency becomes standard inarticulacy and it is that perception that stands behind regular criticisms of the lexis, especially as tied into the currently dominant form of slang – that found in rap music – as underpinning illiteracy, joblessness, street crime and even riots.

This is a lexicographer's history and not a linguist's. Its subject is the words, not pictures of words. Its aim is therefore the accretion of the lexis and the background to that accretion rather than the linguistic status of the register. For all the criteria, for all the inconsistent yet ultimately similar definitions, one is left, like the judge who knows pornography but still cannot say exactly what it is, as knowing it when one meets it. Michael Adams, whose own interest in slang includes his study of the language used in the TV show *Buffy the Vampire Slayer* (*Slayer Slang*, 2003), agrees: 'Slang is what it is. You'll know it when you hear it.'[25] For him much is down to context and the need to create a social link to those with whom one is speaking. Simply checking a dictionary definition, let alone multiple definitions, offers no help. As fellow slang expert Connie Eble puts it: 'Slang cannot be defined independent of its functions and use.'[26] And both cite James B. McMillan from 1978: 'the basic problem of slang lexicology – definition of the class – has not been solved […] Until slang can be objectively identified and segregated (so that dictionaries will not vary in labeling particular lexemes and idioms) or until more precise subcategories replace the catchall label SLANG, little can be done to analyze linguistically this kind of lexis.'[27]

Etymological Roots

Slang, and cant before it, has always been promiscuous in its accretion of sources. At the time of writing my current database runs to approximately 54,000 headword entries (derivations, compounds and phrasal uses bringing the total slang lexis to approximately 125,000 terms). Setting aside some 33% of the etymologies which cross-refer to another slang headword, the first and foremost of these sources is standard English, the twisting, tweaking and otherwise ludic exploitation of which accounts for at least 15% of the vocabulary. In terms of register, rhyming slang and abbreviations offer around 5% each, and lesser roles are played by puns and plays on words (c. 1,400 entries), dialect (870 entries), proper names (375 entries), echoic uses (257 entries) and brand names (90 entries). In terms of languages, the most influential has been French with 400 etymologies, followed by Scottish (305), Latin (241), Irish (220), Afrikaans (212), Yiddish (199), German (195), Italian (162), Dutch (152), Romani (117), Hindi (79), Hebrew (44), Greek (40), Welsh (31), Twi (25), Spanish (21), Zulu (20), Yoruba (14) and Arabic (7).

2 In the Beginning: The Pre-History

As we have seen, John Camden Hotten, writing in 1859, believed that slang was not simply old, but almost pre-historical. 'For aught we know,' he suggested, it was used in Nineveh, Babylon and ancient Egypt.

For aught we know, indeed, but the problem is that we do not know, and while one wishes to state unequivocally 'In the beginning', the story of the earliest slangs might just as well be prefaced 'Once upon a time'. The problem for the lexicographer is that even had such lexes been used, no one seems to have bothered to have acknowledged them, at least for the record, and slang's invariable identification with and use by the less privileged classes of society meant that such texts – one could hardly at this early stage talk of books, nor indeed of publishing – that were set down, eschewed it. It is frustrating, but it would seem that whether or not such *ur*-slangs existed, their vocabulary will remain a secret.

Where, then, can we start? Since one requires evidence, then the best place would seem to be Classical Rome. Yet even here what we are observing is still not the spoken language of the streets, but primarily the image-filled language of literature, delivered in a consciously lower register than the standard and used, as often as not, for conscious effect. But as for spoken Latin, which might provide examples of non-standard usage, the true 'vulgar Latin', as L. R. Palmer has made clear, 'we have no text which is a faithful record of even one mode of contemporary speech […] It is only through their inadvertences, almost willy-nilly, that the writers give us hints that their natural speech deviates from the language of the schoolroom which they are at pains to use.'[1] Certain authors are more useful than others. The comedies of Plautus, the erotic verses of Catullus, the epigrams, often obscene, of Martial, even certain comments by Cicero. Equally productive is *The Priapeia*, a collection of short Latin poems in the shape of usually coarse epigrams affixed to the statues of the god Priapus, itself invariably adorned with an outsize phallus; translated by the orientalist Sir Richard Burton (of *Kama Sutra* fame), it was issued in 1890 by Leonard Smithers, the period's best-known publisher of pornography (as well as of the works of Aubrey Beardsley, Max Beerbohm, Aleister Crowley and Oscar Wilde). Editions had been available, in part or whole, since the mid-fifteenth century. We may also look profitably at some of the insults used in the classical period.

At first glance the Latin vocabulary provides us with the desired evidence. If sufficient proof of slang's origins was to be found in the display of its under-pinning themes, then Latin is undoubtedly a precursor of modernity. As James Allen has laid out in *The Latin Sexual Vocabulary* (1982), terms for the penis, aside from its primary names of *mentula* and *verpa* (an erect or circumcised penis), can be categorized variously as sharp or pointed instruments (*colcata cuspis,* a pointed stem), weapons (*arcum,* a bow, *ensis* and *machaera,* a sword, *sicula,* a dagger), household objects (*pilum,* a pestle, *pondus,* a weight, *rutabulum,* an oven rake or poker), poles and stakes (*caduceus,* a wand, *radius,* a rod, *virgo,* a rod, *virgula,* a wand), agricultural implements (*ligo,* a mattock, *raster,* a hoe, *subucula,* an awl), personifications and animal metaphors (*anguis,* a snake, *passer,* a sparrow, *titus,* a dove, *natrix,* a water-snake or whip; the snake imagery can be found in similar uses in classical Greek), anatomical metaphors (*venus,* literally a vein, *cauda,* a tail, *neruus,* a sinew), tools, implements and vessels (*capula,* a handle, *falx,* a sickle, *vas,* a vessel, *vomer,* a ploughshare), private property (*peculum,* 'the private thing'), as well as metaphors drawn from food (*cuculis,* a cucumber, *olera,* herbs), nature (*curculio,* a corn-worm, a weevil, *caulis,* a cabbage stalk, *thyrsus,* a plant stem), the sea and from music (*pecten,* a plectrum used in playing the lyre). The euphemism *pudenda,* the parts of shame, was still used in slang dictionaries well into the twentieth century. Even the *one-eyed trouser snake* may have a Latin 'ancestor' in the one-off use of *monstrum* by Ausonius:[2] the 'monster' in question, referring in context to the penis, was stolen from Virgil, who was referring to Polyphemus, who of course had but a single eye. It has been argued that *futuo*, used specifically of a male client copulating with a whore, is one of the etymologies of the modern *fuck*. It is unlikely, even if the word was undoubtedly obscene, and lies behind sixteenth-century Italian's *fottuere*, which the Anglo-Italian lexicographer John Florio gave in 1598 as one of his synonyms for *fuck*, and thence French *foutre*.

Looking at my own *Slang Down the Ages* (1986), which deals with the modern lexis, one can find a similar list of penis-metaphors, typically: weapons, knives and daggers, guns, sticks, the hunter, food, proper names, nursery terms, anatomy and euphemism. As in Latin, large, small, erect and flaccid members are also dealt with. If one moves from the penis to the remainder of the sexual world, the situation is the same: the images found in Latin that stand in for the vagina (animals, fields and similar spaces, ditches and pits, caves, containers, doors and pathways) and for sexual intercourse (among them eating, striking, cutting and splitting, digging, wounding, grinding, kneading, ploughing, fighting, working, killing, riding and playing) are similarly echoic across the centuries.

Trium litterarum homo is how Plautus, in *Aulularia* (The Pot of Gold), describes one character. The term is literally a 'man of three letters', and the phrase reappeared in the mid-twentieth century, even if Plautus' acronym spelt F-V-R, a thief, and the modern *three-letter man* has meant F-A-G or G-A-Y, a homosexual. Insults, while sometimes quite formal, can also foreshadow slang's future. And as in modern slang, they use terms of sexuality, criminality and stupidity. Among those listed by Eleanor Dickey[3] are *asine* (ass), *canis* (dog), *cucule* (cuckoo), *excetra* (water-snake) and *vipera* (viper); *furcifer* (one punished with the *furca*), and its superlative *trifurcifer*; *levis* ('light', fickle), *moriture* and *periture* (about to die), *pestis* (plague), *putide* (rotten), *scelerum caput* ('head of crimes'), *mastigia* and *verbero* (one who merits a whipping), and *verpe* (the erect/circumcised penis). The epitome, but far from as common as its successor uses, is *cunne*, literally a cunt. Such are among the standard terms of abuse, but the imagery, again, has continued into modernity. The negative personification of penis has given *prick, cock, knob, dork* and many more. Those who are deemed worthy of death or punishment include the *canary* (as in prisoner) -*bird* and the *gallows-bird*; the use of 'bad' animals, e. g. a *snake*, remains a way of identifying 'bad'; humans, and senses similar to the 'head of crimes' can be found in a range of negative terms using -*head* or -*face* for a suffix.

Yet we must not be seduced too easily. Latin vulgarisms and insults, however much they can be seen as presaging terms that emerge in modern slang, are just that: vulgarisms and insults used in Latin. It is possible that on occasion they were those of the street, and some are borne out in collected graffiti, but compared to the steady drumbeat of modern slang usage they are few and they are far between. That their imagery is familiar is hardly surprising; humanity has not changed that much and the goods and bads of language, any language, tend to reflect similar moral and emotional positions. Not only that, but these early instances of such terms are far from widespread. To return to Professor Palmer, what one is seeing is not consistent use, nor, of course, can one prove that this is language as spoken. As Palmer puts it, within 'the dead landscape of literary Latin' there are 'seismic areas where occasional eruptions reveal the intense subterranean activity'.[4]

These seismic areas, these occasional eruptions, do not increase in volume for virtually 1,400 years after Christ. They remain elusive, even if they may well be active beneath the 'seen' language. And when they do make the surface they generally do so, it should not come as any surprise, as representative of the real underworld, that of crime. Given that as regards the West the Middle Ages were for the slang researcher, as Eric Partridge has said, 'the dark ages',[5] if one seeks slang at that time then one must look East and to the Arabic world, which as in medicine and mathematics was not subjected to the limiting obscurities of omnipresent Christianity. Here the world of the beggars, rogues, criminals and confidence tricksters, known as the *Banu Sāsān*[6] (the Sons of Sāsān), evolved their own slang, or more properly, since it was restricted to that world, criminal jargon or argot. And more vitally, such jargon was recorded in a number of *Quasˌīda Sāsāniyya*, ('Poems about the Banu people'), lengthy poems recounting the underworld life, and larded, naturally, with its terminology. The first of these, by the traveller and physician Abu Dulaf, appeared in the second half of the tenth century, probably in western Iran. A second was written in Iraq four centuries later by the poet Safi d-Din al Hilli. Between them they offer some 540 specific terms. And as such they can be seen as the direct precursors of the European 'beggar books' (see Chapter 3) that are in turn the first emanations of 'slang lexicography'. As well as listing a variety of occupations – snake-charmers, the exhibitors of bears or monkeys, doctors both qualified and quack, a variety of those extolling and exploiting religion, even those who perform 'moonlight flits' to avoid their bills or rent – Abu Dulaf offers beggarly tricks that seem quite timeless.

> 35. And the one who simulates a festering internal wound, and the people with false bandages round their heads and sickly, jaundiced faces. *Al-hājāur* is the person who pierces a hole in an egg, which he secretes in his bosom, so that it oozes out as a yellow liquid. *Al-kadhdhābāt* are bandages which the beggars tie round their foreheads, and in this way make people think that they are ill. [...]

> 37. *Maisara* is when a person begs, alleging that he has come from the frontier region [...] *Makht‚ara* is when a person swallows his tongue, and gives people the impression that the Greeks have cut it out. [...]

> 66. *Wa minnā kullu mamrūr.* These are a group of people who wear ragged clothes and shave off their beards, thereby creating the impression that their minds are deranged through melancholia and have an excess of bile. [...] The generality of people account them mad, and no one punishes them for what they say.

> 67. *Wa-man yakalu.* This is the person who has with him a piece of cotton dipped in olive oil, which he rubs over his eyes to induce a flow of tears. He sets about lamenting his wretched state and accosting people for money, relating the story of how he has been set upon by brigands or how his property has been unjustly confiscated. These *musta'ridūn* are the real aristocracy of the beggars.

All remains, nonetheless, quite fragmentary. In 1200 the West makes its first scratch on the record, and that is only debatable. Around that year one Jehan Bodel (1165–1210), a poet from Arras in north-eastern France and best known for his *chansons de geste* memorializing in verse the derring-do of various kings and knightly nobles, wrote *Le Jeu de Saint Nicolas*. The poem, considered as the first French miracle play, recounts the saint's successful campaign to persuade four thieves to restore a stolen treasure. Within the play, alongside the saint's activities, are those of three villains, found predictably in a tavern, who perform the robbery. Scholars have long since argued as to whether certain of their lines included terms that could be categorized as argot, i.e. criminal language. The glossary to Albert Henry's 1981 edition marks such terms as *geugon* (a potboy), *teme* (to open, lit. to broach), *santissiés* (be quiet, shut up), *asemer* (to render thin), and *dap/paier un dap* (a blow/to cut), as unequivocal 'argot'. However, the argot specialists of the late nineteenth and early twentieth centuries, notably Francisque Michel, Marcel Schwob and Lazare Sainéan, were less impressed. For them argot begins in 1455 with the trial of the Coquillards, posing as legitimate merchants but preying on unfortunate travellers.

Before looking at that, perhaps the first major way station in the collection and assessment of any criminal language, one should re-cross the Channel. The twenty-four stories that make up *The Canterbury Tales*, by Geoffrey Chaucer (*c.* 1343–1400), began appearing in manuscript around 1387. And among them there are undoubtedly what appear to be slang usages, notably in the *Reeve's* and *Miller's Tales*, predictably the most bawdy of the collection.

Given that bawdiness it is unsurprising that the terminology of sex plays a major role: *swive* (to have sexual intercourse), *prick* (to enter a woman), *belle-chose*, *quaint* and *quoniam* (the vagina; all euphemisms, the latter pair playing on *cunt*), *fire* ('of Saint Anthony', i.e. a venereal disease), *gay* (of a woman, leading an immoral life or working as a prostitute), *hot* (sexually aroused and/or available), *honey* and *pigsnyes* (terms of endearment), *loteby* (a mistress), *malkin* (a female) and *wench* (a woman). Defecation was the source of various jokes, and Chaucer uses *arse* and *tail* (the anus or buttocks), *hole* (the anus), *gong* (a privy), *jordan* (a chamberpot), *fart* and *piss* (both found as nouns and verbs), and *shitten* (covered in excrement, filthy). And there were oaths: *Christ!* *cock* (euphemizing God), *for Christ's sake! Gad*, as in *Gad's precious* and *Gad's bones*, and *nails!* which referred to 'god's nails', i.e. those of the crucifixion.

But if Chaucer, as defined by the nineteenth-century literary historian Frank Chandler,[7] 'depicts vice humorously with all the tolerance of a great artist', then one who might be seen as his opposite number, another fourteenth-century author, William Langland (*c.* 1330–*c.* 1386), also offers a small 'slang' lexis. In his great religious allegory of *Piers Plowman*, which appeared in various revisions between 1367 and 1386, he is 'intent upon preaching penitence',[8] but before penitence must come sin, and Langland shows readers 'the arts, lies, hypocrisy, wealth and pride of [...] archdeacons, summoners, pardoners, monks' and the rest of the ecclesiastical hierarchy. In so doing his terminology at times overlaps with that of Chaucer: among the shared terms are *arse, malkin, placebo* and *wench*, the oaths *Jesus!* and *by Christ!* Langland also offers *bacon* (human flesh, and thus a human being), *bitch* (used derogatorily of a woman), *buzzard* (a weak foolish person, a gullible dupe), *catchpole* (a sergeant or bailiff, especially one who arrests for debt), *bad penny* (an unpleasant, untrustworthy person), *daffy* (an eccentric, a mad person and as such used some 520 years before it was next recorded), *dead as a door-nail, grope* (to fondle sexually), *guts* (the stomach), *land-loper* (a vagabond), *lubber* (a fool), *tail* (in his use the vagina), *troll* (to wander around) and *weeds* (clothes).

Nor was the use of such terms restricted to purely canonical writers, although the nature of 'publishing' meant that what has lasted from the period must imply a certain literary longevity. It was certainly far from the streets. The thematic groups that would underpin slang gradually fill out as the fourteenth and fifteenth centuries pass. There is the penis: *bow, cock, lance, pin* and *sword*; the testicles: *ballocks* and *eggs*; the genitals: *privates* and *jewels*, albeit not yet 'family' ones. *Gear, lap, socket*, and *trench* meant the vagina; a *game* was an act of sexual intercourse, as was a *ride*, also found as a verb, *clicket* (usually used of animals), and *jape* (lit. 'to play'). The *horn* stood for cuckoldry, while to *burn* was to be infected with VD.

The prostitute has her role: a *cat*, a *hackney*, a *kate*, a *ramp* and a *tickle-tail*. A *mare* was a mistress while a female *mackerel* ran a brothel;

to be *light*, of a woman, was to be seen as promiscuous and referred to the 'lightness' of her heels, so easily raised towards the ceiling. There were terms of communication: *blow* (to discredit, to defame), *cackler* (a tale-teller, one who talks 'out of turn'), *capron hardy* (an impudent fellow; calqued from the synonymous French *capron hardi*, lit. 'a bold hood', the garment metonymizing the man), *choking oyster* (a reply that silences one's opponent), *sneck drawer* (a flatterer), *tilly-vally* (nonsense). *Mompyns* were teeth, *muzzle* the face. And there was naturally crime: *barker* (a thug), *bell-wether* (the leader of a mob), *lime-twig* (a thief; their 'sticky fingers'), *moocher* (a petty thief), *pilgarlic* (an outcast), *scour* (to wear fetters).

That these terms would in time enter the slang dictionaries is unarguable. But we must still ask: at the time that they were used, the mid to late fourteenth century, can they be classified as 'slang'. Unlike the beggar books of the sixteenth century, they are undoubtedly nearer to what would become 'civilian' slang, France's *langue populaire* or *argot commun* – there is no criminal jargon in either list – and their preoccupations are very much those that continue to underpin the slang lexis seven centuries later: the parts of the body, sexuality, defecation, misogyny, insults. They are also voiced by the lower classes of society. Again, a near prerequisite of slang. And it is true that for research purposes they offer the lexicographer some very early uses of the terms in question. Nor, in certain cases, are they even the oldest uses. Abbot Aelfric's Latin to Anglo-Saxon *Glossary* (*c.* 1000) translates podex as *ars* and testiculi as *beallucas*, the 'ancestor' of the modern bollocks. No one would pretend that the writer-theologian was an adept of the counter-language.

One might argue that because there yet exists no definition for a phenomenon, in this case slang, that is not to say that it does not exist in itself. And again, one can say that because of the topics and themes with which they were concerned, when slang was defined and corralled off from standard English these words would qualify for that lexis. But at a time when there was no such concept as slang, they were not slang. What they were, at a time when the elites still spoke Norman French, or even Latin, was *English*, in linguistic terms Middle English, and still something of an upstart. This was not the vocabulary of elite speakers, but of the wider population, who had not fallen prey to the French cultural ascendancy that had followed on the Norman Conquest. Like slang, English, it might be suggested, started in the street. What they spoke was the vulgar tongue, the idea of which in 1785 provided Francis Grose with a title for his influential slang dictionary. Vulgar as in Latin's *vulgus*, the crowd.

Seventy years after Chaucer, and back again across *La Manche*, we finally reach the first concrete examples of what, if not slang, would in lexicographical terms be its immediate precursor: criminal jargon, known, since the backdrop is France, as *argot*. The document in question, while not a beggar book as such — it was taken from evidence given at a trial — can be linked directly to those pamphlets that emerged across western Europe over the next century and beyond. The subject was undoubtedly criminal vagabonds, though they posed as merchants rather than beggars, and the language was theirs.

The trial, held in 1455, was that of the Coquillards, a gang of criminal wanderers made up mainly of ex-soldiers of the Hundred Years War, which had effectively ended a decade earlier. The source of their name is debatable. The obvious root being the 'coquille' or cockle, as worn by genuine pilgrims to the shrine of St James of Compostela. However, while there were undoubtedly some fake pilgrims, who sported the 'coquille', the Coquillards were as much violent robbers as they were merely con-men. Writing in his *Anthologie de la Littérature Argotique* (1985), Jacques Cellard offers an alternative root: the popular saying that all merchants of cockles were liars and tricksters who ate the flesh of an oyster and left their foolish customers nothing but the shell. And Marcel Schwob, in a detailed discussion, refers the reader to such phrases as *vendre coquilles* and *dresser un coquille*, both of which idioms mean to trick or con, presumably from the same imagery. The link to real-life merchants is underpinned by the French lexicographer Pierre Guiraud,[9] who notes that far from being mendicants, the Coquillards presented themselves as successful merchants, often accompanied by a servant, who dealt in gold and precious stones. He also makes a link, which he admits might be considered 'poetic', between the *escargot* or snail, which has its *coquille*, or shell, and the word *escargueter*, to set a trap.

Whatever their etymology, the Coquillards, anything from 500 to 1,000 in number, plied their trade from the 1440s around Dijon, in eastern France. Not a gang as such, they still boasted a degree of organization, including in their ranks a variety of criminal specialists, whether violent or otherwise. By 1450 they were considered a major problem; the Dijon authorities demanded an enquiry, to be led by one Jean Rabustel. In 1455 he arrested a dozen Coquillards, and with them some of their otherwise respectable bourgeois accomplices, but all maintained their *omertà*. Only when he offered to set free the youngest of the band, one Dimanche le Loup, in return for betraying his companions did Rabustel achieve a breakthrough. (Le Loup, it appears, was still one of those hanged after the trial.) After Le Loup came another informer, the barber Perrent le Fournier. The two volunteered much information, notably a list of names and, more importantly for lexicographers, the language or private jargon that the Coquillards used. The accused were tried: three were hanged, the rest banished from Dijon.

Other than a few words encountered in the mouths of brigands, hangmen and robbers in the 'mysteries' of the early fifteenth century (e.g. *marié*, hanged, in the *Geste du Nobles* (1408), or *beffleur*, a robber, in the *Mistère du Vieil Testament*), this was the first occasion on which a substantial body of argot was recognized. Yet it would be 400 years before the trial's records were unearthed, in 1842, and published as *Les compagnons de la Coquille, chronique dijonnaise du XVe siècle*, and a further forty before in 1880 Marcel Schwob, researching the poet-criminal François Villon, appreciated the linguistic importance of what had been revealed in 1455.

Contemporaneous with the Coquillards, indeed more than likely one of their number or certainly their associate, is François Villon, the other indicator of early argot. Villon (born 1431 and last recorded as active in 1463) is probably the best-known poet of his era. (The line '*Mais où sont les neiges d'antan?*' in his 'Ballade des Dames du Temps Jadis' – translated by D. G. Rossetti as 'Where are the snows of yesteryear?' – remains one of the best-known, if somewhat impenetrable lines of poetry yet written.) A student at the University of Paris, he became Master of Arts in 1452 but at the same time was increasingly involved in the period's outbreaks of student rioting. In 1455 he was implicated in a murder; he pleaded self-defence but his accuser died and Villon fled Paris. He was pardoned in 1456 but as a killer he had to give up his high-status teaching post at the College of Navarre and henceforth scrape a living singing in taverns. That year he was in trouble again: accused of leading a gang of students who broke into the chapel of the same College of Navarre and stole 500 gold crowns. He left Paris once more and for the next five years survived on the road. It may be that it was during this time that he joined, however marginally, the Coquillards. Certainly he had a number of unarguably villainous friends. He suffered further accusations of criminality in 1461 and 1463. This last led to his banishment; thereafter he vanishes from history.

His works, however, do not. In 1460 he began the composition of his magnum opus, the 2,023 verses of *Le Grand Testament*, filled with bitterness, invective, lamentations for a wasted life and an imminent sense of death on the gallows. For the student of early argot, of which Villon's work is, to quote Sainéan, 'one of the most important monuments',[10] his work is irresistible, however much of it remains a challenge to modern readers. The *Testament* was published in 1489; the edition included a group of *ballades argotiques* entitled *Le Jargon ou Jobelin de Maistre François Villon* ('the slang or cant of Master François Villon').

This, however, is now accepted as a misattribution: Villon, it is acknowledged, was not their author. The actual writer is unknown, his identity as hard to discern as the argot the work contains.

> A parouart la grant mathegaudie
> Ou accollez sont duppez et noirciz
> Et par les anges suivans la paillardie
> Sont greffez et print cinq ou six
> La sont bleffieurs au plus hault bout assis
> Pour le euaige et bien hault mis au vent
> [Escheques moy tost ces coffres massis
> Car vendengeurs des ances circuncis
> Sen brow et du tout aneant Eschec eschec pour le fardis].[11]

Terms include *paroir* and *montjoye* (the scaffold), *collez* (hanged; slang 'scragged'); *riflart* is a police-officer, *abroieart* fog. A few words from foreign languages occur: *audinos* (prayer) is the Latin *audi nos* of the litanies; *arton* (bread), is Greek. *Moller* (to eat), may perhaps be the Latin *molere*, to grind. *Anse* (the ear), is the Latin *ansa*, handle.

No one has recorded Villon's death, or even later life. Branded a criminal, he disappears and leaves only his semi-penetrable linguistic legacy. And with Villon we also leave this introductory, fragmentary search for early examples of slang. Henceforth, in the late fifteenth and far more so the sixteenth centuries, one sees a concrete attempt, visible across Europe, to tackle the new sub-set of speech: the language of criminal beggary. From now on, while there are lacunae, and as is ever the case with slang there will always be aspects that defy us, the story of the counter-language takes real form.

3 Lewd, Lousey Language: Beggars and Their Books

Without the sort of wide-ranging publishing that has come to display every register of language – from high to low, and literary to popular – we have no choice but to look to lexicography, the making of dictionaries, for the early records of modern slang, or what at least count as its earliest roots. Not that it appeared in any form of dictionary yet. Bilingual lists, usually combining a national vernacular with the scholars' language Latin, had become well established by the sixteenth century, but other than in Italy, where a pair devoted to the 'lingua vulgare' appeared in 1543, monolingual dictionaries would have to wait until the seventeenth, which saw every major European country (with the exception of the Netherlands) offer a local version, whether through individual scholarship (as in England and Germany) or under the auspices of an academy (in France, again Italy and Spain). Vernacular lexicography was still coming up to speed, and its products were seen in a variety of specialist glossaries. These did not include slang, as yet an unknown or at least uncategorized quantity, but since every country had criminal beggars the language of these vagrants was duly researched and set down. It was these glossaries, known as *beggar books*, that formed the foundations of slang collection, gave the first insights into the vocabulary of the 'counter-language' and would dominate the 'slang lexicography' of the sixteenth century.

The European Background

> Probably for the last time, it was through the beggars' books
> that Europe found that unity of interests and readers which
> would appear unthinkable only a few years later.
>
> Piero Camporesi Introduzione, in
> *Il libro dei vagabondi* (1973)

There are no unimpeachable statistics for how many beggars, whether
'deserving', i.e. genuinely poor, or 'sturdy', i.e. supposedly capable of
earning a living and thus 'fraudulent', roamed Europe in the fifteenth and
sixteenth centuries. Historians offer a variety of figures based on valiant
research, totals usually running to the tens of thousands, but nothing
can be comprehensively offered. What one can say, however, is that the
image of the beggar, once seen as a legitimate and deserving beneficiary
of charity – itself one of the cardinal Christian virtues – which had thus
often been ecclesiastical, had taken on a new, and often negative image.
A variety of social and economic changes had substantially increased the
numbers of those who begged, adding impoverished small tradesmen
and women to the traditional ranks of workless peasants. The changes
had been underpinned by natural calamities (the Black Death) and man-
made ones, e.g. the Hundred Years War, which ended in 1453, releasing
a tide of henceforth unemployed soldiers; or the enclosure of land,
which replaced the old feudal divisions, and again deprived peasants of
a livelihood. Further to this, England's Dissolution of the Monasteries
(1536–41), while not perhaps unleashing thousands of now homeless
monks on to the road, as was once believed, undoubtedly rendered
jobless many whose incomes had depended on providing the religious
foundations with a wide range of service industries. To compound the
problem, prices were rising, perhaps doubling during the half-century
of Elizabeth I's reign, and the population at large was increasing.

The result of these changes was that the once-efficient charitable
institutions were overwhelmed and those who might once have received
alms and shelter had no alternative but to take to the road. And once
on the road, at least in a substantial number of cases, to turn to one or
another form of crime, be it out-and-out robbery, or a variety of forms

of deception. In society at large the beggar, thus categorized, became a pariah.

While much of the response to this explosion of vagabondage was in the form of legislation, one can see a major cultural impact, nowhere more than in a new genre of writing, subsequently bracketed either as 'rogue literature' or the 'literature of roguery'. It was not an entirely new phenomenon. Nor was it by any means restricted to England. The criminal vagabond – 'the rogue' – had been a stock figure for some time, often in folklore but also as the subject of tracts that urged repentance for such sinning. He can be seen as far back as the Latin author Lucian's dialogue 'The Parasite: A Demonstration that Sponging is a Profession' (second century CE). He also appeared in such picaresque (from Spanish *picaro*, a rogue) tales as Spain's anonymously penned *La Vida de Lazarillo de Tormes*, published in 1554 and generally seen as the first of a much-copied type, and Mateo Aleman's *Guzman de Alfaracke* (1599–1604, published in English as *The Rogue* in 1623). In the latter the hero is 'educated' by the boss (the *protopobre*), who explains to him the various types of beggar. Two major sources were the multi-tale epic – Boccaccio's *Decameron* and Chaucer's *Canterbury Tales*, in both of which a number of stories are devoted to a variety of roguish trickery – and the jest book, a compendium of anecdotes (the first English example *One Hundred Merry Tales* appeared in 1526) that often focused on the victimization of the gullible sucker by the artful villain.

Perhaps the most important literary work, and as such one that might be positioned as bridging the gap between the Medieval style and that of Early Modernity, appeared in Germany in 1494: *Das Narrenschiff* (The Ship of Fools), by the German theologian and satirist Sebastian Brant. A number of later editions followed, among them that of 1497, retitled with a Latin synonym: *Stultifera Navis*, which brought it to the attention of the learned, while most of the seventeen editions that appeared in the next century were in a variety of people-friendly vernaculars. The first English version appeared in 1509, translated, with an admitted freedom, by the poet-clergyman Alexander Barclay (c. 1484–1552). It offered 113 linked rhyming satires and displays the author's denunciations of what he saw as contemporary corruption and immorality; it was also notable for being the first book to offer woodcuts by Albrecht Dürer. Brant, and after him Barclay, targeted 'fond parents and ungrateful children, inconstant and evil women, all who wore extravagant clothes, pluralist clergy, ignorant gentlemen, avaricious merchants, corrupt lawyers and physicians, riotous servants, and sturdy undeserving beggars'.[1] Thus among the original Dürer illustrations is that of 'The Beggar', which depicts among other things – an ass-load of small children in baskets, a female companion tipping a wineskin to her lips – the beggar himself, in a belled cap that denotes his role as fool, leaning on a stick and displaying a patently false peg-leg, the real one openly bound up to disguise the truth.

Brant's take on begging was acerbic, reflecting the popular disdain for 'sturdy beggars' who could work but preferred the greater financial rewards of professional, criminal begging. Such views were those of many, including Erasmus and Protestant reformer Martin Luther, who stated in 1520, 'It is not seemly that one man should live in idleness on the labors of his fellows or possess wealth and luxury through the hardships which others suffer, as is the prevailing perverse custom.'[2] But it happened, and to an increasing extent. To quote a modern translation of Sebastian Brant:

> For begging has become the rule
> And ranks among our best professions …
> To beg some men will always choose,
> Though they could work if but they would
> They're young and strong, their health is good,
> Save that their back they won't incline …[3]

What links *Das Narrenschiff* to the 'beggar books' that would follow is Brant's delineation of the various begging specialities, a taxonomy that would underpin a number of European 'rogue' works in the making.

> They carry on much rowdy work,
> They have their thieves' slang everywhere,
> It helps them out where'er they fare.

[…]

He uses crutches when he's out,
But not when no one is about;
He throws a fit before a crowd
So everyone will shout aloud;

[...]

He limps, he's hunched and very sick,
He ties his leg to crutch or stick
Or hides a bone 'neath garments thick.
Should anyone inspect his wound
He'd find it very shrewdly bound.[4]

These verses 'On Beggars' were, however, a small section of Brant's work. The concept of the 'beggar book', versions of which would be published across Europe, with its attempt to set out the ranks of criminal mendicants and to itemize their jargon, aimed not for satire, but for a rudimentary form of criminology. The first such analyses seem to have emerged in Germany, although the early works do not offer any vocabularies. Germany's cant was known as *Rotwelsch*, from *rot* (cunning; literally 'red', coincidentally or otherwise the stereotyped hair colour of the Jew, also seen as cunning), and *welsch* (unintelligible language). In 1932 D. B. Thomas noted that '[Hans] Vintner [*sic*; usually Vindler or Vintler] uses a few Rotwelsch words in his *Blume der Tugend* ('Flower of Virtue', 1411), and others occur in the anonymous *Des Teufels Notz* (*ca.* 1420). About 1425 the Lübeck Dominican Herman Komer relates in his *Chronica Novella* a story of a band of murderers with a peculiar language of their own.'[5]

The mid-fourteenth century saw a variety of ordinances issued by German cities in which lists of begging specialities were enumerated, along with statutes prohibiting any of their practitioners to enter the city. The Konstanz *Ratsbuch* of 1381 was perhaps the first ever to list the categories of rogues. In 1479 the Basel *Kronik* included a document entitled 'The devices with which vagabonds and blind men extort alms'; some thirty categories of beggars are mentioned, and there are translations from their jargon (Rotwelsch) into standard German. This was presumably a later version of *Die Basler Betrügnisse der Gyler* (*The Deceptions of Beggars (in Basel)*), allegedly published *c.* 1450 in Basel, Switzerland. It appears to have been the work of a clergyman, John Knebel, who, like those who noted the language of the Coquillards, picked up his material at a series of criminal trials aimed at controlling vagabondage. Three manuscripts of *The Deceptions* survive; at some later stage it went into print and was still appearing as late as 1749. This 'beggar book' or 'rogue pamphlet', as the genre became known, set out, as its opening lines explain, to inform the law-abiding citizen of 'the deceptions which beggars and blind men practise, and especially all the dodges, as they call them, by which they make their living'. Like its many successors, *The Deceptions* goes on to list the types of beggars, the tricks they use and the language they adopt to deceive the authorities and the gullible public. It was this document, much amended, that would become the first widely known beggar book: the *Liber Vagatorum* (1509). This 'Book of the Beggars' also enjoyed a number of editions, perhaps the best known of which was that of 1528, which boasted a preface by none other than Martin Luther.

The *Liber Vagatorum* offers some 295 words, of the roots of which just over half are German, followed by 22.1% Hebrew, 6.8% Dutch, 6.4% Latin, and small specimens (all under 2%) drawn from Romani, French and Spanish. Nearly 30% have no ascertainable etymology. Among the words are *hanfstaud* (a shirt; lit. 'hemp-rub'), *kabas* (the head; from Latin *caput*), *betzam* (an egg; from Hebrew), *diftel* (a church; from German *stiftel*, lit. a small cathedral), *dotch* (the vulva; possibly a corruption of German *tasche*, a pocket), *mess* (money; German *messing*, brass), and *schöchervetzer* (an innkeeper; German *schenken*, to retail liquor).

In addition to these general terms, there are those that denote the beggars' tricks. *Wilners*, those who like the English *ring-dropper* pretended to 'discover' a piece of silver, which they then sell to a victim; *Joners* (perhaps linked to French *jouer*, to play), card-sharps; *Sönzen-goers*, prototype begging-letter writers, and armed with false documents; *Schwanfelders*, who stripped naked in the hope of exciting pity and thus alms. There are the *Lossenders*, lit. the 'let-loose', who claim to have been imprisoned in far-off countries and there persecuted for their Christian faith; the *Klenkners*, those who pretend to wounds the gruesomeness of which is balanced only by the ingenuity that conjures them up from perfectly healthy flesh; the *Grantners*, who pretend to the 'falling sickness', again a form of epilepsy; the *Gickisses*, or beggars who pretend to blindness, and claim to be on a pilgrimage to Rome or Compostela; the *Dallingers*, posing as ex-hangmen and now repentant; and the *Schweigers*, who concoct a case of jaundice, using a mix of horses' dung and water.

The *Liber Vagatorum*, then, set the pattern, and it was widely emulated. Before turning to the English beggar books, and confining this history to the Anglo-Saxon world, it is worth surveying what else Europe had to offer.

The Coquillards had offered, as it were, an *argot* glossary by default. The first conscious effort to categorize the world of the *argotier* and the language that they employed comes thirty years after the English magistrate Thomas Harman had offered *c.* 1566 his *Caveat for Common Cursetors*, and contemporaneous with the 1590s 'coney-catching' pamphlets of the ne'er-do-well playwright Robert Greene. *La Vie généreuse* (= 'heroic') *des mercelots, gueux, et Boesmiens, contenans leurs facons de vivre, Subtilitez et Gergon* (i.e. jargon) was published in 1596. Its pseudonymous author called himself Péchon de Ruby (roughly equivalent to 'The Smart' or perhaps 'Naughty Kid'). As was now well established, he lays out a hierarchy of villainy and offers a glossary of criminal argot. And while Harman's work purported to be culled from the magistrate's one-to-one interrogations of a variety of villains, Péchon de Ruby's is presented as pure autobiography. As he explains in his extended title, he is a Breton *gentilhomme*, who associated with criminals in his youth. A dictionary *en langue Blesquien* (in the language of criminals) is added, 'with an explanation in the vulgar tongue', i.e. vernacular French, as opposed to Latin.

La Vie généreuse also differs from Harman in its open celebration of the vagabond life, a latitude that eclipses the belief that those beggar books written in Catholic countries were 'more moralistically committed and more severe'[6] than those produced in Protestant ones. As he makes clear, 'nostre vie estoit plaisante' (our life was pleasant), and he recounts a picturesque existence, even if there are scenes of horror and cruelty and the gallows, inevitably, casts its lengthy shadow. This picture of a parallel, organized criminal underworld, with its hierarchy and its initiatory rites, not that dissimilar from the fantasy Mafia so beloved of Hollywood, is perhaps, as Jacques Cellard has suggested, 'too good to be true'. It is perhaps a rebellious young man's fantasy viewed through the roseate lens of middle age.

For the purposes of argot, however, it is worth taking note. Again like Harman and his peers, but quite unlike Villon, Péchon de Ruby sets out to inform. Thus the 'memoirs' are filled with argot, but a translation of that argot is included. Useful? Possibly – it would be useful for 'civilians' to know what those who wanted to rob them were saying amongst themselves – but equally voyeuristic. It is, as such books were, as much a book of titillatory sensationalism, an embryonic tabloid exposé, as a piece of disinterested research.

As well as vocabulary, Péchon de Ruby establishes, believably or not, a distinct hierarchy of crime. At the top stands *le Grand Coesre*, the king of the beggars and presumably cognate with such rulers as a *Caesar* or *Tsar*. 'A very good-looking man, with the majesty of a great monarch [...] and a great beard.' His coat, if we are to believe the author, consisted of six thousand coins sewn together. Beneath him, the *Cagous* ('hooded ones'), his immediate assistants. In addition are some six 'façons de suyvre la vertu' (ways of pursuing virtue), in fact far from virtuous, but methods of extracting money from the foolish. Finally, in the true tabloid tradition, Péchon de Ruby, having laid out a world of glamour and excess, concludes with a warning: 'Ces folies meslees de cautelles, c'est afin que chacun s'en donne garde.' In other words, these tricks are dangerous for you (and, he implies, for society), be on your guard.

Italy would also contribute to the genre, albeit later still. The primary work was *Il vagabondo, ovvero sferza de' bianti e vagabondi* ('or the scourge of bandits and vagabonds') by the Roman Dominican friar Giacinto de' Nobili alias Rafaele Frianoro; it appeared in 1621 and enjoyed at least seventeen editions, in Italian and French, by 1700. Again, less censorious than its Protestant peers, *Il Vagabondo* is as much a series of anecdotes as it is a tract against beggary. Its author claims that it has been written 'for entertainment rather than health'. However, it is possible that this was in fact no more than a vernacular translation of an earlier Latin original: a manuscript by one Teseo Pini from Urbino entitled *Speculum cerretanorum* (The Mirror of Beggary). Although this was not published until 1973, by the historian Pietro Camporesi, it would appear to have been written between 1484 and 1486, thus making it one of the earliest examples of the genre. Its structure is certainly exactly that of later German and English books. Compared with *Il Vagabondo* it is tougher on crime, its author justifying his work, stating that he had published it (as supposedly would many successors) in order 'that honest good people may learn how to defend themselves from the falsehood of the dishonest'.

Slightly earlier than Italy came Spain's contribution to the genre. This was Juan Hidalgo's *Vocabulario de germanía* (1609, 'brotherhood' in Catalan and thence *hermanos*, brothers), published in Barcelona by Sebastián Cormellas. The glossary was appended to his *Romances de germanía*, a collection of canting ballads. According to Hidalgo (whose name may in fact have been a pseudonym of Cristóbal Chaves), all the words in the *Vocabulario* (some 1,272) are taken from ballads, although the author provides no specific sources. A second edition, published in Zaragoza, appeared in 1644, with a reprint in 1654.

The English Development

It is possible that, Barclay aside, another English author, forever unknown, offered a take on the *Ship of Fools*. This was *Cock Lorel's Bote*, published sometime prior to 1513. The name Cock Lorel, used in slang to mean the leader of a gang of rogues, combines the adjective *cock* (first-rate), and *losel* (a worthless rogue, a profligate). It is usually found as a proper name and features largely in the literature of Elizabethan villainy. As described in the anonymously written verses, he is a 'shipmaster', whose 'crew' is a group of rogues drawn from the workshops and gutters of London. Together they 'sail' the country, engaging in a variety of villainies. He appears in a number of works, as well as in the glossaries compiled by Awdeley (whose *Fraternity of Vagabonds* (c. 1561) was 'confirmed by Cock Lorel') and Rowlands (in *Martin-Mark-all: Beadle of Bridewell*, 1610), who suggests that while he was 'the most notorious knaue that ever lived'),[7] his 'captain's' role was purely allegorical and he was, in fact, a tinker. In all mentions he remains at the head of his marauding beggars, sometimes plotting against the state, on one occasion even entertaining the Devil to dinner. According to Rowlands's generally fictitious 'history' of the canting crew, Cock Lorel's reign supposedly lasted *c.* 1511–33. As well as supposedly establishing a number of rules whereby his villains should conduct themselves, he was the first to lay out the 'quartern of knaues called the five and twentie orders of knaues', a hierarchy of beggary much imitated in a succession of canting dictionaries.

'Come any mariners hither of Cock Lorel's boat?'[8] asks *Copland* of the Spytell-Hous *Porter*, and with that we enter, finally, on what is seen as the first English beggar book. Robert Copland's *Hye Waye to the Spytell-Hous* (loosely translated as 'The Road to the Charity Clinic'; a *spytell-house*, synonymous with a lazar house or poor hospital, was a form of charity foundation, dealing specifically with the poor and indigent and especially with those suffering from a variety of foul diseases). It was written between 1529 and 1534 and probably published in 1535.

Copland's birth-date remains a mystery, but his known professional career as a printer, bookseller and stationer, as well as a collector of cant, covers the years 1508–47 (when he seems to have died). He worked primarily as an assistant to the printer Wynkyn de Worde (d. 1535), who had been William Caxton's principal assistant from 1476. Copland claimed to have worked for Caxton too, but given their respective dates, this relationship is more likely figurative than factual.

Sometime between 1529 and 1534 Copland created the work for which he remains known. The *Hye Waye* is a lengthy verse dialogue, supposedly conducted between Copland and the Spytell House Porter. The clinic in question, while not named by Copland, is generally accepted to have been St Bartholomew's Hospital, London's oldest, founded in 1123 near the open space known as Smithfield, now London's central meat market. Trapped in the hospital porch by a snowstorm, Copland strikes up a conversation with the Porter, taking as their subject the crowd of beggars who besiege the Spytell House: 'Scabby and scurvy, pock-eaten flesh and rind / Lousy and scald, and peeléd like an apes / With scantly a rag for to cover their shapes, / Breechless, barefooted, all stinking with dirt.'[9] The pair then discuss why some are allowed in and others rejected. Within this framework Copland notes and the Porter

describes the various categories of beggars and thieves, as well as the
tricks and frauds that are their stock in trade. They further note the way
folly and vice lead inevitably to poverty and thence disease and finally,
willy-nilly, to the Spytell House.

The *Hye Waye* falls into two halves, the first focusing on beggars, the
second on fools. Whatever the source of the 'criminological' verses, the
second half would appear to have been influenced by Robert de Balzac,
one of the minor French writers whose work Copland would have
known, and author of *Le chemin de l'ôpital* (The Road to the Hospital,
1502). And while de Balzac's catalogue of fools does not deal in crime,
it undoubtedly gave the English author his title.

Unlike the beggar books that would succeed Copland's work, the
Hye Waye does not offer a 'canting vocabulary', but it does provide vivid
descriptions of a wide range of what would be known as 'the canting
crew', 'diddering and doddering, leaning on their staves, / Saying "Good
master, for your mother's blessing, / Give us a halfpenny"'.[10] Some,
explains the Porter, are justified in their beggary. Others are not.

> By day on stilts or Stooping on crutches
> And so dissimule as false loitering flowches,
> With bloody clouts all about their leg,
> And placers on their skin when they go beg.
> Some counterfeit lepry, and other some
> Put soap in their mouth to make it scum,
> And fall down as Saint Cornelys' evil.
> These deceits they use worse than any devil;
> And when they be in their own company,
> They be as whole as either you or I.[11]

The Porter also describes such 'nightingales of Newgate' as those
who claim to have been imprisoned in France 'and had been there
seven years in durance', or falsely imprisoned in London only to face
poverty on their release. And explains how, once enough money has
been earned, all such villains repair to brothels and taverns, dressing
up in far from ragged finery and making 'gaudy cheer'.[12] As in *Das
Narrenschiff*, upon which Copland undoubtedly drew, there are false

scholars, and quack doctors, and, inevitably, corrupt clergy, whom the Porter characterizes as monks, driven from the dissolved monasteries and posing as Pardoners. And as his descriptions reach their end, the porter offers a list:

> For by letters they name them as they be
> P a Pardoner; Clewner a C;
> R a Roger; A an Aurium, and a Sapient.[13]

The *clewner*, a senior villain, may be linked to the Gaelic *cluainear* (a cunning fellow, a hypocrite), Erse *cluanaire* (a seducer, a flatterer), or Manx *cleaynagh* (a tempter). The *roger* pretended to be a poor scholar from Oxford or Cambridge; pronounced with a hard 'g', the word is ostensibly a version of SE *rogue*, but may be linked to Gaelic *ruaigair* (a pursuer, a hunter), and Lowland Scottish *rugger* (an outlaw). The *aurium* is a fake priest, possibly from Latin *aurius* (an ear), i.e. that which hears confession, and the *sapient* is a travelling quack, from Latin *sapiens* (a wise man), a term also found, with the same meaning, in the *Liber Vagatorum*.

In all, Copland offers fifty-one examples of cant, though they must be disinterred from the rhyming text. Among them is *pedlar's French* (thieves' jargon), only the second printed use: the first had been in Palsgrave's bilingual dictionary *Lesclarcissement de la langue francoyse* (1530).

Other than his work, we know little of Robert Copland. Of his successor in cant-gathering, John Awdeley, also known as John Sampson, we know little more. The son of the verger of Westminster Abbey, he was born in or before 1532 and died in 1575. He was another printer turned writer, and from 1561 to his death he ran a thriving business in Little Britain, around the corner from Copland's Spytell-Hous, Bart's. He published much popular material, often ballads or news sheets, some sermons and studies of 'algorism' (the decimal system) and the highly popular *Fitzherbert's Boke of Husbandry*. Nor did he overlook the potential profits of sensationalism. His *Description of Swedland* (1561) concentrates on 'the moste horrible and incredible tiranny of the second Christern kyng of Denmarke against the Swecians', while the broadsheet *Cox's Retraction* (1561) set in print 'the vnfained retraction of Francis Cox, which he uttered at the Pillery in Chepesyde, and els where … being accused for the vse of certayne sinistral and Diuelish Artes'. His most important work, a primary source for much that followed, was *The Fraternity of Vagabonds* (1561). 'As wel of ruflyng Vacabondes, as of beggerly, of women as of men, of Gyrles as of Boyes with their proper names and qualityes.'

If Copland's interlarding of his text with cant can be cited as the first attempt in England at any such collection, then Awdeley's glossary is the first proper listing of the cant vocabulary. It is brief – its nine pages contain but forty-eight headwords, mixing the occupational names of beggars and rogues with those of sluggish and slovenly servants – but highly influential. Awdeley's researches appear time and time again, embellished and substantially expanded no doubt, but still undeniably plucked from his files. If one is to trust his rhymed preface '*The Printer to the Reader*', it would appear that he gathered his material, like several European predecessors, from court records. As he tells it, a vagabond appeared before the magistrates,

> Who promysde if they would him spare,
> And keepe his name from knowledge then,
> He would as straunge a thing declare,
> As euer they knew synce they were men.
> 'But if my fellowes do know,' sayd he,
> 'That thus I dyd, they would kyll me.'
>
> They graunting him this his request,
> He dyd declare as here is read,
> Both names and states of most and least,
> Of this their Vacabondes brotherhood.
> Which at the request of a worshipful man
> I haue set it forth as well as I can.[14]

Frustratingly for the researcher, Awdeley goes no further as to detail. The work falls into three parts: the first deals with rural villains – some nineteen in all; the second with their urban cousins – the 'Cousoners and Shifters', i.e. con-men of various sorts; and the third is Awdeley's list of 'the xxv. Orders of Knaues, otherwyse called a Quartern of Knaues Confirmed for euer by Cocke Lorell'.

The Fraternity proper, the criminal mendicants, form the core of all later canting lists. That Awdeley's definitions are relatively brief led for some years to the mis-dating of the work and suggestions that he had plagiarized that of Thomas Harman. But as Thomas Harman, whose work actually followed Awdeley's by around four years, would note in his 'Epistle dedicatory', 'There was a fewe yeares since a small breefe [i.e. pamphlet] set forth of some zelous man to his countrey, – of whom I knowe not, – that made a lytle shewe of their names and vsage, and gaue a glymsinge lyghte, not sufficient persuade of their peuishe peltinge and pickinge praetyses, but well worthy of prayse.'[15]

Thus it is in Awdeley that one first encounters what would become a recognized taxonomy. Among the rogues that he defines are:[16]

An Abraham Man is he that walketh bare-armed and bare-legged, and feigneth himself mad, and carryeth a pack of wool, or a stick with bacon on it, or suchlike toy, and nameth himself Poor Tom.

A Ruffler goeth with a weapon to seek service, saying he hath been a Servitor in the wars, and beggeth for his relief. But his chiefest trade is to rob poor wayfaring men and market women.

A Prigman goeth with a stick in his hand like an idle person. His property is to steal clothes off the hedge, which they call 'storing of the Rogueman,' or else to filch Poultry, carrying them to the Alehouse, which they call the 'Bousing Inn,' and there sit playing at cards and dice, till that is spent which they have so filched.

A Whipjack is one that by color of a counterfeit License, which they call a 'Gibe,' and the seals they call 'Jarks,' doth use to beg like a Mariner. But his chiefest trade is to rob Booths in a Fair, or to pilfer ware from stalls, which they call 'heaving off the Booth.'

An Upright Man is one that goeth with the truncheon of a staff, which staff they call a 'Filtchman.' This man is of so much authority that meeting with any of his profession he may call them to account, and command a share or 'snap' unto himself of all that they have gained by their trade in one month. And if he do them wrong, they have no remedy against him, no, though he beat them, as he useth commonly to do. He may also command any of their women, which they call 'Doxies,' to serve his turn. He hath the chief place at any market walk and other assemblies, and is not of any to be controlled.

A Kintchin Morts is a Girl; she is brought at her full age to the Upright Man to be broken, and so she is called a Doxy until she comes to the honor of an Altham.

Awdeley offers only three con-men: the *Courtesy-man*, who inveigles his way into the victim's home, and steals what he can before slipping away; the *Cheater* or *Fingerer*, who persuade suckers to join in fixed games of 'chance'; and the *Ring-faller*, who supposedly 'finds' a gold (actually copper) ring, and persuades a passer-by to purchase it from him. They are all given substantial, quasi-anecdotal descriptions, while Awdeley returns to his abbreviated format for the final part: 'The quartern of knaues'. These, paradoxically, were not villains as such, but ill-behaved servants – the original meaning of knave – who may or may not have descended into actual crime. Typical among them are the '*Bawde Physicke* … is he that is a Cocke [cook], when his Maysters meate is wyll dressed, and he challenging him therefore, he wyl say he wyll eat thye rawest morsel thereof him selfe. This is a sausye knave, that wyl contrary his mayster alway' and the '*Esen Droppers* … bene they, that stand under mens wales or windoes, or, in any other place, to heeare the secretes of a mans house. These misdeming knaves wyl stand in corners to heare if they be evill spoken of, or waite a shrewd turne.'[17] This latter section, while amusing, did not survive its coiner other than in dictionaries and is very much tied to its time (although the characters of the scheming or lazy servants seem to be enshrined in literature); indeed a number of the names, suggests Partridge, may well be nonce-creations of Awdeley's own.[18]

Before turning to the work of Thomas Harman, there remains one more mid-sixteenth-century work worthy of consideration: *A Manifest Detection of the most vile and detestable use of Dice-play, and other practices like the same*. This pamphlet, which appeared in 1552 (there may have been an earlier edition in 1545), has been attributed to one Gilbert Walker. It was subtitled 'A mirror very necessary for all young gentlemen and others suddenly enabled by worldly abundance to look in'. Unlike Awdeley or Harman, Walker, for whom no biographical details exist, focused on a single topic: gambling with dice. It takes the form of a dialogue between 'R', the unfledged young man, and 'M', who is up to every gamblers' trick.

Unsurprisingly the predominant vocabulary concerns the dice themselves: depending on the way they have been loaded, or if their sides have been slightly misaligned – in both cases leading to throws that the cheat can therefore predict – such dice as *cheaters*, *doctors* or *flats* can be *bars*, *bristles*, *cater-treys*, *contraries*, *demies*, *fulhams* or *fullams*, *gourds*, *graviers*, *high men* and *low men*, or *langrets*. The dice sharp himself is a *cheator*, a *foister*, an *old cole* (a veteran), or a *workman*. Those who draw the victim into the game are *setters*, *barnards* (thus *barnard's law*, the whole world of dice-sharping), *snappers* and *takers*, while the *verser* is he who actually plays. To *cog* is to cheat, while to *crossbite* is to cheat a fellow-sharp.

In 1566 or 1567 there appeared the most influential of any English beggar book: Thomas Harman's *Caveat or Warening for Commen Cursetours Vulgarely Called Vagabones*. It reproduces the now regular beggar book pattern, and for all that it lists but 114 terms other than those of the begging specialities themselves (there are also such words that are not listed but encountered within the narrative), in its socio-linguistic rigour it would play a greater role in the canting collections that followed than any predecessor.

Harman was the grandson of one Henry Harman, who was clerk of the crown under King Henry VII and was granted the estates of Ellam and Maystreet in Kent around 1480. Harman's father, William, expanded the family lands by buying another estate, that of Mayton or Maxton, also in Kent. Thomas himself, the heir to this not inconsiderable property, and certainly not the 'poor gentleman' that he liked to style himself, lived nearby, in the town of Crayford. He remained in the country from 1547 until his death, the date of which remains unknown, but is presumed to have followed not so long after the appearance of his book. Never a well man, or so he claims, he preferred the fresh air of Kent to the less salubrious atmosphere of the metropolis. That said, Harman was more than happy to pursue the insalubrious side of language. He interrogated the beggars who appeared at his door, offering food or money in exchange for linguistic information. He apparently knew his local villains so well that he lists them in his book: 'Harry Smith, hee dryveleth when he speaketh' and 'Richard Horwood, wel neer lxxx. yeare old, he will bite a vi. peny nayle asunder with his teeth and a baudy dronkard.'[19] He would also pay regular visits to London to double-check his information. He was not, however, immune to deception. On occasion beggars presumably fed him any old words in order to pick up their fee, but Harman had clout. He was a magistrate, and thus charged with putting into practice the new laws against beggary. As he explains, he was not above depriving some particularly mendacious traveller of his licence, confiscating such money as he had and distributing it among the honest poor of his neighbourhood.

Sometime before 1566 Harman had completed his labours: he had the manuscript of a substantial treatise on beggars and their ways, complete with a brief glossary and the lengthy list, with less than flattering descriptions, of the individuals who made up his primary sources. The Caveat appeared either in 1566 or possibly a year later. No copy of the purported first edition has survived; the first available is dated 1567.

As he puts it in a burst of alliterative disdain, Harman offered his readers 'the leud lousey language of these lewtering [loitering] luskes [idlers] and lasy lorrels [blackguards] where with they bye and sell the common people as they pas through the country. Whych language they terme Peddelars Frenche, a vnknowen toung onely, but to these bold, beastly, bawdy Beggers, and vaine Vacabondes ...'[20] He prefaces his work with an 'epistle' to Elizabeth, Countess of Shrewsbury, to whom the book is dedicated, and thence the readers, followed by some twenty-four small essays, each dealing with a different rank of villain, from the 'upright man' (the leading rank of villainy) to the 'counterfeit crank' (bedecked with repellent sores) and from the 'dummerar' (feigning dumbness and claiming to have been mutilated by the infidel Turk for denying Mohammad) to the 'fresh-water mariner' (whose 'shippes were drowned in the playne of Salisbury'). He offers a list of 114 canting terms, very briefly defined, usually with a single synonym, and grouped loosely into themes: the body and its parts (plus its clothing, which in turn moves on to linen and bedding); money; food; animals; buildings and their contents; day and night; and a hierarchy of people (from top to bottom). Following these, all nouns, are a cluster of verbs, mainly dealing with criminal activity but including terms for drinking, sex and sleep.[21]

The book also features a number of woodcuts, notably portraits of Nicolas Blunt, an upright man, who as Nicolas Genynges (Jennings) sought alms as a fake invalid, a *counterfeit crank*. There are also illustrations of whips, fetters, a pillory and a gibbet. The book concludes with a cant dialogue in the beggars' 'pelting [worthless, contemptible] speche', purporting to be between a pair of criminals. These contrived exchanges, laying all his favourite terms out on display, include for example, 'Maund of this morte whate bene peck is in her ken', and translates as, 'Ask of this wyfe what goode meate shee hath in her house.' Elsewhere he throws in the oath-ridden 'Gerry gan the Ruffian cly thee', which becomes 'A torde in thy mouth, the deuill take thee'. And on they go. 'By this lytle ye maye holy and fully vnderstande their vntowarde talk and pelting speache, mynglede without measure,' promises Harman, but he acknowledges that cant is always changing and 'as they haue begonne of late to deuyse some new termes for certien thinges, so wyll they in tyme alter this, and deuyse as euyll or worsse'.[22]

Certain of Awdeley's terms make their way into Harman's lists, but 'honest Harman', as Partridge described him[23] moved a substantial distance beyond Awdeley's pioneering efforts. He may have hoped, as he states in his epistle, that his socio-linguistic efforts would provide a useful sourcebook for his fellow-magistrates, as well as for interested members of the public, but the long-term beneficiaries of his manual were his lexicographical successors. The Harman lists would re-occur, albeit playing a decreasing part, in a succession of cant or slang dictionaries: they are still there today.

As so central a text, Harman, who positioned himself as having written a guidebook to contemporary crime, has been subjected to substantial critiques. Writing in the introduction to their reprint of the *Caveat*, in *The Rogues and Vagabonds of Shakespeare's Youth* (1869), Frederick

Furnivall and Edward Viles apostrophize him as a 'wise and practical man' and a 'keen inquiring Social Reformer'[24] and add, affectionately, 'We've some like you still, Thomas Harman, in our Victorian times. May their number grow!' This opinion, echoed in Partridge's 'honest Harman', was until the late twentieth century very much the orthodox view. Writers on the period drew heavily on Harman's gospel, accepting him without question as an unimpeachable source. A. V. Judges, who reprinted the *Caveat* in his *Elizabethan Underworld* (1930), was typical in stating that Harman had produced 'the best sixteenth-century account of vagabondage and roguery' and that the magistrate had 'all the deftness of the trained sociologist'.[25] Other writers, such as Frank Aydelotte in *Elizabethan Rogues and Vagabonds* (1913), and more recently John L. McMullen, in *The Canting Crew* (1984), and Gāmini Salgādo, in *The Elizabethan Underworld* (1992), have all been satisfied that what Harman wrote was a legitimate historical document.

But this assessment has not lasted, and while literary critics find Harman a useful non-canonical source of the sixteenth-century treatment of vagabondage, and see links to representations of beggary such as Shakespeare's street-wise pedlar Autolycus in *The Winter's Tale*, others, usually historians, are less convinced. Since the 1980s Harman has been criticized in sociological studies of his era on the grounds of his accuracy, of his method, of his 'classism', and of his 'patriarchal' take on the female beggars, to whom he spoke, some have suggested, for the voyeuristic thrill of hearing them 'talk dirty'.[26] He has been analysed through Freudian eyes and found much wanting. For such critics Harman's pamphlet is nearer to a traditional, and of course wholly fictional jest book, with perhaps an above-average emphasis on sensational crime and on sex. Nor are the historians satisfied. It has been suggested that the image of vagabonds, laid out in beggar books as inspiring (and deserving) both fear and loathing, far exceeded in its threat their reality. That threat, if any, was psychological: the establishment's disapproval (backed by a succession of suppressive legislations) of their marginality to the status quo rather than any idea that they could, let alone would overthrow it. Harman's 'elitist' narrative simply backed up the ruling class's hostile perceptions. And the point of many such historical criticisms was that the formal, hierarchical

'Elizabethan underworld' that was represented by Harman's and before him Awdeley's claimed researches simply didn't exist.

Harman's chief critic on this score is Linda Woodbridge, in her article on Jest Books (2003).[27] Drawing on a supportive selection of historians, she states:

> There is little evidence that real vagrants spoke thieves' cant, a notion fostered by rogue literature. [...] Beier's essay on canting reports only six cases in Renaissance England in which references to thieves' cant occur in court depositions rather than in imaginative literature, and all six occur after the publication of Awdeley's and Harman's cant lexicons [...]. Paul Slack harbors a shrewd suspicion that thieves' cant was simply made up by writers of rogue pamphlets, noting that 'references to ['Pedlar's French'] outside literary contexts are extremely rare' [...] Noting that the first recorded use of thieves' cant in English occurs not in a court deposition but in rogue literature (Robert Copland's *The Highway to the Spital-house*), Beier acknowledges that evidence for real-life canting is slim, 'largely anecdotal,' and 'second-hand.' Although he cautiously concludes that 'there is probably sufficient documentation to support the view of literary sources that canting existed' [...], it looks to me as if independent evidence, indisputably uncontaminated by rogue literature, is practically non-existent. Not only are Harman's assertions often contradicted by the findings of modern historians, but his claim to first-hand experience is also undermined by the fact that much of his 'information' is borrowed from earlier rogue literature going all the way back to the fifteenth-century Liber Vagatorum.

Setting aside the fact that Professor Woodbridge appears to ignore the fact that the *Liber Vagatorum* was written in German, and no authority has found direct borrowing in Harman or his English predecessors, this seems as unprovable as is the contrary thesis that she is at pains to decry.

Some terms can be found, in the way of all lexicography, in previous collections. There are those from Copland (*make*, a halfpenny, *nab-cheat*, a hat, *patrico*, a priest, and *Salomon*, the mass); he has drawn on Awdeley's list of villains to compile his own, and includes a number of other terms (e.g. *autem*, a church, *filch*, to beat or to rob, *gybe*, 'a writinge', and *jarke*, a seal) from Awdeley's narrative. A number of other terms, e.g. *bouse*, as noun or verb, and *cut* (to speak), 'are antedated in the OED and found in a variety of colloquial and popular texts'.[28]

Looking in detail at Harman's lists, Julie Coleman has decided[29] that, 'perhaps, with a little help from Awdelay [*sic*], Harman did compile his list in the manner he describes'. She notes that a number of his entries can be found in dialect dictionaries, although their citations occur several centuries later and it is thus impossible to establish continuity, but Harman may well have met dialect-users and the words they used, which he would have found strange, would have been noted down. But in the end, while 'this may indicate that people from around the country came begging at Harman's door, it does not demonstrate that the vocabulary he noted was a language common between them'. The 'formal' vocabulary, one infers, may be as dubious as the 'formal' hierarchy.

Examples are notoriously hard to disinter from this period. A marginal language used by marginal people in a way that was consciously secretive: such difficulties are hardly surprising. Looking at the period between 1500 and 1567, the date of the second edition of Harman and the only one of which copies exist, the database on which I base my dictionaries offers some 761 discrete terms. Subtracting from those the vocabularies on offer in Copland, Awdeley and Harman (260 terms in all), one is left with 501. The entire sixteenth century, with no exclusions and thus including Robert Greene, author of several 'coney-catching' pamphlets, can only muster 1,552 items.

Among other pertinent authors are the playwrights Thomas Nashe and Thomas Marston, the Italian-English lexicographer John Florio, John Lyly, and the proverb collector John Hayward; there are many minor contributors. These are not absolute figures – almost inevitably some sources may have been left unresearched – but it gives an adequate impression of the relative paucity of available material. We have little choice but to trust our lexicographers in embryo. I have cited Harman as the first record of 144 terms and/or sub-definitions. If one turns to the *OED*, Harman, although not only for his canting terms, is cited 253

times as a first use of a given definition. His researches may not have
been quite as cut-and-dried as he sets out, but the words he includes
are valid.

Coney-catching

Harman's is the last of the sixteenth-century English beggar books,
but his is not the last work to look at cant. His 'borrowers' – the
playwright and pamphleteer Thomas Dekker, Samuel Rowlands or Rid,
the picaresque 'novelist' Richard Head and the criminal John Hall who
turned to lexicography in the death cell – will be dealt with in their place.
Before that one needs look at the era's final exploiter of the cant lexis,
the writer Robert Greene, whose series of 'coney-catching' pamphlets,
written to expose the world of confidence trickery, were published in
the century's final decade.

While Greene's work can be bracketed with that of his predecessors
– it offered specimens of the canting lexis as had theirs – it differs in
important ways. He does not offer a vocabulary, nor does he include
the usual 'order of villains'. He does not deal with the 'underworld' at
large, but instead sticks with its con-men and women. The terms he
explains are very focused: lists of the names given various teams of task-
specific tricksters, such as those pursuing *Barnard's Law*: card-sharping;
the *Cross-biting Law*: the modern 'Murphy game', i.e. the robbery of a
whore's client by a supposedly aggrieved 'brother' or 'boyfriend'; the
Figging Law, pickpocketing; the *Sacking Law*; prostitution and *Vincent's
Law*; cheating at bowls, and later cards. And while his pamphlets pretend
to virtue, warning the unwary by means of lengthy anecdotes or via
supposed conversations between concocted protagonists, of the perils of
such trickery, the reality is a far more naked sensationalism. With Greene
one enters the world of the tabloid exposé, having one's voyeuristic
cake, while eating one's supposed condemnations of the subject of
one's report.

Robert Greene (*c.* 1558–92), the last of the sixteenth century's
cant collectors and publicists, is a far more accessible figure than any
predecessor. After two printers and a magistrate Greene represents
literature, ranking among the major playwrights of the period. His

brief life was a mixture of rackety self-indulgence and hard, productive work. His death, in poverty and supposedly accompanied by his fear of a much-merited descent into hell, was subject to the emotionally charged arguments of friends and enemies almost before he was buried. And although his work has slipped from view, he remains an important figure in any studies of the period.

Greene was first and foremost a writer on demand. As John Clark Jordan noted in 1915, 'Whatever literary form he took up, it was for exploitation; whatever he dropped, it was because the material or the demand was exhausted. He did what no man before him in England had done so extensively: he wrote to sell.'[30] And Greene was undoubtedly good at what he did. His peers may have exceeded him for quality – the Shakespearian scholar Stephen Greenblatt has dismissed him as 'by no means the most accomplished'[31] of the [Cambridge University] Wits – but Greene's quantity was what made him popular. Whatever was needed – drama, poetry, romances, social pamphlets, treatises, even death-bed repentances – Greene could and did knock it out, and deliver to the deadline. As Nashe put it in his defence of his newly dead friend, *Strange Newes, of the Intercepting Certayne letters* (1592), 'In a night and a day he would have iarkt [written, literally counterfeited] vp a pamphlet as well as in seauen yeare'. Printers, it was said, would 'pay him deare for the very dregs of his wit'. Yet, whether journeyman hack or prolific author, Greene was not especially obsessed with fame. 'He made no account of winning credite by his works,' adds Nashe, '... his only care was to hauue a spel in his purse to coniure up a good cuppe of wine at all times.' He wrote some thirty-eight works (although the manuscripts of others may have vanished, as did a variety of literature, during the Great Fire of London), of which twenty-eight appeared in his lifetime and ten more were attributed to him later. His eight plays were published after his death: the best known are *Orlando Furioso* (1594), *Frier Bacon and Frier Bungay* (1594, in which the real-life mage Roger Bacon, 'Dr Mirabilis', conjures up the Devil), and *James the Fourth* (1598). Perhaps his most important work, other than his four 'rogue pamphlets', is the *Groats-Worth of Witte, bought with a Million of Repentance*. This autobiographical prose tract, which appeared in 1592, the year of his death, was one of a pair of pamphlets (the other is *The Repentance*) composed on his deathbed. The *Groats-Worth* tells the story of one 'Roberto' (Greene himself) and his gradual decline into debauchery. The piece ends with an Address to his fellow playwrights; Greene cites Marlowe, Lodge and Peele, urging them to use their brains for something better than the writing of plays.

Greene also excoriates 'the upstart Crow, beautified with our feathers, that with his Tygers heart wrapt in a Players hide, supposes he is as well able to bumbast out a blanke verse as the best of you: and being an absolute Johannes fac totum (a 'Jack of all trades'), is in his owne conceit the only Shake-scene in a countrey'. Unsurprisingly, it has been assumed that this is an attack on William Shakespeare, newly arrived in London from the Midlands and looked down upon by the Wits as one who lacked the advantages of an Oxbridge education. Certainly it is the first ever mention of Shakespeare as a working dramatist. Whether Greene's attack hurt Shakespeare is unknown; more usefully, his prose romance *Pandosto* (1588), itself based on a Polish folktale, provided his greater contemporary with the plot for *A Winter's Tale* (1610). Professor J.M. Brown, writing in *The New Zealand Magazine* (April 1877), suggests that Greene should be seen as 'the father of Shakespeare – as far, at least, as an ordinary man may be said to be the father of a giant'. He also suggests that Shakespeare paid Greene back, mocking him through the character of Bottom, in *A Midsummer Night's Dream*, and burlesqued both Greene and his sworn enemy Harvey in *Love's Labours Lost*. It was further suggested in 2004, by Stephen Greenblatt, that Shakespeare used Greene for his own purposes, creating from his character that of that 'bolting-hutch of beastliness',[32] the libidinous, drunken and cynical Sir John Falstaff.

It is in the latter role – Greene the debauchee – that he presumably amassed the material upon which he based his four 'coney-catching' pamphlets, published between 1591 and 1592. And however substantial or otherwise may have been Greene's influence on Shakespeare, and however successful a celebrity author he may have been to the late sixteenth century, it is in the sphere of the popular 'rogue pamphlet' that he is possibly best remembered now. The first such pamphlet, *A Notable Discouery of Coosnage* [cozenage, or trickery], 'Now daily practised by sundry lewd persons called Connie-Catchers [confidence tricksters] and Cross-biters [swindlers] …', appeared in 1591. It was followed by *The Second part of Conny-catching* and the *Thirde and last Parte of Conny-catching*, all published in the same year. These in turn were followed by *A Dispvtation between a Hee Conny-catcher and a Shee Conny-catcher*, 'whether a Theefe or a Whoore is most hurtful in Cousonage … ' *The Black Booke's Messenger* and finally *The Defence of Connycatching* 'by Cuthbert Conny-catcher', all 1592. The proposed Black Book never appeared, nor did a tract entitled *The Connycatcher's Repentance*. Greene did not sign the pamphlets, other than setting his initials on the title-page of the *Disputation*, but he did acknowledge that the prefaces were his. He fooled no one, if he even wished to: as he would in his final work, the self-excoriating death's-bed *Repentance*, Greene, claiming that his work would benefit the Commonwealth, was playing the dual role of repentant degenerate and guide to the excitements of that shamefully exciting world. And as with his 'straight' works of prose and drama, the pamphlets were highly successful, with rival stationers, the 'publishers' of the era, competing for the texts.

The essence of all these is the parading by Greene of what he claims are his first-hand reminiscences of and insider tips on the underworld and its language. Like some sixteenth-century precursor of *True Detective* magazine, Greene gleefully peddles his downmarket sensationalism, larded with cant and anecdote, but carefully quarantined with pious distaste. Greene positions himself as a lone fighter against crime, protesting somewhat over-enthusiastically the way in which he has risked the wrath of the coney-catchers, and indeed his own life, by breaching their tavern-bench *omertà* and revealing their masonic secrets. But nothing is as important as getting out the story. He compares himself to the Roman hero Scaevola, who sacrificed his own hand in order to save Rome, claiming that despite their most blood-curdling threats 'these vultures, these fatall Harpies' will not still his tongue.[33] *Nascimur pro patria*: 'We are born for the good of our country', trumpets the title page of each pamphlet, and Greene's ostentatiously public-spirited sentiments dominate every page. Greene also parades, in *The Second Part*, a variety of 'testimonials' from potential coneys, whose money had been saved thanks to a timely encounter with his efforts: 'Maisters, I boughte a booke of late for a groate that warnes me of Card-playing … I have foresworne cards ever since I read it';[34] another, who had not been so fortunate, meets Greene and sees his book: 'Sir, said he, If I had seen this booke but two dayes since, it had saved me nine pound in my purse.'[35] That the *Notable Discouery* in fact makes no mention of card-playing is neither here nor there. This is the commercial world.

Like Thomas Harman, who similarly advertised his labours 'for the proffyt of [my] naturall Countrey',[36] Greene played the reformer's card, but unlike his forerunner, the deck he used was distinctly corrupt. Nor was Harman the only source on which he drew. Substantial pieces of Greene's 'revelations' had appeared around forty years earlier in *A Manifest Detection of Dice-Play*.

Greene's works further resemble those of the restrained Harman in ways that exceed his simple pilfering of the earlier writer's glossary. When in *The Second Part* he rejects the criticisms of those who regret the absence of 'eloquent phrases' in these pamphlets, he is echoing Harman's celebration of his own decision to employ 'plain terms … Eloquence have I none; I never was acquainted with the muses; I have never tasted of Helcyon …' Instead he has preferred to write 'simplye and truelye, with such usual words and termes as is amongst us wel known …'[37] Greene offers a somewhat different justification for his plain language. Self-serving as usual, he explains that he has deliberately rejected the florid niceties of which he is undoubtedly capable, since 'a certain decorum is to bee kept in everie thing, Therefore I humbly crave pardon and desire I may write basely of such base wretches'.[38]

Yet failings of style and motives can be ignored in the face of what Greene's pamphlets actually offer the collector or historian of cant. Rodomontade aside, Greene's lexicography is impressively systematic. In the *Notable Discouery*, for instance, he deals one by one with the varieties of fraud: 'High Law: robbing by the highway side; Sacking Law: lecherie; Cheting Law: playing at false dice; Cros-biting Law: cosenage by whores; Coneycatching Law: cosenage by cards; Versing Law: cosenage by false gold; Figging Law: cutting of purses and picking of pockets; Barnard's Law: a drunken cosenage by cards.' He then lists the essential 'players' of each variety of fraud; thus when he expounds upon the 'Cross-biting Law', 'cosenage by whores', or what, in modern terms, would be the 'badger' or 'murphy game', he lists the whore herself, here known as the traffique, the sucker or 'coney', this time termed the simpler, and the cross-biter, who beat and robbed the unfortunate punter. The system is sustained through each type of trickery. Only when faced with what he calls the 'Cheting Law' does Greene, otherwise so determined in his efforts to reveal every facet of villainy, show himself strangely reticent, and declares, 'Pardon me, Gentlemen, for although no man could better than myself discover this law and his termes, and the names of their Chetes, Bar'd-Dice, Flats, Forgers, Langrets, Gourds, demies and many other ... yet for some speciall reasons, herein I will be silent.' It has been suggested that this silence stems from plain ignorance of all but the names themselves; more likely, surely, is that here was an area of fraud which Greene not merely knew but practised, and saw no reason to reveal himself as an adept. Similar analysis is offered in *The Second Part*, where he deals with the Prigging Law (horse-stealing), Vincent's Law (deceit at bowls), the world of the Nip (a cut-purse) and the Foist (a pick-pocket), Lifting Law (larceny), Courbing Law (hooking items out of open windows) and the Black Art (lock-picking). He also appends nine salutary tales. *The Third Part*, which contains only tales and no glossaries, is essentially an addendum to its predecessors; he had exhausted his canting vocabulary but Greene appreciated the popularity of his pamphlets and saw no reason to turn off the supply.

Whether Greene wrote what would be the final 'coney-catching pamphlet', *The Defense of Conny-Catching, or A Confutation of Those two injurious Pamphlets published by R.G. against the practitioners of many nimble-witted and muysticall Sciences*, remains unresolved. The author purported to be one 'Cuthbert Cunny-catcher', a 'Licentiate in Whittington College' – a joke aimed foursquare at the underworld: Whittington College being in fact Newgate Jail, its name taken from the celebrated Richard 'Dick' Whittington, he of pantomime and actual fame; Whittington's executors had used his legacy to refurbish the prison in 1422. Cuthbert is furious, railing against this 'cursed book of Conycatching' and reviling 'this R.G. that had made a publike spoyle of so noble a science ...'[39] Not only has he revealed many secrets of the criminal fraternity, but he has missed out on a number of even grosser ones. Why persecute the poor coney-catcher? There are many more despicable villains. In fact the book is low on hard information; it is basically a collection, like *The Third Part*, of more or less relevant tales. Perhaps the most interesting passage is that in which Cuthbert teases R.G. 'Aske the Queene's Players if you sold them not Orlando Furioso for twenty nobles, and when they were in the country sold the same play to the Lord Admirals men for as much more. Was this not plaine Conny-catching R. G.?'[40] This is a genuine enough gripe, but was there a real Cuthbert or, despite an elaborate rejection of the theory both by the nineteenth-century Elizabethan specialist A. B. Grosart and by Professor H. C. Hart in Notes and Queries,[41] was Greene the author of this pamphlet too? For all its pious indignation, 'Cuthbert' is surely just one more way of milking a profitable genre. In the end, Greene was most likely as much the author of this refutation as he certainly was of the two pamphlets against which it pretends to rail. Teasing himself in print, revealing his own duplicities, it all seems totally in the character of a man who liked to sail close to the wind.

Whether as straightforward beggar book, or as the focused coney-catching pamphlet, these explications of the underworld and its by-product cant proved an increasingly popular addition to publishing. They represented the shift of printing, once restricted, to that of a mass medium, and the appetite of its new consumers for something beyond the simple moralizing that had informed earlier works. Such a shift was by no means invariably welcomed. Thus the earliest authors of the genre, seeking to deflect criticism, had opted to position themselves as 'sociological' commentators. Greene's pamphlets might be seen as nearer that type, with their succession of anecdotes featuring unfortunate coneys or occasional stories that showed how the criminal biter might themselves be bit. At the same time, in the same way that a number of his romances and plays were based on the 'prodigal son' trope that underpinned many contemporary works, Greene, claiming to have taken his information from personal experience, was far more tolerant of the villains he portrayed. He enjoys their trickery. While he still claimed, as had his predecessors, that his work offered a social good by alerting the innocent to the tricks they might encounter, he also ensured that readers would be both amused and titillated. And ultimately, as Anna Bayman[42] stresses, 'entertainment dominates, often subsuming the conventional moralizing. The indulgence with which Greene handles his rogues – we are invited to admire their inventiveness – is enhanced by his tendency to represent the victim as culpable. Many of the conies are caught because of their own greed, lust, vanity, or willingness to play tricks on others.'

However, the moralizers remained. Pamphleteering became identified with its subject and arguments were proposed whereby the fact of detailing tricks would encourage hitherto law-abiding individuals to try them for themselves. Rather than warn, the pamphlets might teach. But the book trade was undeterred. Their primary concern was profit and their commercial instincts saw how well the pamphlets sold. There might be those, such as Samuel Rowlands, who told readers that 'If any with the spider here seeke to sucke poison, let such a one take heed, lest in practising his villainy he chance commence Bachelor in Whittington Colledge.'[43] But the genre continued. As will be seen in Chapter 4, another hit playwright, Thomas Dekker, some of whose most popular scripts were infused with cant, also saw the charm of pamphleteering. The pattern would persist whether in villainous 'confessions', gallows repentances, street-sold ballads or in today's criminal memoirs.

The extant lexicography of the sixteenth century is usually linked to the lexes listed and re-listed by the canonical quartet of authors: Copland, Awdeley, Harman and Greene, with a minor role for Gilbert Walker. The concept of 'slang', as used by the butcher, the baker and their non-criminal peers, tends not to be considered. But it did seem to exist, even if its sources are far more varied. Of the 1,355 contemporary terms included in my own database, there are around 400 that appear in none of these writers. And of the terms they use themselves, not all are specifically cant. It would appear that approximately 50% of the total are not underworld usage. The sources are varied: Sir Philip Sidney's *Arcadia*, Philip Stubbes's *Anatomy of Abuses*, Shakespeare's plays, and Florio's Italian-English lexicon *The New Worlde of Wordes*, in which he used many non-standard English terms (including the first use of *fuck* in a dictionary), among many others. That these early examples of the 'counter-language' are not codified does not mean that they did not exist. It would still require a further century before they were properly acknowledged, at least in a dedicated dictionary.

4 Crime and Punishment: The Vocabulary of Villainy

The Attention of the Publick is naturally excited towards those, who, by violating the Laws of their Country, are become liable to Punishment ... (N)ot only the Crime, but the Connexions and most private History of the unfortunate Delinquents, are eagerly enquired into, and become the Subjects of every Conversation. To be ignorant of, or to have nothing new to offer upon these Topicks, almost excludes us from Society.

The Authentic Trial and Memoirs of Isaac Darkin, alias Dumas, capitally convicted for a highway-robbery, at the Lent Assizes, Oxford, 1761

While neither language nor the sources that create and drive it are bound to chronology, one can see in the seventeenth century a series of developments that set off the steady increase of what would become known as slang, i.e. language that was not used strictly by criminals, and a gradual diminution of the role that cant would play in the dictionaries. When, *c.* 1698, the otherwise anonymous B. E. Gent. published his *New Dictionary ... of the Canting Crew* not only did the overall count of entries greatly exceed his sixteenth-century predecessors, but its 4,000+ headwords displayed a wide variety of non-criminal, but equally non-standard usages. It would be half a century before the word 'slang' was coined, or at least first recorded (in 1756), and the eighteenth century's first slang dictionary, published in 1725, would do no more than plagiarize B. E., but the change was undoubtedly under way.

The road to B. E. is marked by a number of developments. If the language that appeared in the sixteenth-century glossaries had been that of a supposedly limited set of criminal vagabonds, that of the seventeenth and beyond that the eighteenth centuries reflected a broadening of the criminal world and thus of its vocabulary.

The beggar books had focused on criminal vagrants, the coney-catching pamphlets on various forms of confidence trickery and sharping; now this was compounded by the language of muggers, housebreakers and highwaymen. At the same time the focus of the cant moved from the towns and villages where such tricksters had gulled the provincial and the peasant, towards London and its environs. The old beggar books themselves would dry up, although the taxonomies of 'the canting crew' would continue to appear up to George Parker's *Life's View of Society* (1781), in which the list reached seventy-four 'job' descriptions.

Individual villains also moved into the spotlight. If Harman had simply listed those he had apparently encountered, London publishers realized that the public, under whatever pretext, were open to what remains a popular genre: criminal biographies and even memoirs. In addition to this was an increasing flow of prison writing. Not invariably criminal – many writers concentrated on the political or religious beliefs that had placed them behind bars – but villains had their say. In addition to these writings came the increasing appearance of 'scoundrel verses', such as those appended to the *New Canting Dictionary* of 1725. And a popular author such as John Taylor, 'the Water Poet', went regularly to the counter-linguistic lexicon to embellish his verse. Equally important was the thriving Jacobean theatre, notably in the work of Thomas Dekker and in the 'city comedies' of Middleton, Jonson and Marston.

London was now the centre of crime. Beggars had been nomadic, ambulatory figures; the coney-catcher practised where he could, but the new criminal and the language he or she used focused on the ever-growing metropolis. To an extent this was the result of the sheer size and wealth of the capital of what remains a small island, but London also provided a number of areas in which a criminal could take refuge from those who pursued him. The concept of *sanctuary* had begun as a religious one, but subsequent to the Reformation it was used increasingly of criminal hideaways, those seemingly unassailable refuges that, in the nineteenth century, would be known as *rookeries*.

Sanctuary was an ancient concept, of late fourth-century origin, and was defined as 'a consecrated place[1] giving protection to those fleeing from justice or persecution; or, the privilege of taking refuge in such consecrated place'. The religious aspects had largely faded, but areas of sanctuary, usually extending for a two-mile radius around a given church, began to attract debtors, and in their wake, villains. There were many such zones: Frank Aydelotte quotes a letter from William Fletewood, Recorder of the City of London from 1571 to 1591, to Lord Burghley, dated 8 August 1575, reporting the progress he has made in the suppression of rogues: 'As for Westminster, the Duchie (the district about the Savoy), St. Giles, Highe Holborn, St. Johne's streate, and Islington, were never so well and quiet, for neither roge nor masterles man dare once to looke into those parts.'[2] The campaign cannot have been that successful. As laid down in a law of 1696–7[3] which sought to suppress such aggregations of corruption, sanctuaries still existed in the Savoy, Salisbury Court, Ram Alley, Mitre Court, Fuller's Rents, Baldwin's Gardens, Montague Close, the Minories, the Mint, the Clink, and Deadman's Place.

Unspecified, but comprising the Savoy area, as well as Mitre Court and Ram Alley, was that known as Alsatia, a name borrowed from the provinces of Alsace-Lorraine, an eternally disputed territory on the borders of what would become France and Germany. Situated in the Ward-of-Farringdon-Without, and occupying land that ran along the Thames from the Temple to Whitefriars Street and from Fleet Street down to the river, the Carmelite monastery of Whitefriars had been founded in the mid-thirteenth century. Dissolved like all its peers by Henry VIII's Reformation, the buildings and land were granted to the royal physician, William Butte. By the late sixteenth century the area was in ruins but it had gained a new, criminal population, the antithesis of the holy brothers. In 1580, pushing the old religious concept of sanctuary to its limits, they petitioned Elizabeth I, claiming to be exempt from the jurisdiction of the City; she allowed their claim and the villains' privileges were confirmed by charter by James I in 1608. The area was expanded by the adjacent Savoy, the site of the old Savoy palace, another decaying victim of modernity.

Little light penetrated its clogged alleys; there was much rubbish and more sewage. Ingress might be through a public house: its front door giving on to 'civilian' Fleet Street, a secret back entrance opening into the sanctuary. Teeming with squalid dwellings and a concomitantly corrupt population, these were not the sort of places where the law-abiding, let alone the law-upholding, could simply stroll. In their turn, a villain or debtor, once entered, need never leave, whether voluntarily, or even under duress. Writing in his *History of England* (1849), the historian Thomas Macaulay noted that 'at any attempt to extradite a criminal, bullies with swords and cudgels, termagant hags with spits and broomsticks poured forth by the hundred and the intruder was fortunate if he escaped back to Fleet Street, hustled, stripped and jumped upon'.[4]

So celebrated was the area that it was mentioned in a number of plays, and most famously provided the backdrop for Thomas Shadwell's 1688 hit *The Squire of Alsatia* (see Chapter 5), which employed so much of the area's vocabulary that printed versions of the play were issued with a prefatory glossary. Its reputation persisted: Sir Walter Scott had his hero flee there for a few chapters in *The Adventures of Nigel* (1822) and Harrison Ainsworth did likewise in *Jack Sheppard* (1839). Both authors larded their books with 'Alsatian' language.

Thugs, villains, no-go areas, all these would continue as part of underworld London. St Giles (near today's Centre Point tower), already well known in the late sixteenth century, would thrive and become the greatest rookery of the nineteenth century. Slang, whether in its canting variety or even more so in general use, would only expand. Alsatia would not. Within twenty years of Shadwell's hit, London's great observer Ned Ward would write of the decline of 'these Infernal Territories where Vice and Infamy were so long Protected, and Flourish'd without Reproof, to the great Shame and Scandal of a Christian Nation', a place whose streets were now 'so very thin of People, the Windows broke, and the Houses untenanted, as if the Plague, or some such like Judgment from Heaven, as well as Executions on Earth, had made a great Slaughter amongst the poor Inhabitants'.[5]

The End of the Beggar Books

The focus of crime had moved, but the desire to exploit what had been proved as a lucrative market ensured that at least in one area of publishing the public were offered more of the same. Almost literally the same, even if the authors and their titles would change. Thomas Harman's 'Epistle' expresses his hope that his socio-linguistic efforts would provide a useful sourcebook for his fellow magistrates, as well as for interested members of the public, but the most immediate beneficiaries of his manual were those who followed in his lexicographical footsteps.

The first 'follower' was the playwright Thomas Dekker (?1572–1632). His birth-date is debatable, and while his death may have come in 1632, it might equally possibly have occurred nine years later. His *DNB* entry is substantial, but the actual biography, rather than the listing and analysis of his works, is frustratingly scant. 'His own words are often the only source for personal details. Nothing is known of his parents, though his name suggests that he was of Dutch descent.'[6] While still a young man he picked up a working knowledge of linen-drapery and shoe-making, as well as of the less savoury end of the law. He apparently knew the Low Countries, could certainly read Dutch, and may have fought in the Spanish wars. He began writing plays around 1598. But if his personal biography is lost, he remains one of the best chroniclers of Elizabethan life. An indefatigable eulogist of the city in which he lived, Dekker hymned London as 'thou Mother of my life, Nurse of my being'[7] and set it at the heart of both plays and prose.

Unlike most of his peers, he lacked any patron, nor was he an actor himself nor did he have money invested in a printing house. His sole income was from writing. Like many after him he suffered from a wearingly fluctuating income and was imprisoned for debt, the 'City gout' as he called it,[8] in 1598 and 1599, and he spent the seven years from 1612 to 1619 in the King's Bench prison in Southwark; his first wife, Mary, died while he was away. By necessity he was prolific, and while primarily a playwright he turned for added income to a variety of genres: non-dramatic pamphlets, mayoral pageants and public entertainments, satires, commendatory and other verses. And he produced a number of 'cant' pamphlets. Like other contemporary prisons the King's Bench was en-slanged 'the college': if nothing else, his time inside had taught him a personal knowledge of the underworld.

Dekker's plays tend to be collaborative efforts; his prose pamphlets are solo creations. Perhaps the best known is his description of an outbreak of the plague, *The Wonderful Year* (1603), while *The Guls Horne-Booke* (literally 'the suckers' primer'), his 1609 translation of Fredriech Dedekind's Latin poem *Grobianus*, remained in print throughout the century. And while the *Horne-Booke* deals in the perils that await the unwary in London, and naturally offers some cant, it is notable for including general 'slang' terms such as *bush* for pubic hair. However, it is in his rogue pamphlets, notably *The Bellman of London* (1608) and *Lanthorne and Candlelight, or, The Bell-Mans Second Nights Walke* (published seven months later in the same year), that he demonstrates his knowledge of cant and its users. *The Bellman* was instantly successful, meriting Dekker's speedy follow-up. The book went into nine editions by 1650, sometimes being retitled, such as in *O per se O ... being an Addition, or Lengthening, of the Bell-Mans Second Night-Walke* (1612) and *Villainies Discovered ... Being an Addition to the Bell-Mans Second Night-Walke* (1616).

Dekker would find his critics, but some were unquestioningly kind. A fellow writer, William Fennor, writing on his prison experiences in *The Counter's Commonwealth* (1617), turned briefly to those who had written on criminal language. He noted the efforts of Robert Greene and of Luke Hutton, author of *The Blacke Dogge of Newgate* (a ballad devoted to the prison's mythical 'black dog', supposedly the ghostly remains of a poor scholar, cannibalized by his fellow prison inmates), but set above both 'the most wittiest, elegantest and eloquentest piece, Master Dekker (the true heir of Apollo) composed, called The Bellman of London' in which Dekker had 'set for the vices of the time so vively, that it is unpossible the anchor of any other man's brain can sound the sea of a more deep and dreadful mischief'.[9]

In fact Dekker was as much recycling as creating. In *The Bellman*, properly titled *The Bellman of London: Bringing to Light the most Notorious Villanies that are now Practised in the Kingdom. Profitable for Gentlemen, Lawyers, Merchants, Citizens, Farmers, Masters of households, and all sorts of servants, to mark; and delightful for all men to read*, he borrows substantially from Harman (as he does from Greene). Where he differs from his predecessor is in the story with which he surrounds his exposition of the vocabulary. Hardly surprising, since Harman was a magistrate and Dekker an accomplished playwright. But many of the characters are the same and Dekker's taxonomy of twenty-seven major villainous types essentially replicates Harman's twenty-four. He uses 144 terms that can also be found in his predecessor. But his aims in displaying this list were somewhat different from those of Harman. Where the magistrate wanted to alert his fellow law-makers, as well as the 'straight' public, to this still relatively secret world, Dekker was more interested in the language itself. His fascination, it appears, was with the fictional possibilities of such a lurid vocabulary.

The pamphlet falls into two parts. Dekker begins with a country episode, in which, after some paragraphs in praise of country life, the author stumbles upon a country cottage where there are gathered a number of criminal beggars. Playing host is an old woman, 'an old nimble-tongd beldam',[10] who hides Dekker, who then watches the initiation of a candidate to the canting crew with the words, 'I doe stall thee to the Rogue, by vertue of this Soueraigne English liquor, so that henceforth it shall be lawful for thee to Cant (that is to say) to be a Vagabond and Beg, and to speake that Pedlers French, or that Canting language which is to be found among none but beggars.' The candidate is then drenched with a pot of beer. The woman then proceeds to inform the playwright of the various types of rural villains (in effect repeating Harman's categories). As had Greene's narrators, she pays lip-service to prevailing morality, and hopes that by speaking out about the rogues she 'may teach others how to avoide them'.[11]

Like Sherlock Holmes in 'The Copper Beeches' ('It is my belief, Watson, ... that the lowest and vilest alleys of London do not present a more dreadful record of sin that does the smiling ... countryside'), Dekker professes himself appalled by rural corruption and declares, 'I have heard of no sin in the city but I met it in the village, nor any vice in the tradesman, which was not in the ploughman.' Disillusioned, he returns to town. Here he meets a new informant, the Bellman, 'a man with a lantern and candle in his hand, a long staff on his neck, and a dog at his tail'. The Bellman, who styles himself 'the sentinel of the City, the watchman for every ward, the honest spy who discovered the 'prentices of the night'[12], plays much the same role for Dekker as the Spytell House Porter did for Copland. In his turn he expounds his own, urban knowledge, running down the world of the London criminal classes for Dekker, and his readers.

So successful was *The Bellman of London* that Dekker quickly wrote and published the sequel *Lanthorne and Candlelight,* which echoed the title of a popular ballad of the late sixteenth century (and seems to have taken its frontispiece from a woodcut used with that ballad) and reintroduced the Bellman. As edition followed edition, sometimes with new titles, the Bellman series took on new aspects, notably the inclusion of another of Dekker's concerns: prison in general and the treatment of debtors, which he knew all too well, in particular. *O per se O* (1612) takes as narrator the 'High Constable', whose information supposedly comes from a 'Divellish Schoole-master, whom I call by the name of O Per Se O'.[13] The next edition, now titled *Villanies Discouered* and published in 1616, added 'Canting Songs and other new conceits never before Printed'. Songs aside, the most important 'new conceit' was six new chapters, dealing with prisons. It was not Dekker's first essay into the subject: in 1604 he had written, possibly with Thomas Middleton, *The Black Book,* which among other revelations showed up the corruption of the authorities both in and out of jails. Prison was also the subject of a portion of *The Second part of the honest Whore* (1604), in which the closing scene is set in Bridewell, the 'house of correction', and two further plays: *Eastward Hoe* (1605) and *The Puritaine* (1607). In all cases Dekker continued to highlight the plight of imprisoned debtors.

In *Lanthorne and Candlelight* Dekker had introduced a new character: the beadle of Bridewell, supposedly the Bellman's brother. In 1610 this figure was taken up by another author, who signs himself only as 'S.R.' and issued his own pamphlet, *Martin Mark-All, beadle of Bridewell; his defence and answere to the belman of London.* The attribution of these initials remains unresolved. Prior to 1913 the general assumption had been that they belonged to the pamphleteer Samuel Rowlands, but in that year Frank Aydelotte, in his study of Elizabethan rogues, replaced Rowlands by a contemporary, Samuel Rid, a figure even less well attested in history. Aydelotte, who dismisses Rowlands as 'a hack-writer, with much less ability than Dekker and no perceptible honesty',[14] based his belief on track record. Rid, he explained, had published 'a vagabond book called the *Art of Iugling* [*or Legerdemaine*], in 1612. From the opening of this pamphlet it is evident that the author had published one before on canting rogues and gipsies (which are treated in the *Beadle of Bridewell*) and had promised another pamphlet. "Here to fore we have run over the two pestiferous carbuncles in the commonwealth, the Egyptians and the common canters: the poor canters we have canvassed meetely well, it now remaines to proceede where I left, and to goe forward with that before I promised."'[15] For Aydelotte this was proof. He notes a discussion of gypsies in *Martin Mark-all* that resembled closely that which had begun *The Art of Iugling*; both pamphlets were heavily indebted to Harman's dedicatory epistle and both offer identical pieces of Harman's text. Not only that, but the authors of both publications sign themselves 'S.R.' And to cap it off, near the end of *The Art of Iugling*, 'S.R.' actually refers to himself as 'the Beadle'. Toss in a reference to 'caprichious coxecombes, with their desperate wits', which Aydelotte saw as a reference to Dekker, and the line 'But I cannot stand all day nosing of Candle-sticks' (seen as a reference to *Lanthorne and Candlelight*) and there you were. Aydelotte, according to the lexicologist Gertrude Noyes, writing in 1941, had 'built up such a good case for Samuel Rid as author that his view is now widely accepted'.[16] Yet it would appear that more recently Rowlands has regained his crown, since most modern scholars attribute the work to him without further comment. And Rid, it might be noted, is wholly ignored by the new *DNB*. The identification with Rowlands will be followed here.

Rowlands (*fl.* 1598–1628) was like Dekker another prolific pamphleteer, his material being mainly satirical, but who could also approach more serious topics. In the context of criminal language he has been associated with the authorship of two pamphlets on the late-sixteenth-century highwayman Gamaliel Ratsey, as well as being posited as a possible author of the prison pamphlet *The Blacke Dogge of Newgate*. Rowlands saw Dekker as a rival in a newly lucrative genre, and set out to see him off. He made it clear that Dekker, for all his popularity, had simply plagiarized Harman and that in doing so he had made no effort to bring up to date a glossary that had originally been composed a half-century earlier. He stressed what he claimed was his own superior knowledge of the criminal world and offers his history of the 'the Regiment of Rogues', in which he lays out the story of canting's supposed founding father Cock Lorel as well as listing those beggar kings who both preceded and post-dated him. He appends a vocabulary list of some 129 entries, of which ten are modernizations of Harman's usage and fifty-three are brand-new expressions. If one adds in the canting material included in the narrative there are some eighty overlaps with Harman, and 156 with Dekker.

Rowlands was also keen to play the moral card. It was not for the first time. In 1602 he had been one those who capitalized on the late Robert Greene's reputation to augment their own income. In his pamphlet *Greene's Ghost Haunting Cony-catchers* – supposedly written up from Greene's unpublished papers but in reality plagiarized without acknowledgement from Greene's *Black Booke's Messenger* and the second and third of his *Coney-catching* pamphlets – he stated that his intention was 'for the good of the commonwealth, both for all men to see, what grosse villanies are now practised in the bright Sunne-shine, that thereby they may be forewarned to take heede how they converse with such cosoning companions: as also a just checke and controll to such wicked livers, that they perceiving their goodness set abroach, may with remorse and penitencie forsake their abominable course of life, and betake them to a more honest and civill behaviour.'[17] While earlier writers had insisted that the dissemination of knowledge would act against crime, he suggested that the reality of such pamphleteering was to increase it. With insouciant hypocrisy he explained that his work was of a different calibre. Previous authors had infected their readers with corruption, now he would lance this plague sore with his revelations. No one should attempt to use his book to learn from the tricks it exposed: 'If any with the spider here seeke to sucke poison, let such a one take heed, lest in practising his villainy he chance commence Bachelor in Whittington Colledge.'[18] That 'Colledge' was, of course, Newgate Prison. Now, in *Martin Mark-all*, Rowlands complained that rogue pamphlets were making cant too easily available to the hitherto innocent: 'These volumes and papers, now spread everie where, so that everie Jacke-boy now can say as well as the proudest of that fraternitie, "will you wapp for a wyn, or tranie for a make?"'[19] That cant catch-phrase, presumably already well known, would be explained by B. E.

in his dictionary of *c*. 1698 as '*If she won't wap for a Winne, let her trine for a Make* If she won't Lie with a Man for a Penny, let her Hang for a Half-penny.' Rowlands's real motives were, as Paula Blank has explained, less honourable. Cant had become something 'civilians' wanted to discover and writing about it made money. But there were too many authors vying for the same audience. 'We don't know how many vagabonds there were in early modern England who were "rich" in canting, but there were certainly several contemporary authors who were. The authors of Renaissance rogue literature do not so much decipher the canting language as reproduce it for their own profit.'[20]

Both Beadle and Bellman had their readers, but the flow of rogue pamphlets, with their concomitant vocabularies and glossaries, faded as the march of Puritanism worked with increasing success to sideline such supposedly corrupting frivolities. In addition, the prominence of the criminal beggar, so central to late Elizabethan life, was much diminished. Thus while mainstream dictionaries continued to appear throughout the seventeenth century, the world of cant lexicography was placed on hold until the Restoration.

Some minor examples of canting studies appeared throughout the century, but it was not until 1665 that the beggar book regained a major publication: *The English Rogue* by Richard Head. Head lived the life on which his books commented. As one critic sniffed, 'His indelicacy pleased the public but he led a wild and dissipated life …'[21] He had been born *c*. 1637 in Ireland to a father who had eloped with his mother shortly after leaving Oxford and subsequently gained employment as a nobleman's chaplain. Brought up in Plymouth, Head followed his late father to Oxford, but left quickly and apprenticed himself to a London bookseller. Here he wrote the presumably salacious *Venus' Cabinet Unlock'd*, then married and opened up his own shop in Little Britain, still a centre of the literary world. It was not a success: its meagre profits were promptly tossed away on the gambling tables and Head judiciously packed up and relocated in Dublin.

There he wrote a play, *Hic et Ubique, or the Humours of Dublin*, which, according to his biographer William Winstanley (in *Lives of the Most Famous English Poets*, 1687), was 'acted privately with great applause'. Armed with this success he returned to London in 1663 and had his hit printed, having removed the more 'licentious' portions. An attempt to rekindle his bookselling career failed: gambling remained both alluring and expensive; this second bookshop collapsed in its turn and Head was reduced to hackwork. He remained a hack, suffering vertiginous ups and downs and 'many crosses and afflictions' for what remained of his life, which ended, according to Winstanley, when in 1686 he drowned on a crossing to the Isle of Wight. John Aubrey, on the other hand, dispatches him ten years earlier, and sets the scene of his drowning off the shore near his childhood home of Plymouth. Aubrey noted that Head had recently been travelling with the gypsies and in a less than flattering aside says that he 'looked like a knave with his goggling eyes' and, somewhat mysteriously, that he could 'transform himself into any shape'.

The English Rogue is the life-story of one Meriton Latroon (from *latron*: a robber), 'a witty extravagant', embellished with 'a Compleat History of the Most Eminent Cheats of Both Sexes', included a seven-page glossary, drawing freely on Harman and Dekker, and the canting song, 'Bing Out Bien Morts', which is dense with cant. Indeed, the glossary which follows it is essential for its understanding. It was not, as these four lines indicate, the simplest of ditties: 'This Doxie Dell can cut bien whids / And wap well for a win: / And prig and cloy so benshiply, / All the Deuse-a-vile within ...'[22] Nor was Latroon's life considered acceptable: it was banned for its indecency and circulated secretly, as one of the recognized 'obscene publications' of its day. Nonetheless, and in time-honoured fashion, the author claimed the usual moral purpose: 'My onely designe was to make Vice appear as she is, foul, ugly, and deformed.'[23]

The *English Rogue* was popular and sold out within a year. There ensued a complex publishing history. The publisher of the first edition, Henry Marsh, died in 1665, deeply in debt to his former partner Francis Kirkman. Kirkman took over Marsh's business and republished Head's work in 1666; still popular, it appeared in three more editions that year, with one more in 1667. As the Epistle Dedicatory to part II explained: 'Gentlemen, it is very well known to you, that the first part of this Book has (notwithstanding many oppositions) done its business, being generally liked and approved of.'[24] Keen to keep capitalizing on the book, Kirkman then persuaded Head to write a sequel, a second part. When Head claimed, less than honestly, that the Rogue's life was not really based on his own, Kirkman added his own explanation. He then asked Head for further instalments. Parts three and four duly appeared, although Head claimed that while his name was on the cover he had written nothing. The new *DNB* is unimpressed and suggests that Head's complex professional life and need for money made his denial implausible. A uniform volume appeared in 1680 but the promised fifth part, in fact no more than a few pages tacked on to an abridged version of parts I–IV, was definitely by neither man.

To bulk out the original, the three new parts had Latroon meeting a number of characters with whom he talked and who recounted their own picaresque adventures, usually, like his, tales of cheating, whoring, stealing and cuckolding. In parts III and IV these characters turn out to be those Latroon has met, and in many cases treated badly, in part I. Their lives are equally squalid, but as G. W. R. D. Moseley has suggested, there may be a moral here: such is the result of dealing with the likes of Latroon.[25]

Compared to beggar books, with their focus on taxonomy-plus-glossary, *The English Rogue*, with its many titillating or amusing episodes, is more in the jest-book tradition, or, given its focus on criminality, the more anecdotally based work of Greene, Dekker and Rowlands. However, Head is at pains to include and explicate cant: like those predecessors, he must have known how potent the thieves' vocabulary was in selling a book. Head overlaps with Harman on 115 occasions, with Greene on 63, Dekker 78 and Rowlands 103. And of course this latter trio had all poached in their turn. Unlike them, however, he frames his canting terms in the larger narrative, the new genre of the rogue memoir: falling in with a gang of beggars, he throws in many of their words and then adds an extensive glossary to his recounting of their lives. All in all, between narrative and glossary, Head offers some 298 terms. In part II Kirkman follows suit, encountering another begging crew, although the glossary is shorter. Readers, it can be assumed, lapped them up, although for the most part as items of exotica, rather than day-to-day usages. It is unlikely that many would have needed to make references to 'High-Padding, Low-Padding, [...] Ken-Milling, [and] Jerk[ing] the Naskin'.

Eight years after the original *Rogue* came Head's solo offering: *The Canting Academy, or the Devil's Cabinet opened* (1673). This too falls within the format of most late-seventeenth-century cant studies: acting as an addendum to the genuine or semi-fictional biographies of notable rogues. Like *The English Rogue* it is a mish-mash of a book, which throws together canting songs as well as some composed by 'the choicest Wits of the Age', the oaths taken by professional criminals, 'the vicious and remarkable lives of Mother Craftsby and Madame Wheedle', the first of whom allegedly 'prostituted herself to anything that had money: nay, a Dog if he had but a shilling in his mouth'.[26] The frontispiece maintains the bawdy, if not pornographic tone, showing a whore and her client entwined on the ground, with her speech bubble proclaiming 'I'll smoke your Iockam' and his 'I'le wap your bite.' (*Jockum* was a penis and *bite* a vagina, an early example of slang's depiction of the female genitals as 'dangerous'; and while *smoke* would come to mean fellate in the 1960s, it must be seen here as the contemporary slang, 'uncover', i.e. pull out). Its most important feature was its glossary, the 'compleat Canting Dictionary'. Head lays out 206 canting terms, many of which simply replicated those found in the *Rogue*.

One extra aspect of the book is that like a traditional bilingual dictionary, Head offers 'Standard English-Cant / Cant-Standard English' sections. For him cant is presented not merely as a parallel vocabulary, but a genuinely 'foreign' one.

Head also pushes slang collection forward. While his title refers explicitly to 'canting' and it is B. E., twenty-five years later, who is credited with such innovation, Head is bringing in non-underworld slang. The ballads on which he draws are not invariably hymning crime. Looking at the first part of the alphabet, these terms include *beau-trap*, a confidence man, *blot the scrip*, to sign into writing, *blow off the groundsills*, to have sex on the ground, *bluffer*, an innkeeper, *booze* and *boozing* (hitherto spelt as *bouse / bousing*), *brush*, to rush off, and *bully-huff*, a prostitute's male accomplice, with whom she practised what would come to be known as 'the Murphy game'. Head was the first to offer *canary-bird*, a prisoner, *chiv*, a knife, *collegian*, a prisoner, *cousin*, a whore, *covey*, a fellow or man, *cracker*, the backside, *cruise*, to beg, *cully*, a man, *ducks*, as a term of affection, *fix*, to prepare a trick, *flash*, to talk in cant, *flog* (not yet SE), to whip, with its compounds *flogging cheat*, the whipping post, and *flogging cull*, one who whips. His inclusion of *flogging cully* is perhaps the first mention of one who enjoys what modernity terms 'fladge' or 'B&D'. Some would never leave cant, many others would move out into more general slang.

Head is perhaps not as original as he claims, and 50% of the book remains indebted to Harman and company. Yet his efforts had an influence of their own. The miscellaneous writer John Shirley (fl. 1680–1702), otherwise known as author of *The Famous History of Palmerin of England* (1685) and *The Illustrious History of Women* (1686), included a canting glossary in his best-selling *The Triumph of Wit* (1688, with eight editions by 1724); it appears to have been stolen wholesale from *The Canting Academy*. Nor was Shirley immune to theft in his turn: the anonymously authored *Scoundrel's Dictionary* (1754), supposedly 'printed from a copy taken on one of their Gang, in the late scuffle between the watchmen and a party of them on Clerkenwell-Green; which copy is now in the custody of one of the constables of that parish',[27] is little more than a reprint of his cant list. Perhaps its sole interest is the format: printing the English words first with a cant translation after and thus helping those who, it must be presumed, wanted to rough up their standard English for a little slumming amid the low life.

More important was Head's wider influence. Mainstream lexicographers had so far averted their gaze from cant and similar vulgarisms. But three years after *The Canting Academy* appeared, that pattern changed, albeit briefly. Elisha Coles published his *English Dictionary* in 1676. In it was included pretty much all of Head's word-list. Coles, unsurprisingly, felt it necessary to note in his preface his deviation from the orthodox. His justification is pleasingly pragmatic: ''Tis no Disparagement to understand the Canting Terms: It may chance to save your Throat from being cut, or (at least) your Pocket from being pick'd.' His innovation did not last. Edward Cocker, primarily known as a mathematician (thus 'according to Cocker'), whose *English Dictionary* of 1704 borrowed extensively from Coles, excluded any such vocabulary (although later editions grudgingly reintroduced 'some few, but omitted a multitude'), while in 1755 Samuel Johnson, eschewing anything that he considered naked vulgarity, had no truck with such material.

Nathaniel Bailey, Johnson's immediate predecessor and sometime rival, did include some of the vocabulary, and offered a separate thirty-six-page list (drawn probably on *The New Canting Dictionary* of 1725, whose anonymous compiler had in turn had plagiarized B. E.) in later editions of his *Universal Etymological English Dictionary*, but he was still the exception. The rule was that cant, like slang, would be left primarily to its devotees for some time to come. A rare exception, and on the surface a surprising one, was *The Ladies Dictionary*, written by the well-known London bookseller John Dunton and published in 1694. This work, which aimed at being 'a Compleat Directory to the Female-Sex in all Relations, Companies, Conditions and States of Life', did include some cant vocabulary, essentially that referring to the ranks of female beggars, and the aim, presumably, was to acquaint its gentle readers with the varieties of female mendicants they might find at their doors. Although the bulk of Dunton's publications (he claimed a list of 600 titles) were religious in content, he was also a keen user of slang, in such books as *The Postboy Robb'd* (1692), *The Whipping-Post, or, A Satyr upon Every Body* (1706), *Bumography* (1707), and above all *The Night-Walker, or, Evening Rambles in Search after Lewd Women* (1696).

The work of George Parker (1732–1800) was published in the 1780s, long after the genre had seemingly disappeared, but its content makes it the last of the beggar books. The criminal world had changed, as had its lexicography, as seen in the work of Parker's contemporary Francis Grose. Criminal cant would continue to appear in slang dictionaries, but Parker's two books fall into a much older style. Parker is an elusive figure and his self-description, 'Librarian to the College of Wit, Mirth and Humour', as appended to the title-page of his *Life's Painter of Variegated Characters in Public and Private Life* (1789), hardly helps. It is known, from a biographical section in his earlier *View of Society in High and Low Life* (1781), that he enjoyed a brief career in the navy, served as a soldier for seven years, and then tried, and failed, to succeed as an innkeeper. He turned actor but that was a patchy career and in 1772 he began touring the country giving lectures on elocution (in 1780 he was involved in the School of Eloquence in the Strand) and readings from popular authors. Parker was an eccentric figure, a friend of such celebrities as

Johnson, Reynolds and Goldsmith, who tried to get him an acting job with George Colman who turned him down for being too fat.

The *View of Society* offers an analysis of the world and language, of a wide range of professional thieves. Like his seventeenth-century predecessors, Parker positioned himself as a reporter. Joining a group of beggars in Dunkirk, he travels with them and notes no less than seventy-four discrete varieties of villain, plus their special techniques. He gives a detailed run-down of their activities, although there is no cant dictionary as such.

Among those he specified are *daisy kickers*, cheating ostlers, the *blue pigeon flyer*, a thief who strips the lead from roofs, *traps*, thief-takers, *maces*, who specialize in the theft of watches, and the *queer rooster*, not a villain but a police spy who frequents thieves' haunts, often feigning sleep in order to listen to their conversations. The *resurrection rig* is a synonym for body-snatching, the robbery of graves to provide corpses for an anatomist; the *crocussing rig* is quackery (from crocus, a quack), to *jibber the kibber* is the wrecker's trick of fixing a lantern to the head of a horse, one of whose legs is bound up that its irregular motion may suggest a vessel's. Parker also offers the *little snakesman*, a small boy who, à la Oliver Twist, is pushed through a small window and then opens the front door for thieves to enter; a *low gagger* creates fake sores to elicit sympathy, while a *buz-napper* is a young or apprentice pickpocket. The tricks are often those of Harman's era; only the terminology has moved on.

Seven years later he published *Life's Painter*, with its aim of exposing 'these invaders of our property, our safety, and our lives, who have a language quite unintelligible to any but themselves, and an established code of laws productive of their common safety at the same time, and live in splendour without the exertion of industry, labour, or care'.[28] In its fifteenth chapter Parker lays out a list of some 125 terms, along with illustrative anecdotes. He shows especial delicacy in his introduction to this section, which starts in Chapter 14. He enters into it, he explains, 'with a fearful foot, and I do beseech my fair readers to shun it, lest, in this primrose path, they meet a snake in the grass', and a few paragraphs later urges again that 'the fair reader will pass over the following pages; for the man who could be capable of instilling poison into the chaste recesses of female breast, deserves not the name of man, nor the happiness a virtuous and fond female can bestow'.[29] And having warned, he titillates: proceeding, as had the sixteenth-century glossarists, to create a dialogue, brimming with cant, and some slang. This is the material which the next chapter's glossary explains.

But if Parker's taxonomies represent a throwback, he was not unaware of a new world, and such terms as *hot* and *flannel* were far from cant. Among the 'variegated characters' is one group particularly worthy of note: '*Slang Boys. Boys of the slang*: fellows who speak the *slang language*, which is the same as *flash* and *cant*.'[30] Flash and slang were not exactly the same as cant: the former had replaced it and the latter expanded into a far larger social arena, but Parker could see what was to come.

Prison Pamphlets

Writing in his *English Villainies* (1632), Dekker itemized those places where such villainies led their perpetrators: London's many prisons. 'Upon one side of the Thames stand, the white Lion, the Kings-Bench, the Marshal-sea, the Clinke, the Counter in South-warke. On the other side, the Gate-house, Ludgate, New-gate, Wood-street Counter, Poultrey Counter, Finsbury, New-prison, Lobs-pound at the hole at Saint Katherines. Fourteen Golgathaes environing one City.'[31] He omitted Bridewell, still seen as a place of reform and as much a workhouse as a full-scale prison. London also boasted Tyburn, the country's largest gallows, with room for twenty-one villains to be 'turned off' at a time. The vocabulary of the jailhouse and of the 'the horse foaled of an acorn' substantially expanded the canting lexis.

Prisons were used sometimes as a backdrop for drama. Dekker's *Second Part of the Honest Whore* (1604) sets its closing scene in Bridewell and he used prison scenes in *Eastward Hoe* (1605) and *The Pvritaine* (17607). Thomas Haywood's *The Second part of King Edward the Fourth* (1599) has two scenes in the Marshalsea while Jonson's *Every Man out of his Humour* (1600) reaches its climax in the Counter.

But Dekker's primary writings on prisons were calculated to expose and to campaign rather than to entertain, and for such campaigns he turned to prose. He had experienced incarceration at first-hand and had found the conditions unpleasant and the administrators corrupt.

It was his aim to make this clear. His first attempt came in 1604 when with fellow playwright Middleton he collaborated on the *Black Book*. In its second part, 'The Last Will and Testament of Lawrence Lucifer The Old Bachelor of Limbo alias Dick Devil-Barn the Griping Farmer of Kent' (which was attributed to Middleton), the author highlighted the dishonesty of those policemen tasked with arresting debtors. It was, suggested Philip Shaw, 'the first work to reveal in detail the roguery of these policemen'.[32] He followed this with *The Seuen deadly Sinnes of London* (1606) and in 1616 issued three prison-based pieces, his output perhaps encouraged by his own residence in the King's Bench, halfway through a six-year term. The first comprised the prison chapters added to a new edition of *Lanthorne and Candlelight*; this appeared under a new title: *Villainie Discovered*. He contributed six prison 'characters' to the Overbury collection of 'Theophrastian characters', inaugurated by Sir Thomas Overbury (1581–1613), for which such fellow playwrights as Webster also wrote. His third prison tract is more debatable: a possible collaboration with William Fennor: *The Counter's Commonwealth: or a Voyage made to an Infernal Island* [see below]. Other pamphlets followed before his last *English Villanies* (1632), in reality the sixth edition of *Lanthorne and Candlelight*. In this the old jail chapters are replaced by three new ones, which showcase the miseries of debtor life in jail; the easy living of their companions, political bankrupts, and finally a special 'supplication to Conscience', supposedly suggested by the Bellman, and intended for delivery to a committee of influential London citizens.

Dekker's prison writings ran through his professional life, but he was not the first to attempt the topic. According to Frank Chandler, the first such writer was Luke Hutton, the son of a senior clergyman (either the archbishop of York or the prebendary of Durham). In 1582 he left Cambridge without a degree; according to Sir John Harington[33] he was already a young man 'so valiant that he feared not men nor laws'. He turned to crime, riding out as a highwayman. His career ended after robbing nineteen men in Yorkshire on his birthday, 18 October, in 1598. Jailed in Newgate, he was transferred to York and tried, then hanged in that city in the following year.

Hutton was supposedly the author of a prison-related book, *The Blacke Dogge of Newgate* (published after his death in *c.* 1600). Hutton's alleged repentance had already appeared, though whether he was the author is unknown. It was registered at Stationer's Hall in 1595. There also exists a black-letter broadside, 'Huttons lamentation: which he wrote the day before his death, being condemned to be hanged at Yorke this last assises for his robberies and trespasses committed. To the tune of Wandering and wauering'. The text details Hutton's fall from grace, and his association with a dozen companions, known blasphemously as his 'twelve apostles'. With much requesting that 'Lord Jesus, forgive me, 'Luke of bad life' bewails his sins, recounts his life story and hopes that 'When on the ladder you do me view, / Think I am nearer heaven than you.'[34]

The Blacke Dogge focuses on Newgate, and the prison is described through the medium of a vision. Much of the story is recounted in verse (some eighty-one six-line stanzas), but the prose portion takes the form of a dialogue between Hutton and a prisoner, one 'Zawny', in which they discuss 'the knauerie, villanie, robberie, and cunnicatching, committed daily by diuers, who in the name of seruice and office were, as it were, attendants at Newgate'.[35] Hutton also talks of those who find out the names of the robbery victims, then persuade them to pay over sums towards arresting the robbers. They then approach the thieves in question and obtain more money: forcing them to pay up or face prosecution. In 1612 and again in 1638 the book was reissued, now entitled *The Discovery of a London Monster*. There were various additions, notably material pertaining to the legend of the Blacke Dogge itself. The original book stated that this was the nickname of the Newgate jailer; now it was maintained, in a conversation between the author and one Thin-gut, that the Dogge was the ghost of a mid-sixteenth-century prisoner killed and eaten by his friends, or if not him, then a black stone against which an unhappy inmate had once smashed open his skull.

Judges takes Hutton at face value, allowing him the actual authorship of both the lamentation and the Black Dogge (although not the ballad). John Lievsay, who tends to attribute much contemporary writing to Samuel Rowlands, adds *The London Monster* to his credits. He suggests that the stories that Thin-gut recounts of various styles of coney-catching have been lifted wholesale from Rowlands's *Greene's Ghost Haunting Cony-catchers*. He sees the patchwork cut-and-paste format of the book as very much in Rowlands's style.

In 1617 there appeared the *Counter's Commonwealth, or, A Voyage Made to an infernal Island*. The author is named as William Fennor. Little is known of his life other than that he married and had children, that he gave a one-man show, and published what were considered inferior verses. He worked on stage with, confusingly, Richard Vennard, and in 1614 was pitted against John Taylor the Water Poet in a contest of wits. When Fennor cried off, Taylor, who had laid out a good deal of money on advertising, was furious. There ensued an exchange of attacks in verse, Taylor's being judged superior in both wit and venom. In 1616 Fennor was imprisoned for debt in the Wood Street Counter. The result was *The Counter's Commonwealth*, i.e. the world of the debtor's prison, of 1617. In ten autobiographical chapters he recounts his experiences, and retells the tales of villainy and deception that he hears. As suggested above, it is possible that Fennor collaborated with the now veteran prison pamphleteer Thomas Dekker. He is certainly fulsome in his praise of the playwright. In Chapter 3 of the *Commonwealth* he finds himself mulcted for a payment of garnish (money extorted from a new prisoner either by a turnkey or fellow prisoners), which is beyond him, and wandering the jail is invited to a drink and a smoke with a band of carousing villains. When their leader offers to 'anatomize the vice, and lay the ulcers and sores of this corrupted age', 'Why sir, sayd I, there is a booke called *Greenes Ghost haunts Conycatchers*; another called *Legerdemaine*, and *The Blacke Dog of Newgate*, but the most wittiest, elegantest and eloquentest Peece (Master Dekkers, the true heire of Apollo composed) called *The Bell-man of London*, have already set foorth the vices of the time so viuely, that it is vnpossible the Anchor of any other mans braine can sound the sea of a more deepe and dreadfull mischeefe.'[36]

In the end he does listen, and the information he receives is entered into his book. It was republished in 1619, as *The Miseries of a Iaile*, and in 1629 as *A True Description of the Lawes, Ivstice, and Eqvity of a Compter*.

Philip Shaw sees Dekker's hand all over the book. He credits him with, at the very least, the narrative framework, and possibly with everything but the smallest details. He identifies Dekker with the veteran whom the narrator meets, and whose revelations (very similar, Shaw says, to those exhibited in Dekker's signed *Villaine Discovered*) he passes on to the reader. He also sees the relationship as a financial one: 'Possibly Dekker persuaded Fennor, his fellow prisoner, to issue a prison tract with his help for a share of the profits and under Fennor's name to capitalize upon the latter's notoriety as the antagonist of William [sic] Taylor in the much advertised wit-contest of 1614 that never materialized, and in the pamphlet war of 1615 that continued the rivalry.'[37]

The prison pamphlet continued through the century, typically in 'The Counter-Scuffle, Whereunto is added the Counter-Rat', set down in verse by one R. S., who took much from Fennor. It was a genre that would not die and one sees it from then on, whether in the nineteenth century's *Five Years' Penal Servitude* by 'One Who Has Endured It' (1877), or in Frank Norman's hugely popular *Bang to Rights* (1958), or Noel 'Razor' Smith's A *Few Kind Words and a Loaded Gun* (2004), which like a number of modern criminal autobiographies combines the prison reminiscence with the rogue memoir.

Rogue Memoirs

The rogue memoir was a direct descendant of the Spanish picaresque tale, of which the most important (as noted in Chapter 3) were the anonymously written *Lazarillo de Tormes* (1554), Mateo Alemán's *Guzmán de Alfarache* (1599–1605), and Francisco de Quevedo's *La vida del Buscón* (The Life of a Swindler), published in 1626. It is possible to place Richard Head's *English Rogue*, with its anti-hero Meriton Latroon, in this category, but its additional focus on the canting language keeps it with the dictionaries. The role of rogue memoir was more than that of acquainting an eager public with activities of this forbidden, alien but wholly exciting world. It brought, at least allegedly, flesh-and-blood villains to the page. Dekker and others had learned the appeal of anecdotally based expositions of cant; the rogue memoirs gave such information a new dimension: the personal. Even if they down-pedalled the actual terms.

The first such memoir appeared in 1605, in the form of two anonymous pamphlets commemorating the highwayman Gamaliel Ratsey: *The Life and Death of Gamaliel Ratsey, a Famous thief of England* and *Ratseis Ghost. Or the second Part of his madde Prankes and Robberies*. He was also the subject of two ballads that were registered at Stationers' Hall that year, but have not survived. The real-life Ratsey, the ne'er-do-well son of a prosperous Lincolnshire family, who had drifted from soldiery into crime, was already dead, hanged in Bedford on 26 or 27 March 1605. The facts of his life are little known, other than that he operated in the East Midlands, and one is forced to rely on the mythologizing pamphlets. 'The pamphlets depict Ratsey as bold, artful, generous to the poor, and possessed of a rough sense of humour. In one tale he bestows 40s. upon an old couple on the road to St Ives, declaring that he would 'favour and pitie them that are poore … for the rich can helpe themselves'.[38] His image was that of a Robin Hood, and as the *DNB* notes, some of his exploits were those included in the popular tales of that much-loved if ultimately fictional outlaw.

Like Ratsey, the mid-century James Hind was a celebrity highwayman. His life ended on 24 September 1652 with the gruesome punishment of being hanged, drawn and quartered. Before that event, and after it, he was much celebrated by the pamphleteers. In 1651, while he was still 'working', one finds a good selection. There was *An Excellent Comedy Called the Prince of Priggs Revels,* which featured 'the practices of that grand thief, Captain James Hind'; his lifestyle was further described in the 'most pleasant and historical narrative' *We Have Brought our Hogs to a Fair Market,* while *Hinds Ramble* brought his 'pleasant jests, witty conceits, and excellent cozenages', labelled as 'A Pill to Purge Melancholy'. There was Hinds's *Last Will and Testament,* promised to be 'full of various conceits beyond expectation', and the highwayman's *Declaration,* his *Humble Petition,* his *Trial and Confession* and a *True and Perfect Relation of the Taking of James Hind.* In 1652 came more, typically the story of his 'merry conceits and pretty pranks' entitled *Wit for Money* and *The English Gusman* by George Fidge, the satirical biographer of John Marriot, *The Great Eater of Gray's Inn.*

The theme was life rather than language, and neither rogue, nor others such as the gentleman highwayman Claude DuVal, whose *Memoirs* appeared in 1670, offered readers much in the way of cant. What they achieved was the further opening up of the alluring world of melodramatic crime. Linguistic embellishments would soon be added.

The *Memoirs of the right villainous John Hall, the late famous and notorious robber,* though appearing in the new century, were more linguistically informative. This alleged death-cell confession, 'penn'd from his own mouth', appeared in 1708. As well as Hall's supposed first-person memoir, the book came complete with a glossary of thieves' terms.

John Hall (c. 1675–1707), who is cited in the new *DNB* simply as 'thief', was born at some undetermined date to poor parents in Bishop's Head Court, Gray's Inn Lane, London. Brought up to be a chimney sweep, he soon turned pickpocket. He was only intermittently successful and in January 1682 was convicted of theft at the Old Bailey, and whipped at the cart's tail. In 1700 he was sentenced to death for housebreaking but won a pardon, on condition that he emigrated to America within six months. He managed to desert the ship which was meant to take him to the colonies, and returned to crime. In 1702 he had a cheek branded and was jailed for two years for stealing a portmanteau from a coach. On his release he formed a burglary gang with Stephen Bunce and Richard Low. They were daring, successful house-breakers who were arrested several times, but never convicted. Hall had few scruples. On one occasion he broke into the house of a Hackney baker. Tossing his apprentices into the kneading trough, Hall grabbed the baker's baby grand-daughter, threatening to put her in the bread oven if the baker did not hand over his cash. He did: some seventy pounds. In 1707, convicted for breaking into the house of Captain Guyon near Stepney, the gang was finally sentenced to death. They hanged at Tyburn on 12 December 1707. Before his death Hall used his time in jail to compose his autobiography. The glossary was taken largely from that issued with *Hell upon Earth* (1703), a study of conditions in Newgate which had been subtitled 'the most pleasant and delectable history of *Whittington's* College, otherwise (vulgarly) called Newgate, giving an account of the humours of those *Collegians*, who are strictly examined at the *Old Bailey*, and take their highest degrees near Hyde Park Corner'. The latter address being, of course, next door to the Tyburn gallows.

Hall was further remembered in a ballad, already well known by the 1780s and which remained popular into the mid-nineteenth century. It has enjoyed remarkable longevity, since the comic minstrel C. W. Ross found it and retitled it 'Sam Hall' in the 1850s. Later still it was rechristened again, as 'Sammy Small', and with its obscene lyrics was much loved by USAF pilots. The original ran, in part, as follows:

My name it is Jack Hall,
And I rob both great and small,
But my life must pay for all,
When I die, when I die
But my life must pay for all,
When I die.

Male villains were by no means alone. The voyeuristic thrills of reading about crime could only be intensified when its villains were women. Thus, in *Peirce's Supererogation, or a New Praise of the Old Asse* (1600), Gabriel Harvey wrote as follows: 'Long Megg of Westminster would have bene ashamed to disgrace her Sonday bonet with her Satterday witt. She knew some rules of decorum: and although she were a lustie bounsing rampe, somewhat like Gallemella, or maide Marian, it was she not such a roinish rannell, or such a dissolute gillian-flurtes, as this wainscot-faced Tomboy.'[39]

The woman to whom Harvey referred was one 'Long Meg', who had become well known during the latter half of the sixteenth century. A Lancashire girl, she had come down to London around 1540 and after tricking the carrier out of his fare took a job at a taphouse. According to Chandler she 'loved good company, especially affecting that of Dr. Skelton, the jester Will Sommers, and the Spanish Knight, Sir James of Castille. She delighted to assume man's apparel, and at last went to the wars with King Henry and returned wedded to a soldier, and set up a public house at Islington.'[40] Her life had already been the subject of a number of chapbooks, and Jonson mentioned her in *The Gypsies Metamorphosed* (1621), where he uses her name as generic for any exceptionally tall woman. The 'definitive version' appeared in 1635: *The life of Long Meg of Westminster: containing the mad merry pranks she played in her life time, not onely in performing sundry quarrels with divers ruffians about London, but also how valiantly she behaued her selfe in the warres of Bolloingne.*

Meg was not the only female villain to win literary fame. In 1651 Thomas Randolph's *Hey for Honesty* had this line: 'She is an Amashon [...] A Mall cutpurse, a Long Meg of Westminster.' If Long Meg had some celebrity then Moll Cutpurse, properly known as Mary Frith (1584–1659), had even more. And like Long Meg she earned a biography: *The Life of*

Mrs Mary Frith Commonly Called Mal Cutpurse. Exactly Collected and now Published for the Delight and Recreation of all Merry disposed Persons appeared in 1662. By then, however, Frith had come to symbolize everything that her male contemporaries saw as disturbing in a woman, and the 'facts' of her published life, a purported autobiography, are less than trustworthy.

Frith was born around 1584 and baptized at the London church of St Martin's Ludgate. Her first recorded appearance was, fittingly, in a court record, accused with two other women of stealing a purse containing 2s. 11d. No verdict is recorded, but there were further court appearances, again for thefts, at all of which she managed to obtain a verdict of 'not guilty'. In 1612, however, her luck seems to have run out. Writing to his friend Sir Dudley Carleton on 12 February, John Chamberlain told him how: 'Mall Cut-purse a notorious bagage (that used to go in mans apparell and challenged the feild of divers gallants) was brought to [Paul's Cross], where she wept bitterly and seemed very penitent, but yt is since doubted she was maudelin druncke, beeing discovered to have tipled of three quarts of sacke before she came to her penaunce.'[41] The punishment was for wearing 'indecent dress': which, as Chamberlain makes clear, referred to Frith's frequent sporting of male clothing.

By then she was a notorious figure, 'perhaps the most notorious Renaissance rogue on record'.[42] In a strictly male-dominated hierarchical society she had come to epitomize much that that world feared and thus condemned. Her cross-dressing was seen as undermining the established separation of genders; her frequenting of tobacco houses – the first woman recorded as so doing – and her boast that it was a lifetime's consumption of the weed that had ensured her longevity, was similarly subversive: women should not smoke. In these contexts, modern studies of her life have claimed her as a proto-feminist. In addition there was her image as a seventeenth-century 'Moriarty', controlling every aspect of contemporary crime. In her role as both receiver and broker of stolen goods she resembled her eighteenth-century successor Jonathan Wild. If one follows John McMullen, who as has been noted takes the picture of the contemporary underworld very much on its own merits: 'Her influence as a receiver and thief-taker was institutionalized. Her informers and accomplices advised her about robbers and pickpockets, and advertised her reputation. She cultivated specific crimes, instigating a lucrative trade in stealing and returning shopbooks and account ledgers that had specific value only to business owners. She established a market in high-value items such as personal jewels, rings, and watches. Her influence in the underworld stemmed from her power as defender of the public interest. After a theft, she guaranteed the recovery of the stolen property. […] As a patron of crime, she provided shape and discipline to thieving gangs and she expanded the frontiers of theft.'[43] Mary's last 'public appearance' came in 1644, when she was listed among those recently discharged from Bethlem Hospital, better known as 'Bedlam'; it appeared that at least for a while she had been considered mad. She died on 26 July 1859.

Inevitably Frith became a symbol, and as such celebrated and/ or vilified in the contemporary media. In 1610 the writer John Day composed, but it would appear did not publish, a pamphlet *The Madde Pranckes of Mery Mall of the Banckside with her Walkes in Mans Apparrell and to what Purpose*. Four years later Thomas Freeman wrote that:

> They say Mol's honest, and it may bee so,
> But yet it is a shrewd presumption no;
> To touch but pitch, 'tis knowne it will defile,
> Moll wears the breech, what may she be the while?
> Sure shee that doth the shadow so much grace,
> What will shee when the substance comes in place?'[44]

And John Taylor, the Water-Poet, a few years later, praised her as a contrast to those whose lives were dominated by ephemeral fads and fashions:

> Moll Frith doth teach them modesty,
> For she doth keepe one fashion constantly,
> And therefore she deserves a Matrons praise,
> In these inconstant Moone-like changing dayes.[45]

However, it was not so much in prose and poetry that Frith was commemorated, but in another art. It is now necessary to move into consideration of another form of popular culture, the theatre.

5 Play's the Thing:
The Stage and the Song

It is not possible to offer an accurate assessment of the way or rate in which cant or slang permeate the language. One can only assess one's sources, count the words that had not hitherto appeared in any recorded use, and brand them 'new' as regards their era. But if one cannot properly assess the end, one can identify the means, the most obvious of which can be found in a variety of mass-market entertainments, be they ballads and songs, plays, popular fiction, movies, TV and more recently the Internet and its social media. The world of what has been known since the term was first defined in the mid-nineteenth century as 'popular culture'. Popular culture does not itself coin many slang words and phrases, but outside the oral use in which slang finds its sources it is perhaps the most efficient means of spreading them. The seventeenth century lacked modern media, but there were other means of proliferation. Aside from the popular rogue memoirs and prison writings, there were street-sold broadsheet ballads (of which some were devoted to canting, and as such found bound with certain 'scoundrel dictionaries', but many were not), a growing degree of general writing which had nothing in common with such tracts or memoirs, and the playhouse.

The Playhouse

Whatever may have become of the theatre under the rule of the censorious Puritans, the seventeenth-century playhouse enjoyed two periods of success, before the Commonwealth and following the restoration of the monarchy in 1660. Thomas Dekker, Thomas Middleton, Ben Jonson and other 'city playwrights' were at work in the first period, while such as Thomas Shadwell wrote in the second. And all of these men used cant as part of at least some of their work. Of these the most important in lexicographical terms and in the dissemination of language were Jonson's *Bartholomew Fair* (1614) and *The Gypsies Metamorphosed* (1621), Beaumont and Fletcher's *Beggar's Bush* (1622), Robert Brome's *Jovial Crew* (1641), and Shadwell's *Squire of Alsatia* (1688).

Before them all, however, came Mary Frith's finest, if fictional hour: Middleton and Dekker's *The Roaring Girle, or Moll Cutpurse*, first performed in 1611. There was no pretence about the heroine's identity and Frith, perhaps egged on by the playwrights and actors for the purposes of publicity, even appeared on stage at the Fortune Playhouse. She was dressed as a man and closed the evening's performance with a jig. Critics have argued over the play: some see it as an early demonstration of feminism in action; others, given the final scenes in which 'Moll' is re-absorbed into law-abiding society, as a sell-out, a means of ensuring that the audience left the theatre in the comforting knowledge that all was right in the larger world and the underworld was no more real, let alone threatening, than a stage performance. In either case, neither argument impinges on Moll's cheerful revelation of the supposedly secret language of the underworld, its cant.

In the first scene of Act V the Roaring Girl meets a couple of fellow low-lifers, Tearcat and Trapdoor, and as her guests, a gaggle of aristocrats, look on, puts them through an interrogation:

> *Moll*: And Tearcat, what are you? a wild rogue, an angler or a
> ruffler ...?
> *Tearcat*: Brother to this upright man, flesh and blood, ruffling
> Tearcat is my name and a ruffler is my style, my profession.
> [...]
> *Trapdoor*: I have, by the salomon, a doxy that carries a kinchin
> mort in her slate at her back, besides my dell and my dainty
> wild dell, with all whom I'll tumble this next darkmans in
> the strommel, and drink ben bouse, and eat a fat gruntling
> cheat, a cackling cheat and a quacking cheat ...

All good stuff no doubt – no less than eighteen discrete cant terms in this brief example, and the whole scene carries on in the same way – but it reads less like a feasible dialogue and more like a cursorily dramatized slang glossary – one needs only alphabetical order and explanatory definitions. In parts it echoes Harman's artificial canting dialogues, throwing as many strange terms as possible into a supposedly spontaneous conversation. Nonetheless Middleton and Dekker, who had already issued his cant-based pamphlets, were making cant available to yet another audience. The on-stage aristocrats are initially appalled by the language: 'The grating of ten new cart-wheels,' complains one, 'and the gruntling of five hundred hogs comming [sic] from Rumford [i.e. Romford] market, cannot make a worse noyse then this canting language does in my eares,' but distaste leads to fascination. It is likely that the off-stage audience were similarly fascinated and equally keen to learn. The play contains some 117 terms, many of them in this contrived scene. Dekker, naturally, drew on what he knew: nearly three-quarters of the words can be found either in *The Bellman of London* or in *Lanthorne and Candlelight*. Several more are pre-dated by his play, *The Second Part of the Honest Whore* (1609). There are eleven first uses, none of them cant. The most important may have been *moll* to mean a woman, usually with overtones of promiscuity. Moll, of course, has lived on, notably in the compound *gangster's moll*. The term was especially popular in the mid-nineteenth century when it was reclaimed by cant, stripped of any sexual overtones and used in such compounds as *moll-tooler*, *moll wire* or *moll whiz*, a female pickpocket, *square moll*, an honest woman and *moll-buzzer*, a street thief specializing in purse-snatching.

Moll was among the first to bring cant to the stage; she was not the last. Before the Commonwealth called intermission on the theatre, other playwrights would make their own contributions. If Moll represents the city, then there were those who set their world against a rural background. The 'country' scripts include Richard Brome's *A Jovial Crew*, Jonson's masque *The Gypsies Metamorphosed* (1621) and *Beggars' Bush* (first performed in 1622 but possibly written in 1612), by John Fletcher with either Francis Beaumont or Philip Massinger. In all of these plays are written scenes in which the beggars introduce the audience and the on-stage characters who have met them to their own language. And although the beggars live 'outside the law', unlike the cony-catchers and kindred urban villains, they are seen as a happy, 'clean' community. Their role in the plays is to emphasize the quaint and sylvan. Thus their language, rather than being a sinister jargon that helps in the commission of crime, is presented as one more part of their romantic image, even if the background reality of the words displayed is still that found in the consciously condemnatory rogue pamphlets.

If the beggars were seen through somewhat romantic, even idyllic eyes, the villains of the city were not. The Jacobean playwrights wrote as commonly of London as they did of the countryside, and brought in language to match. Jonson's *Bartholomew Fair* (1614) epitomized the type, laying out some ninety-nine terms, the majority showing the kind of slang that was in contemporary use. Among them: *Bankside lady*, a whore working in one of the popular Southwark brothels such as the Rose or the Holland's Leaguer (which in 1631 earned its own eponymously titled play, by Shackerley Marmion); or the *Bermudas*, hideouts where certain well-connected debtors fled to avoid their creditors. London's Bermudas were either the alleys and passageways running near Drury Lane, Covent Garden, and/or the Mint in Southwark. Jonson, a prolific slang user, offers *jordan*, a chamberpot, *pimp*, yet to become standard English, *punk*, a young whore (plus twenty-three other synonyms), and *whip the cat*, to vomit. These were not exotic, criminal-only terms; these were the currency of everyday life.

Fifty years on, the Commonwealth finished and the Restoration assured, London continued its role as a theatrical backdrop, with language to match. The criminals, of course, still had their place, in entertainment as on the street. By the 1670s the term *Alsatia* was a regular in theatrical scripts. The reality was that the criminal sanctuary was somewhat past its peak, but audiences were well aware of its notoriety. But most were throwaway references. Not so the script that Thomas Shadwell penned and which in 1688 London's playgoers so hugely enjoyed (crowds of disappointed playgoers were turned away night after night): *The Squire of Alsatia*. It was, perhaps, the great London popular fiction until in 1821 Pierce Egan published *Life in London*, another huge hit on the page and on stage. A benefit night for the play netted £130 (worth nearly £20,000 today), and like other popular plays, the take could be around £100 a night. A decade later, around 1698, the term would be embodied thus in a new slang dictionary, B. E.'s *New Dictionary of the Canting Crew*: '*Squire of Alsatia*, a Man of Fortune, drawn in, cheated, and ruin'd by a Pack of poor, lowsy, spunging Fellows, that lived (formerly) in White-Fryars. *The Squire*, a Sir *Timothy Treat-all*; also a Sap-Pate. *Squirish*, foolish; also one that pretends to Pay all Reckonings, and is not strong enough in the Pocket. A *fat Squire*; A rich Fool.'

Shadwell's plot, calling on the self-explanatory names that contemporary playwrights loved, included four *Alsatians*, as those who used the sanctuary were termed: He offers four typical locals – Cheatly, 'who by reason of Debts dares not stir out of White-fryers'; Shamwell, 'who being ruin'd by Cheatly, is made a Decoy-Duck for others; not daring to stir out of Alsatia, where he lives'; and Captain Hackum, 'a Blockheaded Bully of Alsatia; a cowardly, impudent, blustering Fellow; formerly a Serjeant in Flanders, run from his Colours, retreated into White-Fryers for a very small Debt; where by the Alsatians, he is dubb'd a Captain'. Finally there is Scrapeall, 'a hypocritical, repeating, praying, psalm-singing, precise fellow, pretending to great piety; a godly knave, who joins with Cheatly, and supplies young heirs with goods, and money'.

Shadwell also drew on genuine local geography. The George Tavern, in which he places some of his Alsatian scenes, was, according to Joseph Moser, an actual place, 'not only the temple of dissipation and debauchery; but also [a house containing] under its ample roof the recesses of contrivance and fraud, the nests of perjury, and the apartments of prostitution'.[1] Above all the play promotes the exotic language of the Alsatians. Writing on 12 May to the Countess of Rutland, Peregrine Bertie informed her: 'We have had since my last another new play, a comedy writ by Shadwell, called the *Esquire of Alsatia*. It has been acted nine days successively, and on the third day the poet got 16 *l*. more than any other poet ever did. When all this is granted, there is nothing in it extraordinary [...] but the thin reason why it takes soe well is, because it brings severall of the cant words uppon the stage which some in towne have invented, and turns them into ridicule.'[2]

The Squire of Alsatia was not the first to include Alsatian terms, but it had the most extensive range. Printed editions of *The Squire* were prefixed with a forty-seven-word canting glossary and the script is heavy with 'the particular Language which such Rogues have made to themselves, call'd Canting, as Beggars, Gipsies, Thieves, and Jail-Birds do'. Thus in virtually the first scene Sir William, entering Alsatia, and meeting Hackum, Shamwell and Cheatly, also encounters their lexicon, including *ready*, *cole* and *rhino* for money; *putt* for one who is easily cheated; *clear* for very drunk; *meggs* for guineas; *smelts* for half-guineas; *tatts* and *the doctor* for false dice. And like Dekker again, Shadwell was largely responsible for introducing such arcane terminology into the non-criminal world. With the exception of *the doctor*, which can be found in Walker's treatise on dice cheating of 1552, all else is little more than a decade in use. Among them *ready* abbreviates SE *ready money*, while *cole*, cognate with modern *bread*, refers to a staple of daily life, i.e. coal; *rhino*, like its adjectival form *rhinocerical*, defeats the etymologists: the best offerings are the fabulousness of this newly discovered beast, or its being 'worth its weight in gold': neither convince; a *meg* is a variant on *mag*, meaning a halfpenny and thus, generically, money; this in turn comes from *make*, another halfpenny; *smelt* is debatable, possible from SE *melt*, i.e. a half-guinea figuratively 'melts down' the larger coin.

Sir William is in search of his son, and when he catches up with him, discovers that he's become a regular expert in the local terminology. 'Mockney' style is perhaps less recent than believed. 'Were you not educated like a Gentleman?' asks Sir William. 'No,' offers the son, 'like a Grasier, or a Butcher. If I had staid in the Country, I had never seen such a Nab, a rum Nab, such a modish Porker, such spruce and neat Accoutrements; here is a Tattle, here's a Famble, and here's the Cole, the Ready, the Rhino, the Darby: I have a lusty Cod, Old Prig, I'd have thee know, and am very Rhinocerical; here are Meggs and Smelts good store, Decusses and Georges; the Land is entail'd, and I will have my Snack of it while I am young, adad, I will. Hah!'[3] It is hardly surprising that his father condemns him as a 'most confirm'd Alsatian Rogue'.

In addition to those noted, these terms were very much of the era. A *rum nab* was a fashionable one (canting's *rum* being the antithesis of *queer*); a *tattle* and elsewhere in the play a *scout* were watches (the first from its 'tattling' or ticking, the second punning on its earlier definition, a watchman); *famble*, otherwise a hand, was a ring; *snack* means a share, a portion. The rest is monetary. A *lusty cod* meant a substantial purseful (*cod* was SE for a bag, it also meant the scrotum); a *george*, worth half-a-crown (12.5p), showed St George on its reverse; the *decus* echoed the motto 'decus et tutamen' (still on the English version of the pound coin), meaning 'an ornament and a safeguard' – it was inscribed around the edge of coins to prevent clipping; *darby* was also money, derived from Father Darby's bands: a moneylender's bond of particular severity, which effectively bound the borrower to the lender while the debt remained outstanding. Such bands are also at the root of *darbies*, handcuffs.

Alsatia faded then vanished, its decaying buildings finally demolished, its denizens scattered across the city. But it lived on in literature. *The Fortunes of Nigel*, by Sir Walter Scott, appeared in 1822. Set in the court of James I, it retailed the youthful career of its eponymous hero, including his flight into the Whitefriars netherworld after he has insulted a protégé of the king's own favourite, Buckingham. Writing in his introduction Scott acknowledges Shadwell as a primary source.

Scott naturally exploits Alsatian language to underpin Nigel's excursion into lowlife. And as he states, in a footnote, 'Of the cant words used [...] some are obvious in their meaning, others, as Harman Beck (constable), and the like, derive their source from that ancient piece of lexicography, the Slang Dictionary.' The dictionary in question was presumably Francis Grose's still reasonably recent *Classical Dictionary of the Vulgar Tongue*, editions of which had appeared between 1785 and 1811. One conversation, between the two bullies, runs thus: 'Tour out,' said the one ruffian to the other; 'tour the bien mort twiring at the gentry cove!' [Footnote: Look sharp. See how the girl is coquetting with the strange gallants!] 'I smell a spy,' replied the other, looking at Nigel. 'Chalk him across the peepers with your cheery.' [Footnote: Slash him over the eyes with your dagger.] 'Bing avast, bing avast!' replied his companion. While the slang dictionary plays its part, there may well be another source, the canting song of 1612 'Bing out bien Morts' with its call to 'Bing out bien Morts and toure and toure' and its 'doxie dell' or young tart, who will 'wap well for a win' or offer good sex for a penny. On the other hand Scott seems to be moving into invention: if *cheery* ever did mean dagger, it eluded the dictionaries. He is not, however, fantasizing with his references to the 'Huffs, the Muns, and the Tityretu's' – three contemporary gangs of upper-class ruffians, whose amusements tended to vandalism and assault. A *Huff* was a bully; *Mun* a face (the thugs enjoyed slashing the faces of passers-by); *Tityre-tu* apparently echoed the opening line of Virgil's first eclogue, 'Tityre, tu patulae recubans sub tegmine fagi', a Latin tag that implied that these privileged rogues were men of leisure and fortune, who 'lay at ease under their patrimonial beech trees'.

Before the end of the seventeenth century many playwrights had come to appreciate the appeal of non-standard language and included it in their work. It was by no means invariably cant, but simply the sort of slang that anyone might encounter. Among them are Thomas Chapman, William Congreve, John Dryden, John Fletcher, George Farquhar, John Marston, John Vanbrugh, just to name the most prolific. The list is far from all-embracing, but theatre-goers were now encountering terms such as *abigail*, a servant-girl (seemingly coined by Beaumont and Fletcher for *The Scornful Lady* [1610]), *all my eye*, *aunt*, a procuress, *bag* for scrotum, *beaver* for a hat, *bogtrotter* for Irishman, *fumbler*, an impotent man, *gizzard* for stomach, *grinders* for teeth, *half seas over* for drunk, *lurch* in the phrase *leave in the lurch*, *mob* for the rabble, the urban proletariat, *petticoat* for a woman and so on.

The century also indulged a variety of oaths, blasphemous or otherwise. Plays were awash with them and as examples these turn up regularly on stage. For instance, *ads* meant God's and came in such compounds as *adsblood! adsbleed! adsbud! Adsbudikins! adsheart! ad's (heart's) wounds!* (also *ad's heartlikins! … heartliwounds! … waudds! … waunds! … wauntlikins!*), *adslife!* (also *adslidikins! ads my life, adsnigs! adso!* (God's oath!) and *adsooks! adzooks!* or *ads wooks! Gad* played a parallel role, giving *gadsbobs!* (also *gadsbud!*) *gadsbodikins!* (also *gadsbudakins!*) *gadslid! gadsnigs! gadsnouns!* (also *gad-zoons! gadzounds!*) *gadso! gadsokers!* (also *gadsookers! gad-zookers!*) *gadsprecious! gadswogs! gadswoons!* (also *gad zoons!*) and *gadzooks!* (also *gadsooks! gadzookens! gadzookikins!*). All these and many more invoked God's blood, body, heart, wounds, nails and the synonymous 'hooks' and so on. 'God' was generally Christ in this context, thus the references to the crucifixion. Only 'nigs' remains a mystery: the *OED* dismisses it as 'not found in other contexts, and probably … corrupt or fabricated'.

Ballads

By the time Shakespeare created the ballad-seller Autolycus (the 'lone wolf'), the self-proclaimed 'snapper-up of unconsidered trifles' of *The Winter's Tale* (*c*. 1610), the sale of these single-sheet entertainments was well established. Shakespeare parodies their content – 'Here's one to a very doleful tune, how a usurer's wife was brought to bed of twenty money-bags at a burthen and how she longed to eat adders' heads and toads carbonadoed'[4] – and the audience would have laughed. The first recorded ballad, entitled 'Judas', appeared around 1300; three centuries later the form represented a widespread medium, though usually focused not on religious themes but on supernatural and historical events, sundered affection and of course crime, usually in the form of either gallows-delivered 'famous last words' (almost invariably concocted) or potted biographies (a mix of ripping yarn and repentance). They were sold in the street, not least that adjacent to the gallows. Aimed at common people, they naturally opted for common language.

Songs about crime were not, however, made by criminals, or those who tried to mimic them. The 'canting song' was a sub-set of balladeering: songs filled with criminal jargon, probably incomprehensible to many of their readers. That may well have made them even more appealing. For example, Dekker offers 'The Beggar's Curse' in *Lanthorne and Candlelight*:

> The Ruffin cly the nab of the harmanbeck
> If we mawned Pannam, lap, or ruff-peck,
> Or polars of yarrum: he cuts, bing to the Ruffmans,
> Or else he swears by the light-mans,
> To put our stamps on the Harmans.[5]

> [The devil take the constable's head!
> If we beg bread, drink, bacon,
> Or milk porridge he says: 'Off to the hedges.'
> Or swears, in the morning,
> To clap our feet in the stocks.]

Rowlands, in *Martin Mark-all*, is more lyrical.

> Towre out ben morts and towre,
> Look out ben morts and towre,
> For all the Rome coues are budgd a beake,
> And the quire coves tip the lowre.[6]

> [Look out good women (twice)
> All the great rogues have slipped away
> And their confederates have the loot.]

In *O Per Se O*, Dekker offered his version, retitled 'Bing Out Bien Morts', in which the 'good women' were urged to 'go away' or 'wander around' rather than to 'look'. Both Fletcher, in *Beggar's Bush*, and Brome, in *The Joviall Crewe*, included ballads, the former with 'The Maunder's Initiation' ('Cast you cares and nabs [hats] away, / The is maunder's [beggar's] holiday') and the latter with 'The Merry Beggars' ('Now bowse [drink] a round health to the Go-well and Com-well, / Of Cisley Bumtrincket [a personification of the vagina] that lies in the Strummel [straw – perhaps literal, perhaps their pubic hair]').

The slang lexicographer John Farmer's *Musa Pedestris* (1896) gathered a number of such canting songs, taking the tradition through to his own time. His collection remains a landmark of the type, but he drew on well-established sources. Canting songs had begun to appear not simply in the street or via plays, but also as appendices to canting dictionaries and to the rogue pamplets and memoirs. Richard Head included Dekker's 'Bing out Bien Morts'; *A Warning for Housekeepers* has 'A Budg and Snudg Song' ('The budg [sneak thief] it is a delicate trade, / And a delicate trade of fame …'); and John Shirley's *Triumph of Wit* has among several other titles 'The Rum Mort's Praise of her Faithless Maunder' ('Dimber damber [beggar chief] fare thee well / Palliards [professional beggars] all thou didst excel …').

The flow of canting songs continued beyond the seventeenth century. They could be independent one-sheet productions, they could be attached to plays. Typical of these were 'Frisky Moll's Song', sung in the dancing master John Thurmond's *Harlequin Sheppard* at Drury Lane

(1725), or '*Ye Scamps, ye Pads, ye Divers*' from James Messink's pantomime *The Choice of Harlequin* (1781). George Parker, of *Life's Painter* celebrity, was very prolific. His work includes the cantata, *The Sandman's Wedding* (1789), which features the meeting and subsequent nuptials of Joe the Sandman and Bess the Bunter (glossed by Farmer as a 'rag-gatherer', but usually defined as a low prostitute) in a booze-ken, i.e. tavern of the St Giles rookery, as well as his 'Masqueraders, or the World as It Wags', 'The Bunter's Christening' and 'The Happy Pair', which addresses itself to 'Ye slang-boys all ...' On a different level was John Gay's huge success *The Beggar's Opera* (1728), which could be said to be entirely composed of canting songs, considering the characters portrayed (although the cant tends to appear in the text rather than the lyrics). The Victorian popular novelist Harrison Ainsworth made up his own, for such historical novels, heavily larded with tales of villainous derring-do, as *Rookwood* (1834) and *Jack Sheppard* (1839). Ainsworth claimed, in the preface to *Rookwood*, to be 'the first to write a purely flash song',[7] but he was fooling himself, if no one else. His creations, such as 'Nix, My Doll, Pals, Fake Away' and 'The Game of High Toby' (both from *Rookwood*, in which he includes some thirty-one songs) push all the right lexical buttons, but they are merely imitative.

Canting songs are by their nature limited: they were artificial creations, aimed often to illustrate a given story or point up an arcane vocabulary. By the mid-seventeenth century the black-letter broadside ballad was sufficiently popular for a number of collections to start appearing: *Wit and Drollery* (1656), *Choice Drollery* (1656) and *Merry Drollery* (1661). There was a geographically named selection which included *Westminster Drollery* (1671–2), *Covent Garden Drollery* (1672), *Holborn Drollery* (1673) and *London Drollery* (1680), plus the provincial *Oxford Drollery* (1671) and *Windsor Drollery* (1672). The climax of all these came in 1719–20 with the six volumes of the playwright/poet Thomas D'Urfey's *Pills to Purge Melancholy*, a title that he had stolen from Henry Playford's similarly named collection of 1699–1700.

These were certainly not repositories of cant. A selection of terms includes *beaver*, a hat, *blue cap*, a Scot, *carpet knight*, a 'lounge lizard', *chink*, money, *dine with Duke Humphrey*, to go without supper, *drunk as a rat*, *tie a garter*, to caress sexually, *hogo*, a stench, *loose-bodied gown*, a whore, *lousy* as a negative intensifier, *Mother Midnight*, a midwife or abortionist, *clear the pipes*, take a drink or clear the throat, *pisspot*, *prinkum-prancum*, sexual intercourse, *ride a St George*, sex with the woman on top, *upsee-freeze*, strong drink and *yea and nay man*, a Quaker. None of these had come from the world of crime.

D'Urfey offers most of his predecessors' examples, and has the same degree of lexical spread as do they, but he seems to be especially enthusiastic for double-entendres. These are a few examples out of dozens:

> 'Some bring him Basons, some bring him Bowls,
> All Wenches pray him to stop up their holes.'

> 'Her Husband she said could scarce raise up his Hammer,
> His strength and his Tools were worn out.'

> 'Margery came in then with an Earthen Pot,
> Full of Pudding that was piping hot.'

Or, from 'The Jolly Trades-men':

> 'Sometimes I am a Butcher,
> And then I feel fat Ware Sir;
> And if the Flank be fleshed well,
> I take no farther care Sir:
> But in I thrust my Slaughtering-Knife,
> Up to the Haft with speed Sir;
> For all that ever I can do,
> I cannot make it bleed Sir.'[8]

'The Jolly Trades-men' delineates many occupations, although they seem to possess a single-track mind: the Tapster who fills his 'Pots' with his 'Spicket of two Handfuls long'; the Baker and his 'Wrigling-pole', the Glover, dressing skins with his 'Needle' (also wielded by the Tailor), the Cook and his 'Spit', the Weaver and his 'Fulling-Mill', the

Shoe-maker and his 'Lasting-Stick', not to mention his leather-softening 'Stones'. Thighs, no doubt, were duly slapped. The rugby song has many antecedents.

Nor was ballad collection limited to the various *Drolleries*. Samuel Pepys collected ballads and published them in five themed volumes, offering material from 1535 to 1639. In the mid-nineteenth century the Reverend Joseph Woodfall Ebsworth (1824–1908), who had also published annotated editions of *Westminster Drollery*, *Merry Drollery* (edns 1661 and 1670) and *Choyce Drollery*, published the last six volumes of the *Roxburghe Ballads*, with examples taken from 1567–1790. The first three had been edited by William Chappell between 1869 and 1879 and Ebsworth's volumes appeared between 1883 and 1899. Ebsworth was a leading member of the Ballad Society (founded in 1868) and was, as his comments included in his Roxburghe editing make clear, 'a man of deep affections and fierce antipathies'.[9] Among those with whom he quarrelled were Leslie Stephen, editor of the *DNB* – after which his contributions were no longer requested – and the lexicographer and founder of innumerable Victorian societies, Frederick Furnivall, or as Ebsworth termed him, 'the notorious pensioner Furnivallus Furioso'.

In the context of slang, what matters is the wide range of language that Chappell's and Ebsworth's efforts reveal. These ballads would have been on the streets and their language would have been common currency. Between the Roxburghe collection, the Drolleries, D'Urfey, Pepys and a variety of less well-known contributions, ballads provide examples of at least 1,000 slang terms in use during the seventeenth century.

Two modern collections – *Court Satires of the Restoration* (ed. J. H. Wilson, 1976) and *Poems on Affairs of State* (ed. G. de F. Lord, 1963–75) – make it clear that not all emerging slang had to depend on the street. These collections are mainly anonymous, though it would appear that their authors include such writers – both aristocratic and already celebrated – as Charles Sackville, Earl of Dorset, John Wilmot, Earl of Rochester, Sir Carr Scroope, John Dryden, John, Earl of Mulgrave, and George Etheredge. The satires and poems dealt with personalities and circumstances that would have meant little beyond the court, but the language was wholly democratic. Looking at terms that had not yet appeared in print, one finds the accent on sexuality. To *bulk*, to *fopdoodle*, to *futter* (from French *foutre*), and to *lig*, (i.e lie with) all meant to have sex; while the *squirter* was a female producing vaginal fluids and to *tap* was to deflower. The vagina was a *figary* and the penis a *gun*. There was much commercial sex, and the satires introduced the *abbess*, a bawd, ruling her *convent*, the brothel, and its collection of *owls*, *monkeys* and *oysters*, all whores. (The synonymous *nun* had been in use since 1515.) A pimp was a *setter*, a term used in cant for one who 'sets up' a victim for robbery or a confidence trick. More general terms included *booby*, stupid, the exclamation *ballocks!*, *phiz* for face, *jemmy*, a dandy, *high-shoed*, unsophisticated (lit. wearing the heavy boots of a peasant), *player*, a participant and the adverb *roaring*, e.g. roaring drunk. It is a mix of terms that have survived and those that vanished fast.

Journalism

The mid-century witnessed some of London's earliest newspapers, properly news-books. They tended to be named 'Mercurius' or Mercury, a brand that had been copied from the *Mercure française*, launched in France in 1611. First to appear was the *Mercurius Britannicus*, which in 1625 became the first English news periodical to carry a regular title. The outbreak of the Civil War created many more, pushing propaganda for one side or the other. Royalist sheets included the *Mercurius Aulicus* (for which John Taylor the Water Poet may have written), *Mercurius Pragmaticus*, *Mercurius Academicus* and *Mercurius Rusticus*. The Parliament had the *Mercurius Politicus* and *Mercurius Publicus*. Readers could also obtain *Mercurius Dogmaticus*, *Mercurius Morbicus*, *Mercurius Honestus*, *Mercurius Jocosus*, *Mercurius Phreneticus*, *Mercurius Phanaticus*, *Mercurius Insanus Insanissimus*, *Mercurius Infernus* and *Mercurius Democritus*. But none lasted.

Better than many was the *Mercurius Fumigosus*, or the *Smoking Nocturnal*, containing 'many strange Wonders Out of the World in the Moon, the Antipodes, Magy-land, Greenland, Faryland Tenebris, Slavonia and other adjacent parts'. It was published for the 'mis-understanding of all the Mad-Merry-People of Great Bedlam'. By contemporary standards it was a stayer and continued to appear for two years from 1654 to 1655. Its editor was the royalist journalist John Crouch, who had already been imprisoned by the Commonwealth for his earlier news-books: *The Man in the Moon* (1649–50) and *Mercurius Democritus* (1652–4).

Among the bawdy revelations, anecdotes of debauchery and coarse humour, plus a ration of nonsense-stories and poems, there was a good deal of slang. Again, looking only at terms that had yet to appear in print, one finds a preponderance of sexual matter. The penis is a *bone*, a *bill*, a *gunstick*, a *staff*, the *marrowbone and cleaver* and *it*; an erection is the *standing ague* while the impotent man occupies *fumbler's hall*, a *fumbler* being the unfortunate man himself. Semen is *oil*. The vagina is a *spitfire*, a *candlestick* (to hold the phallic *candle*), the *loom*, the *whirlpit* and the punning *Holloway*. A dildo is a *mandrake*, and a *dick* a man as a sexual partner. To have sex was to *do the job*, to *turn up one's tail* and to *knock*. *Fuck* makes an early appearance as 'Madame Fuck-a-Venter [at a venture]. To *crack one's pipkin* was to lose one's virginity, *flats* was lesbian sex (no protruding phalluses), *frigate* a woman and *forest* her pubic hair. The brothel and inmates offered *pie-woman* and *she-trooper* for the whores, *firemonger* for a bawd and *fireship* for a diseased prostitute. The place was a *topping school* or *smock shop*.

Not everything was sex. Among other new coinages were *bub* or *wet one's tonsils*, to drink, and *elevated*, drunk; *bum-fodder*, any form of trashy writing, *cuff*, a jolly old man; *gregory*, the hangman and the *Gregorian tree*, his gallows; a hanging was a *nubbing*; there appeared *cit*, a London citizen, and *louse*, a contemptible or untrustworthy individual; *flash* meant ostentatious or showy.

General Writing

Looking at those sources from which I have taken slang in my lexicographical researches, I find over 300 seventeenth-century writers. Setting aside the dictionaries, and those writers, primarily of drama – alongside poetry, the era's main form of literature – who have been mentioned, it is impossible to itemize each contribution to what was becoming an increasingly solid vocabulary, or would appear so from the acceleration and intensification of its recording. I have thus chosen a pair of authors to stand for the rest: for the first half of the century John Taylor, the Thames boatman whose day-job won him the name 'The Water Poet', and, following the Restoration of 1660, the gentleman poet and translator Charles Cotton, best known for his coarsely bawdy burlesque of Virgil: *Scarronides* or *Virgil Travestie*.

John Taylor was an Elizabethan, in time a Jacobean and always a staunch Royalist. Born in 1578 in Gloucester, there is no record of his parents but his father may have been a barber-surgeon. He was educated in the town but abandoned school when he found Latin grammar too challenging. In the early 1590s he moved to London and was apprenticed to a waterman, one of those, in an era when the river offered only a single bridge, who rowed passengers between the two banks of the Thames. Watermen were considered as a naval reserve; Taylor took part in the 1596 expedition to Cádiz and a year later sailed to the Azores. In all he made sixteen trips for the Royal Navy. His first job, other than cross-Thames portage, was as a 'bottleman' at the Tower of London, going out to wine-carrying vessels and bringing back to the Tower governor his 'fee' of two 'blacke leather bottles or bombards' (containers the size of a high boot) per cargo. The job lasted, on and off, until 1617, when a rival outbid him for the sinecure; Taylor memorialized it in his verses 'Farewell to the Tower Bottles' (1622).

More intelligent and apparently more affable than most of his fellow boatmen, a profession which, according to Taylor employed some 40,000 souls between Gravesend and London Bridge, he ingratiated himself with his clients. He struck up acquaintance with passing courtiers, and with some of the actors and writers whom he regularly rowed to the theatres of the Bankside. In 1613 he was made one of the King's Watermen, and would be involved with the Watermen's Company for the rest of his life. Meanwhile his theatrical connections led him to attempt a literary career of his own. Styling himself the 'Water Poet', he collected his verses and in 1612 published them as *The Sculler, rowing from Tiber to Thames with his Boate laden with a hotch-potch, or Gallimawfrey of Sonnets, Satyres, and Epigrams*. The mix of poet, however uncultured, and waterman appealed and, backed by complimentary verses from such as Samuel Rowlands, his writing was launched.

The poetry, republished in 1614 as *Taylors Water-worke*, was never going to enshrine its self-taught author amidst the literary canon but it romped along and seemed to hit the popular nerve. Equally important, Taylor proved himself a superb and dedicated self-publicist. When one of *The Sculler* verses poked fun at the more established poet Thomas Coryate, the pair became embroiled in a pamphlet war. There were rival petitions to the King and one of Taylor's pamphlets was burnt by the common hangman. It was all good for the Taylor brand. Nor did it suffer when in 1614, after another poet, William Fennor, allegedly stood him up rather than attend a planned and much-publicized trial of wit at the Hope theatre, Taylor launched another paper war with the pamphlet *Taylors Revenge: the Rimer William Fennor firkt, ferrited and finely fetchd ouer the Coales*. 'Come Sirrha, Rascall, off your clothes Sr, strip, / For my Satyrick whip shall make you skip ...' it begins. Fennor fought back, but Taylor cracked his whip again and claimed victory. His rival retreated and devoted himself to penning his prison memoirs.

In a fifty-year long literary career Taylor wrote widely and prolifically and took on any topic. Four centuries before Amazon he made self-publishing into a success. Among his writings (of which some sixty-three were collected in an omnibus of 1630 – another self-published enterprise that required four separate printers – and a further eighty-seven would appear before his death) are *Taylor's Urania*, *Against cursing and swearing*, *The Begger, or the praise of beggers beggary and begging*, *A Dogge of Warre*, *Laugh and be Fat*, *The World Runnes on Wheeles* (against hackney coaches), a number of funeral elegies, and the group of 'characters' of 'A Bawd very modest, A Whore very honest, A Thief very true and A Hangman very necessary'. Even when the subscribers failed to pay up he could turn problems to advantage, as in *A Kicksie Whinsie, or a Lerry cum Twang* (1619), 'Whercin John Taylor hath Satyrically suted seuen hundred and fifty of his bad debtors, that will not pay him for the returne of his journey from Scotland'. His palindrome 'Lewd did I live & evil I did dwel' is one of the first recorded. He wrote a number of nonsense verses, notably *Sir Gregory Nonsense His Newes from No-Place* (1622), making himself one of the founding fathers of a strain of English writing that would include Edward Lear and Lewis Carroll.

For publicity purposes none of this equalled his travels both in Britain and abroad, first sedulously advertised to obtain subscriptions, and subsequently written up to collect the money. As he put it in one preface, 'Thus Gentlemen amongst you take my ware, / You share my thankes, and I your moneye share.' He seems very modern. A 'literary entrepreneur', as the new *DNB* calls him, Taylor 'found his own solution [to literary ups and downs], by promoting his image as a "personality" and turning it to financial account. His greatest success lay in designing a series of exotic journeys, publicizing them in advance, and persuading large numbers of acquaintances to sponsor him in return for a copy of a published account of his adventures following his return. The destination was usually of little importance; the point lay in the mode of travel, and the mock-heroic account of his adventures on the way.'

He stands among the earliest of travel writers. His first trip was to Hamburg in 1617 and the years that followed would see ten trips, including a walk to Edinburgh from London, *The Pennylesse Pilgrimage, or the Moneylesse Perambulation*, carrying no money or supplies and depending on his wide range of acquaintances and admirers to keep him in food and shelter. There was a journey to Prague, where in the face of the Bohemian revolt of Protestants against the Catholic Habsburgs, Taylor's writings carried the flavour of prototype war reporting. At home he made trips via inland waterways or along the coast, using a waterman's wherry, and once rowed some forty miles in a boat of varnished brown paper, kept buoyant by eight inflated bullocks' bladders, and powered by 'oars' made of giant dried fish tied to canes. It was written up as *The Praise of Hempseed*, 'with the voyage of Mr Roger Bird and the writer hereof in a boat made of brown-paper from London to Quinborough in Kent'. When the boat, inevitably, began sinking and Taylor and Bird managed to drag it to land, a crowd tore it to pieces for souvenirs.

According to the verse 'A Taylor's Bill', in which he again had to chide subscribers for failing to pay up, he noted that 'Twelve Voyages and Journies I have past'. Typical were 1623's 'A Disouerie by Sea from London to Salisbury and 1632's Taylor on Thame Isis: or the DESCRIPTION of the Two Famous Riuers of Thame and Isis [...] 'With all the Flats, Shores, Shelues, Sands, Weares, Stops, Riuers, Brooks, Bournes, Streames, Rills, Riuolets, Streamlets, Creeks, and whatsoeuer helps the said Riuers haue, from their springs or heads, to their falls in to the Ocean'. Taylor's topography may have fallen below professional standards, but his relish for the adventure and indefatigable enthusiasm for telling his tale still resound today.

As one might expect from someone so involved with every aspect of daily life, pitching himself into it with such enthusiasm and wit, Taylor's language, even when constrained by rhyme schemes, is invariably lively. He writes elaborate dedications to his noble patrons, but his own writing is far more down-to-earth. His background does not permit elaborations. He lards his texts with allusions to figures of myth and legend, and favours lists, such as those of the menus consumed by Nicholas Wood, the 'Great Eater' of Kent, or things he 'knows', 'wants' or 'cares' in *Taylors Motto*, but his vocabulary is if not exactly 'street' then willing to encompass everyday English. Nor does he sidestep slang and his texts include some 300 terms. His favourite topic is fools and foolishness, and among much else his work employs some thirty terms for 'drunk' alone. Nonetheless, he is relatively prudish: he writes of 'A Whore' and 'A Bawd,' and has a few terms for the vagina and penis, but nothing exhibits the level of sexual terminology that one might find in a ballad, with its double-entendres, or a *Mercurius*, with its open vulgarity.

In 1640 Charles I was replaced by parliamentary rule and in 1642 the Civil War began. Taylor, no revolutionary, could still appreciate certain aspects of the new situation, but he continued writing political squibs and as an avowed royalist was both attacked by a mob as he drank in a Guildhall tavern, and arrested and interrogated over alleged sedition. London was too dangerous: Taylor left, and made his way west to the royalist headquarters in Oxford.

Taylor survived the war but his king did not, and his aristocratic patrons were in no place to help him. The Water Poet had returned to London in 1647 and taken a lease on an alehouse near Covent Garden. Its name, the Crown, drew hostility after Charles's execution. Taylor renamed it The Poet's Head, its sign his own portrait. He continued to write and to journey but while he could still find friends to feed him, his income had declined badly. He lived out his life in poverty, with gradually failing health. He died in December 1653. In time Southey, a genuine romantic, would sneer at him as 'uneducated [with] low breeding and defective education'. His near contemporary John Aubrey seemed to get the point: Taylor, he would note in *Brief Lives*, 'was very facetious and diverting company, and for stories and lively telling them, few could outdo him'.

Charles Cotton (1630–87) was born into the country gentry, the son of another Charles who combined a scandalous private life with an intimate acquaintance with his great literary contemporaries. Like his father Cotton benefited from friendships with the social and literary elites, including Izaak Walton, and added a 'second part' to the 1676 edition of the *Compleat Angler*. He also built a fishing house, ornamented by their joint initials, on the Cotton estate in Staffordshire.

Cotton wrote a number of poems, plus a generally reviled prose celebration of the restored monarchy, and a mildly pornographic work *The Valiant Knight* (1663), but his literary celebrity came when his burlesque *Scarronides* appeared in four books between 1664 and 1665. This scatological rewriting of Virgil was not the first of its kind, and its name paid tribute to the earlier efforts of Paul Scarron's *Virgil Travestie* (launched in instalments in 1648), but it was wholly his own work. The lengthy poem was vastly successful, its faithful playing on the original Latin winning especial praise. There were a succession of reprints and a number of second-rate imitations. Samuel Pepys bought a copy on publication day and was delighted. A follow-up, *Burlesque upon Burlesque, or, The Scoffer Scoft* (1675), which drew on another Latin author, the satirist Lucian, was less successful.

Of the near 200 slang terms Cotton included, his first uses are as follows: *arse about, blind harper* (a beggar who fakes blindness, distracting attention from the disguise by playing a harp or fiddle), *cut away* (to run off), *double jugs* (the buttocks), *drumstick* and *drum* (the penis), *as easy as kiss my hand, fall* (an act of sexual intercourse), *tools of generation* (the testicles), *guts* (coverage), *jiggumbob* (the vagina), *lay up in lavender* (to put out of harm's way), *by the mack!* (i.e. the mass), *mump* (to cheat), *mutton-fist* (a large, coarse hand), *odd fish* (an eccentric), *pippin* (as a term of address), *porthole* (the anus), *poundrel* (the head), *privy counsel* (the vagina), *scut* (the buttocks), *shaver* (a roisterer), *shit-breech* (a term of abuse), *throw the snot about* (to weep), *squitters* (diarrhoea), *swabber* (a promiscuous woman), *tatterdemalion* (a rascal), *toby* (the female genitals), *truck* (to have sex), *hold one's water* (to contain one's emotions), and *whip* (to steal).

The Scoffer may have been less successful, but it was equally productive of slang, and offered these first uses: *bull* (to have sex), *bumfiddle, butt* (the posterior), *change one's note* (to alter one's opinions), *dimple* (the vagina), *pig* (to live with), *pigeon* (to trick), *make a pot with two ears* (to set one's arms akimbo), *punker* (a chaser of whores), *tantrum* (the penis), *tipple* (one's choice of drink as in 'my tipple'), *toast* (a lively old man), *trapes* (a slattern) and *what!* (as an abbreviation of 'what did you say?). Cotton was also responsible, in 1674, for *The Compleat Gamester*, a guide to gambling. Here the language is necessarily more technical, but he introduced a number of terms to the lexis: *biter* (a card-sharp), *bleed* (to extort money from) and *bleeding cully* (a gullible victim), *bully-hack* (a pimp), *flick* (to cut, e.g. a marked card), *mouth* (a dupe), and *on the square* (honestly). His use, with reference to the card game hazard, of *little Dick-Fisher* for the four, may be a distant antecedent of craps' *little dick*, a throw of four.

As the increasing range of non-glossarial sources makes clear, the seventeenth century shows a marked increase in the growth of slang. This development of the 'civilian', general-purpose lexis would expand even further in the eighteenth century and remains, of course, a constant. Cant too would develop, though to a great extent in coining new words for traditional practice, be it that of prostitution, confidence trickery or the mechanics of theft and house-breaking. The element of secrecy remained important and new terms were required to replace those that had been 'smoked out'.

Popular culture has always run hand-in-glove with slang. Such mass-market pleasures were not born in the seventeenth century but the volume of terms show that for the first time it was acceptable to use the terminology at least for entertainment. It is possible that the use of slang, as had cant in its own context, gave an added authenticity to ballads or plays that aimed to please an audience that used such language. By the turn of the century there was sufficient 'civilian' slang to interest the lexicographers. That interest was embodied in or around 1698 by a new lexicon, which embraced both the expected cant, and many hundreds of general slang terms. Written by an author known only by his initials, and still using the term 'canting crew' in its title, its contents took slang collection on to a new level. As the subtitle of its twenty-first-century reprint proclaims: it was 'the first dictionary of slang'.

A New Dictionary of the Terms, Antient and Modern, of the Canting Crew, in its several Tribes of Gypsies, Beggers [sic], Thieves, Cheats, &c. with an addition of some proverbs, phrases, figurative speeches &c.: useful for all sorts of people (especially foreigners) to secure their money and preserve their lives besides very Diverting and Entertaining, being wholly New was published c. 1698 by the otherwise unidentified B. E. Gent[leman].

Like Francis Grose, who in 1785 would produce the next important way-station in slang dictionary-making and whose work may be seen as a non-standard parallel to his predecessor and acquaintance Samuel Johnson's *English Dictionary* of 1755, B. E. did not operate in a lexicographical vacuum. His dictionary's nearest 'standard' equivalent was John Kersey's 1702 revision of Edward Phillips's *New World of Words* (1671), and where Kersey had expanded the older 'hard word' dictionary by including many examples of the everyday vocabulary, so did B. E. expand the old cant glossaries by including more general slang and colloquialism. His title may have implied a continuation of the cant tradition, but his word-list was far more adventurous and for the first time cant began to be absorbed into the larger slang lexis. Like Elisha Coles, from whom he extracted a number of headwords, he suggested to readers that his book was worth reading for purposes of self-preservation since by understanding its vocabulary, they might 'secure their *Money* and preserve their *Lives*'. He added that the book was 'wholly New'.[10] This may have been a slight exaggeration, but there is no doubt that in offering a vocabulary of some 4,000 headwords, a vast increase on Richard Head's 265, he took slang lexicography into a new world. The slang vocabulary had long expanded beyond the confines of cant; if the mainstream 'hard words' might be seen as the scholars' equivalent of cant, then the gradual inclusion in 'straight' lexicography of everyday vocabulary is logically paralleled by the inclusion of everyday slang.

The primary importance of B. E.'s work was that he produced for the first time a slang dictionary that was not merely an appendage to another work. As John Simpson's recent edition (2010) subtitles it, this was 'the first English dictionary of slang'. As such it is far from faultless: the headwords often insufficiently differentiate the various meanings; nor is the same part of speech always chosen for the headword (today one would expect the nominative noun or first person singular verb) and there is a good deal of material that is strictly ephemeral – but that is a problem that every slang lexicographer has to face, so inevitably transient is a proportion of what, properly, is a spoken rather than written tongue.

For lexicographers there was much else to consider. As Professor Julie Coleman's detailed analysis of B. E. has made clear,[11] the *New Dictionary* moved away from simple A = B entries, the staple of its glossarial predecessors, to making the first attempt, however limited, to offer citations and etymologies. Neither of these were extensive. As regards the citations, these were generally not those of modern dictionaries prepared 'on historical principles'. Few authorities or their works are named, and even then the reference is most likely to be on the lines of 'according to the observation of a late Learned Traveller' (for a phrasal use of *cut*) or 'as Sir P[hilip] Sidney calls it' (for *sparrow-mouth'd*). Most citations seem to be simply sentences that illustrate usage, with no further information attached. 'It is tempting,' notes Professor Coleman, 'to assume that B. E. just made them up'; however, she believes that some, 'which continue after they have served their immediate purpose, suggest that B. E. was not always creating but sometimes quoting.'[12] A further novelty was etymologizing; B. E. offers seventy-nine examples, a proportion of which would be confirmed by the *OED* (which includes 1,096 of his headwords, nearly all of them first recorded uses of the term). Perhaps most important, and that aspect of his work that makes the dictionary so definite a step forward, is in the range of areas from which the author takes his headwords. Cant has its place, but it is much reduced. Of the terms that are included there are those from hunting, fencing and duelling, and references to human intelligence, emotions and physiognomy; to sports, games, jokes and various forms of entertainment; to sex, to animals, to national and international politics, to religion, to warfare and to seafaring, including smuggling and the language of shipbuilding. In addition he borrows in its entirety the list of terms that Shadwell included with *The Squire of Alsatia* (and extracts a number more from the text, including the names of such characters as 'Captain Hackum'); it is possible that he also took material from *The Beggar's Bush*.

One might, justifiably, suggest that these 'professional slangs' are effectively jargon, the closed terminology of a given occupational group, but one cannot deny B. E. his innovative expansion of the dictionary. In addition he has included a number of terms that fall into no specific job description nor into cant but that are simply part of everyday life, including such vulgarisms as *bear garden discourse*, 'common filthy, nasty talk,' *cacafuego*, 'a shite fire', *cracker*, 'an arse', and *fizzle*, 'a little or low-sounding fart'. From a sociolinguistic point of view what B. E. is doing is to fold together all these vocabularies as a single non-standard 'vulgar' language, in which vulgar is not defined as 'low-class' but as 'that which is common use'. To that end B. E. offers none of the moralizing that his predecessors found so necessary. The cant terms are included but they are not larded with disapproval. B. E. was offering a descriptive dictionary, another pattern for the slang lexicographers of the future; he was not, as had such as Dekker or Rowlands, quietly but consciously combining titillation with his explaining. As Janet Sorenson says, 'B. E.'s use of the word "cant" in the title of his work resembles Johnson's *Dictionary* entry for "cant," which lists not only "a corrupt dialect used by beggars and vagabonds" but also "a particular form of speaking peculiar to some certain class or body of men"'.[13] And while the 'vulgar' seem, via their choice of language, to be separated from the standard English speaking elite, the criminals amongst them are no longer segregated into their own enclosure.

Like Thomas Harman before him, B. E. initiated a new chain of slang dictionaries. His inclusion of 'civilian' slang brought to an end the Copland–Awdeley–Harman progression and initiated a new one. As Eric Partridge makes clear,[14] both Grose and Hotten are hugely indebted to B. E.; so too are Farmer and Henley, and so too, though he had yet to embark on his own work, which takes as its base Farmer and Henley, was Partridge himself. The book was reprinted *c.* 1720 and in 1899 John Farmer included it as one of his *Choice Reprints of Scarce Books and Unique MSS* (1899). Among the immediate plagiarisms of B. E. was *The*

Regulator (1718), written by Charles Hitchin, which offered 'An Account of all the Flash Words now in vogue'. Hitchin was a corrupt City Marshal who doubled as a receiver of stolen goods. His pamphlet was written as an express attack on his rival Jonathan Wild, who combined *his* receiving with a position as a 'taker' of the very thieves with whom he cheerfully traded. B. E. was also the source of the self-promoted 'Captain' Alexander Smith, the fifth edition of whose *Compleat History of the Lives and Robberies of the Most Notorious Highwaymen, Footpads, Shoplifts, & Cheats of Both Sexes* (1719) has a 200-word glossary, all lifted verbatim. The book also offers the *Thieves' Exercise*, a list of thirty cant commands, which are supposed to be practised by 'Young Beginners' under the tutelage of their criminal 'Superiors'.

Of Smith, other than that he had no right to his captaincy, little is known. The *Compleat History* ran to five editions and, as thc *NDNB* puts it, 'once he had found his formula, Smith stuck to it [...] the work is derivative and unreliable, embroidering on the known facts freely'.[15] He specialized in group biographies, among which were *The Secret History of the Lives of the most Celebrated Beauties, Ladies of Quality, and Jilts* (1715); which was expanded a year later as *The Court of Venus* (1716). Anecdotes included in *The comical and tragical history of the lives and adventures of the most noted bayliffs in and about London and Westminster* (1723) were picked up by the nineteenth-century novelist Harrison Ainsworth for his own *Jack Sheppard* (1839). Finally there was the *Memoirs of the life and times of the famous Jonathan Wild, together with the history and lives of modern rogues* (1726).

In 1725 there appeared the *New Canting Dictionary*: its anonymous author eviscerating B. E. without credit. He was pillaged in turn, typically in *The History and Curious Adventures of Bamfylde Moore Carew, King of the Mendicants* (1745). Many editions of this picaresque 'autobiography' append a 300-word glossary, drawn mainly from the *New Canting Dictionary*.

Carew's tale made for a remarkably successful book. Its appeal is best summed up in the title of the expanded reissue, in 1749: *An Apology for the Life of Bamfylde-Moore Carew (Son to the Rev. Mr. Carew of Bickley) commonly known throughout the West of England by the Title of King of the Beggars; and Dog-merchant-general. Containing an Account of his leaving*

Tiverton School at the Age of 15, and entering into a Society of Gypsies; his many and comical Adventures, more particularly a full and faithful Relation of his Travels twice thro' a great Part of America, his manner of living with the wild Indians, his bold Attempt in swimming the River Delaware, and many other extraordinary Incidents; his Return home, and Travels since, in England, Wales, Scotland and Ireland. The whole taken from his own mouth. Sales were good enough for another, even longer, edition in 1750 – the first to carry the canting glossary – and new editions, expanded by yet more picaresque adventures, appeared until 1779. The book was reprinted regularly throughout the nineteenth century, the last version appearing in 1882. Carew was a real person, a clergyman's son born in 1693 near Tiverton, in Devon. Falling in with the inevitable 'bad company' he quit school and soon encountered a band of gypsies, whose apparently unfettered existence seemed to him irresistible. In time he would become their 'king' and advertise himself as such. He died around 1770. Given the seemingly infinite potential of its expansion, one must assume that his 'life story' is largely fictitious; like such predecessors as Gamaliel Ratsey or Mary Frith, Carew became a useful repository for whatever tale the current embellisher wished to tell.

But while these eighteenth-century dictionaries were happy to copy B. E.'s content, they eschewed his form. His pioneering attempt to re-position non-standard speech in a neutral zone was rejected: the 'cant' in the *NCD* and its emulators had firmly returned to Johnson's primary sense, and the negative assessment that accompanied it. The editor of the *New Canting Dictionary* may have added terms to those included in B. E., written an introduction that informed his readers, and appended nineteen canting songs but if anything he reversed B. E.'s advances. Many of the colloquialisms were excluded and cant once more gains primacy. Entries in which B. E. extended the simple cant definition were brusquely lopped back. The appended canting songs were edited so as to seem more condemnatory of those whose stories they told. As was the custom, the author promoted his work as a prophylactic against theft: with this vocabulary 'an Honest Man, who is obliged to travel … may secure himself from Danger; which is the principal design of compiling this Vocabulary'.[16] He was pitiless in his condemnation and exclusion of those he saw as beyond the pale of respectable society: 'No country in the world, has within itself, better opportunities than England, to imploy and make useful the poor of all degrees … that notwithstanding … no country in the world abounds so much with … the clamourous and often insolent, petitions of sturdy beggars.'[17]

In the end, the greatest importance of the *New Canting Dictionary* is in its adoption by Nathan Bailey, who used it as the foundation of the thirty-six-page slang appendix that he included in the later editions of his *Universal Etymological English Dictionary* (1727). This would be one part of Bailey that Johnson, who kept open a copy as he researched his own work, would resist.

6 The Sound of the City: No City, No Slang

Slang's literary origins are widespread and ever-expanding. Its social roots, however, are narrow and focused: the city. If, as has been suggested, the story of standard English is that of a London language, so too is that of English slang. And the pattern would be repeated elsewhere as colonies became independent and rural settlements became major conurbations. London's chroniclers had always noted the urban vocabularies, though none before the eighteenth century had rendered their discoveries lexicographical. The pioneer of such investigations, John Stow, laying out Elizabethan London in his *Survey of London* (1598), had barely touched on language (his text offers *gong farmer*, a latrine cleaner, *night-walker*, a thief, and *white money*, meaning silver coins). In time those who told London's story would offer a far more central position to the city's speech, alongside its population and topography. The first of these were the Jacobean city playwrights, but they suborned the language to their plays. For those whose work helped showcase the city's particular way of speaking, one must look at the turn of the seventeenth century's Ned Ward and Thomas Brown, and on to their successors.

Ned Ward declared himself 'The London Spy', while Tom Brown was a satirist of the city's 'Amusements Serious and Comical'. The works of both make clear the extent to which slang was interwoven with the metropolis which both created it and used it as part of daily life. Neither author was remotely canonical. In 1726 the New England puritan Cotton Mather bracketed their works with those of Samuel Butler (author of *Hudibras*) – all three sold well in the colonies – and enjoined his readership against 'such Pestilences, and indeed all those worse than Egyptian Toads (the Spawns of a Butler, and a Brown, and a Ward ...)'.[1] Lord Macaulay, in his *History of England* (1849), would sneer at both: of Ward he wrote, 'I am almost ashamed to quote such nauseous balderdash; but I have been forced to descend even lower, if possible, in search of materials,' while Brown was 'An idle man of wit and pleasure, who little thought that his buffoonery would ever be cited to illustrate the history of his times'.[2] He then used them both, as have historians ever since.

Edward Ward, known invariably as Ned, was born in the Midlands to an unknown family, though he always claimed a noble background. Others were unconvinced, and Theophilus Cibber in his *Lives of the Poets* dismissed him as 'of low extraction and irregular education'.[3]

He had arrived in London by 1691 (the date of his first published work: *The Poet's Ramble after Riches*, a verse lament describing his own poverty). In 1697 he set out for Jamaica but as described in his pamphlet *A Trip to Jamaica* (1698) the trip was a failure and he was back in London the same year. It is assumed that this was a genuine trip; its successor, *A Trip to New-England* (1699), was pure imagination. However, the literary trip continued to appeal, although he restricted himself to what he really knew: London. Between 1699 and 1700 he produced, in eighteen monthly parts, the *London Spy*, a work that seems to have been based on a French original, supposedly authored by one 'Mahmut' and titled *Letters writ by a Turkish Spy. Who lived five and forty years, undiscover'd, at Paris* (translated between 1687 and 1694). As Roy Porter put it, this guide to metropolitan high and low life was 'lapped up' by Ward's fellow-citizens.[4]

Ward's portrait, resplendent in full-bottomed wig, may be designed to emphasize his literary side, but pamphleteering, even for one who had written some 100 examples of the genre over fourteen years and achieved at least one best-seller, cannot have brought him sufficient money; in 1712 he embarked on a parallel career: as a publican, opening a punch-house near Clerkenwell Green. As he teased himself in *The Hudibrastick Brewer* (1714), '*Men* of *Sense* must *own* 'tis *better* to *live* by *Malt*, than *starve* by *Meter.*' He was obviously conscious of the job's lowly image. When Alexander Pope, far more famous but still willing to engage in a feud with a lesser scribbler, mocked him as an ale-house keeper, Ward hit back with *Apollo's Maggot in his Cups*, verses that added a prose postscript denying the poet's allegations. He did not sell lowly ale, his house, the Bacchus, was a tavern rather than a pub and anyway, Pope had drunk there himself. Ward was one of several victims attacked in *The Dunciad*, where Pope claimed that Ward's verses were only good to be sent off to the colonies, where they were traded for second-rate tobacco. It was a long-term feud: in 1705 Ward had published the satirical *Hudibras Redivivus*. In 1706 he was charged with seditious libel for this anti-government attack and fined 40 marks (£26 13s. 4d.) and condemned to stand twice for one hour in the pillory. Here he was given a hard time by the mob, so much so that Pope had coined the term 'as thick as eggs at Ward in the pillory'.[5] Ward's best shot came in 1729, but his anti-Pope play *Durgen: a Plain Satyr upon a Pompous Satirist* flopped. 'Durgen' meant 'dwarf' – Pope was tiny – but Ward lacked his rival's literary stature.

He died in 1731 at the British Coffee House in Fullwood's Rents near Gray's Inn, where he had moved around 1730 after some thirteen years at the Bacchus, and is buried in St Pancras churchyard. A dedicated High Tory, Ward is an important source for social historians: 'Though vulgar and often grossly coarse,' sniffs the original *DNB*, 'his writings throw considerable light on the social life at the time of Queen Anne, and especially on the habits of various classes in London.' These writings, while not invariably so, are regularly repositories of slang, and while the eighteenth-century lexicographers might ignore them, their successors were more appreciative. These few titles give a taste of what he offered, and there was much: *Female Policy detected, or the Arts of a designing Woman laid open* (1695), *A Step to Stir-Bitch* [i.e. Stourbridge] *Fair, with Remarks upon the University of Cambridge* (1700), *Adam and Eve stripped of their Furbelows, or the Fashionable Virtues and Vices of both Sexes exposed to Public View* (1710), *The Secret History of Clubs* (1709), *The Delights of the Bottle, or the Compleat Vintner* (1720) and fifty-four *Nuptial Dialogues and Debates* (1710).

Like John Taylor, another 'explorer' who turned his travels into pamphlets and poems, Ward appreciated the appeal of popular language. His works offer nearly 1,000 slang terms, of which almost 250 come from the *London Spy* alone.

He eschews most obscenity, although one does find *arse* (and *bum*), *balls* and *fart*, but is compendious in his references to low life. A prostitute is variously an *apron, baggage, bangtail, belfa, blowse, brimstone, commodity, crack, doxy, Drury Lane vestal, flap-cap, jilt, ladybird, lechery-layer, mumper, night walker, petticoat, quean, socket, suburb-jilt, tickle-tail* and *tickle-tail function, trugmoldy, trull* and *wagtail*. He notes their male accomplices the *town stallion, town-bully, town trap,* or *cock-bawd* (all pimps) and the *bully-huff,* who specializes in intimidating the client, the *cully*. The *flogging-cully* is a fan of modern 'fladge'. Intercourse is almost as well represented: the verbs *bounce, bum-feague, clip, have, pump, shoot, sink, tread,* plus nouns *basket-making* and the *buttock-ball* (an orgy). And he enjoys a little literary euphemism: to *dance Adam's jig, Sallinger's round* or *the shaking of the sheets,* as well as the nudge-nudgery of the whore who can 'show you how the Water-men shoot London-Bridge, or how the Lawyers go to Westminster', eighteenth-century forbears of 'Agnostics do it disbelievingly', 'drillers do it boringly' and so on. There are madams: *Mother Damnable, Mother Knab-Cony, Mother Midnight,* and *mother of the maids,* and homosexuals: the *boretto-man,* the *buggeranto* and the *bum-firker,* and sodomy is defined as 'Italian'. There are plentiful terms for the vagina and the penis.

There is, unsurprisingly, a good deal of drinking. One may be *addled, boozy, bottlenosed, drunk as a lord, elevated, foggy, fuddled, liquored, mellow* and *pot-valiant*. Alcohol itself is *belch, brewer's fizzle, the devil's piss, go-down* (i.e. the throat), *guzzle, nappy ale, tipple, tiff,* and when hungover, *the hair of the dog* (*that bit one*). To drink is to *swill*. He is not a great recorder of novelties – 30% of his uses can be found in the still recent B. E. – but there are some. Looking at the letters F–H, one finds these: *fat-arse* (fat, large-buttocked), *fig-leaf* (an apron), *flame* (venereal disease), *flash in the pan* (an abortive effort or outburst), *frontispiece* (the face), *fuddle* (an act of drinking, a state of intoxication; also to make drunk), *funk* (tobacco and as a verb to smoke or to make a stink), *goggle-eyed* (wearing spectacles), *grizzle* (a whinger or grumbler), *guzzle* (beer), *half-pint* (undersized), *Her Majesty's pictures* (money and thus a distant predecessor of rap's dead presidents), *hole* (any small, dirty, clandestine place) and *huffle* (to fellate; to perform frottage with the armpit).

Tom Brown, born the son of a Shropshire farmer in 1663, may have

had a marginally better reputation than Ned Ward, but he is perhaps
even less well remembered. The verse

> 'I do not love thee Dr Fell
> The reason why I cannot tell;
> But this I know and know full well,
> I do not love thee, Dr Fell.'

was his, and is still well-known, but few would know its writer. Brown
penned this parody of Martial's epigram 1.32 ('*Non amo, te, Sabidi*')
around 1680, in a successful attempt to save his career at Oxford,
where he had antagonized his college dean, Dr John Fell, and faced
being sent down. He arrived in London in 1684 and though his first
publication was a poem, his skills were soon diverted to satire with
the first of several attacks on Dryden: *Reason of Mr Bayes Changing
his Religion*. Unlike Ward (whose *London Spy* was for some years mis-
attributed to his contemporary – even so far as the fact being chiselled
into his gravestone), Brown had been educated in the classics and
used his skills to make a number of translations; classical knowledge
underpinned much of his prose and verse. In an era when for the first
time a writer could attempt to exist without patron or private wealth,
Brown survived by producing a wide range of material, often at his
booksellers' dictate. Before his early death in 1704 he wrote prose, verse,
squibs and pamphlets, as well as three stage plays: *Physic Lies a Bleeding,
or, The Apothecary Turned Doctor* (1697), *The Stage Beaux Toss'd in a Blanket*
(1704), and *The Dispensary* (1697), and in 1692 co-authored a journal,
the short-lived *Lacedemonian Mercury*. He was the first person to adopt
what would become the default satirical style: removing the vowels from
proper names when their use might have brought legal problems. Thus
in 1717 Addison commented in the *Spectator*: 'Some of our Authors
indeed, when they would be more Satyrical than ordinary, omit only
the Vowels of a great Man's Name, and fall most unmercifully upon
all the Consonants. This way of writing was first of all introduced by
T-m Br-wn of facetious memory, who, having gutted a proper name […]
made as free with it as he pleased without any danger of the statute.'[6]

Yet Addison, and others including Swift, are now seen to have been indebted to Brown, whose own work may not have survived, but whose methods of satire, hitherto unexplored, lie behind a number of their own, far more polished and incisive productions. Swift mentions Brown in the introduction to *A Treatise on Polite Conversation* (1738). Writing as 'Simon Wagstaffe, *Esq.*' he boasts of having read 'Mr. *Thomas Brown*'s works entire', and even having had 'the honour to be his intimate friend, who was universally allowed to be the greatest genius of his age'.[7] 'Wagstaffe' also claims to have read 'Mr *Ward*'. But Swift was being satirical in his turn and he had been openly critical in the pamphlet of 1713 in which he put forward plans to establish an English Academy. Here he attributed much of what he saw as slovenly modern speech to 'monstrous productions, which, under the name of *Trips, Spies, Amusements*, and other conceited appellations, have overrun us for some years past. To this we owe that strange Race of Wits, who tell us they write to the *Humour of the Age*.'[8]

Swift was right: Brown as much as Ward was willing to embellish at least some of his work with slang when he saw that it did indeed reflect 'the humour of the age'. Brown had an intimate acquaintance with low-life London, and it is perhaps symbolic that although he had a wife and children, they remain wholly anonymous. He used his experiences to pen some of his most popular works: *Amusements Serious and Comical* (1700), *Comical View of the Transactions That Will Happen in the Cities of London and Westminster* (1705), and the posthumous *Letters from the Dead to the Living* (1708). Of these the *Comical View* represented cod-astrological prognostications (for instance 'Doleful procession up Holborn-Hill about eleven. Men handsome and proper [...] arrive at the fatal place by twelve.' [...] 'If rainy, few night-walkers in Cheapside and Fleet-street.' [...] 'Shoals of country-puts come to town about five'). With the *Amusements* Brown echoed Ward in more than just offering a supposed *tour d'horizon* of louche London. Just as Ward had cribbed from a French work that was allegedly penned by an Arab, so did Brown use as his inspiration the French author Charles Dufresnay's *Amusements Sérieux et Comiques* (1699) supposedly written by '*un Siamois*'. Large portions were simply translated direct.

On the whole slang is a bottom-up creation, a language of the streets. Ward's and Brown's writings – in which the slang speakers are never of the élite – make that clear. But it is not invariably so. Swift's *Treatise on Polite Conversation*, ostensibly a satire on what was known as 'courtesy literature', shows that the nobs can enjoy slang as much as the yobs. Eric Partridge, in the introduction to his 1963 edition of the book, believed that Swift's pages 'manifestly … contain large chunks of conversation that bears every mark of having been recorded verbatim' and as such form 'by far the best single record of polite English spoken at any given period, not merely up to and including that of Swift himself, but also, indeed, after him'.[9] The majority of commentators see it is deliberately contrived and far from reportage. As Swift himself notes, 'The Flowers of Wit, Fancy, Wisdom, Humour and Politeness scattered in this Volume, amount to one thousand, seventy and four.'[10] Partridge notwithstanding, it is hard to believe that the three conversations that make up the book were anything but 'set pieces'. Swift's parade of proverbs and clichés also place him in the line of Flaubert's *Dictionnaire des idées reçues* (written c. 1870, published 1911) and Bierce's *Devil's Dictionary* (1911), both of which mock in their own styles the banalities of received wisdom.

Swift's book can be seen as complementary to an earlier pamphlet: *A Proposal for Correcting, Improving and Ascertaining the English Tongue*, which had appeared in 1712. In this Swift had suggested that Britain set up an Academy on the lines of the *Académie française*, which had been established since 1634. It would not happen, although there were those who believed that Samuel Johnson's *Dictionary* would set out language as it should be, even if Johnson himself, while excluding what he termed 'cant', still admitted that the likelihood of freezing a 'perfect' language had as little chance of success as catching the ever-moving sun. Swift's campaign had begun in a *Tatler* essay (28 September 1710), in which he railed against declining usage and specified such terms as *mob, phiz, pozz, rep, banter* and *bamboozle* as symptomatic of that decline. For Swift, a good Tory, imperfections in language marked those of a society increasingly filled with *nouveaux riches* whose advance, and detestable linguistic innovations, undermined the established order.

Written by 'Simon Wagstaffe, Esq.', presumably one of those same *arrivistes* (and, given that *staff* was well established as a slang synonym for penis, possibly a coarse joke), the 10,000 word introduction to *Polite Conversation*, set down in the finest mock-pompous style, brought such terms up again. This time, however, Swift posed them as exemplars of refined speech. Taking the 'Stamp of Authority from Courts, Chocolate-Houses, Theatres, Assemblies, Drawing-Rooms, levees, Card Meetings, Balls, and masquerades',[11] 'Wagstaffe' attributed his linguistic advice to 'the chief Patterns of Politeness, at Court, at Levees, at Assemblies, at Play-houses, at the prime visiting Places, by young Templers, and by Gentlemen Commoners of both Universities, who have lived, at least, a Twelve-month in Town, and kept the best Company'. He promised to spell 'the Words in the very same Manner that they are pronounced: such as Jommetry for Geometry, Verdi for Verdict, Lard for Lord, Larnin for Learning', and added 'some Abbreviations exquisitely refined: As, Pozz for Positively, Mobb for Mobile, Phizz for Physiognomy, Rep for Reputation, Plenipo for Plenipotentiary, Incog for Incognito, Hipps, or Hippo for Hypocondriacks, Bam for Bamboozle, and Bamboozle for God knows what'.[12]

The supposedly sophisticated interchanges between his stereotypes Mr Neverout, Lords Sparkish and Smart, Colonel Atwit and Sir John Linger, the Ladies Smart and Answerall and Miss Notable contain a good deal of contemporary slang. As one would expect, and as 'Mr Wagstaffe' makes clear, it is almost always genteel, with none of the usual double-entendres ('they often put Ladies upon affected [...] Ignorance'[13]) or oaths ('because both the Male and Female Oaths, are all perfectly well known'[14]).

The *Treatise* was responsible for the first recorded use of a number of slang terms: to *live high*, i.e. comfortably and securely; *dead*, of an empty bottle (Swift also has a *dead man* for the empty), *no chicken*, a woman, no longer young and/or attractive, *spill*, to cause to fall, and phrases such as *all the world and his wife*, *is your father a glazier?* used to embarrass one who is obstructing one's view, the *devil's books*, a pack of cards, *drive one's hogs to market*, to snore, *stare like a stuck pig* and *quarrel with one's bread and butter*, to act against one's own best interests. His talkers were keen drinkers, and knew its terminology: have a *drop in one's eye*, to be tipsy, *put a churl upon a gentleman*, to drink ale immediately after drinking wine (which reflects the supposed links between social class and drinking habits) and *whip-belly vengeance*, very thin beer which 'revenged itself' upon the digestion. There are the *brimmer* and the *bumper*, both full glasses, *half seas over* for drunk, the *hair of the dog* (*that bit one*) and the phrase *drunk as David's sow*.

Swift's use of slang extended beyond the *Treatise* and can be found in *The Tale of a Tub* (1704) and in his *Journal to Stella* (1710–36). To look only at terms that he was the first to record, one finds *spalpeen*, a rogue and doubtless picked up in Ireland, a *thumper*, a major lie, a *clinker*, something exceptional of its type, to *palm on*, to pass something off, to *dish out*, to apportion or hand out; while *yahoo*, a boorish lout, was of course of his own invention for *Gulliver's Travels*. He uses *shit on*, albeit as *beshit on*, to mean to humiliate or abuse, and the phrase *burn it blue*, to act outrageously, possibly by speaking coarsely, may be the first instance of *blue* meaning obscene.

Yet Swift's focus on the slang of society is ultimately anomalous. Slang still found its roots and its home much lower down the social order. A playwright such as Samuel Foote might follow in Swift's footsteps, using their language to tease the pretensions of the rising bourgeoisie in such plays as *The Englishman in Paris* (1753), *The Minor* (1760), *The Mayor of Garratt* (1771) and *The Bankrupt* (1773), and in *Tom Jones* (1749) the novelist Henry Fielding might parody the riper expostulations of a country squire, as well as including the slang his hero encounters in London society, but slang's reality lay on the ground. For all society's 'politeness' much of London remained rough and tough and had the language to accompany it.

Symbolic of this other London was Newgate, the great prison sited in the Old Bailey, on the western edge of the City and just to the south of Smithfield, where not that long before martyrs had been burnt at the stake. Newgate, known as *Whittington's College* or *The Whit*, had been exploited in a variety of seventeenth-century prison writings, and regularly featured in a number of ballads and gallows-side 'last words' and 'confessions', but it had yet to attain the stage. This now changed. Writing on 30 August 1716, Swift suggested to Pope, 'What think you of a Newgate pastoral among the whores and thieves?' and wondered whether 'our friend [John] Gay could fancy it'. Gay rejected the pastoral, but opted for a comedy: *The Beggar's Opera*. Premiered on 29 January 1728, the *Opera* was phenomenally successful, enjoying what was then a lengthy run of sixty-two nights in its opening season. Like

Pierce Egan's *Life in London* almost a century later, Gay's satire, mocking the fashionable contemporary obsession with Italian opera (which the smart set promptly abandoned), and with its plot set against the London underworld, inspired an infinity of clones, parodies and what would now be termed merchandising tie-ins, such as playing cards, fans and fire screens. Gay was already successful, but the opera made him richer: he took £693 13s. 6d (approximately £73,000) from the production, a then substantial sum. Lavinia Fenton, who played the heroine, 'Polly Peachum', did perhaps better: she became the mistress of the Duke of Bolton with a stipend, so Gay claimed, of £400 a year.

The *Beggar's Opera* terrified the moralists who found it subversive, especially since 'the agreeableness of the entertainment, and its being adapted to the taste of the vulgar, and set to easy tunes (which almost every body can remember) makes the contagion spread wider'.[15] Equally bad was the way criminals, its subject, loved it. In his supposed 'autobiography,' *The Life and Actions of James Dalton* (1730),'[16] the author claimed that he and his gang 'used to go to the Play-house, dressed like Gentlemen', and that once, during *The Beggar's Opera*, 'Captain Macheath's Fetters happening to be loose', one of them 'call'd out, *Captain, Captain your Bazzel is undone*'. As Andrea McKenzie, who recounts this anecdote, concludes, 'The real thieves, having shown up the actors with their superior knowledge of both irons and cant, then retired in style to an alehouse, "in four Chairs, with six Lights before each Chair"'.[17] This was not what the theatre was supposed to inspire.

Dalton's tale is, of course, exactly the kind of thing that those who attack slang claim is one of its failings: it keeps such objectionable company. Foreshadowing Egan again, Gay used slang to increase the *Opera*'s appeal, and underline the knowingness of his work. As he had used well-known popular tunes for the songs (which were originally to be sung unaccompanied, an extension of the plot's overall rawness), so did he use popular language. Though for a plot that made a highwayman its hero, and featured the doings of whores, pickpockets, beggars and sundry villains, plus a 'Mr Big' who was a thinly disguised version of the recently hanged fence and thief-taker Jonathan Wild, there is little cant. This was no *Squire of Alsatia* where the audience had to be helped out with a glossary.

A good deal of the cant that Gay did use is in his cast-list. The chief villain Mr Peachum comes from *peach*, to inform; among his gang are Nimming Ned (*nim*, to rob), Ben Budge (*budg*, a housebreaker) and Harry Paddington (reminiscent of *padding*, highway robbery, though the then village of Paddington was synonymous with the Tyburn gallows, upon which one might 'dance the Paddington frisk'). Of the female characters, the surnames *Trapes*, *Doxy*, *Slammekin* and *Trull* all signify whore and/or sloven. Mrs Coaxer, Molly Brazen and Sukey Tawdrey are self-evident, if in standard English. And Jenny Diver was the criminal pseudonym, literally 'Jenny Pickpocket', of the real-life Mary Young (born *c*. 1700), who was hanged for street robbery in 1741. Other canting terms that the audience may or may not have understood included *bit*, robbed, *fetch*, a trick, *filch*, a thief, *in keeping*, used of a prostitute who is kept by a client, *lock*, a repository for stolen goods, *nick* and *pick*, to steal, to *speak to*, an ironic euphemism for to rob and *wheedle*, to cheat.

In the main the *Beggar's Opera* uses more general slang, a number of which terms have survived. Examples include the era's seemingly inevitable *bamboozle*; *beast*, an unpleasant person, *chap*, *charmer*, *come down with*, to hand over (usually money), *deep*, sly, *hard*, to a great extent, *mechanic*, used as a term of abuse, *pump*, to interrogate, *puss*, a whore, *set upon*, *shotten herring*, a good-for-nothing, *sou*, a small amount of money, *tally-wife*, the woman with whom one cohabits, *tip*, to give a gratuity, *tip off*, to die, *on the town*, working as a prostitute, and the *Tyburn tree*.

The seventeenth century had ended with a major slang dictionary; the eighteenth followed suit. If B. E. had shown the way in which the language of crime and that of the mass of non-elite speakers had begun to overlap during the seventeenth century, then his late-eighteenth-century successor Francis Grose would take the process a step further. It is immediately obvious in the title of his dictionary. The word 'slang', first recorded in 1756, was yet to be used in a dictionary title (and would not be until John Camden Hotten's work of 1859), but Grose abandoned his predecessors' usual 'canting', opting instead for 'the vulgar tongue', a use of vulgar that was, as has been noted, synonymous with 'the mass of people'. The *OED*'s first citation for the concept is dated 1513 and defined as 'commonly or customarily used by the people of a country; ordinary, vernacular'. As for the 'classical', this must be the *OED*'s sense 2.a 'constituting an acknowledged standard or model' or 2.b 'representative, typical; archetypal, traditional'. In either case Grose was bringing the non-standard lexicon up to date.

Grose is one of slang lexicography's most satisfyingly three-dimensional figures, certainly the first of such in a lineage too often forced to fall back, albeit in dealing with an elusive human biography rather than a rootless word, on the disappointing 'etymology unknown'. If John S. Farmer would, a century on, be slang's equivalent of the *OED*'s James Murray, then Grose was slang's Johnson. A cheery Johnson, by all accounts, a more comfortably-off Johnson (from his own salary and from inheritances), and seemingly a Johnson unafflicted with the Great Lexicographer's problems of emotions and health. A less grand and influential Johnson, of course, although Grose had his own reputation within the world of antiquarianism. Looking at his two surviving portraits it is hard to resist at least a nod towards the fanciful thesis that an individual's character is determined by his or her surname. Grose was indeed gross – and he apparently appreciated the pun, although he preferred others to resist it – an outsize figure in every way. A veritable Falstaff of lexicographers, whose servant allegedly strapped him into bed to prevent the covers slipping from his vast belly; he was well known for his conviviality and his consumption of porter (a dark, bitter beer à la Guinness). He was born in late 1730 or early 1731 in Broad Street, London. His father, also Francis, a Swiss from Berne, was a jeweller who fitted up the coronation crown either of George II, as suggested in the *Gentleman's Magazine*, or George III as the *DNB* had it.

Grose Jr was classically educated, but preferred enrolment at Shipley's drawing school to entering a university. In 1766 he was elected a member of the Incorporated Society of Artists; from 1755 to 1763 he was Richmond Herald (a position purchased by his father); in 1757 he became a member of the Society of Antiquaries and in 1759 he was commissioned into the Surrey regiment of the militia. Becoming paymaster, he declared, he needed only two account books: his left and right hip-pockets. Receipts went into the right one, and disbursements appeared from the left. It was a characteristically unfussy attitude, but perhaps not wholly prudent. 'The unscrupulous', says Partridge, 'imposed upon him,'[18] and he became heavily indebted to his fellow officers. The regiment was disbanded in 1762, although his salary was continued. His income was boosted by his father's death, in 1769, but his inheritance only lasted so long. (There was a further inheritance on his wife's death in 1774). Grose was forced to rejoin the militia when in 1778 it was re-embodied and remained there, although in training camps rather than on active service, until 1783. As a result, he found himself, as he wrote to a fellow-antiquary, 'tied by the leg to the drudgery of the Drill, endeavouring to teach a parcel of awkward and vicious boobies their right hands from their left, without being able to steal one hour for the pencil'.[19]

Parade-ground tedium notwithstanding, Grose always managed to find some time 'for the pencil'. The first part of his *Views of the Antiquities of England and Wales* appeared in 1773; the complete work was finished fifteen years later. He was responsible for many of the illustrations, although the text was created by a number of other hands. Two studies of military antiquities, of which he was especially knowledgeable, appeared between 1785 and 1789. A trip to Scotland resulted in *The Antiquities of Scotland* (1789–91) and in 1791, after making a brief visit the previous year, he began what would have been *The Antiquities of Ireland*. It did not appear: on 12 May, while dining in Dublin, he suffered a fatal apoplectic fit. He is buried in the graveyard of Drumcondra Church, near Dublin. Noting his series of 'Antiquities', the *St James Evening Chronicle* suggested these lines as his epitaph:

> Here lies Francis Grose,
> On Thursday, May 12, 1791,
> Death put an end to his
> views and prospects.

Like Johnson, Grose established his own coterie, which met in a specially reserved private room on the premises of his publisher Samuel Hooper's bookshop in High Holborn. He also patronized the King's Arms in Holborn, a popular haunt of literary men, journalists, actors and similar figures. Unlike Johnson, Grose was especially happy in Scotland. His antiquarian researches had taken him north in 1789 and soon, while meeting a variety of fellow devotees, he was introduced to the poet Robert Burns. The two men hit it off at once, and Burns capped their acquaintance with a poem: 'On Captain Grose's Peregrinations Through Scotland', a tribute that includes the oft-quoted couplet 'A chiel's among ye, takin notes / And, faith, he'll prent it'. In this same poem he describes the Falstaffian Captain as 'a fine, fat, fodgel [squat and plump] wight / of stature short, but genius bright'. Burns's affection for this friend who displayed such a 'sterling independence of mind'[20] is displayed once more in the later 'Ken Ye ought o' Captain Grose?':

> The Devil got notice that Grose was a-dying
> So whip! at the summons old Satan came flying:
> But when he approach'd where poor FRANCIS lay moaning,
> And saw each bed-post with its burden a-groaning,
> Astonish'd, confounded, cry'd Satan: 'By God,
> I'll want him, ere I take such a damnable load!'

It was also in honour of his friend's powers as a story-teller that Burns wrote the ghostly narrative poem *Tam O'Shanter*, his last major work, in 1791.

In its notice of his death, the *Gentleman's Magazine* praised Grose's antiquarianism, and delighted in his good nature, but turned fastidiously from his slang lexicography, allowing only that 'in 1785 he published "A Classical Dictionary of the Vulgar Tongue" which it would have been to his credit to have suppressed'.[21]

It passes without even a denunciation over his *Provincial Glossary* (1788). (The new *DNB* is no more interested and dismisses the works in two lines.) Yet at two centuries' remove, it is as a lexicographer, as much as an antiquary, that he matters. Building on B. E., but appealing to a much wider audience, and providing them with a substantially larger word-list, Grose's work made it even more clear that there was more to slang than the professional jargon of thieves and beggars. Cant's usual suspects are duly rounded up – *abram-cove, autem bawler, bawdy basket, bene darkmans* and their roguish like – all culled from the sixteenth-century glossaries, but like B. E. he has taken on board the larger world of general slang. In Grose the reader has moved beyond the surreptitious whispering of sixteenth- and seventeenth-century villainy and into the wider arena, where 'civilians', as well as crooks, use the 'parallel' vocabulary of slang. It is in Grose that readers first discover *birthday suit* (although Smollett appears to have been the actual coiner), *chop and change, gam* (a leg, long since exported to America), *shag* (to copulate), *slag* (a pejorative common to the twentieth-century works of both Frank Norman and Robin Cook) and much, much more.

What Grose had done was to remove slang from its association with criminals and put it, with a much enlarged lexis, into the mouths of the common people. On occasion he did this literally, taking terms that had been labelled as cant and re-defining them as 'vulgar'. Like B. E. he finds a place for a good deal of what would now be defined as occupational jargon, whether the words of soldiers and sailors or those of Billingsgate fishwives, long celebrated – typically in Ned Ward's *London Spy* – for the acerbity, not to mention coarseness, of their epithets. For Grose this vulgar tongue was an essential part of British freedom: in this case of speech. Not for Britain the artificial restraints of the *Académie française* and similar 'un-British' institutions. Garrick had praised Johnson for his success when with his *Dictionary* he had 'beat forty French and could beat forty more' (the number being that of the members of the *Académie*). Grose's dictionary, while unsung, attained a similar image of Britishness.

Slang is a man-made language, a gendered vocabulary that while it does not exclude women, is keen to keep them in their place: the nagging wife, the sexy ingénue, the whore, the hag. Grose embraces this wholeheartedly, perhaps most obviously in his self-censored entry at '*C**t*: a nasty name for a nasty thing'. As Janet Sorenson[22] notes, the dictionary offers many examples of intra-male socializing, with terms and definitions that underline the locker-room misogyny of such relationships. Typically he offers thirty-seven other synonyms for the *monosyllable*, including the *bite, Buckinger's boot, Hans Carvel's Ring*, the *man-trap* and the *miraculous pitcher* (*that holds water with its mouth down*). The penis is good for only seventeen, and as ever in slang, they tend to the self-congratulatory: the *matrimonial peacemaker*, the *sugar-stick* and the *arbor vitae*. He also offers such sexual exotica as the *burning shame*, 'a lighted candle stuck into the parts of a woman, certainly not intended by nature for a candlestick', or the *gormagon*, 'a monster with six eyes, three mouths, four arms, eight legs, five on one side and three on the other, three arses, two tarses, and a **** [i.e. cunt] upon its back' and defines it as 'a man on horseback, with a woman behind him'. This was no longer a language for mixed company. Although the pirated edition of his work, the *Lexicon Balatronicum*, suggested that one could in fact use such terms since 'it is impossible that a woman should understand the meaning of *twiddle diddles*, or rise at the table at the mention of *Buckinger's boot*'.[23] Respectable women may have chosen or perhaps pretended to agree but the whores that the male readers frequented, and for whom the *Lexicon* gives seventy synonyms, might have begged to differ.

This maleness also reflects another change: the increasing importance of the city as a coiner of language. The city with its speed, its constant change, is another image of masculinity. The country, where tradition and nature ruled, was seen as more feminine. Egan's *Life in London* (1821), and its several clones, show the way that a city-based male society could cross classes in its movement around town; and that the language of high life and low could be the same. As Egan's hero Corinthian Tom, the epitome of the knowing city sophisticate, explains to his up-from-the-country friend Jerry Hawthorn: 'A kind of *cant* phraseology is current from one end of the Metropolis to the other, and you will scarcely be able to move a single step, my dear JERRY, without consulting a *Slang* Dictionary, or having some friend at your elbow to explain the strange expressions which, at every turn, will assail your ear.'[24]

Grose too had made his way 'from one end of the metropolis to the other'. He may have taken slang out of the 'padding-ken' and placed it more firmly in the public eye, but in one aspect of his lexicography he was linked most definitely to his predecessors. Modern slang collection tends, like its mainstream equivalents, to rely on printed and now digital material for its researches. Such twentieth-century specialists as the late David Maurer have indeed pursued hands-on fieldwork, eliciting slang, or more properly cant, from a wide variety of criminal or quasi-criminal sources, but they remain the exception. Grose was hands-on. He picked up much of his research first-hand during his nightly wanderings through London's criminal slums, accompanied, so it has been claimed, only by his man Batch and later by his companion, 'a funny fellow' properly named Tom Cocking, whom he christened 'The Guinea Pig'. He wandered the low-life streets of London, or indeed whatever town in which he might temporarily find himself, in search of the *echt* vocabulary of the gutter.

His book went into several editions: that of 1785 was followed by another, a major expansion, in 1788 and a third, posthumously, in 1796, by which time the original 3,000 headwords had been increased to 4,000. This third edition was pirated (and only marginally expanded) in 1811, when its title page declared it to be 'a Dictionary of Buckish Slang, University Wit, and Pickpocket Eloquence'. Retitled as the *Lexicon Balatronicum* ('the jesters' dictionary'), it acknowledged Grose's original efforts, but cited this edition as being 'considerably altered and enlarged, with the modern changes and improvements, by a Member of the Whip Club'. The *Lexicon* also claims to be targeting a classier audience than did Grose, whose 'circulation was confined almost exclusively to the lower orders of society. [Captain Grose] was not aware ... that our young men of fashion would at no very distant period be as distinguished for the vulgarity of their jargon as the inhabitants of Newgate ...' However, the real target was the uninitiated, 'the cits of Fish-Street [and] the boors of Brentford ... the whole tribe of second rate Bang ups' who were to be 'initiated into all the peculiarities of language by which the man of spirit is distinguished from the man of worth. They may now talk bawdy before their papas, without the fear of detection, and abuse their less spirited companions, who prefer a good dinner at home to a glorious *up-shot* in the highway, without the hazard of a cudgelling.'[25]

In 1823 Egan himself brought out what was a fourth 'official' edition, with more revisions, often reflecting the relatively new 'flash' language of the Regency sporting world in which as a sporting journalist and the best-selling author of *Life in London* (1821) he was an expert. In addition he cut the '*coarse* and *broad* expressions'[26] which Grose had allowed and noted the way that some slang terminology, typically *rum* – once a positive term, but by 1820 generally the reverse – had altered.

The third edition of Francis Grose's *Classical Dictionary of the Vulgar Tongue*, published in 1796, provides an unrivalled check-list of the level of slang's expansion as the eighteenth century draws to a close. Yet

Grose, for all his lexicographical energies, couldn't list everything and a dictionary can only ever be a mirroring detail of a larger picture. What has become apparent was that slang had by now spread hugely from its original emergence. Setting aside the 400-odd canting terms, still working from the sixteenth-century core, one can see that the major themes that inform slang are all well established. The world of alcohol offers 165 terms, that of the genitals and buttocks 325 and sexual intercourse a further 200; 130 terms stand for fools and the foolish, there are 220 prostitutes working in forty brothels and accompanied by thirty-five pimps. Men and women of assorted types are good for 160 terms apiece. Terms for the mad, the fat, and the unattractive are still relatively limited, none exceeds twenty synonyms, but there are forty-two oaths and thirty thugs.

Slang was now available on all sides. As well as plays, always a showcase, however artificial, of non-standard language, the long-established ballads and the burgeoning 'new medium' of the novel, slang might now be found in magazines, notably the country's first 'general interest' monthly, *The Gentleman's Magazine*, which had been founded in 1731 and had employed Samuel Johnson as a parliamentary reporter, and the slightly more raffish *Sporting Magazine*, first published in 1792. There was also a pioneering women's journal, *The Female Tatler*, edited by one 'Phoebe Crackenthorpe' from 1709–10. There was a healthy trade in pornography, such as 1740's *Description of Merryland* by one 'Roger Pheuquewell'. Alongside this were guides to city brothels, such as *Harris's List of Covent-Garden Ladies* (1773), the publisher of which was prosecuted for obscenity, and Charles Walker's *Authentick Memoirs of Sally Salisbury* (1723), charting the exploits of one of the capital's most celebrated madams. Slang also lent itself to parody, such as that of Thomas Bridges (*c.* 1710–*c.* 1775), who had been a wine merchant and unsuccessful banker before he turned to rewriting the classics. In 1762, as 'Caustic Barebones', he produced his *Homer Travestie*; it reappeared in a number of enlarged editions for the rest of the century, the last in 1797. Each relied at least in part for its appeal by filling the mouths of gods, goddesses and heroes with slang. It appeared in the ever-popular jest-books, notably *Penkethman's Jests* (1721). Even nursery rhymes played a part: *Tommy Thumb's Songbook* (1744) by the pseudonymous

'Nurse Lovechild', offered 'all little Masters and Misses' *bubby*, *bum*, *butt*, *poop*, *piss*, *hole* and *pissabed*. And to keep an eye on criminality there were the Proceedings of the Old Bailey, which had been recording trials at London's most important court since 1674, and the *Account of the Malefactors executed at Tyburn* written up by the Ordinary of Newgate from 1676. The Ordinary was the prison chaplain, and among his perks was that of publishing his clients' final speeches, along with their supposed biographies.

The eighteenth century also boasts one unrivalled milestone: the first appearance, at least as so far recorded, of the word *slang* in print. It is found in William Toldervy's *History of Two Orphans* (1756) and runs thus: 'Thomas Throw had been upon the town, knew the slang well; [...] and understood every word in the scoundrel's dictionary.'

Whether or not the dictionary in question was the anonymously authored *Scoundrel's Dictionary* which had appeared just two years earlier, this remains the first recorded appearance of the word 'slang' as regards language. We know very little of Toldervy (1721–62), other than that he was born in Shropshire, came to London, worked unsuccessfully in the linen trade and wrote a single four-volume novel. But lexicographically he has assured his memorial. The word had been used around fifteen years previously, to mean nonsense or rubbish, and to refer to a line of work or an occupation, but its appearance as a synonym for cant is sudden. And it is not recorded again until the 1780s.

Recorded or otherwise, the reality is that by the eighteenth century slang was ever more embedded into London life. It had crossed classes, and was found in the mouths of workers, 'cits' – tradesmen and merchants who could often be substantially wealthy but were still not deemed 'gentlemen' – as well as those of the gentry and aristocracy. The slang of the upper classes was not that of the market or public house, but neither were standard English and both were prevalent. The traditional canters were almost an afterthought, although cant-specific dictionaries continued to appear and as has been seen, it was not until Grose that the new reality was made clear. The eighteenth-century slang vocabulary can be assessed at over 5,000 terms, and a vast range of authors were now using it as a natural representation of the language of a variety of

English speakers. Among them are the playwrights Richard Sheridan, both the Elder and Younger George Colmans, Susanna Centlivre, Samuel Foote, John Vanbrugh, Oliver Goldsmith and Colley Cibber, and the novelists Henry Fielding, Daniel Defoe, Samuel Richardson and Tobias Smollett, plus essayists such as Jonathan Swift and, as noted, the parodist Thomas Bridges, who like Charles Cotton en-slanged the classics. There were many more. In addition, for those who preferred to pluck their slang directly from the gutter, there were the anonymous pamphleteers offering *The Bog-House and Glass-Window Miscellany* (1744), *The Fifteen Comforts of Cuckoldom* (1706), *The Gentleman's Bottle Companion* (1760), or *The Ladies' Evening Book of Pleasure* (1775); there were dozens of these and their works delighted in raffish terminology. If slang's ever-expanding ubiquity had not been sufficiently noted by 1700, it was irrefutable a century later.

7 Flash:
This Sporting Life

> Prepare for death if here at night you roam,
> And sign your will before you sup from home;
> Some fiery fop with new commission vain,
> Who sleeps on brambles till he kills his man,
> Some frolick drunkard, reeling from a feast,
> Provokes a broil, and stabs you for a jest.[1]
>
> Samuel Johnson 'London: A Poem' (1738)

If Samuel Johnson experienced mugging, it was in print, and from his literary peers. But the city in which he lived was acknowledged as less than safe, irrespective of one's status. In his *Enquiry into the Cause of the Late Increase of Robbers* of 1751 Henry Fielding wrote, 'Whoever considers the Cities of *London* and *Westminster* with the late vast increases of their suburbs the great irregularity of their buildings, the immense number of lanes, alleys, courts and bye-places, must think that they had been intended for the very purpose of concealment, they could not have been better contrived. Upon such a view the whole appears as a vast wood or forest in which the thief may harbour with as great security as wild beasts do in the deserts of *Arabia* and *Africa*.'[2] Fielding was focused on the working-class villain, the stereotyped criminal, but as Johnson's poem on the city underlined, the aristocratic villain, running in gangs and with no need for money but a desire for unrestrained self-indulgence, was just as threatening a figure.

The existence of such gangs was noted in the late sixteenth century.

The *roarer*, from SE *roar*, to riot, entered the slang vocabulary in 1586, and meant a riotous hooligan, a roisterer; by the turn of the century it had been extended to a *roaring boy*. The first named gang appears to have been 'The Damned Crew', as noted in a sermon given in May 1598 by Bishop Stephen Gosson: 'There was some years since a prophane company about this Cittie which were called the damned Crewe, menne without feare or feeling eyther of Hell or Heaven, delighting in that title.'[3] Their pleasures were random violence, usually when drunk; their targets were civilians of any age and both genders. Watchmen were especially unpopular. By the 1620s a new gang had taken over: the Tityre Tu's, and henceforth the period was bedevilled by gangs of gentlemanly thugs known as Bugles, Scourers, Hectors, Dammee-boys, Swashes, and Tuquoques. The early-eighteenth-century version was the Mohocks, tipping their hats to the Mohawk tribe of North America.

They all worked on similar lines: in 1655 appeared a pamphlet, *A Notable and Pleasant History of the Famous renowned Knights of the Blade, commonly called Hectors, or, St. Nicholas Clerkes*. Hector, an ironic use of the Trojan hero Hector, meant a blustering, swaggering bully (later it became a brothel bouncer). The author laid down the names, lifestyle and rules of such gangs and continued, 'All that I can say to their maner of life is, that it consists much in cheat and cousenage, gaming, decoying, pimping, whoring, swearing, and drinking, and with the nobler sort, in robbing.'[4]

By the end of the eighteenth century the gangs had abated their activities, but the link between dissolute members of the upper class and the language of the proles was never stronger. And that language had gained a new name: *flash*. Although not everyone seemed to have sorted it out. 'All England Are Slanging It', included in *The Universal Songster* of 1825,[5] explained that 'Flash is cant, cant is patter, patter is lingo, lingo is language, and language is flash.' And it was not only the language that offered, one might suggest, some paradoxical relationships. The early eighteenth century, at least among the middle and upper classes, was an era devoted to a new social phenomenon: politeness. So why this fascination with the sordid? Perhaps like the counter-language itself, the one impelled the other. If there is a standard – politeness – then there must be an antithesis – social and linguistic slumming. It takes form in the 1720s and lasts for around a century, when it was undermined and then destroyed by the new moralizing that accompanied the advent of Queen Victoria and the growth of evangelical religion. Even Victoria did not wholly crush it: readers of the late-nineteenth-century *Sporting Times*, a racing paper that, from the colour of its stock, was better known in the subaltern's mess as 'The Pink 'Un', could enjoy the same degree of rich-meets-poor adventuring.

Hotten, in the first edition of his *Slang Dictionary* (1859), states that 'flash' was coined in 1718 by Charles Hitchin in *The Conduct of Receivers and Thief-Takers*, but as he notes, 'FLASH' is sometimes exchangeable with 'fancy'. Hitchin's senses were those of 'belonging to or connected with the underworld,' thus the 'flash gaming house', or of being expert, 'knowing the ropes', specifically those of the underworld: 'The Cull is flash alias that is he Associates himself with Thieves.' In *The Regulator* (1718) Hitchin offers the *flash case*, a criminal pub, and the *flash cull*, a 'civilian' who hangs around with criminals; but he does not specify the language as such. Flash as a synonym for cant was seemingly born in the celebrated Covent Garden coffee house run by Tom King and his wife Moll. Open from midnight, when the taverns shut, till dawn, the coffee house, which Moll ran solo after her husband died of alcoholism in 1739, was a local fixture for customers both rich and poor. It was never much more than a shack, and had little in common with such respectable centres as Will's, popular with Dryden and other wits, or Lloyd's, the first home of what would become London's insurance centre, but it offers its own louche charms. In 1732 Henry Fielding asked in his *Covent-Garden Tragedy*, 'What Rake is ignorant of King's Coffee-House?'[6] *King's College*, as it was known, can be seen in Hogarth's engraving of 'Morning', the first of his series *Four Times of the Day* (1738). Outside a couple of rakes are pawing a pair of whores (or maybe market girls), while a cluster of waving sticks and a wig flying through the doorway show that a fight had broken out within.

'Flash' ran through a number of definitions. In *The Life and Character of Moll King* (1747), 'This Flash, as it is called, is talking in Cant Terms, very much us'd among Rakes and Town Ladies.' Grose, from 1785, defined 'FLASH LINGO' as 'the canting or slang language'. By 1789 in George Parker's *Life's Painter*, it is lumped together with slang and cant: the reader is advised that 'The explanation of the Cant, Flash and Slang terms [...] gives at one view, a perfect knowledge of the artifices, combinations, modes and habits of those invaders of our property, our safety and our lives, who have a language quite unintelligible to any but themselves.'[7] Finally, in its last incarnation, laid down in W. T. Moncrieff's 1821 play *Tom and Jerry* (the dramatic version of Pierce Egan's *Life in London*), the man-about-town Corinthian Tom pronounces that, 'Flash, my young friend, or slang, as others call it, is the classical language of the Holy Land; in other words, St. Giles's Greek [...] a species of cant in which the knowing ones conceal their roguery from the flats.'[8] What is clear from the words themselves is that while as a vocabulary it is essentially the old cant made new, it has taken on an important new aspect: as Julie Coleman points out, 'What has happened is that cant has become stylish; it has become flash. Where the earlier glossaries presented the secret language of thieves and beggars, many of the later ones list the slick lingo of London's ultra-fashionable world.'[9] Flash dealt with some of the same topics as cant – typically money, drink, criminal types and their schemes – but its use did not automatically brand one as a criminal. To use flash was to be in the know; it was, logically, to be *flash to*.

That vocabulary is set out in this dialogue, between Moll and 'one of her best Customers, before her House was frequented by people of Fashion'. This was Harry Moythen, a man who was 'stabb'd some Time ago by *Dick Hodges*, the Distiller'.[10] The dialogue was originally published fifteen years earlier, in a lost pamphlet, *The Humours of the Flashy Boys at Moll King's*:

Harry. But who had you in your Ken last Darkee?

Moll. We had your Dudders and your Duffers, Files, Buffers and Slangers; we had ne'er a Queer Cull, a Buttock, or Porpus, amongst them, but all as Rum and as Quiddish as ever *Jonathan* sent to be great Merchants in *Virginia*.

Harry. But Moll, don't puff:-You must tip me your Clout before I derrick, for my Bloss has nailed me of mine; but I shall catch her at *Maddox's* Gin-Ken, sluicing her Gob by the

Tinney; and if she has morric'd it, Knocks and Socks, Thumps and Plumps, shall attend the Froe-File Buttocking B[itc]h.

Moll. I heard she made a Fam To-night, a Rum one, with Dainty Dasies, of a Flat from T'other Side; she flash'd half a Slat, a Bull's-Eye, and some other rum Slangs.

Harry. I'll derrick, my Blood, if I tout my Mort, I'll tip her a Snitch about the Peeps and Nasous. I shall see my jolly old Codger by the Tinney-side, I suppose with his Day-Lights dim, and his Trotters shivering under him.—As Oliver wheedles, I'll not touch this Darkee, I'll nap the Pad, and see you in the Morning.[11]

All of which is explained in the 'KEY to the Flash Dialogue', which holds thirty-eight entries (with fifty-two terms in all). '*To hike, is,* To go home.—*A Grunter's Gig,* a Hog's Cheek.—*Si-Buxom,* Six-pence.— *A Cat's Head,* a Half-penny Rowl.—*A Whyn,* a Penny.—*A Gage of Rum Slobber,* a Pot of Porter.—*Thrums,* Three-pence.—*Max,* Geneva.—*Meg,* a Half-penny.—*A Traveller,* a Shilling.—*Kinchin,* a little Child.—*Doss,* to sleep.— *Pad,* a Bed.—*Grapple,* to lay hold on.—*Trotters,* Legs.—*Bilby's Ball,* Tyburn-House.—*Ken,* a House.—*Darkee,* the Night.—*Dudders,* Fellows that sell Spital-fields Handkerchiefs for India ones.— *Duffers,* Those who sell British Spirituous Liquors for Foreign.—*Files,* Pick-pockets.—*Buffers,* Affidavit-Men.—*Slangers,* Thieves who hand on Goods from one to the other, after they are stole.—*A Buttock,* a Whore.—*Porpus,* an ignorant swaggering Fellow.—*Rum or Quiddish,* Goodnatur'd.—*To puff,* to impeach.—*Clout,* a Handkerchief.—*Derrick,* to go away.—*Sluicing her Gob,* wetting her Mouth, or drinking.—*Tinney,* the Fire.—*Froe-File-Buttock,* a Woman Pick-pocket.—*A Fam,* a Ring.—*Dasies,* Diamonds.—*T'other Side,* Southwark.— *Half a Slat,* 10 s. 6. d.—*Bull's Eye,* 5 s.—*To tout the Mort,* to find out the Woman.—*Snitch about the Peeps and Nasous,* a Fillip on the Nose and Eyes.—*Old Codger,* an old Man.—*Day-lights,* Eyes.—*Oliver wheedles,* the Moon shines.—*To nap the Pad,* to go to Bed.'[12]

This, explains the anonymous editor, ' was part of the cant that the gentry of King's College were mighty fond of; and which too many people now scandalously affect to practise; but by persons of modesty and understanding, those that are so ridiculous as to use it, are looked upon not to be very well bred'.[13]

The idea of 'knowingness' underpins flash. One sees it again in one of the definitions offered by the three-times transported James Hardy Vaux, who had appended a 'New and Comprehensive Vocabulary of the Flash Language' to his *Memoirs*, first published in 1812. While flash could also be 'the cant language used by the *family*', i.e. the underworld, and that 'a person who affects any peculiar habit, as swearing, dressing a particular habit, taking snuff, *&c.*, merely to be taken notice, is said to do it *out of flash*', it is the adjectival use that clearly crosses classes. 'FLASH, to be *flash* to any matter or meaning, is to understand or comprehend it, and is synonymous with being *fly*, *down*, or *awake*.'[14]

One also found it in the canting song that Byron included in canto XI of *Don Juan* (a work which in 1819 Keats described as 'Lord Byron's last flash poem'[15]):

> Poor Tom was once a kiddy upon town,
> A thorough varmint and a real swell ...
> Full flash, all fancy, until fairly diddled,
> His pockets first, and then his body riddled.
>
> [...]
>
> Who in a row like Tom could lead the van,
> Booze in the ken, or in the spellken hustle?
> Who queer a flat? Who (spite of Bow Street's ban)
> On the high-toby-splice so flash the muzzle?
> Who on a lark, with Black-eyed Sal (his blowing)
> So prime, so swell, so nutty, and so knowing?

The authorship has been attributed to John Jackson (1769–1845), an ex-prizefighter (champion from 1795 to 1803) who taught Byron and a number of his friends. The aristocratic poet termed him his 'old friend and corporeal pastor and master'[16] and noted in his 'Hints from Horace' that 'men unpractised in exchanging knocks / Must go to Jackson ere they dare to box'.[17] It was a quintessential flash relationship: the lord and the butcher's son turned publican, united no doubt in language as much as in friendship.

Prize-fighting was a perfect complement to flash. It was not wholly illegal – although beadles and bailiffs would attempt to curtail matches if they could. Its fans, known as the Fancy, were a socially mixed group which brought together the fighters themselves, their professional handlers, a collection of more or less honest bookmakers, a range of noble supporters, and anyone – in and out of the underworld – who appreciated 'the Manly Art'. Writing 'Tom Crib's Memorial to Congress' (1819), his satirical account of that year's congress of Aix-la-Chapelle, Byron's friend Tom Moore – 'passing from the Academy of Plato to that of Mr Jackson—now indulging in *Attic flashes* with Aristophanes, and now studying *Flash* in the *Attics* of *Cock Court*'[18] – signed himself 'One of the Fancy' and cast the diplomatic encounter as 'The Grand Set-to between Long Sandy and Georgy the Porpus' (i.e. Tsar Alexander and King George IV). Among its flash-filled verses were such as this:

> Neat *milling* this Round – what with *clouts* on the *nob*,
> Home hits in the bread-basket, clicks in the gob,
> And *plumps* in the *daylights*, a prettier treat
> Between two *Johnny Raws* 'tis not easy to meet.[19]

His preface gave a mini-glossary and the verses were properly footnoted.

A year later there appeared *The Fancy* or 'The Poetical Remains of the late Peter Corcoran', which pseudonym masked John Hamilton Reynolds (1794–1852), poet, satirist, critic and playwright, and friend of Keats. The hero is a young poet, whose growing obsession with prize-fighting takes over from his writing, his job as a lawyer and his sweetheart who, seeing him with a pair of black eyes, breaks off the relationship. In the end Corcoran, whose 'memoirs' are filled with flash, dies of brain fever. His cranium, it is noted, has an unusually large organ of combativeness. Pugilistic poetry, this time by real-life authors, could be found in magazines such as *Blackwood's Edinburgh Magazine*, which also serialized Egan's work and stated that 'The man who has not read *Boxiana* is ignorant of the power of the English language.'[20]

Not everyone appreciated this socially transgressive world. The US writer Washington Irving's 'Buckthorne: the Young Man of Great Expectations', in his *Tales of a Traveller* (1824), was unimpressed: 'I know it is the opinion of many sages [...] that the noble science of boxing keeps up the bull-dog courage of the nation; and far be it from me to decry the advantage of becoming a nation of bull-dogs; but I now saw clearly that it was calculated to keep up the breed of English ruffian. "What is the Fives Court [London's leading boxing school]," said I to myself [...] "but a college of scoundrelism, where every bully ruffian in the land may gain a fellowship? What is the slang language of The Fancy but a jargon by which fools and knaves commune and understand each other, and enjoy a kind of superiority over the uninitiated? What is a boxing-match but an arena, where the noble and the illustrious are jostled into familiarity with the infamous and the vulgar? What, in fact, is the Fancy itself, but a chain of easy communication, extending from the peer down to the pickpocket, through the medium of which a man of rank may find he has shaken hands, at three removes, with the murderer on the gibbet?"'[21] His assessment may have been spot-on, but what the priggish Yankee missed was the appeal of the Fancy to both noble and vulgar. Not to mention its slangy language.

Byron was an aristocrat and a renowned if controversial poet, but the Fancy's true laureate was less socially distinguished. Pierce Egan (1772–1849) was born in the London suburbs, where he spent his life. By 1812 he had established himself as the country's leading 'reporter of sporting events', which at the time meant mainly prize-fights and horse-races. In the words of the modern journalist A. J. Liebling, his spiritual if not actual successor, 'Egan [...] belonged to London, and no man has ever presented a more enthusiastic picture of all aspects of its life except the genteel. He was a hack journalist, a song writer, and conductor of puff-sheets and, I am inclined to suspect, a shake-down man.'[22] Most important for Liebling, who wrote for the *New Yorker* on boxing among much else, was that 'In 1812 he got out the first paperbound instalment of *Boxiana; or Sketches of Ancient and Modern Pugilism; from the days of Brougham and Slack to the Heroes of the Present Milling Aera.*'[23] The journal lasted until 1828, its fifth volume, and established its editor as the foremost authority on what in the fourth volume (1824) was termed 'the Sweet Science of Bruising'.[24]

As John Camden Hotten put it, writing the introduction to his 1869 reprint of Egan's 'novel' *Life in London* (1821), 'In his particular line, he was the greatest man in England. [...] His peculiar phraseology, and his superior knowledge of the business, soon rendered him eminent beyond all rivalry and competition. He was flattered and petted by pugilists and peers: his patronage and countenance were sought for by all who considered the road to a prizefight the road to reputation and honor. Sixty years ago, his presence was understood to convey respectability on any meeting convened for the furtherance of bull-baiting, cock-fighting, cudgelling, wrestling, boxing, and all that comes within the category of "manly sports".'[25]

Like Tom Moore's satire, *Boxiana* was a showcase of 'Fancy slang'. As the writer Don Atyeo has explained, '"Ogles" were blackened, "peepers" plunged into darkness, "tripe-shops" received "staggerers", "ivories" were cracked, "domino boxes" shattered, and "claret" flowed in a steady stream.'[26] Egan's synonymy made him the father of every sportswriter who has followed. But by its nature it was restrained to the topic in hand. Seven years after the launch of his boxing journal Egan achieved a best-seller that packed in even more flash, and proclaimed itself as a very Bible of Fancy goings on, both high and low.

In 1821 he announced the publication of a regular journal: *Life in London*, to appear monthly at a shilling a time. It was to be illustrated by George Cruikshank (1792–1878), who had succeeded Hogarth and Rowlandson as London's leading satirist of urban life. The journal was dedicated to the King, George IV, who at one time had received Egan at court. The first edition of *Life in London* 'or, the Day and Night Scenes of Jerry Hawthorn, esq., and his elegant friend, Corinthian Tom, accompanied by Bob Logic, the Oxonian, in their rambles and Sprees through the Metropolis' appeared on 15 July. Egan's creation was an enormous, instant success, with its circulation mounting every month. Pirate versions appeared, featuring such figures as 'Bob Tallyho', 'Dick Wildfire' and the like. Print-makers speedily knocked off cuts featuring the various 'stars' and the real-life public flocked to the 'sporting' addresses that Egan had his heroes frequent. There was a translation into French. At least six plays were based on Egan's characters, contributing to yet more sales. One of these was exported to America, launching the 'Tom and Jerry' craze there. The version created by William Moncrieff, whose knowledge of London and of its slang equalled Egan's, was cited, not without justification, as 'The Beggar's Opera of its day'. Moncrieff (1794–1857) was one of contemporary London's most successful dramatists and theatrical managers. His production of *Tom and Jerry, or, Life in London* ran continuously at the Adelphi Theatre for two seasons; it was Moncrieff as much as Egan who, as the original *DNB*, in turn quoting Charles Hindley's *True History of Tom and Jerry* (1890) had it, 'introduced slang into the drawing room'.[27] And, à la Shadwell, some theatrical versions (of 1822 and 1823) felt it worth offering audiences a small glossary, mainly derived from the footnotes in Egan's prose original. In all, Egan suggested in his follow-up *The Finish to the Adventures of Tom, Jerry and Logic* (1830), some sixty-five works were created on the back of his own. And added that, 'We have been *pirated*, COPIED, *traduced*; but, unfortunately, not ENRICHED.'[28]

'We' had also come to epitomize a whole world. The adjectival use of *Tom and Jerry* lasted into the mid-century. Young men went on 'Tom-and-Jerry frolics', which usually featured the picking of drunken fights and the destruction of property, and in 1853, in Surtees's *Mr Sponge's Sporting Tour*, the ageing rake Mr Puffington, ever assuring his friends that, like Corinthian Tom, he could show them 'Life', can be found reminiscing and '[t]elling how Deuceace and he floored a Charley, or Blueun and he pitched a snob out of the boxes into the pit. This was in the old Tom-and-Jerry days, when fisticuffs were the fashion.'[29] There were *tom-and-jerry shops*, which were cheap, rough taverns, *tom-and-jerry gangs* of rowdy, hedonistic young men, and a verb use which meant to go out on a spree. By 1840 the names had come to christen a highly spiced punch, still being served up by Damon Runyon in 'Dancing Dan's Christmas' a century later. It was adopted by London costermongers to mean a cherry in rhyming slang.

Life in London appeared until 1828, when Egan closed it down. The journal was incorporated into the sporting magazine *Bell's Life*, which would last until in 1886 it too was bought up, by the *Sporting Times*.

Egan's prose style was incorporated as well, and it was seemingly still popular thirty years on. When, during his freshman term at Oxford, set *c.* 1850, the fictional 'Mr Verdant Green' tries some genteel prize-fighting, it ends, as do most of his sporting efforts, in disappointment: In 'the sporting slang of *Tintinnabulum's Life* [...] his claret had been repeatedly tapped, his bread-basket walked into, his day-lights darkened, his ivories rattled, his nozzle barked, his whisker-bed napped heavily, his kissing-trap countered, his ribs roasted, his nut spanked, and his whole person put into chancery, stung, bruised, fibbed, propped, fiddled, slogged, and otherwise ill-treated.'[30]

If slang, or rather flash, did manage to reach the essentially female arena of the drawing room, it would have appeared only in a very few, and most likely those of the better class of brothel. Flash remained a male delight. And a raffish one. Egan uses it in many of his London scenes, but they are invariably those where our heroes encounter the low end of the city's life. Indeed sophisticate Tom is constantly warning country Jerry to mind his language when voyaging amongst 'the ROSES, PINKS and TULIPS, the *flowers* of SOCIETY'.[31] It is when they visit All Max, the East End gin shop and encounter such members of the '*flash* part of mankind' as Bob the Coal-Whipper and Black Sal that the racy slang comes out; in the fashionable West End club Almacks, 'we must mind our P.'s and Q.s'.[32] Not merely that but the trio arrange a fail-safe, a murmur of 'lethe' (Greek for forgetfulness) if any of them are heard to fall from social grace. As Tom says, 'Indeed, if it were possible to call to your aid the waters of LETHE, to cleanse your pericranium of all ideas of "the slang" for a night, upon entering those regions of refinement, [...] it would be highly advantageous towards your attraction.'[33] Code-switching is not a modern invention.

In All Max (flash for 'all gin') things were different. 'Lascars, blacks, jack tars, coalheavers, dustmen, women of colour, old and young, and a sprinkling of the remnants of once fine girls, &c. were all *jigging* together, provided the *teazer of the catgut* was not *bilked* of his *duce*. [...] *Heavy wet* was the cooling beverage, but frequently overtaken by *flashes of lightning*. The *covey* was no *scholard*, as he asserted, and therefore he held the pot in one hand, and took the *blunt* with the other, to prevent the trouble of *chalking*, or making mistakes. [...] no one could read his customers better than Mr. *Mace*. [...] His motto was "never to give a *chance* away;" and Mr. *Mace* had long-been christened by the *downies*, the *"dashing covey."* He was *"cut out"* for his company; and he could *"come it well"* upon all points. On the sudden appearance of our *"swell* TRIO," and the CORINTHIAN's friend, among these unsophisticated sons and daughters of NATURE, their *ogles* were on the roll, under an apprehension that the *beaks* were out on the *nose*; but it was soon made "all right," by one of the *mollishers* whispering, loud enough to be heard by most of the party, "that she understood *as how* the *gemmen* had only dropped in for to have a *bit of a spree*, and there was no doubt they *voud* stand a *drap of summut* to make them all *cumfurable*, and likewise prove good customers to the *crib*." On the *office* being given, the *stand-still* was instantly removed ; and the *kidwys* and *kiddiesses* were footing the *double shuffle* against each other.'[34]

They may be slumming, but Egan implies that Tom, Jerry and Logic are as aware of this vocabulary as are their low-life companions. It is, as Gregory Dart suggests, 'a kind of classless language, a polyglot vocabulary that was not tied down to any particular social milieu'.[35] It was this lack of properly defined borders, both social and linguistic, that worried Egan's critics. *Blackwood's* magazine, for instance, shrank from the idea that the high and low might mix so cheerfully and that Egan, unlike for instance Dickens, offered up the working-class and criminal world without the slightest desire to make moral judgements thereupon. Flash, in conservative eyes, represents slang as pure subversion. 'The deep fear was that [Egan] might form part of a growing army of literary rabble-rousers dead-set on putting Cockney self-confidence to political ends.'[36] To Egan, however, as it had been to Grose, the use of flash, by no matter whom, was proof that free-born Britons could speak freely, unlike the French, enslaved to the Académie's linguistic diktats.

In 1823 Egan consolidated his role as a leading purveyor of flash with his revision of Francis Grose's *Classical Dictionary of the Vulgar Tongue*. It is effectively the dictionary's fourth legitimate edition, although as Julie Coleman points out, Egan's direct source was the pirated *Lexicon Balatronicum* of 1811.[37] 'Egan's Grose', as it is generally known, embellished its predecessor with the inclusion of a variety of mainly sporting Regency slang. He also cuts the 'coarse and broad expressions' and 'neglected no opportunity of excluding indelicate phrases [...] nor of *softening* down others[38] which Grose had allowed and notes the way that some slang terminology, typically *rum* – once a positive term, but by 1820 generally the reverse – had altered its sense. At the same time he hoped that in sum his efforts work 'to improve, and not to degrade mankind; to remove *ignorance,* and put the UNWARY on their guard; to rouse the *sleepy,* and to keep them AWAKE; to render those persons who are a *little* UP, more FLY: and to cause every one to be *down* to those tricks, manoeuvres and impositions practised in life, which daily cross the paths of both young and old'.[39] Among the headwords he excluded was the linguistic sense of slang (he defines it only as meaning fetters and as the verb to cheat), which Grose had listed, although at *flash,* defined as 'knowing', he offers *patter flash,* 'to speak the slang language'.

Perhaps Egan's most original contribution was the eleven-page 'Biographical Sketch of Francis Grose, Esq.'. The sources for this have vanished, and it has come to be queried by modern researchers, but the picture he paints of the bonhomous, rotund lexicographer making his nightly tours of London's taverns and rookeries is undeniably appealing.

Egan was respected and successful, even if he might have preferred that his honours had taken on more material form. It was inevitable then that he would have rivals, and one in particular. The career of the shadowy figure of John Badcock (fl. 1813–30), professionally known as 'Jon Bee' and latterly as 'James Hinds', seems to mirror that of Egan. Like Egan, Badcock himself regularly wrote on boxing and racing. As he states on the title page of his slang dictionary, he edited variously *The Fancy, or true Sportsman's Guide,* a monthly part-work offering 'authentic Memoirs of Pugilists', *The Annals of Sporting and Fancy Gazette* (1822–8, 13 vols) and *The Living Picture of London* (1818). The fact that these had actually come out before the far more successful Egan efforts must have been embittering. To be then forced, as he was with *Real Life in London* (2 vols, 1821), published under the name of 'An Amateur', to ape his rival, must have made it even worse. The fourth volume of *Boxiana* was also apparently his work. His last effort, a study of the works of the dramatist Samuel Foote, appeared in 1830. Since nothing else followed it is assumed that he died then or soon after.

It was inevitable that he should try his hand exploiting flash in a dictionary. *Slang,* 'a Dictionary of the Turf, the Ring, the Chase, the Pit, of Bon Ton and the Varieties of Life', compiled by 'Jon Bee, Esq', duly appeared in 1823. It formed, claimed the title page, 'the completest and most authentic Lexicon Balatronicum hitherto offered to the notice of the Sporting World' but this latter comparison was pure commercial flummery, although like Egan Badcock seems to have used the 1811 lexicon as his main source. Any comparison of any pages drawn from the two volumes shows how far Badcock's attempt to improve upon the original has only diluted its quality. Merely to take the respective opening pages: the *Lexicon* starts by listing 'abbess, abel-wackets, abigail, abram and abram cove'; Bee has 'Abatures, abbess, Abbott's Priory, ABC-darian, abigail, abrac and abrahamers' before reaching 'abram'. Of these the first is stag-hunting jargon, the fourth standard English and the sixth and seventh, which appear in no previous slang dictionary, are not considered worthy of inclusion by either Hotten or Farmer and Henley, although Partridge, generous to a fault, does revive them, more than a century later. The pattern persists throughout the dictionary.

As for flash itself, Bee defines it thus: '*Flash* – the language we here explicate is *"flash lingo,"* to be up to which is the earliest desire of all *flashy covey* who may not yet be *fly* thereto. The acquisition of *flash* puts many a man *fly* to what is going on, adversely or otherwise. [...] Again, the language of persons whose transactions demand concealment, yet require that they should mix with those from whom it should be concealed, is *flash*. [...] They were invariably thieves and gamblers who used flash formerly; but other kinds of persons, now-a-day, who may be rippishly inclined, adopt similar terms and phrases, to evince their uppishness in the affairs of life; especially those of the less honest part of the community, who, in this particular, run the risque of being foiled at their own game by means of this dictionary of modern flash. [...] of course, those words and sayings which are appropriate to the turf, the ring, and field-sports, are equally considered as flash by them, and the word has been applied (too generally we allow,) to all this species of quid pro quo lingo.'[40]

For a man whose work falls markedly beneath that of his peers, or perhaps for that very reason, Badcock is insufferably pleased with himself. Running down his near contemporaries, and explaining the rationale behind his own work, he remarks that 'Captain Grose was much too gross, even for his day, besides which, his work is become antiquated, stale, and out of date; the *Count's* ... were indeed *vaut-rien* [the reference is to the wholly unaristocratic James Hardy Vaux], as that *life* had been; and our friend Dr [Hewson] Clarke's augmentations [of Grose for the *Lexicon Balatronicum*] ... added to the structure lead, rather than beauty or strength. Nat Bailey should be forgotten: he is even older than Grose, and twice as nasty.'[41] Badcock goes on to savage Egan, whose edition of Grose he sets in December 1822, 'undertaken in great haste, the printer thereof learning that the materials for the present dictionary were in train ... How it has failed a comparison will show.'[42]

Aside from correcting the inadequate and trumpeting himself, Badcock explains that while every other profession has gained a dictionary, laying out what he terms its 'slangery', or more accurately its jargon, the occupations of the sporting gentry have been overlooked. It is his intention to remedy the omission. What is true is that his dictionary went beyond any contemporary. Many entries add anecdotes, social commentary and material that would have worked better in an encyclopaedia. Many such entries, for instance 'jargon-writer', which occupies two-thirds of page 103, or 'Jack Ketch', nearly a whole page from 108, are disproportionately long, and often not truly slang. Badcock has few defenders, though Julie Coleman is one of them. For her 'Jon Bee' far surpassed Egan. His problem, however, was, as ever, timing. 'Egan was "the Fancy"'s favourite; Bee a mere also-ran.'[43]

There were other dictionaries of flash, including Humphrey Potter's *New Dictionary of All the Cant and Flash Languages* (1795), the anonymously written *Flash Dictionary* (1821), and George Kent's *Modern Flash Dictionary* (1835), which in turn was plagiarized almost complete for the 'Flash Dictionary' included in *The Sinks of London* (1848). Finally, and perhaps oddest, was John Duncombe's *New and Improved Flash Dictionary of the Cant Words* (c. 1850). Duncombe, who made his money as a publisher of pornography in Holywell Street, the trade's contemporary centre, was Kent's publisher, and drew heavily on that work, but some 40% of the entries are wholly new. For instance, there are a group that use the preface abb-, all referring to prison: *abb-clouts* (prison dress), *abb-discipline* (whipping in the prison courtyard, either publicly or privately), *abb-gammonry* (a condemned sermon), *abb-tanger* (the passing bell at execution), and *abb-whack* (gaol allowance). He also offers hitherto unrecorded nicknames for places in London: *Burrowdamp Museum*, Newgate; *Conjuror's Abbey*, Guildhall; *Cowboy Castle*, the Mansion-house; *Culpgill college*, Giltspur-street compter, and the *Tower of Babel*, the Mansion-house.[44] None of these terms have survived, other than in subsequent dictionaries.

Flash remained a force until the mid-nineteenth century but it is best seen in fictional rather than lexicographical contexts. The public appetite for such melodramas was clear. And writers saw a profit in satisfying it. They also knew the necessity of 'realistic' props, among them linguistic. Dominating popular fiction during the 1830s to 40s was what became known, and excoriated, as the 'Newgate Novel'. The 'Newgate' of the novels was not in this case directly the prison, but the accounts of criminals that appeared in the *Newgate Calendar*, also known as *The Malefactors' Bloody Register*, first published in three volumes 1774–8 and appearing in new editions up to 1841. (The calendar was not the first such collection, but the latest version of a number of collections of criminal biographies the first of which, the *Tyburn Calendar*, had appeared in 1705.) The Newgate novelists might have argued a sound pedigree. Walter Scott, in *Guy Mannering* (1815) and as has been seen in *The Adventures of Nigel*, used a good deal of cant and / or flash even if, in the former, after offering a good deal, he dismisses this 'gibberish' as not worth recording – and does not help the reader by translating it. (This was changed in later editions.) The canonical Newgate novels, by authors such as Harrison Ainsworth and Edward Bulwer-Lytton, generally concentrated on the quasi-fictional exploits of popular villains-cum-folk heroes, such as Dick Turpin and Jack Sheppard, even if Lytton's *Eugene Aram* (1832) focused on a notorious killer who had not been overlaid with the patina of public affection, although Judith Flanders has shown how Aram (executed in 1759) was recreated in the Victorian popular mind not so much as a murderer, but a tortured soul whose philosophizing in some way excused his crime.[45] The novels, already much criticized by moralists, slumped from favour subsequent to the murder, in 1840, of Lord William Russell by his valet Benjamin

Courvoisier, who claimed in his unsuccessful defence that he had been influenced by Ainsworth's *Jack Sheppard* (1839).

In 1846 an author styling himself 'The Hon. F. L. G.' produced *The Swell's Night Guide*. This vade-mecum to London's lubricious pleasures included what must be the most artificial of all slang's concocted 'conversations'. Purportedly conducted by the *Gonniff* (from Yiddish, a thief), his girl the *Shickster* (again from Yiddish *shicksa* and strictly speaking a female gentile), with interruptions from their pal the *Cracksman*, it represented flash taken to its limits. For instance: 'Ve vas in a swanky ken, flashing the broads, nix of bevey an nanty denarly; in comes a green, multa beargred, flashes his skin of tin; we cops that; patters about his crib, we tumbles to the pitch; so we plants ripping Sall on the bloke, she flokessed his nibs, and hooked it off to his crib, unscrewed the drum, made the lob and scarpered.'[46]

It was perhaps this that provided a source for Thackeray, who parodied the Newgate melodramas in a wonderfully plausible episode called 'The Night Attack' which was published in the early editions of *Vanity Fair* (1849) but removed from that of 1853 and subsequent editions:

> One, two, three! It is the signal that Black Vizard had agreed on.
>
> 'Mofy! Is that your snum?' said a voice from the area. 'I'll gully the dag and bimbole the clicky in a snuffkin.'
>
> 'Nuffle your clod, and beladle your glumbanions,' said Vizard, with a dreadful oath. 'This way, men: if they screak, out with your snickers and slick! Look to the pewter-room, Blowser. You, Mark, to the old gaff's mopus box! and I,' added he, in a lower but more horrible voice, 'I will look to Amelia!'
>
> There was a dead silence. 'Ha!' said the Vizard, 'was that the click of a pistol?'[47]

The Newgate genre was that of ripping yarns but in one way at least prefigured modernity, not merely in placing villains at the heart of the plot, but like *romans* and *films noir*, in accepting moral ambiguities: the author refused to take on the black and white dichotomy of 'goodies' and 'baddies'. Writing in a note to his own version, the supposed

Newgate parody *Catherine* (1839), Thackeray was indignant. 'Let your rogues in novels act as rogues and our honest men as honest men; don't let us have any juggling and thimblerigging with virtue and vice.' But as he continued: 'We know what the public likes and have chosen rogues for our characters and have taken a story from the Newgate Calendar.' The difference, he promised, was that his rogues would 'have nothing that shall be mistaken for virtues'.[48]

The Newgate novels were undoubtedly enlivened by their use of cant and flash. However, the century-old setting of their stories ensured that much of the terminology was anachronistic. None of it was actually contrived, it can all be found in the canting dictionaries, but those consulted had as often been published in the early eighteenth century as more recently. Ainsworth even went so far as to compose his own set of canting songs, found in *Rookwood* (1834). There were twenty-three in the first edition, and he added seven more for the fourth. Typical was 'Jerry Juniper's Chant', otherwise known as 'Nix My Doll, Pals':

> In a box of the stone jug I was born,
> Of a hempen widow the kid forlorn,
> Fake away,
> And my father, as I've heard say,
> Fake away,
> Was a merchant of capers gay,
> Who cut his last fling with great applause,
> Nix my doll pals, fake away.[49]

Quizzed as to whether, like Lytton who claimed to have sought out gypsies and villains to find his vocabulary, he had actually done any fieldwork, Ainsworth replied, 'Not at all. Never had anything to do with the scoundrels in my life. I got my slang in a much easier way. I picked up the Memoirs of James Hardy Vaux – a returned transport. The book was full of adventures, and had at the end a kind of slang dictionary. Out of this I got all my "patter." Having read it thoroughly and mastered it, I could use it with perfect facility.'[50] Vaux' dictionary had appeared in 1812, but it largely mimicked its predecessors. Keith Hollingsworth has suggested that 'such a highly respectable answer may be open to doubt'[51] but it has some validity: of the 270 cant terms used in *Rookwood* Vaux has 114.

Dickens had been a mere reporter when Ainsworth, in time to be among his closest – if short-lived – friends, was already a bestseller. By 1837, when he published *Oliver Twist*, the Newgate novel was fast becoming discredited and he was keen to disavow any links with his own crusading work. Dickens notoriously pandered to his middle-class readers: flash, he stressed (though he resisted naming it), had been inserted only for verisimilitude and to heighten the unpleasantness of Fagin's and Sikes's world.[52] As he put it in 1841, 'I endeavoured, while I painted it in all its fallen and degraded aspects, to banish from the lips of the lowest character I introduced, any expression that could by possibility offend; and rather to lead to the unavoidable inference that its existence was of the most debased and vicious kind, than to prove it elaborately by words and deeds. In the case of the girl, in particular, I kept this intention constantly in view.'[53] Dickens was invariably careful. As early as *The Pickwick Papers* he stated, 'Throughout this book no incident or expression occurs which would call a blush into the most delicate cheek or wound the feelings of the most delicate person.'[54]

Presumably his readers had no problems with Oliver's egregiously impeccable diction and the fantasy that Nancy was not employed at the lower end of prostitution. Yet Dickens's nay-saying – and in September 1853 he published G. A. Sala's long denunciation of slang in his own *Household Words* – does not convince. Comparing the book's vocabulary to that of its peers – Dickens uses just under 200 terms – his uses seem as widespread as those of any Newgate author. And whether or not he picked up terms in his wanderings through night-time London, the bulk of his material, as did theirs, probably came from printed sources. The difference, of course, was his quality as a writer.

The slang of sporting men, a subset of flash, persisted on the race-course and the hunting field. Dickens's Pickwick drew on Robert Smith Surtees's serialized tales of 'jaunts & jollities', the 'eccentric and extravagant exploits of that renowned sporting citizen, Mr John Jorrocks of St. Botolph Lane and Great Coram Street', which appeared through the 1830s and beyond. Surtees, who in 1831 co-founded the *New Sporting Magazine* with fellow sporting journalist C. J. Apperley ('Nimrod'), wrote a number of successful 'hunting novels' including *Handley Cross* (1843), *Mr Sponge's Sporting Tour* (1853) and *Mr Facey Romford's Hounds* (1865). Surtees, who never actually signed his work and led a parallel life as a Co. Durham squire and M. F. H., offered an unvarnished world: his rakes were rakish and his women far from simpering caricatures. Kipling, in 'My Son's Wife', has a priggish character shudder from 'a foul world [...] a heavy-eating, hard-drinking hell of horse-copers, swindlers, match-making mothers, economically dependent virgins selling themselves blushingly for cash and lands, Jews, tradesmen and an ill-considered spawn of Dickens and horsedung characters'.[55] Surtees knew the sporting world at first hand and duly satirized it, matching an accuracy of observation that rivalled that of Dickens with an acid wit. His language was suitable. 'His books ran counter to the currents of his age in their lack of idealism, absence of sentimentality, and almost wilful flouting of conventional moralism. His leading male characters were coarse or shady; his leading ladies dashing and far from virtuous; his outlook on society satiric to the point of cynicism.'[56] Frustrated by the seeming popularity of so reprehensible a figure, critics attributed it to his illustrator, John Leech, a regular at *Punch*. Victorians were far happier with such as George Whyte-Melville (1821–78) and his successor Hawley Smart (1833–93), both ex-officers, both hunting novelists, and both far more willing to 'play the game' of contemporary self-censorship. Nonetheless, there was usually a chapter where the young master, paying for his father's self-indulgence and fallen into the hands of the Jews, was forced to assume a pseudonym and mingle with stable-boys, touts or worse before winning the Derby and thus enough money to cast off his proletarian disguise, pay his father's debts and marry the heroine. Such chapters always yielded flash.

By the mid-nineteenth century flash was effectively dead. But it was preserved, if only in the cheap fiction popular among the working class. Writing in his sociological study *The Seven Curses of London* (1869), Mayhew's heir James Greenwood, 'The Amateur Casual', claimed to have witnessed this conversation during a prison visit:

'This is a very bad lad, sir,' remarked the governor sternly; 'he only came in yesterday, and to-day, while out for exercise with the others, he must misconduct himself, and when the warder reproved him, he must swear some horrible oath against him. It is for that he is here. How many times have you been here, lad?'

Lad (gulping desperately). 'Three times, sir!'

Governor (sternly). 'What! speak the truth, lad.'

Lad (with a determined effort to gouge tears of his eyes with his knuckles). 'Four times, sir.'

Governor. 'Four times! and so you'll go on till you are sent away, I'm afraid. Can you read, lad?'

Lad (with a penitential wriggle). 'Yes, sir; I wish as I couldn't, sire.'

Governor. 'Ah! why so?'

Lad (with a doleful wag of his bullet-head). 'Cos then I shouldn't have read none of them highwaymen's books, sir; it was them as was the beginning of it.'[57]

And in 1886, in an article entitled 'What Boys Read',[58] Edwin Salmon described the story of a young clerk 'who had devoted his leisure to a study of Harrison Ainsworth's novels' and was arrested for a failed attempt to rob his employer. Inspired, it appeared, by the likes of Turpin and Sheppard, he had lured his boss from his bedroom by mewing like a cat and then tried to knock him out with a handkerchief drenched in chloroform.

'Them highwayman's books' were what were known as 'penny dreadfuls', and before that 'penny bloods'. The middle classes might have absorbed flash through Dickens, they did not do so through the works of such as Edward Lloyd, Edwin Brett and Charles Fox, the best-known publishers of such cheap blood-and-thunder 'literature'. But these were not aimed at the middle classes; their readers were working-class children and teenagers, of whom by the 1870s more than two-thirds were able to read. This was a new mass-market and it was happy to be exploited. The 'dreadfuls' that they consumed were the easy-read successors to the Newgate novel, and unlike those relatively expensive volumes, their weekly eight pages came at just 1d, well within the pocket of the young people at whom they were aimed. Like the Newgates the 'dreadfuls' delighted in the exploits of highwayman and robbers, and like them and the 'video nasties' and computer games of modernity excited a contemporary moral panic. The stories were bad enough; what was worse was that they often focused on a young man, once a humble clerk, who tossed aside respectability and his few shillings a week, wilfully embracing the romantic pleasures, and far greater financial rewards, of criminality. They featured such as Charley Wag, 'the boy burglar' (whose 'portrait' fitted him with the carefully curled lock of hair known as a 'Newgate knocker'), Spring-heeled Jack, 'the Terror of London', and the Wild Boys of London or The Children of the Night. They also republished such as Ainsworth, and of course a wide range of stories dedicated to Dick Turpin and his many clones. Charley himself was described as 'pugnacious, great at punching heads and bunging up eyes' and in a fight with a youth of 'Slogger's Alley' tipped his hat not merely to Ainsworth but further back to *Boxiana*, when he gives his opponent 'one of those heavy taps upon the nasal organ which is, I believe, in the language of the prize ring denominated "a smeller"'.[59]

That the 'dreadfuls' of the 1860s were still using the slang of a good thirty years past is predictable if, given the fuss they caused, ironic. Their middle-class writers were not interested in presenting real working-class culture. That would not come until the 'Cockney novels' of later in the century. Their readers would have been infinitely more fluent in contemporary slang and if criminals themselves, cant. Rhyming slang and back-slang, the reasonably new coinages of the period, do not appear amongst the fictional *gentlemen of the pad*. But the hacks who put the tales together would not have cared. They may have claimed, as did the blurb-writer for one edition of Charley Wag, that 'In this Work, upon which the Author has been employed almost night and day for the last two years collecting the necessary information, will be found the most graphic and reliable pictures of hitherto unknown phases of the DARK SIDE OF LONDON LIFE. Not exaggerated and distorted by the wild imaginings of the Novelist's brain, but rendered in stern, truthful language, by one who has studied, in all its blackest enormity, the doings of secret crime,'[60] but unlike Ainsworth and Co. they would have done little research and their slang presumably came second-hand from their Newgate predecessors.

In the end flash was only a name, a temporary description of something much bigger. The aristocracy might back away from slang as Victorian society, rather than indulge in their pleasures, began to see the proles as something not merely 'lower' in class but also dangerous and unclean. But slang was unfazed. It continued to grow and to expand. And for the first time, and initially using the same vocabulary as had informed Francis Grose's dictionary and the fiction of Pierce Egan, it emigrated: to the empire's latest penal colony: Australia.

8 Down Under: Larrikin Lingo

> 'Tis the everyday Australian
> Has a language of his own,
> Has a language, or a slanguage,
> Which can simply stand alone.
> W. T. Goodge, 'The Great Australian
> Slanguage', in *The Bulletin*, 4 June 1898

The 'First Fleet', captained by Arthur Philip and bringing with it in its eleven vessels some 148 male and 188 female convicts, all sentenced to transportation from England to New South Wales ('discovered' by James Cook in 1770), made landfall in Botany Bay on 20 January 1788 and arrived in Port Jackson, modern Sydney Harbour, six days later. It was the first such convoy to bring British criminals to Australian shores — transportation to America having ceased in 1776, a substitute had urgently to be found; its successors would continue coming until the 1840s and the system would not be wholly abandoned until 1868. Some 165,000 prisoners would arrive to fill the penal settlements. They were not alone: an increasing flow of free settlers would join them: in 1852 alone, drawn by the contemporary gold rush, 370,000 would make the journey and by 1871 Australia's population had reached 1.7 million. By 1900 there were around 3,788,000 Australians and the current statistics show just over 22.5 million. It remains a country that draws in immigrants: figures for 2010 show that judged by 'country of birth' former citizens of some fifty nations chose in that year to start new lives 'Down Under'.

James Hardy Vaux arrived in New South Wales in 1801. He was nineteen and about to serve the mandatory minimum term of seven years' judicial exile. He had been born in Surrey, the son of a butler and a house steward, had been apprenticed to a linen-draper in Liverpool and then fallen amongst the obligatory 'bad company' that gave him a taste for cock-fighting, and thus gambling, and thence launched him on his criminal career. Moving to London, living on his wits and rarely employed for long, Vaux was not violent, but ran the gamut of petty crimes, with a lucrative sideline in peddling plausible sob-stories in return for his victims' charitable donations. He had survived unscathed, despite an arrest for pilfering, but in 1801, convicted of stealing a handkerchief, was charged, tried and sent to what was still a relatively new-formed colony.

Here Vaux was lucky: rather than labour, and thanks to penmanship skills that he regularly employed in forgery, he was employed as a clerk and in 1807 was able to sail back to England. He returned promptly to criminal form, and 'exercised alternately the following modes of depredation [...] *buzzing, dragging, sneaking, hoisting, pinching, smashing, jumping, spanking, starring,* the *kid-rig,* the *letter-racket,* the *order-racket,* [and] the *snuff-racket*'. It is in character with *The Memoirs'* invariably self-serving style that he adds that 'considering our youth and inexperience, [we] evinced a good deal of dexterity'. He also, 'least the reader be unprovided with a cant dictionary',[1] explains them all.

Not enough dexterity, it seems. He was re-arrested and as a second offender, now facing the more serious charge of stealing jewellery, was sentenced to transportation for life. He returned to New South Wales in 1810. A year later he was sentenced again, this time for receiving stolen property, possibly via a judge's servant, and sent to Newcastle (north of Sydney), known as a 'place of secondary punishment' and a hard-labour prison within the country's greater one. This 'hamlet of punishment', as Robert Hughes has termed it, was designed to make incorrigible criminals suffer. 'Everything seemed either exhausting or boring, but that was what commended it to the authorities.'[2] Yet again Vaux seemed to have been lucky. Rather than logging in the fast diminishing cedar forests, or suffering in the mines or at burning lime – and despite an abortive escape attempt for which he received fifty lashes – he managed to obtain another clerking job.

Writing in 1792, in *A Complete Account of the Settlement at Port Jackson*, Watkin Tench, a young officer of marines who had volunteered for a posting in Botany Bay and had sailed in the First Fleet, had noted that:

> A leading distinction, which marked the convicts on their outset in the colony, was a use of what is called the 'flash', or 'kiddy' language. In some of our early courts of justice an interpreter was frequently necessary to translate the deposition of the witness and the defence of the prisoner. This language has many dialects. The sly dexterity of the pickpocket, the brutal ferocity of the footpad, the more elevated career of the highwayman and the deadly purpose of the midnight ruffian is each strictly appropriate in the terms which distinguish and characterize it. I have ever been of opinion that an abolition of this unnatural jargon would open the path to reformation. And my observations on these people have constantly instructed me that indulgence in this infatuating cant is more deeply associated with depravity and continuance in vice than is generally supposed. I recollect hardly one instance of a return to honest pursuits, and habits of industry, where this miserable perversion of our noblest and peculiar faculty was not previously conquered.

The equation of slang with vice was nothing new. Vaux, no doubt unconsciously, took up where Tench had indicated. Though not with plans for abolition of the 'flash' language, but for its explication. It was during his time in Newcastle, 'during his solitary hours of cessation from hard labour', that Vaux produced what continues to be credited as the first dictionary of any kind with reference to the Australian language: *A New and Comprehensive Vocabulary of the Flash Language*. The preface, dedicated to the then governor of Newcastle, Thomas Skottowe, is dated 5 July 1812. 'I trust the Vocabulary will afford you some amusement from its novelty,' said Vaux, 'and that from the correctness of its definitions, you may occasionally find it useful in your magisterial capacity.'[3] The *Vocabulary* did not appear in print, however, until 1819, when it appears as an addendum to Vaux's unashamedly picaresque *Memoirs*, published in London by John Murray.

Although Julie Coleman has suggested that life in the Newcastle camp would have been too tough to allow for writing,[4] and opts to date the *Vocabulary* alongside the later *Memoirs*, the dedication to Skottowe (replaced as governor before 1819) and more importantly the terms included suggest the earlier date. Noel McLachlan, who edited both works in 1964, has no problem dating them separately. And Professor Coleman herself, who provides a detailed breakdown of Vaux' 332 entries, notes that one third of the entries could be found in either Humphrey Potter's *New Dictionary of the Cant and Flash Languages* of 1790 or the *Lexicon Balatronicum* of 1811. (However, as she adds, this does not prove that Vaux had actually consulted either work.) To what extent the moonlighting clerk drew on his personal experience of the criminal world – which was undoubtedly wide enough – or on 'field-work' among his fellow-transportees is unprovable. But while his work is credited as the first dictionary of any kind to have been published in Australia, it cannot be seen as a dictionary of homegrown Australian language. It is, rather, a somewhat abbreviated selection of what was available in the late-eighteenth and early-nineteenth-century London underworld.

One can also assume that in common with the readers of most canting dictionaries, those who obtained copies of Vaux were not those whose jargon filled its pages. Amanda Laugesen, in an essay in the Australian Dictionary Centre's newsletter *Ozwords*, on 'Botany Bay Argot',[5] has suggested that Vaux's glossary was as much a reflection of the continuing British upper-class fascination with the criminal world and its language – thus Tench's observations – as it was a record of actual convict speech as found in the penal settlements.

He was not making it up. Whether or not it was current in New South Wales, this was an established vocabulary used by a recognized group. That terms such as *charley* ('a watchman'), *pall* ('a partner, companion, associate, or accomplice'), *stick* ('a pistol'), *crib* ('to die'), or such terms for money as *bean, bender, bob, coach-wheel, crook, rag* and *quid* made their way across the seas was hardly surprising. These and others were terms prisoners would have known and continued to use. In addition Vaux offers certain terms that came directly from the convict experience. For instance *bellowser*, originally a prize-fighting term for a blow to the stomach, but now a sentence to transportation: both 'take one's breath away'. Similar is *nap a winder* (to be transported); a winder also deprived one of breath, but as with *bellowser*, there is also the image of the wind in the prison ship's sails. The word *lag* was not coined in Australia (it is recorded in 1760 with reference to America) but became identified with its penal settlements. Vaux has *lag* as 'a convict under sentence of transportation' and is first to record the *old lag* ('a man or woman who has been transported, and is so called on returning home'). The term would go on to mean any veteran prisoner, incarcerated or (currently) free, and be used in the UK as often as in Australia. He also has *lag ship* ('a transport chartered by Government for the conveyance of convicts to New South Wales; also, a hulk, or floating prison, in which, to the disgrace of humanity, many hundreds of these unhappy persons are confined, and suffer every complication of human misery').⁶ Vaux's second voyage out had been prefaced by a period in the hulks: he knew of what he wrote.

Where Vaux does demonstrate that language was altering (and thus defies the belief of some negative critics that his was merely a pseudonym for some London hack) was in his appreciation of the way in which certain terms, while already common in London, had undergone a change in their new environment. These were nowhere as radical as the renaming of flora and fauna that provided much new and truly 'Australian language', but they showed the way words, like people, were in transition. The emblematic example being *swag*. Swag had meant criminal booty since the mid-eighteenth century; prior to that it had first been used as a shop (and its stealable contents) and then to mean money. Vaux has that sense ('The *swag*, is a term used in speaking of any booty you have lately obtained, be it of what kind it may, except money, as *Where did you lumber the swag?* that, is, where did you deposit the stolen property? To *carry the swag* is to be the bearer of the stolen goods to a place of safety'') but he also offers, as his first definition, 'a bundle, parcel, or package; as a *swag of snow*' (i.e. of linen or washing). It was this swag, denoting the pack carried by an itinerant, that would, with such derivatives as *swaggie*, *swagger*, and *swagman*, become Australia's primary use.

Vaux made some £33 (now approximately £2,000) from his memoirs (half the profits). His career is unknown after the publication but he absconded from New South Wales sometime before 1830 and made his way to Dublin. Arrested again, he was transported, for an unprecedented third time. Nothing more is recorded, other than a brief court appearance, and it is assumed he died in Australia. The *Vocabulary* did not appear in the second, 1827 edition of the *Memoirs*, but Vaux, at least as a character, did appear in William Moncrieff's 'serio-comical, operatical, melodramatical, pantomimical, characteristical, satirical, Tasmanian, Australian extravaganza' *Van Diemen's Land! or Settlers and Natives*, which played London's Surrey Theatre in early 1830. The fictional Vaux leads his fellow-convicts in the egalitarian verse, 'Ne'er droop brother convicts, but keep up the ball, / For in court, or in cottage, in hovel or hall, / Mankind, as occasion permits, are rogues all, / Sing Tantarantara, rogues all, &c.', delivers a couple of speeches and joins the 'convict galopade' that concludes the scene.

Moncrieff is better known for his stage version of 'Tom and Jerry'. In 1843 Egan's London picaresque was cloned for Australia when it was announced that the burletta *Life in Sydney; or, the Ran Dan Club* by the otherwise anonymous 'A. B. C.'[8] was due for production in the city from which it took its name. It did not appear, being one of only three plays banned between 1841 and the 1850s by the Colonial Secretary, who claimed it was libellous (in its unrestrained satire of the current colonial way of life), but the surviving script shows it to have taken Egan's Corinthian duo to Australia. Tom is now a Sydney resident, Jerry the 'new chum' and Logic 'leader of the Ran Dan Club'; But 'A. B. C.' did not have London's variegated life to play with. Sydney provided fewer excitements. Still, the script does indeed skate near the libellous with its barely disguised references to real-life characters, including policemen, entertainers and well-known sporting gentry. However, unlike Moncrieff's London original, *Life in Sydney* does not moralize.

Flash was also noted, in 1827, by the Royal Navy surgeon Peter Cunningham in his book *Two Years in New South Wales*: 'A number of the slang phrases current in *St. Giles's Greek* [from the London criminal 'rookery' at St Giles; elsewhere Cunningham refers to 'Billingsgate slang'] bid fair to become legitimatized in the dictionary of this colony : *plant, swag, pulling up*, and other epithets of the Tom and Jerry school, are established – the dross passing here as genuine, even among all ranks, while the native word *jirrand* (afraid) has become in some measure an adopted child, and may probably puzzle our future Johnsons with its *unde derivator*. In our police-offices, the slang words are taken regularly down in examinations, and I once saw a little urchin not exceeding ten years *patter* it in evidence to the bench with the most perfect fluency.'

The convict world did not only produce or use flash – there was a wide range of standard terms developed within the institution – and its use gradually petered out. This was not the end of criminal-specific slang, but of its current style. The natural turnover of any jargon was partially responsible, but Dr Laugesen also suggests that the gradual movement of convicts into civil society, where once freed they were known as 'emancipists', meant that they left behind their old vocabulary as determinedly as they had their shackles. As in Britain flash survived as much through literary use as through currency.

Some crime-writing authors, however, were more adventurous. In 1868 Marcus Clarke wrote a series of 'Sketches of Melbourne Low Life' for the *Australasian*; he would use some of the terms he uncovered in his popular, convict-centred novel *For the Term of His Natural Life* (1874). A seeming intimacy with the underworld gained him the authenticity that crime writers before and after him have always sought. Among the words for which his is the first recorded use are *canary* (a convict's yellow jacket), *come the drops* (to burst into tears), *gaff* (to talk loudly) and *stow your gaff!* (be quiet!), *hang one's jib* (to look miserable), *jump it* (for a convict to become a warder), *muggy-pated* (stupid), and *Norfolk Dumpling* (a prisoner on Norfolk Island); others used include the *echt*-Australian *tucker* (food), *Miss Nancy* (an effeminate man), *area-sneak* (a robber of basements), *bolter* (one who runs from their responsibilities), *moisten one's chaffer* (to take a drink), *hocus* (to drug [someone's drink]), *knuckler* (a pickpocket), and *lifer* (coined for the Australian experience of those who suffered a more severe punishment than a 'seven-year man'), *neddy* (to hit with a blackjack), and *obstropolous* (i.e. obstreperous). Ironically, since the novel is set between 1827 and 1846, not all of Clarke's Melbourne terminology might have been chronologically accurate.

After the convict, the bushranger. Australia's version of the highwayman, the bushranger (sometimes known, like his British antecedents as 'Captain' this or that), has gained much of the same mythology, with his 'Bail up!' replacing 'Stand and deliver!' and the outback taking the place of London's notorious Blackheath. The supreme example is of course Ned Kelly, whose reputation – either gloriously independent epitome of Australia's national myths, or psychotic, heartless thief and killer – continues to divide the nation. Distance seems to have increased his appeal: contemporaries used the verb to *Ned Kelly* as a synonym for rob; the congratulatory *game as Ned Kelly* does not appear for half a century after his death. (The rhyming slang, meaning both 'belly' and 'telly', seems simply disrespectful on either level.)

The great fictional treatment is Rolf Boldrewood's *Robbery Under Arms* (1883). Boldrewood, real name Thomas Browne (1826–1915), had been a pastoralist, a police magistrate and gold commissioner by the time in 1878 he began writing fiction. In 1882, since 'a man with eight children and a limited income must do all he can to supplement the income', he began writing what he termed 'rather a sensational novel [...] called "Robbery Under Arms"'.[9] First serialized in the *Sydney Mail*, then published in full in 1883, the book was hugely successful, first at home and then across the anglophone world. As the English critic Henry Green would put it, Boldrewood's heroes, the Marston brothers, were 'the first thoroughly Australian characters in fiction'.[10] The atmosphere was intensified by the introduction of the honourable bushranger 'Captain' Starlight and his aboriginal sidekick Warrigal. Dan Moran, another bushranger, offers the downside, doubtless more realistic, of the criminal type.

Whether it directly contributed to the book's popularity is unknown, but *Robbery* was the most slang-laden book yet to appear in Australia, offering some 360 discrete terms. And although a portion is inevitably imported from English, there is a very minimum of outmoded cant. And Boldrewood is responsible for a number of first uses: among them were *at full bat* (at top speed), *boxed-up* (confused), *break-out* (a bout of drunkenness or insanity), *bullock* (to perform heavy manual labour), *bush* (uncivilized, inferior, rough-and-ready), *cook* (to overcome), *cut out* (to finish, to complete a job), *dead house* (a room in an outback public house set aside for those who are incapably drunk), *derry* (an aversion towards, a feud with), *dingo* (a cheat, a scoundrel, a traitor or a coward), *dinkum* (hard work, a due share of work), *knockabout*, (an unskilled labourer or handyman on a sheep station), *mix it* (to cause trouble for), *on the grass* (released from prison), *ringer* (the fastest and best shearer in a shed), *roll into* (attack), *shook on* (infatuated with), *straight-ahead* (committed, reliable), *straighten* (to defeat, to beat up), *try-on* (any form of attempt at something), *turn out* (to leave home and become a bushranger), *wag it* (to play truant), *whole box and dice* and *wood-and-water joey* (a general labourer).

The century began with one dictionary and culminated in another: E. E. Morris's *Austral English* (1898). Morris had responded to James Murray's appeal for Australianisms that might be included in the *OED*. He found that he had collected enough to create his own lexicon (and Murray, in his initial invitation to Morris in 1882, had noted that 'It might even be possible, with sufficient co-operation, to produce an Australian dictionary on the same lines as the *New English Dictionary* by way of supplement to it'[11]). Morris's strength is in listing the new names of Australia's flora and fauna. He offers less than forty examples of slang, among them *Australian flag* (an untucked shirt-tail), *Bananaland* (Queensland), *Barcoo spew* (severe vomiting brought on by drinking bad water and often accompanied by attacks of dysentery), *cronk* (dishonest, illegal), *gluepot* (a near-impassable muddy road), *Jack the painter* ('very strong bush-tea, so called from the mark it leaves round the drinker's mouth'), *joey* (a child), *old identity* and its antonym *new iniquity*, *overlander* (a tramp), *pannikin-boss* (a minor official), *scrubber* (a rough, unkempt person, thus an outsider), *shepherd* (to follow someone who has been targeted for robbery), the drinking ritual of *shilling in and the winner shouts*, *stick up* (to extort money), and *take down* (to swindle).

There had, however, been a couple of dictionaries of Australian slang since Vaux. The first of these, the ambitiously titled *Sydney Slang Dictionary*, is in fact an eleven-page pamphlet that offered some 558 entries, plus material on back slang and prostitution and 'some specimens of slang talk'. It is dated to 1882, although it bears no actual date and this is simply the year of its accession to the Mitchell Library, which holds the only two surviving copies. It also claimed to be a 'new edition', but as Bruce Moore, who has discussed it at length in *Ozwords*,[12] has suggested, this may be no more than an advertising ploy. It is largely a work of plagiarism, with the bulk of its words stolen either from John Camden Hotten's *Slang Dictionary* (1859 et seq.) or George Washington Matsell's *Vocabulum* (1859, and itself deeply indebted to 'Egan's Grose' of 1823). 'Much of the material is simply the slang of the London or American underworld, which may or may not have been used in Australia. Only about 50 of the 558 entries turn out to be Australian, and half of these were taken from the plagiarised texts.' Of the remaining twenty-five 'it is possible that these are the compiler's own original contribution to the pamphlet. Most of them are obscure, and probably the only two that a modern audience would recognise are *putting on jam* 'assuming a false air of importance' and *yacker* 'to talk'.[13]

Writing in his introduction, Morris noted that while a great deal of slang is used in Australasia, 'very much less is generated here than is usually believed. In 1895 a literary policeman in Melbourne brought out a small *Australian Slang Dictionary*. In spite of the name, however, the compiler confesses that "very few of the terms it contains have been invented by Australians." My estimate is that not one word in fifty in his little book has an Australian origin, or even a specially Australian use.'[14]

The dictionary to which he referred was that product of a Melbourne policeman and campaigner against his own force's corruption, Cornelius Crowe (1853–1928), whose bearded portrait adorns the front cover. Its full title runs: *The Australian Slang Dictionary containing the words and phrases of the thieving fraternity, together with the unauthorised, though popular expressions now in vogue with all classes in Australia*. Its target readership can be deduced from the advertisements that top and tail the text: alongside those for a variety of hotels (i.e. pubs), for tobacconists (including Harry Lewis's 'Ally Sloper Cigar Divan') and one for an undertaker, is *The Newest Woman: The Destined Monarch of the World*, explained as 'MILLIE FINKELSTEIN'S Theatrical, Sporting and Sensational Story. A tale dealing with all phases of MODERN SOCIETY, moving from the Aristocratic Halls of Rupertswood to the Hovels of Melbourne; now dealing with the feverish Follies of Flemington, now Peering from the prison cells of Pentridge.'

The reality is somewhat more sober. Offering some thirty-three varieties of slang – including that of auctioneers, bootmakers, clergymen, football, hotel, imposters, lawyers, shooting, and undertakers (geared, perhaps, to bringing in ads) – Crowe's A–Z work runs to ninety-six pages, and is rounded off with a heavily contrived 'flash' text (with translation), comments on back slang and rhyming slang (brief and British: the homegrown lexis had yet to develop) and a pair of canting poems. A final verse – 'The Convict's Dream' – is slang-free.

Like many predecessors, Crowe's aim was 'to place in the hands of the police and the public a work through which they become conversant with the slang terms used by the rogue fraternity as a medium of communication with each other. [...] I trust the circulation of this work will have the desired effect of preventing criminals, rogues and gamblers from conversing with impunity in the presence of the police and public.'

He also admits what Morris would repeat: 'Although I have entitled this book the "Australian Slang Dictionary", I would ask the reader to bear in mind that but few of the terms it contains have been invented by Australian criminals; the most of them have been brought into use by the criminal classes who have emigrated here from different parts of the world where criminals have had a language of their own for centuries past.'[15] Few terms indeed. Of the 2,688 entries some 2,574 have been borrowed: again from Hotten and from Trimble's *Slang Dictionary of New York, London and Paris* (1880), again based heavily on Hotten.[16]

There was also the unpublished manuscript entitled *Materials for a Dictionary of Australian Slang*, collected between 1900 and 1910 by Alfred George Stephens and S. J. O'Brien. Stephens (a fervent Australian nationalist with the motto: 'Muscle and Pluck forever!'[17]) had been until 1906 a sub-editor on the Sydney *Bulletin* and manager of Bulletin Publications; O'Brien was a house-painter, political hopeful and, as 'Jack Shay', a *Bulletin* contributor. Despite the title, of the 221 entries only approximately half can be considered as 'Australian'. They include such well-attested staples as *act the angora* (to play the fool), *barmaid's blush* (a drink composed of ginger beer/rum and raspberry cordial), *jackaroo* (a new arrival on a sheep station), *lamb down* (for a landlord to persuade a customer to keep spending money on alcohol), *offside* (an assistant), *robbo* (a cab), and the drinking game *Tambaroora*. However, Judith Robertson, in her analysis of the entries, pinpoints a number for which 'there is no evidence of the existence of the terms apart from the entries in the manuscript'[18] and suggests that due to the authors' background, many of these apparent nonce-words are better described as 'Bulletinisms' than as widely used Australian slang.

Reading the press, and in particular the Police Court 'Sketches' retailed from 1845 in the 'sporting journal' *Bell's Life in Sydney* (motto 'Hark Forward, Australia'), one also finds that while local slang's origins may have not been indigenous, Australians seemed less inhibited in recording what *Bell's* termed 'the language of the people'. A wide range of terms find their first recorded use in the mouth of one defendant or another, sometimes decades before they were written down back in Britain. This is not, again, to say that they were coined in Australia but they had been imported there, whether by convicts or free settlers, and were central to the speech of the urban working class.

Although the Australianism *sly-grog* was first recorded in 1825, the making and consumption of illicit liquor found a home in another important area of the mid-century: the gold rush that followed the metal's discovery near Bathurst, New South Wales, in 1851. The majority of terms, which Bruce Moore has glossed in his book *Gold! Gold! Gold! A dictionary of the nineteenth-century Australian gold rushes* (2002), were miners' jargon, words that dealt with the process of extracting the precious metal from the earth. But some entered the larger vocabulary. One was *joe*, at first a cry to warn that the troopers were on their way to check for unlicensed excavations. The term came from Charles Joseph LaTrobe, Lieutenant-Governor of Victoria from 1851 to 1854, familiarly known as 'Charley Joe'. It was his regulations that bedevilled miners who found the licence fee, £18.00 per year payable in advance, too onerous. The meaning was soon extended to mean any officer of the law, and beyond that a general term of abuse. *Shicer*, borrowed from English slang, meant a worthless and/or worked-out mine. Most important, and longest-lasting, was *digger*, a simple description of those who mined: the gold-diggers. Digger would not achieve its mythical apotheosis until World War I, but as Bruce Moore notes, 'its appearance in that war owes much to the analogy drawn between the often deep holes that had to be dug arduously in the search for gold, and the trenches that the soldiers had to dig'.[19]

If English slang arrived in Australia unaltered, then British dialects also made the trip and in some cases added to the local slang vocabulary. Among the best known is *sheila*, Australian for a woman (first recorded in 1832), which is generally seen as a generic use of the Irish proper name. Other terms include *boomer* (something large of its kind), *shivoo* (a celebration), and *ringer* (one who excels at their occupation). As the century progressed, and with it more free settlers – many drawn by the gold rush – made their way to Australia, more dialect words came with them, especially from Scotland and the north of England. These include *chook* (a chicken), *skerrick* (a low-value coin), *shanghai* (a catapult), *stoush* (a fight), *wowser* (a puritan), *googie* (an egg), *knockabout* (a manual labourer), *skite* (to boast), *dag* (an eccentric; or a piece of matted hair around a sheep's tail). Three of the most 'Australian' of terms arrived quite late. *Cobber*, a close friend, has been tied to dialect but seems more likely to have been based on the synonymous Yiddish *chaver*; its first appearance in 1893 suggests a link to Jewish immigration, though that had been in progress much earlier. *Dinkum*, as in genuine or reliable, appears in Boldrewood's *Robbery Under Arms* (1883) (its extension *dinkum oil*, reliable information, is listed from 1915; *fair dinkum* is found as an exclamation from 1894 and an adjective from 1912), while *dunny*, first an outside lavatory and subsequently any such appliance, is not recorded until 1933. It abbreviates *dunnaken*, first recorded in England in 1790, which combined *danna* (dung) and *ken* (a house).

To round off a very random list was *larrikin*, variously a hooligan, a rascal, a villain, a Bohemian, and in general one who acts without regard for conventions. The word most likely comes from the Warwickshire / Worcestershire / Cornish dialect *larrikin*, a mischievous or frolicsome youth, and itself rooted in *larking*, as in playing around. It is recorded from the 1860s, and might be seen as one of the prototypes of many threatening 'youth cults' to come; certainly it underpinned one of the country's first moral panics, seeing the native-born youthful hooligans as the product of parental laxity, not to mention a throwback to their convict origins. Larrikins associated in a *push*, a term first recorded in England in 1672 as meaning a press of people or a crowd; its Australian use, as a criminal gang, appears in the 1880s, as does a parallel meaning of a non-criminal crowd or clique, among the most celebrated of which was the Sydney Push, or Sydney University Libertarian Society of the early 1960s; a *pushite* (1897) was a member of a gang or 'crowd'.

As a type he was seen as the negative side of the country's own sons, the boisterous, but unthreatening 'currency lad', infinitely preferable to effete 'sterling' settlers. His antecedents can be found in the *cabbage-tree mob* of the mid-century, named for the hats they wove from cabbage-tree leaves. His own origins have been attributed to the lowlife area of

Sydney known as The Rocks, which in *Life in Sydney's* Tom terms 'The St. Giles of Sydney, where you may see life as low as ever you did in St Giles in London'.[20]

Larrikins were unashamedly public: drunken, tobacco-spitting, noisy (with plenty of obscenities), fighting among themselves and jostling and heckling middle-class passers-by; careless of the authorities, they offered a threatening invasion of public spaces. And as a youth gang must, they sported a uniform. As explained by John Rickard, 'He wore distinctive high-heeled boots [known as 'Romeos'] and bell-bottomed trousers. The boots, finely cut and pointed, were handy, so to speak, for putting the boot in; it was also said that there was sometimes a mirror embedded in the toecap, so that, as James Murray archly puts it, "observation of the mysteries hidden under girls' skirts might be contrived". The high heels had the advantage, too, of adding height. The trousers, flared over the boots, were tight around thighs and bum. The shirt was usually white and collarless, worn sometimes with a vivid neckerchief; the jacket short and loose. The hat was black, round and firm [...] And in an age when beards or whiskers were the norm, the larrikin was defiantly clean-shaven. With this appearance went a certain manner, the swaggering walk, the 'leery' look.'[21] He was accompanied by his girl, the larrikiness, known as his *donah* or *clinah* (both borrowed from London costermonger use, as perhaps was the predilection for flared trousers, gaudy neckerchiefs and boots –listed by Henry Mayhew as basic to the Londoner's dress code[22]).

To what extent the larrkins originated their own slang is debatable, although they certainly used a good deal. W. T. Goodge's 'Great Australian Slanguage' has been seen as representative, and sample verses run:

> And his naming of the coinage
>   Is a mystery to some,
> With his 'quid' and 'half-a-caser'
>   And his 'deener' and his 'scrum'.
> And a 'tin-back' is a party
>   Who's remarkable for luck,
> And his food is called his 'tucker'
>   Or his 'panem' or his 'chuck'.

A policeman is a 'johnny'
    Or a 'copman' or a 'trap',
And a thing obtained on credit
    Is invariably 'strap'.
A conviction's known as 'trouble',
    And a gaol is called a 'jug',
And a sharper is a 'spieler'
    And a simpleton's a 'tug'.

If he hits a man in fighting
    That is what he calls a 'plug',
If he borrows money from you
    He will say he 'bit your lug.'
And to 'shake it' is to steal it,
    And to 'strike it' is to beg;
And a jest is 'poking borac',
    And a jester 'pulls your leg'.[23]

Of these terms *panem*, as *pannum*, can be found in Harman, meaning bread, while *jug*, as *stone jug*, is early seventeenth-century and *quid, deener* and *caser* are all London coinages as are *chuck, johnny, plug, strike* and *shake*. *Spieler* is international. *Poke borak* is homegrown, as are *bite your lug, copman, scrum*, and *tug* (in this sense).

Like the portrayal of the Cockney costermonger in the London music-hall, 'larrikin acts' developed on the popular stage of the 1890s and the performers sprinkled their sketches with appropriate terms. There were songs such as 'I've Chucked Up the Push for My Donah' (1893), and 'The Woolloomooloo Lair', now categorized as an Australian folksong, and which ran in part:

Oh my name it is McCarty & I'm a rorty party
I'm rough & tough as an old man kangaroo
Some people say I'm crazy, I don't work because I'm lazy
And I tag along in the boozing throng, the Push from
    Woolloomooloo.

This was most notably performed by a Londoner, E. J. Lonnen, in 1892; Lonnen dressed the part, and like a number of stage larrikins of the day performed in blackface.[24] Seemingly bizarre at a century's distance, larrikins saw themselves, and were often described – though less positively – as Australia's blacks: socially marginalized, stereotyped as pursuing 'black' i.e. criminal activities, and simultaneously feared and despised. The music-hall minstrel's blackface dandy, with his smart suits, rousing songs and his outlaw, macho posing, was not so far from the flashily adorned larrikins, 'with their well-oiled heads and their high-heeled boots, / Bell-bottomed pants and very loud suits!'[25]

Of the language used, *boozing* is English, and *rorty* is a London coster word, meaning either splendid or rowdy; *strike me blue* is primarily Australian, as are *push* in this context and *old man*. *Lair* is also Australian, but its origin, *lairy*, in the earlier sense of knowing, conceited, cheeky, can be found in *Oliver Twist* (1838). The Australian use tends more to an idea of ostentation and showiness.

The real-life larrikin was a constant subject of journalistic study, invariably portrayed as a barely restrained thug. His fictional evocation, however, emphasized the gentler side: 'larking' rather than 'larceny'. The work of Edward Dyson (*Fact'ry 'Ands*, 1906; *Benno and Some of the Push*, 1911; *Spats' Fact'ry*, 1922), Louis Stone (*Jonah*, 1911) and C. J. Dennis (whose *Songs of a Sentimental Bloke*, 1915, and *The Moods of Ginger Mick*, 1916, can sometimes suggest an influence of the more sentimental side of British music-hall) does not completely romanticize him – there can be violence, especially on behalf of a 'mate' or of a wronged female – but it ultimately emphasizes the positive. In this it echoes the contemporary treatment of East Enders by such humorous Cockney novelists as William Pett Ridge or Clarence Rook, rather than following the grim chronicles of Arthur Morrison. Even Dyson's 'Chiller Green', who arrives as a 'sinister youth' dressed in the larrikin garb of 'soft black felt hat [...] trousers very skimped in the waist, and high-heeled boots' and who has 'eyes full of truculence', is found a page later to be 'really a jaunty, companionable youth'. Even if, in a recent set-to he knocked a rival 'fair off his trolley' with 'er half Brunswick' and 'got four moon'.[26] And he ends up, in the story 'The Wooing of Minnie', thoroughly domesticated and pushing 'er peramberlater'.[27]

The atmosphere in the paper-bag 'fact'ry' is ultimately good-natured, if boisterous, and if any of the males does get above himself, then one of Spats's 'beauties' – the packers – will soon take him down a peg. Domesticity seems the fate of every fictional larrikin. Stone's duo Jonah and Chook transcend the push: one to become rich, the other to marry his larrikiness Pinkey. As for Dennis's 'Bloke', his titulary adjective gives him away. He may have done a stretch inside for 'stoushin' but what really matters is his donah Doreen. And in due course their child. The rabbit-oh Ginger Mick is similarly besotted, beating up 'a shickered toff' who 'slings Rosie goo-goo eyes', but if he greets the war by questioning Britain's need for imperial troops, then at the end of the poem cycle he dies 'a gallant gentleman', killed in action at Gallipoli and a symbol of many thousands of other working-class Anzacs.

All three authors wrote phonetically, Dyson perhaps the most emphatically so, though all attempt to reproduce the contemporary working-class accent. 'A' becomes 'er', 'you' 'yer' and 'of' 'iv'; 'h's' are invariably dropped, as are 'th's'. Syllables vanish. More pertinent is the high level of slang. Dennis appends a 485-word glossary to *The Sentimental Bloke*. Dyson's works produce almost as many terms, by no means all overlapping. If Stone is the least slangy, it is perhaps because he is the least prolific of the three.

The larrikin, of course, was a creature of the city. There was another side to Australia: the bush, and it boasted its own population and its own concerns. It found its voice in the poet Andrew 'Banjo' Paterson, in Henry Lawson, both poet and short-story writer, in 'Price Warung' (William Astley) with *Tales of the Old Days* and in 'Steele Rudd' (Arthur Hoey Davis), creator of *On Our Selection*, where his characters Dad and Dave, along with Mum and Mabel, became the country's best-known bushies and in time a radio favourite. Edward Dyson, better known for his urban fables, had also offered tales of the bush. All of whom, and many more, sometimes rejoicing in such nicknames as The Giaour, The Dipsomaniac, Scotty the Wrinkler and Rose de Bohème, were alumni of an astounding, unique magazine – The *Sydney Bulletin* – and of its outstanding editor J. F. Archibald (1856–1919), who may have been born as prosaic John Feltham, but adopted the more exotic Jules François.

It was to Archibald that another chronicler of bush life, Joseph Furphy, wrote his celebrated self-introduction in April 1897: 'I have just finished writing a full-sized novel; title, "Such Is Life"; scene, Riverina and northern Vic; temper, democratic; bias, offensively Australian.'[28] And 'offensively Australian' is a good way of summing up Archibald's creation.

An editorial of 2 July 1887 laid out the *Bulletin's* stall. Under the headline 'Australia for the Australians', it declared: 'By the term Australian we mean not those who have been merely born in Australia. All white men who come to these shores – with a clean record – and who leave behind them the memory of the class-distinctions and the religious differences of the old world [...] all men who leave the tyrant-ridden lands of Europe for freedom of speech and right of personal liberty are Australians before they set foot on the ship which brings them hither. Those who [...] leave their fatherland because they cannot swallow the worm-eaten lie of the divine right of kings to murder peasants, are Australian by instinct – Australian and Republican are synonymous.'

All white men. Archibald's paper, which he co-founded in 1880 and for which he worked until his health collapsed in 1902, was a paradoxical blend of beliefs: anti-hanging, nationalistically Australian, disdainful of British influence, in favour of socialism and egalitarianism and devoted to the Zola school of realism, yet unswervingly racist (especially as regarded the Chinese), anti-Semitic and casually misogynistic. In these latter opinions it echoes London's *Pink 'Un* – and both appeared on pink stock, and used the illustrator Phil May (London-based but temporarily in Australia for health reasons) – but the one was sporting and gossipy, and the latter political, however harum-scarum the politics, and, in its literary Red Page (launched in 1896), the cradle of many Australian writers. Known from 1890 as 'the Bushman's Bible', it did not so much echo bush concerns – though the work of Lawson, Paterson and the rest was imbued with bush life – but acted as the bushman's cultural gateway to the world, both local and international.

Henry Lawson (1867–1922) was just twenty (though Archibald's prefatory note claimed him as seventeen) when in 1887 he made his first contribution to the *Bulletin*. His career would collapse into alcoholism and poverty, but his works – the poetry collections *While the Billy Boils*,

Over the Slip-Rails, On the Wallaby Track, plus prose stories featuring recurring characters such as Joe Wilson, Jack Mitchell and the two swaggies Steelman and Smith – made him one of Australia's best-known writers. The books are filled with slang, though being slang and thus innately urban it is not especially bush-related. Unlike his fellow *Bulletin* poet and slangster Andrew 'Banjo' Paterson' (1864–1941), who preferred to romanticize the glories of the bush in such collections as *Clancy of the Overflow* and *The Man from Snowy River*, Lawson was deeply pessimistic. Lawson's 'Romance of the Swag' (1907) may have featured the tramping life, as did Paterson's 'Waltzing Matilda' (1895), but the two men took very different positions. Paterson pushed seasonal variety and resilient farmers; Lawson saw none of it: for him the bush was unforgiving, no place for human happiness and offering at best hard-grafted subsistence. It was a tough, cynical view, but accorded with the paper in which it appeared. The *Bulletin* may have been the bushman's bible, but its testaments remained creatures of the city and the writers not rural 'cow-cockies' but urban Bohemians.

The paper absorbed many influences, often those already filtered through its editor's own life as a jobbing journalist in both bush and city. Most of these were Australian, but Archibald's biographer has suggested 'that it would not be fanciful to observe also traces of that New York *Sun* which took such pleasure in words like "twaddle", "humbug" and "grovel"'.[29] The *Bulletin* printed thousands of slang terms over the years. Many of them had not yet been recorded. To look merely at a very small sub-set of the letter S (words *sa-* to *sh-*) one finds these 'first uses': *sail* (walk, travel), *sample* (caress), *sandbag* (dispose of), *Satan* and *Sheol* (euphemisms for hell), *sausage* (used affectionately to an animal), *scaler* (a cheat on public transport), *hot school* (a challenging environment), *scoop the pool*, *on the scoot* (on a spree), *score on* (inform against), *scotty* (tetchy), *scragged* (dead), *chuck a scrammy* (to pretend to have a withered arm so as to shirk work), *scrapings of the pot* (i.e. of the barrel), *scratch off* (to resign), *screw* (a station overseer or an unpleasant old woman), *screw* or *have a screw at* (to stare at in an aggressive manner), *scribe* (a journalist), *scroucher* (a general derogative), *go out to 'see a man'* (to urinate), *sell* (a swindler), *sell the pony* (to buy a round), *send along* (to berate), *send it down, Hughie!* (an appeal for rainfall), *have a set on* (to bear a grudge), *put a set on* (to bring to an end), *have someone set* (marked for punishment or revenge), *settled* (finished, 'done for'), *shanghai* (to trick, cheat), *sheepo* (a shearer), *sheila* (a woman), *shelf* (to inform against), *shell* (a corpse), *on the shicker* and *shickered* (drunk), *shift someone's ears* or *jaw* (to knock down), *shirt-tail* (a distant relation), *shook* (very excited), *shoot* (to hurry someone along), *shoot down in flames* (to humiliate or ridicule), *shoot for* (to aim at), *shoot in* (to imprison), *shop teeth* (dentures), *shoppie* (a shoplifter), *have a shot at* (to attempt), *show a point to* (to swindle or deceive), *show one's cards* (to reveal oneself), *shrewd-head* (a cunning person), *shutters* (the eyes), and *sign up* (to write a confession).

In addition there were the nonce-words, which came to be known as 'Bulletinisms'. From the same alphabetical spread one finds: *salvarmy*, *sandgrope* (pertaining to Western Australia), *scripture-tickler* (a preacher), *scupperer* (a killer), *second* (a girlfriend), *Set o' Sun* (a distant place), *shandygaff* (an uneasy compromise), *shanghai* (a ramshackle vehicle), *hang a shanty on* (give a black eye), *she-oak* (beer), *shearer* (bookie), *shell* (a coffin), *shicker saloon* (a pub), *shindykit* (a business consortium), *shiner* (attractive girl), *Shivery Isles* (New Zealand), *shoppying blue* (a confession) and *shriek* (something fashionable). Some of these may have entered general use, but they were coined by Archibald's men.

As it would be for every anglophone nation (and indeed all others who participated), the next great way-station for Australian slang creation after the efflorescence of the late nineteenth century was World War I. What a post-war author would term 'Digger Dialects' will be treated along with the language of Tommies and doughboys.

That burst of coinage, fuelled as it was by the need to create a national language (by no means all of it slang). would not be repeated. There is a steady procession of authors whose books offered slang usage, to varying extents, but one can do little more than mention them. They include Kylie Tennant, X. Herbert, K. S. Prichard, Lenny Lower, Norman Lindsay, Dal Stivens, Eric Lambert, T. A. G. Hungerford, Ion Idriess, Lawson Glassop, D'Arcy Niland, Frank Hardy, Dymphna Cusack, 'Miles Franklin' (Stella Franklin); playwrights David Williamson, Henrietta Drake-Brockman, Jack Hibberd, Alexander Buzo and more recent novelists Tim Winton, Kathy Lette, and for crime both fictional and confessional Shane Maloney, Robert G. Barrett and Mark 'Chopper' Read.

There has also been both slang lexicography and slang lexicology. The primary work was that of Sydney J. Baker, Australia's equivalent of and sometime collaborator with Eric Partridge (both were originally New Zealanders), whose *Australian Language* appeared in 1945 (revised editions 1966, 1978), and whose dictionaries of first New Zealand and then Australian slang were published in 1941. In his introduction to the former – which was not a dictionary as such but a disquisition heavily underpinned by lexical examples – he suggested that it was an 'offshoot'[30] of an on-going work aimed to cover all 'Australasian Colloquial Speech', but that never materialized. Further studies – *Australia Speaks* (1953) and *The Drum* (1959) – followed, increasing and refining the word lists and expanding Baker's commentary. His take on Australian speech has been described as a 'monument of Australian linguistic nationalism'[31] and is notable for the author's equation of national characteristics – the tough, no-nonsense Aussie bloke with a bit of larrikin in him – with at least the colloquial end of the national language. Of the dictionaries that followed the most scholarly have been works by G. A. Wilkes and Gary Simes, both of the University of Sydney. Wilkes's work, *A Dictionary of Australian Colloquialisms* (1978 et seq.), has now reached its fifth edition (2008). Almost all entries are accompanied by citations. That Wilkes chooses 'colloquialisms' rather than 'slang', even though many terms would otherwise be labelled as the latter, suggests that in his opinion there is no discernible, or perhaps no easily identifiable difference. Simes's *Australian Underworld Slang* (1993) draws on two important glossaries of Australian cant – one collected in 1944 by a young conscientious objector, Ted Hartley, who served time for his beliefs; the other in 1950 by a prisoner calling himself 'Thirty-five' and entitled *The Argot*. As well as laying out the full text of both glossaries (*The Argot* was in the process of revision and altered entries are noted), Simes has subjected them to a degree of 'historical principles' lexicography, offering wherever possible a number of additional citations for the core terms.

One cannot assess the slang contributions of every Australian writer, but it is worth pausing for two names. Both have leant heavily on slang and/or colloquialism, Broad Australian as it was known, and both have disguised themselves under a pseudonym. The first, John O'Grady, brother of the 'straight' novelist Frank, broke every Australian publishing record for both sales and his own celebrity when in 1957 he published *They're a Weird Mob*, written under the name of 'Nino Culotta', a pseudonym he later 'translated' as 'big backside'. The second is Barry Humphries, known worldwide for his rendition of Edna, now Dame Edna Everage, the muse of Moonee Ponds, of the foul-mouthed Australian Cultural Attaché and boss of the nation's 'yartz', Sir Les Paterson, and, between 1963 and 1974, of the ex-pat Aussie Barry McKenzie, as portrayed with the illustrator Nicholas Garland in a comic strip in London's satirical magazine *Private Eye* and later elevated to the big screen.

'Nino Culotta' was supposedly an Italian journalist, sent to Australia to report on the local culture, with the intent of informing his fellow Italians, many of whom were thinking of emigrating in the aftermath of World War II. To get the story 'Nino' takes a job as a brickie's labourer, and the fulcrum of the plot is his attempt to understand working-class Australian speech. The novel had begun, so it was claimed, as a result of a £10 bet between the two O'Grady brothers. It was John's first novel, but not his first publication: he had placed both prose and verse in, unsurprisingly, the *Bulletin* among other vehicles. However, he was currently working as a New Zealand government pharmacist in Samoa. The initial print run was 6,000 hardbacks. After six months there had been reprints and sales stood at 74,000, rising to 150,000 in the first year. It topped the bestseller lists for two years. When O'Grady died, in 1981, the book had notched up forty-seven impressions and sales were pushing one million. It was an unprecedented success: the readers moved beyond the predictable book-loving demographic and out among the people of whom 'Nino' was writing: the suburb-dwelling Australian male. There was a follow-up, *Cop This Lot* (1960), which sold 150,000 copies; further sequels followed, although O'Grady bucked against their writing: *Gone Fishin'* (1962) with *Gone Troppo* (1968) and *Gone Gougin'* (1978). Over the next twenty years O'Grady published eighteen more books, including studies of *Aussie English* (1965) and *Aussie Etiket* (1971). *Weird Mob* became a movie in 1966, and while O'Grady vetoed plans for a musical a single was released. The author wrote a play script and in 1967 visited Australian troops in Vietnam with a 'Weird Mob Show'.

As regards its slang – praised as 'the best collection of Australian colloquialism one has seen' in the *Bulletin*, but decried as 'phoney' in the literary journal *Meanjin*[32] – 'Nino' was not creative – most of his usage is well-established – but he undoubtedly knew the core terminology, the vernacular nuts and bolts of Aussie popular speech, and the books remain a valuable source for the lexicographer.

'Barry McKenzie, Australian at Large' made his debut in the 10 July 1964 issue of London's satirical fortnightly *Private Eye*. His first words, 'Excuse I, what's gone flaming wrong?', informed readers that they were in the presence of an Australian Candide, the classic hick, come to the big city and ready to surf on a tide of Fosters Lager into what within a year would be apostrophized (in the *Observer*) as 'Swinging London'. Identified in this first strip as 'a strapping young specimen of Australian manhood' and self-described as 'an ordinary honest working-class bloke', McKenzie has many roots, not least among the larrikins of a century earlier. The *ocker*, another larrikin descendant, would not appear until 1968 (named for a yobbish character portrayed by actor Ron Frazer in the mid-Sixties TV series *The Mavis Bramston Show*), but Humphries's naïve and noisy ex-pat is the type *avant la lettre*. McKenzie would spend the next nine years enmeshed in London's wonder and weirdness, going out from his base in Earls Court (otherwise known at the time as 'Kangaroo Valley' in honour of its Antipodean population) to act as the vehicle of his creator's satire of both Australians and Londoners. Played by Barry Crocker, he would feature in two movies: *The Adventures of Barry McKenzie* (1972) and *Barry Mckenzie Holds his Own* (1974). Between the strip and the films McKenzie became, for many, an archetype of the young Australian, though his compatriots back home were less than amused.

As laid out by Paul St Pierre in his study of Humphries's life and work, 'In the first Private Eye strip Barry McKenzie, on arriving in England mistakes Southampton for Dover, has a confrontation with a class snob, is "fleeced" at customs, has his transistor radio nicked on the train, is over-charged by a taxi-driver, is clipped for a dingy hotel room, and is "poisoned" by [...] tepid English beer.'[33] In time he turns the tables, becoming a trickster whose cunning tests out the tropes of English life, but the figure who first adorned the *Eye* was rube all the way.

But for all his naiveté, in one respect at least Bazza, as he became known, was entirely citified from day one: his slang-laden language burst into the *Private Eye* reader's consciousness fully-formed and quite astounding. It would take a few years to come fully up to steam, but by 1968 Bazza was offering, among much else, *freckle puncher* for homosexual, *smell like an Abo's armpit, bang like a shithouse door, dry as a nun's nasty, shake hands with the wife's best friend, siphon the python* and perhaps the most celebrated; the *Technicolor yawn* (also known as the *liquid laugh* or the *big spit*). With its concentration on defecation and urination, drinking and the seemingly inevitable vomiting it induced, and copulation (even if Bazza remains the eternal virgin), Humphries either created or collated a vocabulary that would not be rivalled until successive editions of *Viz* magazine's 'swearing dictionary' *Roger's Profanisaurus* began appearing in 1997.

Barry McKenzie was canned by *Private Eye* in 1973. In 1975 Humphries introduced a new character: Dr Sir Lesley Colin Patterson, better known as Les Patterson, supposedly Australia's Cultural Attaché for the Arts. Sir Les 'exists' primarily on stage, often serving as an MC for Humphries superstar Dame Edna Everage, although books (notably *The Traveller's Tool*, 1978) and records (e.g. *12 Inches of Les*, 1985) would appear. Like Bazza, but devoid of the slightest innocence, this culture-free, burping, farting, nose-picking monster, suit invariably stained with nameless detritus, mouth crammed with comedy teeth and foul with double-entendres, promoted a vocabulary dedicated to sex (unlike Bazza he boasts of many sexual triumphs, notably with his seemingly pliant 'Girl Friday'), drinking and wide-spectrum excess.

The question for fans of both characters was to what extent the language given McKenzie and Patterson represents established Australianisms and to what extent the products of Humphries's mind. *Chunder*, for instance, another synonym for vomiting and undoubtedly introduced into British consciousness via the strip, had been around since at least 1950; *Edgar Britt*, rhyming on *shit*, since 1960, and if Humphries coined *one-eyed trouser snake* for the penis, then he drew on imagery (*trouser serpent, one eyed rattlesnake*) that can be traced to the mid-nineteenth century.

The blend of novelty and elaboration holds good for many of Humphries coinages. Among them are *aim Archie at the Armitage* (to urinate), *dark as an abo's arsehole, blow the beef bugle, bent as a two-bob watch, hawk one's brown* (to work as a male prostitute), *bugle duster* (handkerchief), *drop a bundle* (to defecate), *call or call Charles* (to vomit), *chocolate cha-cha* (anal sex), *chemise-lifter* (homosexual), *doover* (penis), *feature with* (to have sex), *giggle factory* (a psychiatric institution), *haricot* (bean = queen, a male homosexual), *go where the big knobs hang out* (to urinate), *flog the lizard* (urinate), *mattress muncher* (a homosexual), *nunga-muncher* (a fellatrix), *nut-chokers* (male underwear), *performer on the pink oboe* (a male homosexual), *snake's piss* (beer), *couldn't go three rounds with a revolving door* (stupid), *throw one's voice* (to vomit), *throttling pit* (the lavatory), *thunderbags* (male underpants), *water the horses* (to urinate) and *yellow velvet* (an Asian woman in context of sex).

These, on the whole, remain Humphries's linguistic property, although one can see that in many cases he is recreating well-worn themes and images. Few appear to have been used outside his work. At the same time he can take credit for the first recorded use of a number of other terms. They include *bang like a shithouse door (in a gale), tummy banana* (the penis), *beef bayonet, bung it on* (overcharge), *chockers with* (full of), *may your chooks turn into emus and kick your shithouse down, chuck* (to vomit, an act of vomiting), *daks* (trousers), *choke a darkie* (defecate), *date puncher, dine at the Y* (to perform cunnilingus), *get the dirty water off one's chest* (to have sex), *cop a dose* (get VD), *fair suck of the (sauce stick/ pineapple), fair crack of the whip, crack a fat* (achieve erection), *full two bob, full as three race trains / a fairy's phone book / a seaside shithouse on Boxing Day, furburger* and *furry hoop* (vagina), *have the flags out* or *the painters in* (to be menstruating), *funbags* (breasts), *go off like a two-bob watch* (of a woman, highly sexed), *go the grope, Honkers* (Hong Kong), *hornbag* (attractive woman), *hurl* (to vomit), *make love to the lav, lonely as a bastard on Father's Day, mutton dagger* (penis), *gnaw the nana* (fellate), *off like a bride's nightie* (fast), *open one's lunchbox* (to break wind), *Mrs Hand / Mrs Palm and her five daughters* (the hand, as used for masturbation), *point Percy at the porcelain, perve* (voyeur), *pillow-biter* (homosexual), *red sails in the sunset* (menstruation), *ripper* (excellent), *rod-walloper* (masturbator), *shake hands with the unemployed* (urinate), *shake hands with the wife's best friend* (urinate / masturbate), *siphon the python* (urinate), *snake's hiss* (beer), *snake's house* (lavatory), *skid marks* (faecal stains on one's underwear), *splash one's boots* (urinate), *big white telephone* (lavatory), *top bollocks* (breasts), *towelhead* (Arab), *crack a tube* (open a beer), *ugly as a hatful of arseholes*, *weak as piss*, *wellington boot* (= root, sex), *William (the third)* (=turd), and *yodel* (to vomit).

Australia remains a major creator of slang, the country's linguistic inventiveness as fecund as ever. To what extent that slang has spread is less certain. The fascination of British readers who encountered Barry McKenzie did not mean that his entire vocabulary entered the Old Dart's slang lexis, though such as *technicolor yawn* and *pointing Percy at the porcelain* proved irresistible. The 1980s arrival on UK television of such Australian soap operas as *Neighbours* and *Home and Away* brought a few terms, though the major influence, it is believed, was in the adoption by the British young of an upwards, semi-interrogative tone at the end of sentences, seen as typical of Australian speech. Some was held up, as it were, for inspection, marvelled at and then discarded. Rhyming slang was thought by some Americans around 1940 to be an Australian creation, but while Australia undoubtedly creates a good deal, it tends to be reserved for domestic consumption. What matters is not export but the abiding flair for the vivid. Like every other form of anglophone slang the Australian version remains tied to the inevitable themes, but nowhere plays such inventive variations upon them.

9 Sex in the City: The Agreeable Ruts of Life

> A young lady was out riding, accompanied by her groom. She
> fell off her horse and in so doing displayed some of her charms;
> but jumped up very quickly and said to the groom: 'Did you
> see my agility, John?' 'Yes, miss,' said he, 'but I never heard it
> called by that name before!' – Another version has it: 'Yes, miss;
> but we calls it cunt in the kitchen!'
>
> 'An English Popular Story', in *Kruptadia* (1888)[1]

Sex runs through slang like blue through Roquefort. It has been a driving
force for as long as the vocabulary has been collected. The first such
glossary, extracted from Copland's *Hye Waye* of *c.* 1535, offers *apple-squire*
(a pimp), *dock* (to have sexual intercourse), and *callet*, *drab* and *dell* (all
whores), while his lesser-known *Complaynte of Them that ben To Late
Maryed* (1505) has *instrument* (the penis), and *stand* (to have an erection).
There would be much more to come. If one looks at even the most
broad-brush of taxonomies, one finds perhaps 7,000 terms referring to
intercourse, to the genitals and what is done with them, to prostitution
and to venereal disease. If one adds women, who are almost always seen
in a sexual context, one is moving towards 10,000 terms, not far below
10% of the entire slang lexis.

Slang, being a language of synonyms and of themes, repeats itself.
The penis has taken on 1,200 aliases in 500 years. The *jockum* becomes
the *instrument* becomes the *pistol* becomes the *beef bayonet* becomes the
purple-headed custard chucker. The imagery draws on Greek (*pego*, literally

a fountain) Latin (*member*, from *membrum virile*), French (*bracmard*, a short sword) and Yiddish (*schlong*, a snake), food (*tummy banana*), proper names (*John Thomas*), on the nursery (*winky*), on hunting (*crack-hunter*), on an armoury of guns (*bazooka*) and clubs (*pestle*), sticks (*gutstick*) and knives (*dard*) and naturally offers a role to euphemisms (*What Harry gave Doll*) and rhymes (*Hampton Wick*). Other images include those drawn from physics (*pendulum*), tools (*derrick*), mechanics (*machine*), animals (*ferret*), music (*skin flute*), botany (*sensitive plant*), invertebrates (*worm*), and human anatomy (*middle leg*). In a rare excursion into mutual pleasure it has been a *lady's delight* and even, uncharacteristically substituting procreation for pleasure, a *baby-maker*. Some terms survive, seemingly the oldest: *cock*, *prick* and *tool* were all available to standard English speakers of the early era and while their register has been downgraded to slang, they remain common. Citations prove them still the port of first call. The more florid variations have their moment and disappear into the dictionaries.

Slang's vagina monologue is equally fecund. There are nearly as many terms as there are for penis. (There are even more for sexual intercourse but while there are phrases using *play* and *dance* there is a single overriding image: man hits woman.) *Cunt* is the great survivor, a survival that is more impressive in that unlike its penile equivalents, the word, while seemingly unexceptional in Middle English, was not transmuted, other than surreptitiously, into the Early Modern or beyond. It is not dignified as for instance are *cock* and *prick* by Shakespeare, although he dances near its edge with Hamlet's 'country matters' and with other puns.

It is nameless (the *monosyllable*), rendered literary (*agreeable ruts of life*), or euphemistic (*down there*), sniggering (*where Uncle's doodle goes*), amatory (*Cupid's arbour*), and metaphysical (*Alpha and Omega*). It has names (*Mother of All Saints*), it is a place for the penis (*pole hole*), it is laboriously punning (*Eve's custom-house*, where 'Adam made the first entry'), it is a repository for semen (*honey-pot*). It is a labourer (*buttonhole worker*), something that one can 'ride' (*town bike*), and on which one may 'play' (*lute*). It is a road (*covered way*) and an entrance (*front door*). It is lucrative (*money-maker*), even if a *Tipperary fortune* is apostrophized by Grose as 'two *town lands* [the breasts], *stream's town* [the pudend] and *ballinocack* [the anus]'). It is a place both specific (*Leather Lane*) and generic (*garden*). The synonymy seems inexhaustible: nature in general (*nature's tufted treasure*) or specific (*gooseberry bush*); water (the *peculiar river*) wherein are many fish (*ling, whelk, trout*); food gives *yum-yum, meat* and *dripping pan*. There are vegetables (*cabbage*) and fruit (*split apricot*). Then the animals, both the *beaver* and the *pussy*.

Above all slang is man-made in the most literal sense and man for all his boasts is frightened. Many vagina images are fearful, suspicious. It is voracious (*snatch*), it is a trap (*fly-catcher*), a carnivore (*snapping-turtle*), it hurts (*rough-and-tumble*), it brings inevitable disease (*claptrap*). It is a hole (*hole of holes*), a sewer (*drain*), a chasm (*pit*) and a slit (*gash*).

One may deplore the stereotyping but it is harder to fault slang's imagination.

The question, however, is not whether or what, but why. Why slang has taken it upon itself to create quite so many variations on the theme. The answer would seem to be, as it is in other multi-synonymic areas such as crime and drugs, the need for secrecy. Or in this case the acknowledgement of what, at least directly, cannot be said (particularly in public) or written for publication. In this such terms differ from those for another vastly synonymized group, the many words for drink, where one wonders if the mass of terms (several thousand, especially as regards drunkenness) suggest that one simply can't have too much of a good thing. Rather than talking behind its hand, slang is shouting about intoxication, celebrating alcohol in all its contradictory moods.

We remain confused by sex and its language. In 1965, appearing on the late night television talk show *BBC3*, the theatre critic Kenneth Tynan suggested that 'I doubt if there are any rational people to whom the word "fuck" would be particularly diabolical, revolting or totally forbidden.' The outraged response proved him wrong. Fifty years later his belief has yet to be wholly sustained. The taboo on 'fuck' and its peers has undoubtedly weakened in the face of a more sexualized culture, but it still can and does provoke. Britain's tabloid media – whether print or digital – to which such sexualizing is often ascribed, still quail from spelling out the 'dirty words', although the former broadsheets appear to consider their supposedly more intelligent audience better capable of encountering such words. America, where religion remains a repressive force, is uniformly prudish, paradoxically so considering the country's thriving pornography industry. In Anglophone countries at least, the use of such a term by a public figure triggers a kneejerk burst of moral condemnation.

Public attitudinizing should not be confused with private practice. In 1965 Leslie Fiedler described 'fuck' as 'the single four-letter word no family newspaper would reprint, though no member of a family who could read was likely not to know it',[2] and if he was correct then, then all the more so now. The press, though still not in America, may have become less fearful, but the reality is that 'fuck', once worthy of court cases, can be found emblazoned on T-shirts.

The 'canonical' obscenities are easy to find. *Fuck* as a verb is first recorded in 1508 (in Dunbar's 'In Secreit Place this Hyndir Nycht') and as a noun in 1654 (in the news-sheet *Mercurious Fumigosus*); it maintains an unbroken record ever since. *Cunt*, for all that it had been tabooed since the mid-fifteenth century, is recorded in 1540 (in Lyndsay's *Satyre of Thrie Estaits*); *prick* in 1556; *cock* in 1450; *arse*, which had been regularly recorded from the late fourteenth century, appeared in a sexual sense in 1512 (it appears far earlier in Abbot Aelfric's glossary of 1000, translating the Latin *nates*); *ballocks/bollocks* has been found since the 1380s (and is also in Aelfric, translating *testiculi* and spelt *beallucas*). There is no sense, reading the citations, that these were as yet segregated from 'proper' language. These were terms for the body and its functions (one finds similarly early uses of the best-known terms for defecation and urination) and one used them unabashed. They seem, even, to predate most of the 'official' terms: one finds *testicles* in 1425 and *copulation* in 1483, but *penis* is not recorded until 1578, *vagina* in 1682, *sexual intercourse* in 1753.

Vernacular use did not preclude the growth of synonyms. Between 1500 and 1600 noun equivalents to 'fuck' were *bob, clipping, dance, falling sickness, hornpipe, leather, pleasure, running at the ring, roust, sport, stroke, tillage, trade,* and *trick*. For the verb there were: *bed, bob, caterwaul, clip, dance, do the deed of darkness, do it, flesh it, foin, foutre, frig, frisk, ginicomtwig, have, jape, juggle, jumble, leap, labour leather, lie on, niggle, nock, occupy, play at* ... in various compounds such as *play at Adam and Eve, at all fours, at belly-to-belly, at blindman's buff, at couch quail, at couple your navels* and several more; the list continues with *plough, rifle, seal, sport, swive, thrum, thump, tick-tack, till, towze, tread, tumble, twang, vault* and *wap*. The terms drew on standard English, on puns, on euphemism, on nature and animals, and on foreign languages. In most cases the woman is passive, even invisible; the idea of physical domination by the male is a constant. These would remain among the primary images. And the same period produces nearly fifty terms for the vagina and around forty for the penis.

Unspecified copulations and the genitals required to perform them, whether encountered in conjugal situations or otherwise, presented only one part of the whole. The commercial variety of sex, for which the lexis would in time amount to many hundred terms, was also establishing itself within the language. By 1600 the prostitute could be a *white apron, hackney* (who like the homonymous horse was both 'hired' and 'ridden'), *picked-hatch vestal, scab, smock servant, smock vermin* and *striker* (who could also be her pimp). The key word was *suburb*, plus its adjective *suburban*. Literally 'beneath the city', such early suburbs – Holborn, Wapping, Mile End, Bermondsey, Clerkenwell– may have become parts of central London but, in the sixteenth and seventeenth centuries, they were beyond the City and its walls, and, as such, were home to various 'stink' industries – tanning, leper hospitals, playhouses and brothels. And most notoriously the last. Thus a whore could be an *aunt of the suburbs*, a *suburb wench*, a *suburban strumpet*, a *sixpenny suburb-sinnet* and a *suburb lady*, while the world of prostitution was the *suburban trade*. Her consort, the pimp, was variously an *apple squire, apron squire, bellswagger, captain, hackney, smell-smock, smock merchant* (or *agent, attorney, tearer* and *tenant*), a *smocker, smockster, smock pensioner* (*smock* in all cases metonymizing the woman who wore it), *striker*, and *suburban roarer* (who could also be a whore).

These terms are all attested in one form of contemporary print medium or another. And with the exception of *cunt*, which as noted would not be retained in standard use after 1450, the supposed 'dirty words' had not been fully prescribed by 1700. Nonetheless there was a growing circumscription, and if in doubt, what might wish to qualify as literature opted for some form of euphemism when it came to matters sexual, if not yet defecatory. Judiciously or otherwise, slang dictionaries have chosen to offer a home to these linguistic hybrids. These are literary creations by canonical authors: they are not be confused with puns nor double-entendres: there is no humour, no nudging nor winking involved, even if such as John Cleland were undoubtedly aiming, like any other pornographer, to achieve that for which 'dirty books' and the 'dirty' words within them are created; the application of male hand to male member and, to offer some pertinent euphemisms, to undertake the *hand-gallop* and ensuing *sailor's joy* that follows.

Take Farmer and Henley's *Slang and Its Analogues*, a seven-volume slang dictionary that appeared between 1890 and 1904 (with a 1909 revision for the letters A and B). The six columns of synonyms for *greens*, sexual intercourse, feature a number of established literary stars. Among them we find Robert Burns (*do a lassie's by-job, a mow,* or *a random push, play at houghmagandie, lift a leg on*), John Marston (*go bed-pressing, vaulting* or *bitching*), Shakespeare (*do a bit of business, make the beast of two backs, take a turn in the lists of love*), Alexander Pope (to *wag one's tail*), and Thomas D'Urfey (*join faces, get what Harry gave Doll*).

Slang is not merely a receptacle of obscenities, for all that its critics might wish to dismiss it as such, but when dealing with euphemisms, the rendering the rough smooth and the bitter sweet, one must accept that the original word must be of such a type that writers had come to recoil from its use within what was known as 'polite company'. Hence the euphemism, and the slang dictionary benefits from a number of such polite necessities. Euphemism was the only way that many writers were able to render sex palatable, or more important, publishable for commercial gain. Of the many users, a couple, one from the seventeenth and one from the eighteenth century, can serve as exemplars.

The first great literary creator of such terms was the word-obsessed courtier and author Sir Thomas Urquhart of Cromarty (1611–60), a 'logofascinated spirit' as he described himself, who took upon himself in 1653 the publication of 'The Works of Master Francois Rabelais doctor in physick ... now faithfully translated into English'. Rabelais (*c.* 1494–1553) was French and had written in a contemporary version of that language the work known as *Gargantua and Pantagruel*, the first books of which appeared in 1534 authored by one 'Alcofribas Nasier' – an anagram of the author's name. The literary merits of his work (among other things one of the more censored productions of the last half millennium) are irrelevant here. What matters is the language he used, or more properly the language into which Urquhart, a devotee of 'metonymical, ironical, metaphysical and synecdochical instruments of elocution' – or 'meaningful words', as the less loquacious might put it – rendered it in his translation.

A good example is this list, all items of which refer to what Urquhart initially terms the 'you know what', a piece of careless vaguery applicable to many aspects of sex, and in this case the giant Gargantua's penis, which is being dandled by an enthusiastic gaggle of court ladies. So gross a member doubtless merited so extensive a list: 'One of them would call it her *pillicock*, her *fiddle-diddle*, her *staff of love*, her *tickle-gizzard*, her *gentle-titler*. Another, her *sugar-plum*, her *kingo*, her *old Rowley*, her *touch-trap*, her *flap dowdle*. Another again, her *brand of coral*, her *placket-racket*, her *Cyprian sceptre*, her *tit-bit*, her *bob-lady*. And some of the other women would give these names, my *Roger*, my *cockatoo*, my *nimble-wimble*, *bush-beater*, *claw-buttock*, *evesdropper*, *pick-lock*, *pioneer*, *bully-ruffin*, *smell-smock*, *trouble-gusset*, my lusty *live sausage*, my *crimson chitterlin*, *rump-splitter*, *shove-devil*, *down right to it*, *stiff and stout*, *in and to*, *at her again*, my *coney-borrow-ferret*, *wily-beguiley*, my *pretty rogue*.'[3]

When Urquhart wrote, aside from its medico-Latin self, the primary synonym for penis was *yard*. Its roots lie in a number of terms, typically the Old Teutonic *gazdjo*, all of which mean a thin pole; which may possibly be linked to the Latin *hasta*, a spear, and even to the Italian *cazzo*, also slang for penis. (Certainly the seventeenth-century *gadso* and *catso* are borrowings from the Italian original and like a number of similar terms mean both penis and rogue or villain.) The first dictionary use comes in John Florio's *New World of Words* of 1598: '*Priapismo*, [...] pertaining to a mans priuities, or the standing of a mans yard)', but it can be found much earlier, e.g. in Wyclif's 1682 translation of the Bible (where, in Genesis, it is found in the story of the first circumcision). Though Urquhart does not disdain *yard*, he had Rabelais' vast linguistic inventiveness to deal with. He proved an able pupil.

Looking at his choice of images, one sees many that would recur in slang's treatment of the penis: the colour of pink flesh (*brand of coral*, *crimson chitterlin*), the idea of consumption whether by vagina or mouth

(the *crimson chitterlin* again, *the sugar-plum*, *live sausage* or *tit-bit*), the idea
of the penis as attacking the woman (*fiddle-diddle*, *tickle-gizzard*, *touch-
trap*, *bush-beater*, *claw-buttock*, *rump-splitter*) or simply interfering with her
garments (*placket-racket*, *smell-smock*, *trouble-gusset*); it can come from
hell (*old rowley*, *bully-ruffin*, *shove-devil*); it can show its shape (*Cyprian
sceptre*, *staff of love*, *stiff and stout*), it can be cunning (*picklock*, *pioneer*,
coney-borrow-ferret, *wily-beguiley*, *my pretty rogue*) and simply metonymize
the rampant male (*down right to it*, *in and to*, *at her again*). And of course
none, none at all actually use the word in question.

On the level of pure imagery Urquhart's coinages are not especially
exceptional. But as noted they represent themes that would embed
themselves (and in some cases were already embedded) in slang. But
the subject of his list – the penis, no more, no less, and taken to such
variegated lengths – certainly was still unique. No slang dictionary –
or more properly glossary, since no dictionary of slang proper would
appear for another forty-five years – had yet approached sex so freely.
The sixteenth-century whores and villains whose careers had been
itemized in Awdeley or Harman obviously had sex, but as regards the
bits and bobs, the human giblets required to get the job done, then the
canting crew, at least in print, were often as puritan as the establishment
they defied. That Urquhart was one of that establishment, a member
of the Scottish landed gentry and intimate of King Charles I, merely
underlines an irony. And the belief that one had to cross the Channel
if one wanted to get that 'dirty' stuff uncensored was a truism (if not a
truth) that appealed to seventeenth-century Britons as effectively as its
always has to their successors.

That is not to say that the early canting glossaries completely by-
passed sex. Harman, in 1666, tells of 'a proud Patrico' [priest] who 'tooke
his jockam [penis] in his famble [hand], and a wapping [fucking] he
went'. He also offers '*to nygle* to have to do with a woman carnally'. An
early seventeenth-century 'canting song' attributed to Thomas Dekker
has 'And wapping Dell [a whore, lit. fucking girl], that niggles well, and
takes loure [cash] for her hire', while B. E.'s dictionary of *c.* 1698 picks
up that same *dell*, citing the dictum: '*If she won't wap for a Winne, let her
trine for a Make*, If she won't Lie with a Man for a Penny, let her Hang
for a Half-penny.' But the very insularity and deliberate obfuscation of

the language involved might well have failed to conjure up the requisite images for those who lacked the insider knowledge. And while *niggle* crops up in a US dictionary of underworld slang in 1931, there are no contemporary cites for any of these terms outside the criminal milieu – and those either in glossaries or in contrived dramatic scenes, e. g. in Beaumont and Fletcher's *Beggar's Bush* (1622) or Middleton's *Roaring Girl* (1611) that were obviously created after reading them. Thus Urquhart had, one might suggest, to start at the beginning.

After Urquhart, John Cleland. Reading his *Memoirs of a Woman of Pleasure* (generally known as *Fanny Hill*), it is hard for what are perhaps the coarser sensibilities of modern life to see quite how anyone derived sexual thrills from his elaborate phraseology and protracted but strangely 'hands-off' copulations. Or if not coarser, then certainly far, far more exposed to what lies at the heart of Cleland's efforts: pornography.

Urquhart's lists are a delight, but they are lists, albeit those dictated by Rabelais, and inevitably appear at times like excerpts from a thesaurus. Cleland had no such restraints: his prose is all his own and the narrative far more 'modern'. Other, of course, than for his stated aim: to write about a whore without using the language that was seen as part of her stock in trade. What he does is to use the usual slang themes, with the concomitant accent on male sexual aggression. Thus the penis ('an object of terror and delight'[4]) is variously an *axe*, a *battering ram* (with, like all the erections we encounter, a scarlet 'head', be it 'ruby', 'vermilion', 'flaming red' or whatever), a *red-headed champion*, a 'delicious' *stretcher*, a 'stiff, staring' *truncheon*, and a 'terrible' *weapon*. It can also be an *engine* (invariably 'wonderful', 'thick', or 'enormous'), a *machine* (whether 'unwieldy' or 'formidable'), an *instrument*, a *picklock* (the labia being 'soft-oil'd wards' which it opens) and a *wedge* with which one *nails* one's partner. And if the penis is a *conduit-pipe* (and elsewhere a *pipe*), then the vagina is the *pleasure conduit*. It can be a *staff of love*, a *sensitive plant* (a contradictory image, since the botanical version shrinks rather than grows when touched), a *wand*, a *white staff*, and, less obviously a *fescue* (an old term that plays on its standard meaning: 'a small stick, pin, etc. used for pointing out the letters to children learning to read; a pointer') which thus is one of the wide selection of penis as pointed instrument images. *Morsel* is also on offer, but doubtless Fanny is only being figurative (in one thing Cleland is faithful to the porn tradition: no one ever has a small penis), and the morsel is being 'engorged' by her *delicate glutton* or *nether mouth*.

Fanny, being a professional, is obliged to be 'up for it' but she differs from most of her peers, at least as recorded, in enjoying the sex and having orgasms. But as slang (and pornography), even euphemized, makes sure, the over-riding image is of the submissive female, even slightly reluctant; her honour or at least her vagina always requiring a degree of force. Thus the vagina is the *ready made breach for love's assaults*, the *furrow*, which 'he ploughs up', the *saddle* ('He was too firm fix'd in the saddle for me to compass flinging him'⁵). Its physical nature and bodily position are emphasized: the *central furrow*, the *centre of attraction*, the 'soft, narrow *chink*', the 'tender *cleft* of flesh', or the '*cloven* stamp of female distinction' with its hint, conscious or otherwise, at the Devil's cloven hoof. It is also a hostess for sexual enjoyment: *mount pleasant* (and Cleland used the plural form to mean the breasts), the *seat of pleasure*, the *pleasure girth* and *pleasure pivot*. It is a *jewel* (though *lady's jewels*, like the later *family* ones, are the testicles), the *maiden-toy*, the *main spot* or *main avenue* and the *mouth of nature* (and as noted above, the *delicate glutton* and *nether mouth*). It is also, and here one cannot avoid Cleland's consciously punning name for his heroine, which might be 'translated' as 'Mount of Venus', the *fanny*. All of which imply pleasure and enthusiasm. Only in the use of *pit*, *slit* and *slash* does he present another slang trope: the vagina as *wound* (and Fanny calls it that too) and threatening, unfathomable hole. The testicles are the tried and tested *balls*, not to mention the *treasure bag of nature's sweets*. The pubic hair is *moss* or a *thicket*. To be naked is to be in one's *birthday suit*: Rochester had offered *birthday coat*, but Cleland seems to have coined this longer-lasting version.

Whether one dismisses Cleland's language as over-wrought and at best material for latter-day parody or, like the new *DNB*, praises 'a stylistic *tour de force*, employing a dazzling variety of metaphors for parts of the body and for sexual acts, with a series of sly comic puns animating the delicately periphrastic prose', its euphemistic role remains undeniable. If anything, and reading ahead, his style seems to set the pattern for the writers of at least some nineteenth-century pornography, typically 'Walter', the name popularly attributed to the anonymous author of the multi-volumed *My Secret Life* (1888–94). He too offers examples of *machine, gristle, thatch* and *thicket*, as well as such terms as *sugar-stick, generation tool, persuader* and *rammer*, which would not have been out of place in his predecessor's work. But there are a vast range of obscenities too: 'Walter' is no euphemizer, and certainly not literary.

We need not wait for the 1890s to abandon euphemism. Whether what follows can be termed dysphemisms, and thus euphemism's antonym, there is not the slightest effort at disguise. From title to last line, nothing is spared. Writing as an aristocratic insider the author gives us what he suggests is the true picture of upper-class, supposedly privileged sex whether among politicians (the 'Council') or at Court ('Whitehall'), from promiscuity in the city, to venereal disease in the country. But this is very far from the sniggering insinuations of today's celebrity mags, who may place the stars (at least the female variety) on pedestals the better to look, and indeed snap pictures up their skirts, but never forget that the pedestal is there. John Wilmot, the Earl of Rochester, who penned these lines, was seemingly more interested in digging a grave for society than raising it on high. And he used the most 'aggressive' terms to do so. Rochester brandishes his obscenities like offensive weapons, rendering himself excessive even in an age, so recently emerged from the Commonwealth's grim Puritanism, that was hardly restrained. His 'Advice to a Cuntmonger' begins:

> Fucksters you that would bee happy
> Have a care of *Cunts* that Clapp yee,
> Scape disease of evill Tarshole,
> Gout and Fistula in Arsehole,
> Swolne Codds, colon descending,
> Prick Still weeping, never spending,
> Pocky Nodes, Carnosityes,
> Cunt botches, Gout and stranguryes:
> Take the Councill I have sent yee,
> Then fuck on and nere repent yee.[6]

'A Ramble in St James' Park', equally coarse, was still banned well into the 1960s. He outdid himself in his single venture on to the stage: *Sodom: or, The Quintessence of Debauchery*. This play in five acts, a prologue and two epilogues, was published in Antwerp in 1684 as a play 'by the E. of R.' Rochester disclaimed responsibility for what the critic Donald Thomas has termed his 'scatalogical romp', and for a while it was attributed to John Fishbourne, a barrister. Neither his contemporaries nor generations of scholars have been willing to accept Rochester's disclaimer, and the original *Dictionary of National Biography* includes *Sodom*, a work of 'intolerable foulness', in Rochester's bibliography. To be fair, a number of modern scholars have supported the earl, claiming on both stylistic and chronological grounds that Rochester was innocent of the play's authorship. But the play appears in the earl's most recent 'Complete Works' (1999) and so be it. It is unlikely that anyone else would wish to lay a claim.

To take it, for a moment, seriously, the play represents the first example of English libertine writing – for instance his contemporary Henry Neville (whose *Isle of Pines* is a salacious pun), Aphra Behn or the work of Thomas Shadwell, whose *Squire of Alsatia* (1688) did for criminal slang what Rochester did for filth, albeit with a great deal more popular exposure. But lit. crit. aside, what *Sodom* is about is filth, and the language in which it is represented. Nowhere more than in its cast list: Bolloxinion and Cuntigratia, 'King and Queen of Sodom'; Pricket and Swivia, 'young Prince and Princess'; Pockenello, 'Pimp, Catamite and Favourite to the King', Buggeranthos, 'Generall of the Army' and the 'maids of honor' ffuckadilla, Clitoris and Cunticula. That is, *bollocks*, *cunt*, *prick*, *swive* (an early synonym for fuck), syphilitic *pocks* or pox, *buggery* and *fucking*. Contemporary feminists doubtless approved the writer's acknowledgement of the clitoris.

The entire play is devoted to debauchery and all characters copulate ceaselessly. As for stage directions, Shakespeare may have had his much-loved 'exit, pursued by a bear', but Rochester offers: 'Six naked men & six naked women appeare & dance. In their Dancing ye men do obeysance to ye womens C[un]ts, kissing & tonguing them often. The women in like manner do Ceremony to the mens P[ric]ks…' That all 'so fall to Copulacion' comes as no surprise. The supreme pleasure, as underlined in the title, is sodomy, although such alternative amusements as incest are not overlooked. The play ends with the apocalyptic destruction of the kingdom.

Rochester's poems would not have reached the street. Readers in search of accessible titillation could turn to the series of five sixteen-page pamphlets entitled *The Wandring Whore*, which appeared between 1660 and 1663. It was sub-titled: 'A Dialogue between *Magdalena* a Crafty Bawd, *Julietta* an Exquisite Whore, *Francion* a lascivious gallant And *Gusman* a Pimping hector. Discovering their Diabolical Practises at the Chuck-Office. *With a List of all the Crafty Bawds, Common Whores, Decoys, hectors, and Trappaners and their usual Meetings.*' John Garfield, its publisher and very likely author, claimed that it had been 'Published to destroy those poysonous Vermine which live upon the ruin and destruction of many Families'. The reality was that like many pornographers before and since, Garfield used his purported disgust to offer as much titillation as he could get away with. The format, a dialogue between the old whore and the novice, aped that of the recently published *La Puttana Errante* and indeed simply Englished its title. Like rival publications such as *The Ladies Champion* and *The Practical Part of Love* it added a list of currently working girls.

The *Wandring Whore* offers a mix of stories, focusing either on criminal trickery or on sexual pleasures, invariably ascribed, however, only to degenerate foreigners. It is full of bawdy humour and uses a number of military and naval images. And like later guides to London prostitutes it names streets and real-life whores such as Damaris Page (mentioned by Pepys) and Madame Cresswell (a successful madam for thirty years until her arrest in 1681). It offers some 130 examples of contemporary slang. There are the first uses, which include *as long as one's arm, tearing*, for impressive, *cock-broth*, a strong soup, and *hit*, to take effect. There were the predictable range of sex-related terms which offer both the obvious: *cunny, cunt, fuck, ride, stallion* and *tail*, and the more imagistic: *the best in Christendom* (usually in a toast; 'the best' referred to the vagina), the *touchhole*, the *fancy bit* and the punning *low countries* for vagina. There were a variety of xenophobic terms for venereal disease: the *French pox* and the *Neapolitan disease*, both of which *burned* the victim, plus the *Italian padlock*, a chastity belt. As well as to be *clapped*, *peppered* and *pocky*. The *Whore* also offered what may be the earliest take on 'as the actress said to the bishop', in this case 'Every man to his trade, as the Rat-trap-maker said to the Parson'. Intercourse was *business, fancy work, knocking* or *dancing* and a prostitute was a *buttock*, a *hackney* or a *trader*; her pimp a *smock merchant* and her client a *rumper*. She worked in a *dancing school*, or brothel. Of particular note was the title's reference to the *chuck office*. This was a 'game' whereby a whore would stand on her head, exhibiting her spread vulva, and clients would throw coins into the vagina. As the first edition of the *Wandring Whore* reported in 1660: 'Witness Priss Fotheringham's Chuck-office, where upon sight thereof, French Dollars, Spanish pistols, English Half-crowns are as plentifully pour'd in, as the Rhenish wine was into the Dutch wenches two holes till she roar'd again, as she was showing tricks upon her head with naked buttocks and spread legges in a round ring, like those at wrestling neer the Half-crown-chuck-office, call'd Jack-a-newberries-six windmills.'[7]

Like their French equivalents, whose scabrous assaults on Marie Antoinette among others have been credited, at least in part, for the growing anti-monarchical sentiments that would lead to the French Revolution,[8] the pornographers of the pre-nineteenth-century era invariably mixed their titillation – such as it might be – with politics and philosophy. Pornography could embrace science (the electrical eel being especially discussed), anti-Catholicism (randy, hypocritical priests, complaisant nuns), and offer a number of utopian fantasies. In many cases the books themselves were translations of Italian and French originals. 'Up, and at my chamber all the morning and the office doing business,' wrote Pepys for his diary entry of 9 February 1667, 'and also reading a little of *L'escholle des filles*, which is a mighty lewd book, but yet not amiss for a sober man once to read over to inform himself in the villainy of the world.' He was not alone. Though in his case, guiltily, he burned his copy. Above all, as Julie Peakman has suggested, 'Writing about sex is a revolt against authority [...] Obscene books, in this context, play the role of opposition.'[9] In this, I would suggest, they find their kinship with slang, that most contrarian and subversive of lexes. But the language was more that of Cleland than of Rochester. Metaphor rather than out and out 'filth'. The writers have moved a long way from the out-and-out bawdy of the Restoration. To take an example, *The New Description of Merryland* (1740) may have been written under the unabashed pseudonym of 'Roger Pheuquewell' but the book is one long metaphor based on the rural landscape. One finds, for instance, that '*Carrots* are no Strangers to this Soil, but are much used',[10] the traveller will encounter 'the smell of *ling*'[11] (one of the many equations of the vagina with fish), and the author has 'indeed heard of a *Mackarel* [i.e. a bawd] being found here',[12] while there is 'A small Animal [...] known by the Name of *PNTL* [*sic*] it is often found plunging about in the great Canal'.[13] Merryland's 'Metropolis'[14] is called *CLTRS*. Within the book we find a *plough* with which one *tills*, a *purse*, *riding*, the *b*[u]*bby mountains*, and the *turnpike* and the *pleasure seat* (both the vagina). And while 'Pheuquewell' cites a 'celebrated *French* Author', who recommends the 'back Way as the best and easiest',[15] the nearest he comes to simple obscenity is in the use of 'shitten', and even this was still considered unexceptionable even in polite speech.

Although Francis Grose's dictionary has its share of sex-related terms, including in his second and third editions the *uber*-misogynistic 'C—T, [...] a nasty name for a nasty thing', and offered sixty-eight terms for the penis, seventy-seven for the vagina and seventy-five for intercourse, eighteenth-century sexual slang still tended to the metaphorical. Egan's augmented version of Grose added the latest flash terms, but these, while dealing with *sport*, used that word only in its literal sense. As noted, he wished to excise the more coarse of Grose's headwords. He added just eleven terms for the penis, ten for the vagina, and seventeen for sex and most of these had already been found in the pirated edition of Grose, the *Lexicon Balatronicum* of 1811. Sex slang had essentially paused, and would not move on again until the Regency gave way to the Britain of Queen Victoria.

Victorian England with its supposedly moral 'values' has been stereotyped as a template for sexual hypocrisy: all child whores on Saturday night and chapel on Sunday morning. Modern historians may have undercut such assumptions, but contemporary commentators were united in one thing: the need to protect the masses from their own excess. Such excess might be physical – be it sexual or violent – but it might also be by way of language:

It is impossible to contemplate the ignorance and immorality of so numerous a class as that of the costermongers, without wishing to discover the cause of their degradation. Let any one curious on this point visit one of these penny shows, and he will wonder that any trace of virtue and honesty should remain among the people. Here the stage, instead of being the means for illustrating a moral precept, is turned into a platform to teach the cruelest [sic] debauchery. The audience is usually composed of children so young, that these dens become the school-rooms where the guiding morals of a life are picked up; and so precocious are the little things, that the girl of nine will, from constant attendance at such places, have learnt to understand the filthiest sayings, and laugh at them as loudly as the grown-up lads around her. [...] How can the lad learn to check his hot passions and think honesty and virtue admirable, when the shouts around him impart a glory to a descriptive song so painfully corrupt, that it can only have been made tolerable by the most habitual excess? The men who preside over these infamous places know too well the failings of their audiences. They know that these poor children require no nicely-turned joke to make the evening pass merrily, and that the filth they utter needs no double meaning to veil its obscenity. The show that will provide the most unrestrained debauchery will have the most crowded benches; and to gain this point, things are acted and spoken that it is criminal even to allude to.[16]

The pioneer sociologist Henry Mayhew, who wrote this attack on the cheap theatre, the 'penny gaff', duly essayed the social depths for his readers, but still infused his findings with his own puritan morality. He had started *Punch* to counter what he saw as the excesses of contemporary satirical papers, and in time would decry the 'penny dreadfuls' so beloved of the youthful working class. Nor could he even face the worst excesses himself: his brother Augustus was deputed to investigate the barbarities of ratting, while the fourth volume of his treatise on *London Labour and the London Poor*, which dealt with prostitution, was attributed to a trio of collaborators. He was not alone in his attitudes. If the Regency aristocracy had been happy to mingle with at least a subset of the masses and even talk their slang, the Victorian middle class were less inclined. It might be, as Michael Mason has argued,[17] that not every piano leg was clad in modest cloth, and that in the UK (though at least some Americans were even more prudish: zealously substituting 'limb' for leg, 'rooster' for cock and so on) such euphemisms as 'inexpressibles' and 'unmentionables' for trousers were at heart a joke, and that a chicken's breast was just that, and not delicately euphemized as 'white meat', but there had been since the 1790s a movement towards greater propriety. To an extent this can be attributed to the growing power of evangelism, but the middle classes, religious or not, had come more and more to subscribe to the identification of the poor with metaphorical and perhaps physical 'dirt'. As Lisa Sigel has written, 'Middle- and upper-class Victorians saw pollution rising off the masses like a miasma'[18] and it was taken as read that among the foulness perceived through that miasma was 'bad language', a concept that was first recorded in the sense of 'obscenity' in 1798.

Much of the so-called obscenity came in the productive and widespread creation of the double-entendre. Try as one might there are only so many sex-related bodily functions (a list augmented by those linked to defecation) and only so many 'official' dirty words to describe them. As we know, they are the great survivors. Among the songs that Mayhew deplored was 'one written about "Pine-apple rock," [which] was the grand treat of the night, and offered greater scope to the rhyming powers of the author than any of the others. In this, not a single chance had been missed; ingenuity had been exerted to its utmost lest an obscene thought should be passed by, and it was absolutely awful to behold the relish with which the young ones jumped to the hideous meaning of the verses.'[19] Doubtless the song included 'cock' but that required no deciphering. It is in his reference to the 'meaning of the verses' that one can see that most of the references would have relied on smutty inference.

There were many such songs, often sold in small booklets at sixpence a time. Mayhew does not mention encountering them in the gaffs, but they were on sale in such places as the Coal Hole or the Cider Cellars– down-market taverns around Covent Garden where singers would keep it clean until midnight and then render it increasingly filthy thereafter. The British Library holds scores of such songbooks. Their names include *The Delicious Chanter* (1834), *The Flash Chaunter* (1834), *The Frisky Vocalist* (1836), *The Gentleman's Spicey Songster* (1841), *The Icky-Wickey Songster* (1837), *Swell!!! or, Slap-Up Chaunter* (1833) and *The Knowing Chaunter* (1835). They were published in London and Edinburgh and Dublin and across the Atlantic in New York; the earliest appeared in the 1770s; among the last was *The Rakish Rhymer, or, Fancy Man's Own Songster and Reciter* (c. 1864).

The primary publisher of these song books was the theatrical printseller William West, of 57 Wych Street, Strand, not far from the pornography centre of Holywell Street. Mayhew interviewed West, who had pioneered the popular toy theatres ('penny plain and twopence coloured'), but they did not discuss this side of his trade. The authors remain anonymous, other than occasional initials. The singers have been recorded; some were 'low' comedians, while others, equally at home with less controversial lyrics, maintained some form of parallel career within the legitimate theatre. John Duncombe, another Holywell Street bookseller and publisher of his own and other slang dictionaries, also issued a variety of 'songsters' and 'chaunters'.

Most songs depended on a 'knowing' audience, i.e. that which appreciated the double-entendres of 'He'll No More Grind Again', 'Mother H's Knocking Shop; or, A Bit Of Old Hat!', 'I Am a Smutty Chimney Sweep' (When up the ladies' flues I creep, / The pleasure it is all my own), 'Nix My Jolly Gals Poke Away' (including the first use of *snatch* for vagina), and 'Rory O'More Had A Hell Of A Bore' (I'm the boy your touch holes to prime; / I never miss fire, or flash in the pan, / When I go shooting it is not my plan'). There was 'The Spring Bedstead' (giving a first recorded use of *glue*, meaning gonorrhoea) and the still-popular 'Job Halls & Mike Hunt'. Thus *The Swell's Night Out* (1841) noted of one dive that: 'The dance was followed by an out-and-out song by Mike Hunt, whose name was called out in a way that must not be mentioned to ears polite.'

Not everyone appreciated the 'entertainment'. Thackeray's Colonel Newcome had 'brought his young son in the expectation of enjoying an evening of glee singing and old English ballads, but when later in the evening Captain Costigan rose to his feet and gave voice to a song, it so offended the worthy Colonel that he called for silence. When some in the room urged the singer to go on, the Colonel retorted, "Does any gentleman say 'Go on'? Does any man who has a wife and sisters, or children at home, say 'Go on' to such disgusting ribaldry as this? Do you dare, sir, to call yourself a gentleman, and to say that you hold the king's commission, and to sit down amongst Christians and men of honour, and defile the ears of young boys with this wicked balderdash?" "Why do you bring young boys here, old boy?" cried one of the diners, as the Colonel stalked, with his son, from the room.'[20]

Looking at a representative selection of terms used in the songs – from the letter 'C', which provides just under 10% of those cited in my database – the majority of the terms remain both single-entendre and on the whole of proven use. Some of these are cant/flash: *charlie* (a watchman), *claret* (blood), *clean* (to rob), *click* (a robbery or theft), *cly* (a wallet), *cracksman* (a housebreaker), *crap* (to hang) and *cull* (a whore's client). The remainder, however, are in general use and while some are relatively recent (to the early- or mid-nineteenth century), there are no examples of first use.

There are fewer terms embracing Mayhew's 'hideous meaning'. Some are used without disguise; the bulk, however, come with the necessary nudge in the audience's ribs: *C* (the vagina), in 'Come, Sleep With Me' (1836): 'And then we'll plough the deep deep C. [...] / Around that secret spot of thine.' *Cabbage* from 'A Parody' (1789): ''T shall go hard, If out of your suit I don't cabbage a yard' which may be literal but the use of *hard* and *yard* make it hard to believe so. *Can* (the vagina) in 'The Chapter of Smutty Toasts' (1837), which tells that 'Here's the thatched house, the miraculous can!' – the thatched house being the pubic hair. Other smut includes *cod* (the penis): 'May the ladies always find plenty of fresh cod in the market', and to *come* (to reach orgasm) which is found both 'straight': 'When I rifled her charms, she so wriggled her bum, / That it was not long before I did come' and disguised: 'Then Mr. Shove, / Said oh, Miss Love, / No longer can I play; / You've beat me quite, / So love, good night! / I'll come another day.' In 'An Out-And-Out Riddle' (1834), *crack* (the vagina) is called 'the funny Magic Crack' while 'Sam Swipes' (1837) echoes the 'tradesmen' puns of the seventeenth century: 'The next was a builder, so stout and so rare, / Who heard that her kitchen was out of repair, / He brought his strong tools, and at it went smack, / And shoved a wedge ten inches long, up her c–.'

Cunt being seemingly off-limits (other than allied to 'Mike'), even in such deliberately bawdy gatherings, the most prevalent term, whether disguised or otherwise, is *cock*. For the former one has, among other examples, these, in which the first title – 'The Plumber's Ball-cock' (1837) – leaves one in no doubt of what is to follow: 'The cock did likewise leak – it was not a good fit: / So he very wisely, with two stones, began to drive it in.' Plumbers are celebrated again in a selection of 'Toasts & Sentiments': 'Here's to the plumbers, / Who are the chaps for a lass, / For their balls are of copper, / And their cocks are of brass.' Disguise is abandoned in this American example, from 'Long Tail Jock' (1838): 'Jim Crow was courting a brown girl, / And he show'd to her his c--k; / But I guess she let the nigga go, / When she saw my long tail jock.' *Jock* (from the older *jockum*) had meant penis since the 1740s.

Not much humour, even less wit, for all that the double-entendres do point towards their comparatively bowdlerized twentieth-century descendants, the *Carry On* movies. The image of drunken provincials clutching their booklets and roaring away in tuneless unison is depressing. Michael Mason seems right to term this a 'shamefaced vocabulary'.[21] If the masses chose not to venture into such gatherings who can blame them.

The alternative source of sexual language was pornography. This was undoubtedly flourishing, and the bookshops of Holywell Street (long since buried beneath the southern end of Kingsway) were justifiably notorious. Bookseller-publishers such as Henry Smith, William Dugdale, and later Charles Carrington and Leonard Smithers carried on a lucrative trade. So too, as a sideline to his general publishing, did the slang lexicographer John Camden Hotten (see Chapter 14). Titles included *The Lustful Turk*, *Flossie, a Venus of Fifteen*, *The Amatory Experiences of a Surgeon*, and *Nunnery Tales*, wherein Dugdale, in a burst of alliterative puffery that Thomas Harman would have appreciated, promised his clients that 'every stretch of voluptuous imagination is here fully depicted, rogering, ramming, one unbounded scene of lust, lechery and licentiousness'. In subject if not style, *Raped on the Railway* offered something new: a tribute to the onrush of technology. There were also a number of 'top-shelf titles': magazines such as *The Pearl*, *The Oyster*, *The Boudoir* and *The Cremorne*, all of which mixed facetious, smutty poetry and jokes with multi-part serials such as 'Sub-Umbra, or Sport among the She-Noodles' and 'Miss Coote's Confessions'.

The language of such volumes was a mix of Cleland and Rochester. On the one hand one still had the flowery, euphemistic side-stepping of the simple four-lettered vocabulary, and on the other, often in breathless dialogue, that vocabulary itself. And again, this was a middle- and upper-class world (as was generally that depicted). The masses could never afford such publications: at a guinea a copy, *The Cremorne* cost more than two week's wages for the average worker, while buying a novel such as *My Secret Life* – its £100 price daunting for even the middle-class buyer – was inconceivable.

There was, however, a world of much cheaper titillation, masquerading as guides to London's louche underside. These papers, appearing between 1830 and 1870, cost a few pennies and offered a mix of scandal and (near-)pornography. Their titles included the *Town*, the *Fly*, the *Star of Venus: or Shew-Up Chronicle*, the *London Satirist*, *Paul Pry*, *Peeping Tom*, and the *Fast Man*. They were short-lived and probably sold relatively few copies. 'What their circulations were, we have no way of knowing. Some were blackmail sheets; all were so scurrilous and licentious that even the most liberal-minded apologist for popular taste could not defend them.'[22] In 1838 Thackeray bought half-a-crown's worth and reported on their content to readers of *Fraser's Magazine*: '... the schoolmaster is abroad, and the prejudices of the people [against wickedness] disappear. Where we had one scoundrel we may count them now by hundreds of thousands. We have our penny libraries for debauchery as for other useful knowledge; and colleges like palaces for study—gin-palaces, where each starving Sardanapalus may revel until he die.'[23]

New York, necessarily on a smaller scale, offered its equivalents. The first of such publications – the *Whip and Satirist of New York*, the *Weekly*

Rake, the *Flash* and the *Libertine* — flourished very briefly, between 1842 and 1843. They were known as the 'flash press', using *flash* in Hotten's sense of 'showy, smart, knowing [...] "fast," roguish and [...] counterfeit or deceptive',[24] rather than the older sense of pertaining to criminality. These too posed as guides to the sexual underworld, with articles on brothels, street whores, masturbation, female underwear, 'the sodomites', the bare-knuckle prize-ring and much else. The difference being that the American magazines also set themselves up as politico-moral reformers: advocating republicanism and democracy as a response to what they pretended were unacceptable excesses. By 1843 they had gone too far: opposition from a coalition of evangelical Christians, conservative lawmakers who disliked the flash papers' attacks on privilege and hypocrisy, and readers who were unable to accept the realities of commercial sex unveiled by the comforting fantasies of romance, ensured that their editors faced trials and the papers were closed. But if the titles were banned the style did not disappear. George Wilkes, formerly of the *Weekly Flash*, went on to found the vastly popular *National Police Gazette*. He also worked for a while with the radical Democrat Mike Walsh on his muckraking magazine the *Subterranean*. Journals such as *Venus' Miscellany*, the *New York Scorpion*, the *Broadway Belle*, *Life in Boston*, Baltimore's *Viper's Sting and Paul Pry* and several others all walked the thin line between allusion and actual pornography.

To see the epitome of Victorian sexual language one needs go back up-market. To *My Secret Life*, of which only six copies were published, and which was written in eleven volumes (totally nearly one million words) between 1888 and 1894. No author was ever declared, although the writer appears, from conversations he recounts, to be called 'Walter'. Current belief, based on the scholarship of the late Gershon Legman, the analyst of erotic folklore, and more recently on Ian Gibson's study *The Erotomaniac* (2002), ascribes the book to Henry Spencer Ashbee, both a respectable businessman and one who as the coarsely punning 'Pisanus Fraxi', compiled three massive bibliographies of erotic literature and whose own collection of 'facetiae' and 'curiosa' forms the core of the British Library's Private Case.

My Secret Life leans heavily on the canonical terms: in its first volume alone *cunt* appears 331 times, *prick* 253, *fuck* 177, *frig* 102.[25]

Like his contemporaries, he relishes the simple obscenities and he enjoys persuading his partners to mouth them as they copulate. But even if the book is, as claimed, a genuine sexual autobiography (it lacks even the rudimentary fantasies of its unarguably fictional equivalents, being a repetitive list of essentially vanilla copulations[26]) 'Walter', like every pornographer, feels it necessary to ring the linguistic changes. He has some fifty-two synonyms for the penis, including *engine, pego, cunt-rammer, doodle, cucumber, stretcher, gristle, frigger, generating tool, persuader, pickle, spindle, spouter* and *truncheon*. Vagina brings in fifty-nine: *grummet, machine, article, sperm-sucker, pin-cushion, pleasure place, pouter, man-trap, horse-collar, tail, purse, scabbard* and *you-know-what*. Sexual intercourse has nearly 100, among them *shove, bullock, bounce, bumbaste, belly-bump, grind, poke, pump, split, strum, whop* and *have a game of fathers and mothers*. A fan of oral intercourse, he gives the lexicographer a first use of *eat* for fellate, and related terms include *suck* and *minette* for fellate, plus *gamahuche*, which worked for either gender and the two-way term *sixty-nine*.

Nor does he relent even in the index, which runs to forty-odd folio columns. 'Sodomites, put pestles up arseholes'; 'Thrusts of prick, number given when fucking' (average forty-five thrusts/min. apparently); 'Fucking, with another man present and sucking man's prick whilst'; 'Farting, one let in a closet by self'; 'Cunts, felt in church by me and frigged'; 'Anus, toothbrush up a man's while he's gamahuched'. Other entries are more arcane: 'Apprentice dress-makers, three in a cab'; 'Barn-loft, page frigging himself in'; 'Champagne and sperm, singular letch'; 'Bloody nose and broken pisspot'; 'Kid gloves and cold cream frigging'; 'Postage stamp, a woman got by gift of' and 'Double-cunted harlot'. The Index also points up another of Walter's pleasures – philosophy: 'Prick, is an emblem of the Deity'; 'Fucking, is obedience to the Divine command "increase and multiply"' (that said, Walter procures as many abortions as he fathers bastards); 'Gamahuching, man is superior to the beasts therein'; and 'Cunts, are divine and not obscene organs.'

To return to Farmer and Henley, whose work began appearing just as 'Walter' completed his, although they do not appear to have used him, or not among their citations, one might suggest that for all that has followed, sex slang had reached its finest flowering by the end of the nineteenth century. Aside from the majestic entry at *greens*, they have, at *monosyllable*, seven columns of vagina terms (plus ten more in French, Italian Spanish, Portuguese and German); elsewhere one finds eight for whores, and nine (under various headwords) for the penis (again backed by substantial lists of European synonyms). The seven volumes can be mined for much more.[27] But modernity, as in so much else, had less time for decoration. The trend, already seen in the late nineteenth century's pornography, for cutting to the chase and replacing the bulk of semi-euphemisms with blunter variations on what Anthony Burgess's *Clockwork Orange* would term 'the old in-and-out', merely developed.

The return to basics can be seen in D. H. Lawrence's *Lady Chatterley's Lover*, at the trial of which in 1960 the prosecution informed the court that there were 'thirty "fucks or fuckings", fourteen "cunts", thirteen "balls"...' and so on. Although Lawrence still managed to include 'John Thomas' and 'Lady Jane' in his adulterous idyll. The synonymy tradition continues, but it is of the ramming and rogering persuasion, rather than that of the *agreeable ruts of life* and the *ladies' pleasure garden*. Typically the 42nd Street 'stroke books' of the 1960s to 1980s kept it simple. For instance, *Hot Young Wife* (*c.* 1976) by 'Ted Leonard':

'Panting hotly, she raised her pussy up and guided his thick, wet cockhead between her cuntlips. When his massive cockhead was firmly wedged into the hot opening of her fuck-channel, she slipped her slender arms around his broad shoulders. [...] When he gladly urged the full length of his slippery cock up into her squirmy little cunthole, she gasped, "Oh — do it, Dad! Ohhh, fuck me! Ohhh, God, what a big cock — give it to me! Fuck it into my cunt, Dad. Ohhh, I'm so fucking horny. Fuck the life out of me! Fuck me, fuck me, FUCK MEEEE!"'

We have come a very long way from *Fanny Hill* or even 'Walter'. Turning to the on-line pornography of such 'adult story' sites as www. asstr.org or www.literotica.com, where amateurs send in a ceaseless flow of self-penned fantasy, one finds the same limited vocabulary; often the story-tellers opt primarily for standard English. Perhaps the modern attention span can't tolerate Cleland's languorous descriptions. The bulk of pornography is now visual: the briefest glance at the net will show that there are very few words needed there. If you show there is little need to tell.

None of which is to deny the influx of new coinages. The themes are long established and variations do keep coming. Since 1990 we find, for penis, *whanger, jimmy, tockley, pant-worm* and *one-string banjo*; and for vagina, *bliff, blurt, pink-eye, glamity* and *badly packed kebab* – but few of these, and the many others to be found in the wonderfully inventive (but perhaps less than wholly trustworthy) pages of successive editions of that 'revolutionary dictionary of bad language' *Roger's Profanisaurus*, are likely to show the staying power of the favoured few. And it may say something of contemporary attitudes to sex that the *Profanisaurus* is even more dedicated to that other sort of 'filth' – scatological – than it is to sex. And when sex is considered, it is often so as to list terms that are anything but exciting. Like the seventeenth-century courtiers whose scabrous poems as often mentioned sexual dysfunction and disease as they did successful and satisfying unions, the *Profanisaurus* concentrates on the downside. Sex still runs through slang like mould in cheese, but perhaps one might question the sell-by date.

10 Cockney Sparrers: Mean Streets and Music Halls

Now kool my downy kicksies – the style for me
Built on a plan werry naughty,
The stock around my squeeze a guiver colour see
And the vestat with the bins so rorty

[chorus]

I'm a Chickaleary bloke with my vun-two-three,
Vitechapel was the village I was born in,
For to get me on the hop, or on my tibby drop,
You must wake up very early in the morning.
　　　　　A. Stephens, 'The Chickaleary Cove', c. 1864

The word *Cockney* has resolutely resisted any simple etymology. It is first noted in 1362, when it meant a 'cock's egg' – that is, a defective one. However, there was an alternative use, first recorded in Chaucer and defined in the second edition of the *OED* (1989) as 'a mother's darling'; a cockered child, pet, minion; 'a child tenderly brought up'; hence, a squeamish or effeminate fellow, 'a milksop'. Hence too the equation, presumably coined by self-aggrandizing countrymen, of the weakling with the townsman, a use initially recorded in 1521. However, that faded, and in 1600 appeared what remains the over-riding usage: a born-and-bred Londoner, in which the initial reference was not merely to the working classes, with which it is now invariably allied, but to any

'Bow-bell Cockney', whether poverty-stricken or a wealthy member of the middle classes.

What is a Cockney? One who has been born within the sound of Bow Bells, a reference not, as often believed, to London's eastern suburb of Bow, but to the church of Saint Mary le Bow, Cheapside, in the City of London. Further to a study carried out in 2000 to see how far the Bow Bells could be heard, it was estimated that they would have been audible six miles to the east, five to the north, three to the south, and four to the west, an area that covers Bethnal Green, Whitechapel, Spitalfields, Stepney, Wapping, Limehouse, Poplar, Millwall, Hackney, Hoxton, Shoreditch, Bow, and Mile End, as well as Bermondsey, south of the River Thames. Nor were the original Cockneys invariably working-class. All sorts of individuals would once have spoken the London dialect, even if the great push for linguistic 'purity' during the seventeenth and eighteenth centuries prohibited such 'vulgarisms' from the aspirant middle class. Even so, as late as the mid-nineteenth century Dickens's Sam Weller, Mr Pickwick's servant, may be a 'typical' Cockney, but so too is Surtees's prosperous sporting grocer John Jorrocks, unselfconsciously dropping his aitches and swapping his 'w' for 'v' with the best of them. But by then Jorrocks, even if he hunted alongside the nobility, was not invited to their tables.

The *OED*'s first recorded use of *Cockney* as language is dated 1776. But it has been suggested that a Cockney style of speech is much older, and William Matthews, in his study *Cockney Past and Present* (1938), offered examples from the sixteenth century onwards. Shakespeare is among those he quotes, although the playwright's Cockneyisms are far from TV's *EastEnders*. Indeed, early Cockney is primarily a matter of pronunciation, as reverse-engineered from the recorded spelling of words such as *frust* (thrust), *farding* (farthing), *anoder* (another), and so on.

The nineteenth century saw the first wholesale attempt to record Cockney as it was spoken. The low-life episodes of Egan's *Life in London* take his heroes deep into the East End and its speech. Dickens, notably with Sam Weller and his father, is keen on setting down the sound of Cockney speech, most obviously in the substitution of 'v' for 'w' and vice versa.[1] The pioneering sociologist Henry Mayhew recorded his impoverished or criminal interviewees in much the same style. Mayhew remains neutral but Dickens implies a moral judgement on those who drop their aitches and reverse their v's and w's: irrespective of their background, 'virtuous' characters, such as Oliver Twist and Nancy, never stray from standard English. It is left to Sikes and the Dodger to display the author's knowledge of underworld cant. Yet 'Dickensian' Cockney was short-lived. By the century's end a new school of Cockney novelists – notably William Pett Ridge, Edwin Pugh, and Arthur Morrison – had emerged. It is 'their' Cockneyisms that are far more like what one hears today. At much the same time London's music-hall was dominated by stars such as Albert Chevalier, Gus Elen, Marie Lloyd and Bessie Bellwood (actually Kathleen Mahoney, but still a Londoner), all of whom promoted themselves by creating personas that appeared to embody the lives of the Cockneys who made up their audiences. Moreover, they did so with songs imbued with that audience's home-grown language.

Criminals would always converse in their own jargon. In the form of flash this would drift on into the nineteenth century, even if most examples were to be found in 'Newgate' fiction and its down-market offshoots. Meanwhile the slang of the wider world continued to expand, and on occasion to take on new forms.

Of these, the most important was a conscious invention: rhyming slang. There are suggestions of the form in the third edition of Francis Grose's *Classical Dictionary of the Vulgar Tongue* (1796), but the author makes no specific mention of the concept and such terms as 'bubbly Jock' (a turkey cock) and 'give hot beef' (to shout 'Stop thief!') are as likely coincidentally rhyming synonyms as rhyming slang proper. Nor do subsequent editions, including that edited and expanded by Pierce Egan in 1823, make mention of slang's new subset. It seems likely that this novel variation emerged sometime before 1830.

In the terse definition offered by the *OED* (3rd edn, 2010), rhyming slang is 'a variety of (orig. Cockney) slang in which a word is replaced by a phrase which rhymes with it, sometimes with the rhyming part of the substituted phrase omitted'. Setting aside the unquestioning assumption of 'Cockney' origins, this provokes no argument. There is nothing that mysterious about rhyming slang. It can, of course, defeat the untutored listener – like all slangs it originated in the desire to create a 'secret' language – a secrecy that was helped by its generally 'clipped' form, i.e. 'Barnet' for hair (rather than the full-out 'Barnet Fair'), but the basic principle is an undaunting one. One takes a word one wishes to describe, and in its place provides a brief phrase, usually of two but also of three words, of which the last word rhymes with the word for which it is a synonym. *Round the houses*, trousers; *Alan Whickers*, knickers; *artful dodger*, lodger ... thus the pattern. Some terms hold greater complexities, usually originating from the layers of rhyme through which the 'translator' need pass. Thus *arris*, meaning the buttocks, makes its way through *arris* which abbreviates *aristotle* = *bottle* which clips *bottle and glass* = standard slang *arse* = standard English buttocks. Nonetheless, despite the somewhat laborious trail, the basic rhyming scheme holds true. There are also examples that, to non-Cockney ears, seem devoid of rhyme: *Charing Cross* does not immediately offer 'horse', not until one recalls the Cockney pronunciation 'crorss'; similarly, once 'Cocknified', *cold potato* ('pertater') is a waiter, *Max Miller* is a pillow ('piller'), *burnt cinder* a window ('winder') and so on. Sometimes the rhyme is less tenable, becoming what linguists would term an 'imperfect rhyme'. Examples include *bronze figures*, kippers; *Jack Jones*, alone (usually in the phrase 'on your Jack', by yourself) and *nanny-goating*, courting. However, given the usual clipping of all but the first element, the rhyme, it might be said, becomes a technicality. This clipping, it should be stressed, is not a product of familiarity, the full phrase has not, as it were, 'worn away': it has been intrinsic to rhyming slang since its creation. Hotten notes the way, for example, in which *nosey-me-knacker* ('bacca', i.e. tobacco) was immediately shortened to *nose-my* and the principle has never been abandoned. It is this clipping, suggests Hotten, that provides such 'secrecy' as rhyming slang may project. As he puts it, 'if there is any secrecy about the rhyming slang it is this – the rhyme is left out.'

Like mainstream slang, rhyming slang covers a relatively narrow waterfront, but it covers it, even within the limitations of its small vocabulary, in depth. Abstracts, once more as in the world of general slang, are short in supply; rhyming slang prefers the concrete: parts of the body; money; sex and alcohol, and the effects (usually deleterious) of them both; food; the house and what goes in it; the family and other humans. These are the main areas. Initially, at least, it avoided obscenities. As one might expect, many definitions offer a number of synonyms: to give just a couple of examples, tea can be *betty lea*, *dicky lee*, *George Bohee*, *glory be*, *Gypsy Lee*, *hay lee*, *jennie* or *jenny lea*, *jimmy lee*, *Mother Machree*, *nancy lee*, *Peter and Lee*, *River Lea*, *Rosie Lea* or *Rosy Lea*, *sailors on the sea*, *split pea*, *sweetpea*, *wasp and bee* or *you and me*. It is all a matter of choice, and as Hotten remarked, 'it must be borne in mind that the rhymes are all matters of individual opinion, and that if one man says Allacompain means rain, another is quite justified in preferring Mary Blane, if his individual fancy lies in that direction'. A single rhyming term may stand for a number of definitions: *Adam and Eve* means leave or believe, *ball* a walk or a talk, *battle of Waterloo* a queue or a stew. As ever in slang, context is all.

As to its creation myth, there seem to be a number, none of them offering incontrovertible proof. Hotten suggests that the language was deliberately covert and was created by street patterers to confuse the police. An anonymous 'patterer' (a street-seller of ballads, dying speeches and melodramatic reports of major events), speaking to Mayhew sometime in the 1840s, seems to underline the point: it was a matter of finding a new way of deceiving the 'flats' (policemen) who had, by now, decoded the older slang of the eighteenth-century villain. For the costermongers, the market traders, the job was achieved by creating backslang (a far less hardy survivor than its rhyming cousin, though some few examples are still to be found); for the patterer it was, logically given the ballads that formed the basis of their profession, in rhyme. Another theory ascribes the original rhyming slang to thieves, whose varieties of slang had by necessity always been at the cutting edge of 'counter-language' coinage. Flash, as seen, no longer fulfilled that role. Julian Franklyn, in his *Dictionary of Rhyming Slang* (1960, 1984), notes the criminal input, but suggests that the villains, while proficient in the new slang, were not its creators. They picked it up from the roving vagabonds. As ever, what had initially been restricted to the criminal classes (and one can see the street sellers as charter members of that group) spread into the wider 'respectable' working class and thence, once the slang collectors sniffed it out, to the dictionaries. Peter Wright, in *Cockney Dialect and Slang* (1981), adds bricklayer's slang (quoting a source who notes it to have been 'the most picturesque, involved and unintelligible' of all rhyming slangs); in addition he suggests a large input from the Irish navvies, recently imported to England to build railways and canals. According to Franklyn it was the linguistic rivalry between these navvies, and similarly recruited Cockneys, who worked alongside them and like them revelled in language, that created rhyming slang. Wright too accepts this theory, but one must wonder, given the relatively minimal use of rhyming slang in modern Irish usage (or at least as collected in Bernard Share's dictionary of Irish slang *Slanguage* [1997]), whether this can be the case.

Backslang has effectively vanished (unlike France's analogous *verlan*, which has moved triumphantly out of the *banlieues* into the bourgeois mainstream); rhyming slang survives; indeed for many (especially tourists to London) rhyming slang *is* slang. More important is that in some ways it is the most accessible of slang. Julian Franklyn has suggested that it is much more humorous than its predecessor, the slang of the villains of the pre-Victorian era: 'The former is grim, harsh and humourless; the latter gay, frolicsome and amusing.'[2] Perhaps, but the slang amassed by Francis Grose or 'Jon Bee' is far from unamusing, especially to those whose sense of humour runs to the cynical and ironic. Among others, the wealth of terms that accrued to the gallows, wretched though their ultimate definition might be, were far from dour. Nor is rhyming slang invariably funny. Like any such creation, not least 'mainstream' slang itself, the best is admirable and witty, the worst – especially in many of its modern iterations – laboured and banal. The primary reason for its longevity is probably its adoption by the world of entertainment and popular media. It was not only Cockneys, already versed in the vocabulary, who appreciated hearing its use on stage. Both the cheap 'penny gaffs' and their more expensive peers, the grand music-halls, paraded artistes who thrived on rhyming slang, an essential part of their own 'coster' persona; in the 1930s the music-hall star Lupino Lane brought the vocabulary to tens of thousands with his hit show *Me and My Gal*. Later still Frank Norman's *Fings Ain't Wot They Used T'Be* (1959), another Cockney saga (albeit set in a Soho 'shpieler') carried on the good work. More recently TV series such as *Till Death Us Do Part*, *Minder* and *Only Fools and Horses* have been similarly revelatory. In the modern literary world rhyming slang is a sine qua non if 'colour' is required; that said, it was much less common prior to the late Sixties, with stand-out titles such as Robin Cook's *Crust on Its Uppers* (1962) being a rare exception.

As for the press, few papers could equal the late-nineteenth-century *Sporting Times*, best known from the colour of its newsprint as 'The Pink 'Un' and perhaps best celebrated as the creator of test cricket's Ashes. Among its roseate pages readers of such authors as 'The Pitcher', 'The Shifter' and 'The Dwarf of Blood' (Pink 'Un authors revelled in their *noms-de-plume*), not merely in London, but in every outpost of the Empire where men sought news of the Metropolitan demi-monde, interspersed with gossip, risqué humour and horse-racing information, would find the products of their much loved poet: 'Doss Chiderdoss'. Chiderdoss – the name allegedly means 'sleep, gently sleep' and refers to the slang *doss*, a bed or a sleep – was the pen-name of A. R. Marshall. Marshall wrote, as Franklyn puts it, 'as though rhyming slang was the only language in the world',[3] and his explorations of the rhyming lexicon appeared as the mainstay of the weekly 'Pome' which adorned the journal's cover.

'Meg's Diversion: A Sonnet in Slang', which appeared in the edition of 4 September 1897, gives a flavour:

> A tear-drop fell from the girl's mince-pie,
> And her raspberry-tart was torn
> With anguish; For she'd an empty sky,
> And nothing to bullock's horn.
>
> But she cooled each mince with a little scent,
> And her Barnet arranged with grace;
> And then down the apples and pears she went
> With a sorrowful Chevy Chase.

Given Hotten's knowledge of his subject, it is unsurprising that the first appearance of the phrase 'rhyming slang' as a linguistic qualifier comes in his *Dictionary of Modern Slang, Cant, and Vulgar Words*. Describing it as 'the secret language of Chaunters and Patterers' (both terms referring to those who sang and sold ballads, broadsides and similar material in the streets), he explained that 'like the costermongers [...] they have a secret tongue or Cant speech known only to each other. The cant, which has nothing to do with that spoken by the costermongers, is known in Seven Dials and elsewhere as the RHYMING SLANG, *or the substitution of words and sentences which rhyme with other words intended to be kept secret.*'

However, Hotten was neither the first to notice the 'new' form of language, nor the first to enter examples into a dictionary. Henry Mayhew, the social commentator whose *London Labour and the London Poor* was initially serialized in 1851 (and was based on interviews garnered over the previous decade), spoke to one such chaunter who explained that 'The cadgers' talk is quite different now to what it was in the days of Billy [William IV]. You see the flats [policemen] got awake to it, so in course we had to alter the patter. The new style of cadgers' cant is nothing like the thieves' cant, and is done all on the rhyming principle. This way's the caper. Suppose I want to ask a pal to come and have a glass of rum and smoke a pipe of tobacco, and have a game at cards with some blokes at home with me, I should say, if there were any flats present, "Splodger, will you have a *jack-surpass* of *finger and thumb*, and blow your *yard of tripe* of *nosey me knacker*, and have a *touch of the broads* with me and the other *heaps of coke* at my drum."'[4] As far as dictionaries were concerned, the first examples of rhyming slang appear in *The Vulgar Tongue* by the otherwise anonymous Ducange Anglicus, some two years before Hotten's work. Its brief vocabulary included some fifty-eight rhyming terms, including the ever-popular *apples and pears* (stairs), *Rory O'Moore* (floor) and *linen draper* (a newspaper) as well as long-obsolete terms such as *Hounslow Heath* (teeth, now *Hampstead Heath*), *split pea* (tea, now *Rosie Lea*, among many others) and *throw me dirt* (a shirt, now *Dicky Dirt*).

But if Hotten is not a pioneer, then he is undoubtedly the first lexicographer to attempt a detailed analysis of rhyming slang. Like Mayhew he believed firmly in statistics and posits some 20,000 'oratorial and bawling wanderers' scattered around the major cities and the large provincial towns, using and coining rhyming slang on a regular basis. He does not see the rhymes as a specifically London, or indeed Cockney, phenomenon – simply the occupational jargon, designed as a deliberate form of obfuscation (since such street patterers often came up against the authorities), employed by these vagabond sellers of dramatic, if ephemeral literature. Nor, at this stage, does it appear that rhyming slang was much used in print; such efforts would not arrive until later in the century and by then rhyming slang was regarded more as an amusing form of communication than a secret code, and very much the property of the 'Cockney sparrer', albeit rarely printed, other than by those who enjoyed the eccentricities of such colourful speech. Hotten's glossary runs to 144 items.

For all its identification with the East End, rhyming slang has long since moved far beyond earshot of the Bow Bells. There was, as noted above, the natural popularization of the form via the media, but an equally important factor can be found in the intermingling of soldiers from all over Britain in two world wars. And rhyming slang, while rooted in England, is not the sole province of native English-speakers. Two countries have taken it on board, not as extensively, nor as enthusiastically as the UK, but a survey of both Australian and American slang will unearth examples.

Setting aside its social spread, its geographical departure led first to Australia, where in time it must have been transported along with the criminals who peopled the new colony's penal settlements. The transportees came from all over the country, but there were many Cockney villains and they doubtless imported their homegrown language. Voluntary immigration would have swelled the lexis further. There are around 635 examples of Australian coinages, and while in his authoritative *Australian Language* (1941) Sidney Baker may have dismissed the style as 'dull, unimaginative [and] foolish' and compared it very negatively with the wider world of general Australian slang, its importance cannot be wholly denied. Given the inventiveness of Australian slang, it would be odd were its coiners to have overlooked so fecund a source. For all his carping, Baker notes the popularity of the form in Australia, and quotes a passage from the Sydney *Bulletin* of 18 January 1902: 'Me mother's away, as I was swiftly-flowing up the field of wheat in the bread-and-jam, a heavenly plan with a big charming mottle of o-my-dear sticking out of his sky-rocket fancy-sashed the girl-abductor on his bundle-of-socks with it cos he wouldn't let him have a virgin-bride for nothing.'

Rhyming slang's arrival in the US came not too long after its appearance in the UK, and its first example was found in an issue of the *National Police Gazette* in 1859. In a move that seems bizarre in hindsight, rhyming slang was known then and for many decades as 'Australian slang'. The belief seems to have originated in the arrival, especially on the West Coast, of a number of Australian criminals, keen to enjoy the rich pickings of the Gold Rush of 1849. With them came rhyming slang and while they would leave, it stayed. At the same time or soon afterwards, rhyming slang began to be seen in Chicago and in New York. In these two cities it was more likely that the users were native American criminals (although some of the late nineteenth and early twentieth century's most successful confidence tricksters, operating all over America, were Australians – not to mention the occasional Britisher), although the regular visits of British sailors to New York must have left their linguistic legacy. Criminals and sailors undoubtedly had their role to play, but according to a source quoted by the slang collector David Maurer, 'The roving British and Australian thief have played their part in bringing the lingo to the racketlands of America, but the ones who have really brought the Australian lingo into our stream of speech have been the roving American thief and the good-time bims (chorus girls and fortune hunters) who have played between Frisco, Shanghai, and Sydney for the past fifty years.'[5] As to the 'Australian' aspect, Maurer's collaborator on this essay, Sidney Baker, had little time for that fantasy. Writing in his book *The Australian Language* (1945), he termed the assumption 'an odd myth' and looked at a list of some 352 allegedly 'Australian' terms forwarded to him by his co-author. Of these he could find only 3% that were 'definitely Australian', 49% that were coined in America and 48% that had come from the UK. Of the 352 some 88% had never been recorded in Australia.

The lexicographer records the vocabulary of slang, but, unless the dictionaries they write also offer citations, they cannot properly record its use. Prior to the work of John S. Farmer and W. E. Henley between 1890 and 1904, one must seek elsewhere for that. As previous chapters have made clear, the sources for nineteenth-century slang are widespread. Ballads and poems, novels and plays, penny dreadfuls and pornography all played their part. Setting aside the proliferating newspapers, magazines and journals, over 700 individual British authors, both named and anonymous, have contributed to the gathering of the era's slang, and they are doubtless no more than a representative sample of the most prolific. The figure more than doubles that of the previous century's sources (although it is more than doubled again in the twentieth century). But a relatively small proportion of these report the language as spoken, the actual sound of the street. One group who did may be termed the pioneer sociologists, or as some prefer it, given that the discipline was still unformed, the higher journalists. There were a number of these, of whom the most notable were Henry Mayhew and his successor James Greenwood. Both spoke to and recorded the slang-makers, those who Mayhew termed 'the street-folk', and both show how widely used their language was.

Mayhew (1812–87) was one of contemporary London's literary phenomena. One of seventeen children, he rejected his father's wish that he enter the law and aged sixteen turned instead to writing. He edited variously *Figaro in London* (1835–8), *Punch*, of which in 1841 he was a co-founder though he departed a year later, the *Comic Almanack* (1850–51), and the *Morning News* (1859). As a freelance he contributed to the *Morning Chronicle, Bentley's Miscellany*, and other journals. In addition he wrote for the stage – the farce *The Wandering Minstrel* (1834) plus a number of productions co-written with others – and with his brother Augustus humorous novels – notably *Whom to Marry and How to Get Married, or, The Adventures of a Lady in Search of a Good Husband* (1848) – and works of travel literature.

His greatest success, and the one piece of work for which he is remembered, was *London Labour and the London Poor* (4 volumes, 1861–5). This in turn was based on some eighty-two articles, published in series between October 1849 and December 1850, entitled 'Labour and the Poor', in the *Morning Chronicle*, of which Mayhew was the metropolitan correspondent. Mayhew was not an original – Ned Ward and Tom Brown had also walked the London streets bringing their inhabitants to life for an interested audience – nor was his focus on the London poor unique – the 1840s government was looking hard at poverty, and produced a series of Blue Books devoted to sanitation,

housing, health, burial and much more. (And Mayhew described his
work as 'the first "blue book" ever published in twopenny numbers'.⁶)
The condition of England, and specifically that of its impoverished
citizens, was becoming of interest: Carlyle had taken a look in his piece
'Signs of the Times' in the *Edinburgh Review* in 1829 and Disraeli's *Sybil*
(1845) was subtitled 'The Two Nations' and showcased the grimmer
conditions of the working class.

Yet in *London Labour and the London Poor*, subtitled 'A Cyclopædia
Of The Condition And Earnings Of Those That *Will* Work, Those
That *Cannot* Work, And Those That *Will* Not Work', and expanded
by a fourth volume devoted to Prostitution, Mayhew offered a picture
of poverty-stricken London that had never been attempted. Writing
in *Punch*, Mayhew's *Morning Chronicle* colleague Thackeray, picturing
Mayhew as an anthropologist travelling in 'the poor man's country', told
how 'a clever and earnest-minded writer [...] reports upon the state of
our poor in London; he goes amongst labouring people and poor of all
kinds – and brings back what? A picture of human life so wonderful, so
awful, so piteous and pathetic, so exciting and terrible, that readers of
romances own they never read anything like to it; and that the griefs,
struggles, strange adventures here depicted exceed anything that any of
us could imagine.'⁷ The flow of praise continued long after Mayhew's
death. E. P. Thompson, writing in 1967, called *London Labour* 'the fullest
and most vivid documentation of the economic and social problems,
the customs, habits, grievances, and individual life experiences of the
labouring people of the world's greatest city of the nineteenth century'.⁸

Not everyone has been convinced. The critic Gertrude Himmelfarb⁹
has savaged the work, maintaining that its title is misleading, its 'sample'
interviewees unrepresentative and its contents and statistical tables
unreliable, tainted throughout by 'fallacies, including arithmetical
miscalculations, questionable sources, data pertaining to different
periods, and categories added together as if they were all distinct and
mutually exclusive'. And for her the very depiction of the 'poor man's
country' was not so much too good to be true, but over-selective, over-
lurid, too much journalism to be sociologically valid.

Urban anthropologist, journalist or sociologist, whatever Mayhew's
motives, however meretricious some might find his presentation or

invalid his statistical evidence, no one would deny the excellence of his interviews. The power of these interviews, and the language in which they are recounted, is at the heart of the work's success. It was, as he explained, 'the first attempt to publish the history of a people, from the lips of the people themselves – giving a literal description of their labour, their earnings, their trials, and their sufferings, in their own "unvarnished" language; and to pourtray [sic] the condition of their homes and their families by personal observation of the places, and direct communion with the individuals'.[10]

As faithful transcription of the interviews required, they are dense with slang, at least 1,250 discrete terms. Mayhew's interest in specific occupations, and his coverage of those who lived on the margins of, if not wholly beyond the law, means that there is a high volume of cant, and it is possible, given the original newspaper publication of the work in 1851, that his are the first examples of many of the words that appeared in the lexicographer's work.

Mayhew's series triggered a number of similar investigations. Among them were John Garwood's *The Million-Peopled City; or, One-half of the People of London made known to the Other Half* (1853); Catharine Sinclair's *London Homes* (1853) and Viscount Ingestre's collections *Meliora: or, Better Times to Come* (in two series 1852, 1854). Mayhew's brother Augustus, who had done some of the research for *London Labour*, published a novel ironically titled *Paved with Gold* in 1857. Of all such writers the best qualified as Mayhew's successor was James Greenwood (c. 1835–1927). Greenwood had worked as a compositor and written a number of adventure stories for boys before joining his elder brother Frederick in founding the *Pall Mall Gazette*. He had already touched on London street life in *The True History of a Little Ragamuffin* (serialized 1865, published 1866), which was set in the Clerkenwell slums, when in late 1865 his brother suggested that he spend a night in the casual ward of a workhouse and report on what he found. Greenwood was allegedly reluctant, but the £30 fee persuaded him, as did a promise of extra payment were the piece to increase the *Pall Mall's* circulation. Accompanied by a stockbroker friend, and dressed down for the occasion in battered hat and greasy coat secured with string, Greenwood spent fourteen hours in the Lambeth workhouse. Three articles, written under the name of 'The Amateur Casual', appeared in January 1866. The revelations of filth, squalor, abject mismanagement and neglect, underlined by Greenwood's personal revulsion at his own immersion in so alien an environment, proved a sensation. The inference of homosexual relations between the tramps was even more shocking. Circulation duly increased, the *Times* reprinted the series and it was issued as a pamphlet. From there Greenwood continued producing what he called 'public faithful photographs, open pictures of daily life in London'.[11] Titles included *The Seven Curses of London* (1869), which he cited as 'neglected children'; 'professional thieves'; 'professional beggars'; 'fallen women'; 'the curse of drunkenness'; 'betting gamblers'; and 'waste of charity'; *The Wilds of London* (1874); *Unsentimental Journeys; or, Byways of the Modern Babylon* (1867); and *Low-Life Deeps; an Account of the Strange Fish to be Found There* (1876).

Although the role of flash in *Oliver Twist* has been considered, it is worth a look at Dickens's wider, and somewhat ambivalent take on slang. In the issue of his journal *Household Words* for 24 September 1853, he published what appears at first to be an outspokenly negative piece, calling for the once pure and undefiled English language to be rescued from 'the sewerage of verbiage and of slang'.[12] Its author believed, like many before and after him, that slang was ruining the language, substituting cheap verbal short-cuts for genuine wit. He blamed America, but the British were equally culpable, employing without discrimination 'every bastard classicism dragged head and shoulders from a lexicon by an advertising tradesman to puff his wares, every slip-slop Gallicism from the shelves of the circulating library'.[13] He accepted that criminals, sailors and others will always need their own cant, i.e. jargons, but complained that 'so universal has the use of slang terms become, that, in all societies, they are frequently substituted for, and have almost usurped the place of wit. An audience will sit in a theatre and listen to a string of brilliant witticisms, with perfect immobility; but let some fellow rush forward and roar out "It's all serene," or "Catch 'em alive, oh!" (this last is sure to take) pit, boxes, and gallery roar with laughter.'[14] Nor was slang merely a working-class sin, it was equally prevalent among the aristocracy, in Parliament, among lawyers, literary critics and so on.

His solution, delivered with unfettered gusto, would have pleased, and may even have inspired Hotten. 'I must express my opinion either that slang should be proscribed banished, prohibited, or that a New Dictionary should be compiled, in which all the slang terms now in use [...] should be registered, etymologised, explained, and stamped with the lexicographic stamp, that we may have chapter and verse, mint and hall-mark for our slang. Let the new dictionary contain a well-digested array of the multitude of synonyms for familiar objects floating about; let them give a local habitation and a name to all the little by-blows of language skulking and rambling about our speech, like the ragged little Bedouins about our shameless streets, and give them a settlement and a parish. If the evil of slang has grown too gigantic to be suppressed, let us at least give it decency by legalising it.'[15]

He continues with lengthy lists for money, for drunkenness, and offers further lists of synonyms for specific drinks, for men, for thieves, and to steal, to run away, to beat, a horse and a donkey, the hands and feet, boots, to pawn, for food, watches, policemen, magistrates and more.

But perhaps the writer protests too much. Of course he has decided that slang is bad, and sets out to establish his case. But there are anomalies. His definition of slang, notably in its lengthy teasing of upper-class affectation, typically the use of unnecessary gallicisms and the drawling substitution of 'w' for 'l', and his critique of those classes very far above slang's usual creators, is surely too broad. Slang in this context is far from restricted to the street; for the author it represents any form of what he dismisses as witless, redundant word-play in any social group. At the same time, as seen in his lists of synonyms his own knowledge of genuine slang, the language of the street, is impressive. All this, he claims, comes off the top of his head, and he acknowledges that his readers will be able to come up with much more. One need only read Dickens' fiction to see that slang plays an important role, if only in characterizing his lower-class players. Perhaps 25% of his uses come in *Oliver Twist*, and a proportion of that is cant, but there are hundreds more. To what extent his middle-class readership, safely barricaded within *Household Words* from the less savoury penny and threepenny papers of such as Edward Lloyd and G. M. Reynolds, knew the slang as well as did its editor is unknown; but at least, thanks to his expertise, they would know it was there.

And what is Sam Weller of *The Pickwick Papers* but the *echt*-Cockney of the mid-century. Not until the arrival of Punch's 'Arry in 1877 would he be replaced as the exemplar of the social type. (Weller was also a best-seller: the fourteenth issue of *Pickwick* ran to 400 copies, the fifteenth, with Sam arrived, increased to 40,000).

Dickens, as both editor and author, was hardly egregious for his time. Hotten would make it clear that slang was primarily the language of the streets, but the concept that equated it with any other form of 'un-British' and thus potentially harmful linguistic affectation was deep-rooted. Grose's belief that the freedom to use slang and cant marked the unfettered Englishman was gone. In 1842 *Punch* printed an alleged letter citing an 'Alarming Prospect' that faced English literature which was 'becoming conversational, and our conversation corrupt. The use of cant phraseology is daily gaining ground among us, and this evil will speedily infect, if it has not already infected, the productions of our men of letters. Unfortunately what is vulgarly termed SLANG is unfortunately very expressive, and there fine peculiarly adapted for the purposes of those whose aim it is to clothe "thoughts that breathe" in "words that burn:".'[16]

Punch was not invariably anti-slang. In 1842 it also published 'Prolusiones Etymologicae' – a specimen of a proposed 'philosophical dictionary' which laid out, with only slightly facetious meta-data, some twenty-three terms for money: *dibs, ready, blunt, rhino, mopusses, stumpy, dust, tin, rowdy, needful, oil of palms, shiners, goldfinches, flimsies, bits of stuff, kites, bulls, hogs, bobs, benders, joeys, bits and browns.*[16] In 1843 it offered several columns 'On the Cockney Pronunciation', and in 1847 'The Fast Man's Phrase-Book', which lists *brick* ('a term of extreme laudation'), *cleaned out* ('his pocket having undergone that operation'), *malt* ('a comprehensive term for beer'), *fresh* ('the state of the convivial Fast Man who has been drinking too liberally of spirituous liquors') and *governor* ('Father is a word always banished from the lips of the Fast Man').[18] Intermittent lists would follow, similarly explained. Slang was not always an 'alarming prospect' for *Punch*, but it was undoubtedly an odd one.

Though sections of *Oliver Twist* might qualify as a 'Newgate novel', as some feel *Barnaby Rudge* is too, Dickens was not of the genre; nor, although his books are filled with Cockneys, on occasion talking slang, was he one of the group who have been labelled by historian P. J. Keating the 'Cockney novelists'.[19] Nor were the many mid-century advocates of temperance and self-denial who wrote novels that were little more than tracts to push their beliefs, nor the industrial novelists, who mainly looked further north than London. They were all in dreary earnest, propagandizing the proles, allowing neither smiles nor jokes, no amusements and certainly no drink or tobacco. For them the working class was either debased or respectable, and the aim of their one-dimensional tales was to move him by whatever necessary means from point A to its sober antithesis.

The Cockney novelists (not to be confused with the earlier 'Cockney school' of poets, among them Leigh Hunt, Keats and Hazlitt) flourished towards the end of the century, with certain titles spilling over into the next one. They included Arthur Morrison, Edwin Pugh, William Pett Ridge and, even if his bestseller purported to be reportage, Clarence Rook. While they dealt with their subject matter in different ways, all can be seen in at least one aspect of their work as combining a fictional form with a new concern with the London working classes, not as comedy walk-ons à la Dickens, or as objects about which one might preach and on whom one might prey, but as three-dimensional figures in their own right and as such the coiners of much slang.

The first such writer was Henry Nevinson (1856–1941), a socialist, feminist and a campaigning journalist who in time covered the Boer War, Russia's 1905 Revolution and, much against establishment wishes, World War I (in which his son C. R. W. Nevinson was a war artist). In 1893 he was commissioned to write a series of sketches on working-class life. Following its author's hands-on researches in the East End, where he had already run a mission and given classes in English literature, this appeared in 1895 under the title of *Neighbours of Ours*. There are a dozen stories, all narrated by the same Cockney speaker. What Nevinson offers is a portrait of a community, as realistic as he can make it, and without falling into stereotypes. He covers a variety of aspects, good and bad, and in 'Sissero's Return' even looks at a cross-race relationship. The book is more dialectal than overtly slangy, but it lays the groundwork for those who followed; Nevinson's East Enders have a language of their own, and there is no need for its recorder to caricature it.

Arthur Morrison (1863–1945) had begun his professional life as a sports writer (boxing and bicycling) before moving on to full-time work at *The Globe* in 1885. A year later he became a clerk to the Beaumont Trustees, a charitable trust that administered the People's Palace – a philanthropically designed educational and cultural centre for the local community – in Mile End in the East End of London. Here he began writing a series entitled 'Cockney Corners' for the Palace's magazine, the *People's Journal* and it was these sketches that would lead him to further writings on the area. A short story, 'The Street', was published by *Macmillan's* in October 1891, followed by fourteen more tales of London's most impoverished area, published in book form in 1894 by W. E. Henley (who was already working with John Farmer on their slang dictionary) as *Tales of Mean Streets*. The book, with its unblinking depiction of East End squalor and the violence, crime and desperation that it engendered, was a controversial success, especially as regarded the story 'Lizerunt' (i.e. Liza Hunt),[20] a young woman, once blithe and flirtatious, who is first beaten by her boyfriend and then forced by him into prostitution. *A Child of the Jago* (1896) was even more controversial, with its exploration of life in an area known as the Jago (in reality the notorious Old Nichol slum off Bethnal Green Road). This story of the street Arab Dicky Perrott laid out even more unmediated violence, criminality, dysfunctional family life and aggressive, fearful insularity. Drunkenness is a given. Despite the presence of a muscular Christian parson (Morrison's portrait of the real-life Revd A. Osborne Jay, vicar of Holy Trinity, Shoreditch, and author of *Life in Darkest London*, 1891), Dicky cannot escape his environment and is murdered, refusing, as the Jago code demands, to 'nark' on his killer. In Morrison's bleak portrait, death is the only escape the Jago will permit.

Slang, or at least cant, had always been used as colour. Morrison's use is different; after all, this is a story of working-class life and for a change it is the middle classes who are allotted the cameos. Conversations are written phonetically, and the use of slang, criminal or otherwise, is common. But it has gradations. When Dicky slips, showing off, into the lexis of crime, his mother, not above profiting from her husband's muggings herself, takes fright.

The boy returned to his box, and sat. Then he said, 'I do n't s'pose father 's 'avin' a sleep outside, eh ?' The woman sat up with some show of energy. [...] 'No, I ain't seen 'im; I jist looked in the court.' Then after a pause, 'I 'ope 'e's done a click,' the boy said. His mother winced. 'I dunno wot you mean, Dicky,' she said, but falteringly. 'You you 're gittin' that low an' — '

'Wy, copped somethink, o' course. Nicked somethink. You know.' 'If you say sich things as that I'll tell 'im wot you say, an' 'e' pay you. We ain't that sort o' people, Dicky, you ought to know. I was alwis kep' respectable an' straight all my life, I 'm sure, an'— '

'I know. You said so before, to father — I 'eard: wen 'e brought 'ome that there yuller prop the necktie pin. Wy, where did 'e git that? 'E ain't 'ad a job for munse an' munse; where 's the yannups come from wot 's bin for to pay the rent, an' git the toke, an' milk for Looey? Think I dunno? I ain't a kid; I know.'

'Dicky, Dicky! you must n't say sich things !' was all the mother could find to say, with tears in her slack eyes. 'It 's wicked an' – an' low. An' you must alwis be respectable an' straight, Dicky, an' you'll get on then.'[21]

It is not the idea of crime – such is her husband's 'job' – but the criminal's language that disturbs Hannah Perrott. It defies respectability, as of course does the whole of the Jago. Morrison does not moralize: the entire text is infused with the deepest irony. But to an even greater extent than Mayhew's readers had believed of the 'street folk', the world of the Jago represents social deviance, uncivilized savagery, something altogether 'other'. Other missionaries were posted to 'darkest Africa'; the East End was also characterized as 'dark' and the 'low' language of its denizens as incomprehensible to the fascinated middle classes as any tribal tongue.

W. E. Henley, reviewing 'Some Novels of 1899' in the *North American Review*,[22] described Morrison's *Child of the Jago* as 'masterly' but equally as 'that terrible work'. Against it he set another book, the popular journalist Richard Whiteing's *No. 5 John Street*, which Henley saw as 'a fairy-tale [and] no mere debauch in sentiment, but— a refined and moving expression of reality'.[23] Whiteing (1840–1928) had been a foster child; he had been apprenticed to a maker of seals and medals, and later attended art school at among other places the Working Men's College in Great Ormond Street, where he met F. D. Maurice, John Ruskin and Frederick Furnivall, one of the pioneers of the *OED* and guiding light of multiple literary societies and journals. Furnivall's ladies' rowing eight, recruited from the New Oxford Street ABC restaurant, would feature in Whiteing's novel *Ring in the New* (1906). Whiteing's journalistic career began in 1866, on the *Evening Star*. Here he wrote a column, supposedly in the persona of one Mr Sprouts, who rose to become an MP and embodied the principles of common sense and plain talk; the collected columns appeared as a book in 1867. Whiteing travelled as a foreign correspondent and wrote fiction and travel literature. *No. 5 John Street* was his best-seller. Somewhere between a Greenwood investigation and a Cockney novel, it followed the author as he lived in the East End slums in order 'to learn what it is to live on half a crown a day, and to earn it'.[24]

Morrison may be seen as a descendant of Greenwood, a reformer's zeal permeating his work. The other three 'Cockney' writers are far more allied to Dickens, most of whose Cockneys (even if he never penetrates the East End) were by no means 'savage'. For all that her home turf is the Cut, near Waterloo, no one could epitomize the 'chirpy cockney sparrer' of popular myth more than the eponymous heroine of Pett Ridge's *Mord Em'ly* (1898). Mord is poor, her mother a nervous wreck and her father 'away' (i.e. in prison), but if she runs in the streets as the junior member of the all-girl Gilliken Gang, there is no malice let alone hard-core criminality in her. (Nor in the gang whose leader subsequently joins the Salvation Army.) Dicky Perrott sees crime as an escape from wretchedness, Rook's 'hooligan' Young Alf is a career villain, but Mord Em'ly is above all a feisty young woman, enjoying life, and giving as good, if not better than she gets. Unsurprisingly she lacks the cant that informs the other two. Her slang is gentler: *act the giddy goat*, *soft* (a weakling), *song and dance*, *stony* (broke), *bounder*; it often appears as interjections: *cheese it!*, *give over!*, *I don't think*, *s'elp me greens!*, *language!*, or in imagery: someone has 'a face on 'im like half-past six'. It represents not her own 'soft' femininity – her verbal sophistication can outwit virtually every male she meets – but her 'civilian' status. Mord's slang would not have defeated the middle classes, and the book was a best-seller.

Edwin Pugh (1874–1930), whose titles include *A Street in Suburbia*

(1895), *The Man of Straw* (1896), *Tony Drum: A Cockney Boy* (1898), *The Spoilers* (1906), *The City of the World* (1912), *Harry the Cockney* (1912), and *The Cockney at Home* (1914), is the antithesis of Morrison. He allows for no irony and makes no attempt at the ultra-realism that his predecessor offers. Pugh is a sentimentalist and his affections veer unashamedly East. His own background – the son of a theatrical prop maker and a wardrobe mistress – may have been an influence. He sympathizes with his characters' problems, and they almost invariably have to battle (often unsuccessfully) against ill fortune and tough lives, but there is no crime, no violence. His Cockneys are the 'deserving' poor; they are prey, not predators. His essay 'Real realism' in *Slings and Arrows* (1916) berates those who only paint the darkest of dark and thus show a false picture, but Pugh, working from the opposite direction, did much the same.

Clarence Rook (1862–1915), American but London-based and prolific in his time, remains something of a mystery, with one bestseller to his name, and a great deal of second-rate work to accompany it. George Bernard Shaw (whom he interviewed) praised him as a 'very clever fellow' but E. V. Lucas, another contemporary, saw him as one who 'never fulfilled his many talents'. Rook wrote the 'By the Way' column for *The Globe* (as would P. G. Wodehouse), contributed freelance journalism, had a number of short stories published and in 1907 wrote a travel guide, *Switzerland: The Country and Its People*. In 1898 he launched the career of one of fiction's earliest female detectives: Miss Nora Van Snoop of the New York Detective Force. All of which was geared to a middle-class audience. *The Hooligan Nights* (1899) was very different, although the readers again were doubtless middle-class, many of whom might have already read Morrison or Pugh. According to Rook this was no novel but a piece of reportage based on 'some sheets of manuscript' shown to him by his publisher Grant Richards. 'They contained certain confessions and revelations of a boy' – named in the book as 'Young Alf' – 'who professed to be a leader of Hooligans'. All else aside, Rook was using his journalistic instincts: the word *hooligan*, still of unknown etymology, had only emerged – first recorded in police court reports – a year earlier. Such early uses were capitalized, suggesting a gang, but no evidence has survived. Rook claimed that Irish Court, in the same area, had once hosted an actual Patrick Hooligan who led the first such gang, and that Alf was 'one on whom a portion at least of [...] his mantle had fallen',[25] but this was merely touting an unproven etymology.

'Young Alf', the star and supposed author of this 'Life and Opinions of a Young and Impenitent Criminal Set Down by Himself', is a south Londoner and lives just down the road from Mord Em'ly, in the Elephant and Castle district. Rook describes him as a 'young man who walks to and fro in your midst, ready to pick your pocket, rifle your house or even bash you in a dark corner if it is made worth his while. [...] It would, I think, be very difficult to persuade young Alf that honesty is the best policy.'[26]

Far more successful than poor Dicky Perrott, and just as cheekily self-confident as Mord Em'ly, Alf is a professional, on however limited a scale. And since there is no moralizing, he declares a frank delight in his occupation. He has, after all, a philosophy:

> Look 'ere [...] if you see a fing you want, you just go and take it wivout any 'anging abart. If you 'ang abart you draw suspicion and you get lagged for loiterin' wiv intent to commit a felony or some damn nonsense like that. Go for it, strite. P'r'aps it's a 'awse and cart you see as'll do you fine. Jump up an' drive away as 'ard as you can and ten to one nobody'll say anyfink. They'll think it's your own prop'ty. But 'ang around and you mit jest as well walk into the next cop you see and arst 'im to 'and you your stretch. See? You got to look after yourself; and it ain't your graft to look after anyone else, nor is it likely that anybody else'd look after you — only the cops. See?[27]

Alf's slang is profuse, but compared with a Dickensian villain, almost devoid of cant. Of the 250 terms he (or Rook) uses, a mere dozen are strictly underworld uses. Indeed, he is very modern: substitute 'nahmean' for 'see' and one could be listening to a young tearaway of today. And while he misuses 'v', it is not to replace 'w', as might Sam Weller, but instead of 'th', still a common Cockneyism.

Nine years later Rook published *London Side-Lights* – thirty sketches including 'The Boxers', 'London Justice', 'Morality and the Cabman', 'Cave Dwellers (woman caretakers of rented houses), 'Animals and Doctors' (the Royal Veterinary College and Hospital), 'The Pirate of

Piccadilly' and 'Ankypankyanner'. In the twentieth, 'To Him Who Waits', we read again of Young Alf who has 'gone away and laid his bones upon a battlefield – for he enlisted in a moment of enthusiasm – and his colonel announced that he had died as a good soldier'.[28]

Whether actual East Enders, rather than middle-class voyeurs, read the 'Cockney novels' is unknown; certainly residents of the Old Nichol would have been more urgently occupied. But if they wished to see themselves portrayed, costermonger finery, homegrown slang and all, there were simpler, and indeed cheaper methods. The most popular was the music-hall, which in the late nineteenth century was enjoying what is seen as a 'golden age'. The music-hall had found at least some of its roots in the free-and-easies of the 1830s, just as those pub and café sing-alongs had in turn emerged, it has been suggested, from the vanishing street ballad singers. The free-and-easies also gave the music-hall some of its flavour. The alternative distractions of a packed night at the Coal Hole or Cider Cellar had necessitated a loud and physically demonstrative delivery. This, in the music-hall context, transmuted into the identification of given performers with a specific character, with dress and diction to match. They might also add a brief spoken interlude between songs, known as patter, perhaps a conscious back-reference to the street balladeer's cant name: a patterer. That both songs and patter might sail a little 'near the mark', albeit in a manner less openly bawdy than had the free-and-easy material, worried no one.

There were a variety of 'characters' but among the most popular, at least for male performers (and the versatile Marie Lloyd would impersonate 'The Coster Girl in Paris'), was the Cockney coster. His primary avatars were Gus Elen, Albert Chevalier and Harry Champion. The first exemplar, however, was 'The Great Vance', properly Alfred Peck Stevens (1839?–1888), a 'lion comique' who had been delighting audiences as early as the 1860s, around the time the others were born. It was for him that Stephens wrote 'The Chickaleary Cove', i.e. the 'knowing fellow', and according to the new *DNB* 'All London rang with [its] words and tune.'

If one wishes to draw parallels with the novelists then the gritty Elen was Morrison, albeit less squalid, Chevalier echoed Pugh's sentimentality, while Champion went for laughs, à la Pett Ridge. Elen's songs were the least slangy of the three, but the persona he offered, with its accentuated Cockney pronunciation (typically, the phrase 'a great big shame' sounds more like 'a grite big shime'), was generally acknowledged as the most 'real'; he was also born in the working-class world he re-created, and claimed to have worked as a draper's assistant, an egg-packer, and a programme seller at the Royal Aquarium, as well as a street barrel-organist before he began his career 'on the halls'. Like gangsters taking tips from *Godfather* movies, East Enders had a role model in Elen from whom they could learn to do it 'proper'. Before he retired in 1914 he had added such classics as 'Never introduce your donah to a pal', "Arf a pint of ale', 'It's a great big shame' and 'If it wasn't for the 'ouses in between' to the national repertoire.

Chevalier, often overly sentimental in songs such as his debut 'The Coster's Serenade', and such classics as 'My Old Dutch' and 'Wot' cher, or, Knocked 'em in the Old Kent Road', was from a middle-class background and combined 'legitimate' theatre with music-hall, in which, although he first resisted it, he worked very successfully for seven years. Unlike Elen he had other characters, including that of a vicar, and his song 'Funny without being Vulgar' sums up his overall style. This did not preclude a wide use of slang.

Champion, who appeared on stage in a rakishly tilted billycock hat and a frock coat, delivering his lyrics at machine-gun pace, was especially known for his elegies of the edible. The most famous was 'Boiled Beef an' Carrots', but there were others which hymned variously 'cucumbers, pickled onions, piccalilli, saveloys, trotters, cold pork, and baked sheep's heart, all basic elements in the cockney's diet'. Champion's biggest hit was so popular that 'about the time of the First World War it was possible to go into a cheap London restaurant and ask for "a Harry Champion" and be given a plate of boiled beef and carrots, echoing the title of one of his most famous songs'.[29]

Alongside all these Cockneys – fictional or theatrical – one representation stands out beyond any other. No coster comedian, no product of a Cockney novelist could rival E. J. Milliken's grotesque, created for the pages of *Punch* in 1877 and strutting there for the next twenty years: 'Arry.

Milliken was *Punch*'s "'Suggestor-in-Chief'" for the major cartoons and also wrote their captions; he was known as one of the most invaluable of Mr. Punch's staff'.[30] 'Arry's first appearance, in a cartoon caption – 'Arry on 'Orseback – of 1874 was a dry run. This was not 'Arry fully-formed, but merely a generic for what the *OED* in 1889, using the caption as the term's first citation, defined as 'A low-bred fellow (who 'drops his h's') of lively temper and manners'. The first 'real' ballad did not appear until 1877. A decade later Jenny Hill could sing of the Cockney toff "Arry' and her music-hall audience knew exactly whom she meant.

Today 'Arry might be bracketed with the chavs, but he rises far above the underclass in aspirations, social encounters and loudly voiced opinions: traditionalist, jingoistic and unashamedly conservative. In his time he was a *cad*, a term that comes ultimately from standard English *cadet*, but more immediately from Eton and Oxford slang, in which a cad was a townsman: the implication being that such a figure could not be 'a gentleman'. He appears in the form of verse letters to his country friend 'Charlie', five or six per year. (Charlie achieved a single reply, in 1877, but that idea was dropped and all else is monologue.) With illustrations by *Punch*'s stable of artists, including Bernard Partridge, George Du Maurier, and Linley Sambourne, Milliken used his creation to sound off on a succession of issues, be they political or social, or simply to air his views on such things as travel. His monster expatiated on class – seeing himself as the equal, if not in many ways the superior of the 'swells' ('o Call me Cad? When money's in the game, / Cad and Swell are pooty much the same'[31]) – on dress ('Yaller ulster and elbows well crook'd on the 'igh-perlite pump-'andle plan'[32]), on "ot and spicy entertainment', on patriotism and on women, whom he loved, or at least flirted with when in what he deemed to be their place, and predictably despised when they turned too clever. A mirror-image girlfriend, 'Arriet, occasionally made her own appearances, but 'Arry's eye was always roving.

Milliken described his creation thus, in a letter:

> 'Arry – as you say – the essential Cad, is really appalling. He is not a creature to be laughed at or with. [...] I have mingled much with working men, shop-lads, and would-be smart and 'snide' clerks – who plume themselves on their mastery of slang and their

general 'cuteness' and 'leariness.' I have watched, listened, and studied for years 'from the life,' and I fancy I've a good memory for slang phrases of all sorts; and my 'Arry 'slang,' as I have said, is very varied, and not scientific, though most of it I have heard from the lips of street-boy, Bank-holiday youth, coster, cheap clerk, counterjumper, bar-lounger, cheap excursionist, smoking-concert devotee, tenth-rate suburban singer, music hall 'pro' or his admirer, etc. etc.[33]

Whatever our reaction to 'Arry, we cannot deny that what makes him is his use of slang. The *Sporting Times* may have had Doss Chiderdoss's weekly shot of its rhyming version, but 'Arry outdid the *Pink 'Un* in every line. Whether he is on the boulevards of 'Parry', punting on the river, commenting on adverse criticism in a literary magazine, or excoriating some threateningly intellectual 'blue', every stanza is loaded down with a generous helping of the counter-language.

And 'Arry is justifiably proud of his own contributions. In 1890 he explained:

> 'Tisn't grammar and spellin' makes patter, nor yet snips and
> snaps of snide talk.
> You may cut a moke out o' pitch-pine, mate, and paint it, but
> can't make it walk.
> You may chuck a whole Slang Dixionary by chunks in a stodge-
> pot of chat.
> But if 'tisn't alive, 'tain't chin-music, but kibosh, and corpsey at
> that.
>
> Kerrectness be jolly well jiggered! Street slang isn't Science,
> dear pal,
> And it don't need no 'glossery' tips to hinterpret my chat to my
> gal.
> I take wot comes 'andy permiskus, wotever runs slick and fits
> in.
> And when smugs makes me out a 'philolergist,'—snuffers! it do
> make me grin![34]

'Philolergist' or not, the ballads are good for 1,000 terms of 'snappy snideness' (although only two might qualify as rhyming). And the bulk were contemporary (even if in his 'transcription' Milliken allows the occasional anachronistic 'w' for 'v'): if he had known a 'Slang Dixionary' it would have been Hotten or perhaps Barrère and Leland (which came out in 1889), and he overlaps with the former but seventy-five times and the latter merely ten. But why disbelieve Milliken: he used what he had found, and there was a great deal. 'Arry would benefit, as would his readers, and in time, though he is lamentably under-used by contemporaries such as Farmer and Henley, so very gratefully would the lexicographers.

The representations of the Cockney used slang on a variety of a levels, and as well as quantity there was also the quality to be considered. There were a number of debates over how the sound of that slang, and of Cockney pronunciation in general, should appear on the page. Dickens, notably in the v/w substitutions of Tony and Sam Weller, did it one way, Milliken's 'Arry another, and Ortheris, the Cockney member of Kipling's *Soldiers Three*, another. The Cockney novelists, whether portraying the violent or more gentle image of the East End, refined things once more. The music-hall had its own ways. The changes came to a head in the late century when what had been a succession of variations of distorted standard English of one degree or another were finally put to rest. Under the influence of the philologist Andrew Tuer, author of *The Kawkneigh Awlminek* (1883) and *Thenks awf'lly* (1890) there developed a full-scale phonetic system for transliteration, which has stayed in place ever since.

One aspect of representation remained impossible to overcome: the level of obscenity in Cockney speech. It was frustrating, and the writers often referred in their texts to their own need to self-bowdlerize, but they invariably held back. Arthur Morrison came as near as was possible, using *bleedin'* and *bleeder*, and including such coarse abuse as calling women *cows* and *'eifers*, but the full-on obscenities remained far off limits. Even *bloody*, already acknowledged as the 'great Australian adjective' (though unprinted even in the poem of that name) is never used (other than by the pornographer 'Walter'). Dickens might use *blank*, as did papers such as the *Sporting Times*, which expanded it to *blankety-blank*, but that was generally an American habit. Kipling used dashes.

Punch dropped 'Arry, the music-hall became another victim of World War I, and the 'Cockney novel' had its day. Novels with Cockneys in them – whether walk-ons or stars – remained. And would be joined by movies, plays, musicals and most recently television – whether soap operas or crime series both dramatic and humorous. And the Cockney would also change: notably in race and religion. Irish, Jews, Bangladeshis, Sylhetis and Somalis have all arrived as immigrants, colonized the area and continue to move through the East End streets. Young Alf has not gone, but he has become Young Ali. Perhaps the least likely arrivals have been the gentrifying middle classes who in the last decade have turned areas such as Hoxton, once synonymous with squalor and violence, into the latest in chic. The old Cockney accent has also gone, but it has been replaced by 'Estuary' pronunciations and, for the young of seemingly every class, London's own multi-ethnic London English. Cockney slang will never be as omnipresent as before World War II, but it remains a part of the area's ever-welcoming linguistic melting pot.

11   America: Pioneers

'Peace, Sirrah! — none of your American phrases!'
Joseph Atkinson, *A Match for a Widow,*
or the Frolics of Fancy (1786)

English, however hotly pursued by Spanish, is America's national language and has been so since independence was declared on 14 July 1776. That this should be so may have been something of an accident. The pattern of exploration by the European nations had been such that the French, who held vast tracts of the interior, the Germans, who had flooded to Pennsylvania and thence to the Mid-West, and the Dutch, who had substantial settlements around the Hudson valley, might each have put in a bid for linguistic pre-eminence. In the event it was English, the language of the chain of states running along the Eastern seaboard, that 'won'. And while the Native American tribal languages were the first to be termed an 'American Language' – by the seventeenth-century settlers who met them – the creation of 'American English' as something quite apart from its 'English English' mother tongue was central to the national project. That homegrown variety of English continues to be enriched, as it has been from day one, by a succession of immigrations, but it remains America's official tongue.

The concept of 'American English' was coined – or at least most noisily advocated – by the fiercely patriotic linguist Noah Webster, who wrote in 1789 of 'the American tongue',[1] and eleven years later published in the *Monthly Magazine and American Review* an essay 'On the Scheme of an American Language'. Webster wrote presciently of the 'future separation of the American tongue from the English' and called for 'a system of our own, in language as well as government'.[2] In 1828, the year in which Webster published his ground-breaking *American Dictionary of the English Language*, the novelist James Fennimore Cooper offered a proud assessment of the new nation's speech: 'If the people of this country were like the people of any other country on earth, we should be speaking at this moment a great variety of nearly unintelligible patois; but in point of fact, the people of the United States … speak, as a body, an incomparably better English than the people of the mother country.'

And, continued the self-styled 'Travelling Bachelor', 'There is not, probably a man (of English descent) born in this country, who would not be perfectly intelligible to all whom he should meet in the streets of London. Though a vast number of those he met in the streets of London would be nearly unintelligible to him.'[3]

It is unlikely that Cooper was referring to the slang that his travelling American would have met in London's streets. But if that traveller was among those who also already used slang in the States, then he would have got by in England. As the decades passed, and America moved gradually from a rural society to one which boasted great cities, notably New York, America's slang would diverge, just as would standard American English. But at independence, and for some time afterwards, the two countries continued to talk much the same language, standard or slang.

To trace the development of slang in nineteenth-century America one is largely forced to draw on a variety of media, mainly printed. To list them all would be otiose; one can, however, assess the various types and genres. It is, to an extent, a matter of reverse engineering: what began as, say, localisms, the jocular stock-in-trade of humorists portraying wily Yankees or the 'wise fool' crackerbox philosophers of the Mid-West or South, might move into mainstream use, but would not proceed beyond slang. There were also the frontier sketches of magazines such as the *Spirit of the Times*, churning out stories of life in the backwoods. Like London, New York lent itself to sociological investigation, and those who dredged the lower depths of the city brought up the language, as well as other facets of the slums. There would be slum fiction, more or less sensationalist, sometimes drawn on personal experience. There was a thriving parade of more or less scurrilous newspapers, usually rooting for one political party or another and in no way bound by fuddy-duddy 'standard English'. In columns and books slang-based humour was always on tap: by the turn of the century George Ade would be perhaps the best-known exponent, but along with him flourished such specifically urban story-tellers as George V. Hobart, Helen Green and Edward Townshend. Purely sensationalist fiction, often purporting to unveil the secrets of the city, developed into the dime novel. By the end of the century there was added a new mass medium, the comic, published in the mass-market press and geared very much towards speakers for whom slang represented a substantial part of their vocabulary.

The earliest instances of slang duly followed the contemporary British pattern. By 1787 the new nation had produced its first play, and within a few decades a couple of criminal memoirs: one a 1791 confession from the gallows and the other, published in 1807, its first homegrown criminal autobiography. All offer embryonic pointers to the development of slang in the country.

In the case of the play, Royall Tyler's *The Contrast*, it accompanies the Yankee 'waiter' (being a proud democrat, he rejects the demeaning name 'servant') Jonathan. *Jonathan* had been in use since the War of Independence as a generic for an American – and thus the antithesis of Britain's personification John Bull – and more particularly a New Englander; its development *Brother Jonathan* would follow in the nineteenth century. Tyler's play, seen rightly or otherwise as deeply indebted to Sheridan's *School for Scandal* (1777), is a comedy of manners. Jonathan is the Yankee hayseed, a character type which would soon play a central role in American humour. His lines are filled with localisms, and some slang. There is not a great deal, just twenty-five terms, but they establish him as very different to his affected social superiors. Of these a number are the first recorded uses: *blueskin* (a moralist), *dang!*, *dumb* (very), *hold the bag* (to take responsibility), *jockey* (to trick), *spark it* (to pay court), *split* (to leave), *tarnation* (as adverb and exclamation), *what the dogs!* and *what the rattle!* There are more exclamations: *by the living jingo!, swamp me!* (his opening words), plus general terms that were already established in the new country: *shooting iron* and *tarnal*. *Cute*, while half a century old and meaning clever or (overly) 'smart', would become the badge of a stereotype Yankee, peddling wooden nutmegs to the gullible in the South and emerging mid-West.

If Jonathan can be seen as paving the way for the nineteenth century's 'local' humorists, then two men, Thomas Mount, whose *Confessions* appeared in 1791, after he had been hanged for burglary in Newport, R.I., and Henry Tufts, whose *Narrative of the Life, Adventures, Travels and Sufferings of Henry Tufts* was published in 1807, point forward to the many dictionaries of cant, criminal confessionals and the vast selection of American crime-related material available in both fiction and non-fiction.

'At my desire,' wrote Mount (or the hack who penned the text), 'the language and songs of the American Flash Company are published to inform the world at large of how wicked that company is and how necessary it is to root them up like so many thorns and briars.' Mount's glossary runs to 108 entries. Half is well-established English cant and can be found in Grose. Of the remainder, while Mount was American-born and made no excursions to London, most still appear to have been imports.

Henry Tufts – who despite so spectacularly unlawful a life still managed to die in his own bed – offered another type of memoir: the rogue picaresque. Like a number of predecessors Tufts appends a glossary to his catalogue of theft, confidence trickery, imprisonment, near-hanging and every other vestige of a godless, wicked, but relatively unpunished life. As listed by Daniel Williams, 'in addition to thief, doctor, preacher, wizard, soldier, deserter, trickster he sometimes posed as a farmer, a land speculator, a Yankee peddler, a wrestler, and even a devoted family man'.[4] He was imprisoned a dozen times, and each time escaped; he was a noted seducer who married twice and promised himself to ten other women. His glossary runs to fifty terms. Of these twenty-one are first recorded (or recorded in this sense) in the *Narrative* while the rest are older, with most of them overlapping – coincidentally or otherwise – with those available in Mount's flash songs and glossary.

While Tyler's 'Jonathan' was a Yankee servant whose straight talk put the verbal fripperies of his supposed superiors to shame, there is little suggestion that he was more than a hick. His visit to the 'devil's drawing-room', as he terms the playhouse, without apparently appreciating where he is, underpins such naïveté, as does his skewed adoption of the methods of fashionable courtship. By the 1830s 'Jonathan' had gained a new image: less of a provincial, and more the smart Yankee. He had become 'cute'. It was a role that was expounded by a succession of American humorists who created characters that might have retained vestiges of rural naiveté, but, as Alan Walker Read put it, combined 'crafty shrewdness, homespun wisdom, involvement in the social issues of the time, and colloquial freedom of speech, along with the outward trappings of bad spelling. They comprise a peculiarly American type known sometimes as [...] the "crackerbox philosopher".' [5]

They found form in the works of such as Charles F. Browne ('Artemus Ward'), J. F. Lowell ('Hosea Biglow'), T. C. Haliburton ('Sam Slick') and Seba Smith ('Major Jack Downing'). While their primary purpose was satirical, their use of colloquialisms, often shading into slang, made them a useful source for lexicographers. Their language is in its way paradoxical, given that they are urban only insofar as they represent the 'sophisticated' world of New England as against the values of the south or mid-West, but it is essential to their personalities. The first of them all appears to have been 'Joe Strickland', who was created in 1826 for the purposes of advertising by the lottery dealer George W. Arnold (1783–1838). Arnold used Strickland's supposed letters to his 'Uncle Ben' to puff his own trade: Strickland, the simple Yankee, was remarkably fortunate in his selections, winning hundreds of dollars at every try. In time the 'Strickland family' expanded, with other members joining in, while rival dealers produced their own equivalents, crying down 'Strickland' and boosting their own tickets. What Arnold might not have predicted was the popularity of his character irrespective of the lottery. The puffs gradually faded, and Strickland the commentator on politics and recorder of public events came to the fore. The final letter, the seventeenth, appeared in 1830.

They make hard reading today. The idea that bad spelling and 'rustic' accents are de facto hilarious has long since vanished. But Arnold had set a pattern which would be rigorously and even more successfully followed by his successors, all of whom delighted their public. The quasi-phonetic orthography, the rustic saws, the Yankee-isms (or what passed for such things, e.g. 'not a bit moor thun yeu koud hoald a wild pig by the tale arter yeu had rub'd Soaft Sope on't'), and the occasional leavening of slang, plus a 'wise' take on local and national events, remained a sure-fire formula. The 'characters' themselves might be different – Major Downing was involved in politics, Sam Slick was a commercial traveller, Artemus Ward the proprietor of a Wax-Works Museum (and whose creator exhibited a series of comic panoramas, and touted his lectures with rowdy processions down the local Main Street) – but all were of a kind. Even accounting for time, it is hard to see, beyond the verbal play, quite what was funny, other, perhaps, than that either in anecdote or in faux-naïve observation 'Joe' or 'Jack', 'Sam' or 'Artemus' tended to 'get one over'.

The Yankees didn't have it all their own way. Frontiersmen, typically Davy Crockett, offered their adventures (in Crockett's case via William T. Porter's *Spirit of the Times*, the US equivalent to *Bell's Life in London*); Charles Henry Smith's 'Bill Arp' offered a Southern point of view; the Ohio journalist David R. Locke used 'Petroleum V. Nasby' to comment on politics and was read by Abraham Lincoln. Mortimer Thompson wrote as 'Philander Q. Doesticks'. Female characters included B. P. Shillaber's 'Mrs Partington', whose *Life and Sayings* were published in 1854, and Frances Miriam Witcher's 'Widow Bedott', whose *Papers* appeared in 1856. There are too many to name, but the last was Bill Nye (1850–96), whose humorous letter to the US postmaster – Nye had been appointed postmaster of Laramie in 1882 – launched him to fame when it was picked up and copied around the country. Another such letter, to the President in 1883, went worldwide. He was syndicated in the international press and his first three books (*Bill Nye and Boomerang*, 1882, *Forty Liars and Other Lies*, 1882, and *Baled Hay*, 1884) each sold 100,000 copies. His last, the *History of the United States* (1894), sold half a million.

Nye was far from unique, and they were all hugely popular: their columns boosted newspaper circulations and many were syndicated abroad; collected into books they sold tens of thousands, sometimes hundreds. They toured and lectured across the States, and the best-known appeared in Europe. The literary elite, naturally, were unimpressed. In a letter to Bayard Taylor of 16 September 1873 E. C. Stedman lamented 'the present *horrible* degeneracy in public taste', complaining that 'The whole country, owing to the contagion of our American exchange system, is flooded, deluged, swamped, beneath a muddy tide of slang, vulgarity, inartistic bathos and impertinence and buffoonery that is not wit.' They were in a minority.

The Yankees, Southerners, mid-Westerners and frontiersmen were of themselves talking in dialect, in which was mixed some slang. It was a portion of their appeal, and the spelling in which their creators set them down was in part an attempt to render such dialects 'audible'. There were, however, other dialects, those of America's European immigrants. And if the non-standard speech of the natives was funny, then that of the Irish, the Germans and in time the Italians and Jews, was funnier still. There was also that of America's black community: that will be dealt with in its place. Two notable exponents – respectively the first and last of the genre – were Charles G. Leland, who would join Albert Barrère in the writing of *A Dictionary of Slang, Jargon and Cant* (1889–90), and Finley Peter Dunne.

Leland's Hans Breitmann appeared in 1857 in the poem 'Hans Breitmann's Barty'. It was the first time an entire work had been composed in a non-native dialect. His hero was by no means despicable or stupid – the stereotype of German immigrants was far more positive than that of Jew or Irishman – and Hans was widely popular even if Leland, who was highly prolific, not least in his knowledge of the Romanies (he wrote two books on them: *The English Gipsies and Their Language*, 1873, and *English-Gipsy Songs*, 1875), came to regret the monster he had created. And like his native peers, Breitmann commented on a variety of political and national events. The primary joke was his heavily accented German English. There was also a good leavening of slang, again in 'German'. Thus Breitmann's use of 'cook one's goose' came out as 'Denn ofer all de shapel / Vierce war vas ragin loose; / Fool many a vighten brinter / Got well ge-cooked his goose',[6] and 'not give a damn' as 'Away down Sout' in Tixey dey'll split you like a clam' — / 'For dat,' spoke out der Breitmann, 'I doos not gare one tam'.[7]

Finley Peter's Dunne's 'Mr Dooley', a philosophical bartender plying his trade in a predominantly Irish area of Chicago, began life as a newspaper column and first appeared in book form in *Mr. Dooley in Peace and in War* (1898). He was, according to his creator, a 'traveller, archaeologist, historian, social observer, saloon- keeper, economist, and philosopher'.[8] Dooley was as Irish as Breitmann had been German. He pontificated, as a vociferous barman, on matters of the time, both great and small, but stood throughout behind the outward persona of the comic Irishman, heavily en-brogued, and not above a good amount of slang. As Dunne explained in an interview in 1899, his intent had always been 'to make Dooley talk as an Irishman would talk who has lived thirty or forty years in America, and whose natural pronunciation had been more or less affected by the slang of the streets'.[9]

Breitmann was one of many Germans who had made their way to the mid-West. Mr Dooley was a Chicagoan. In time Chicago would expand and provide the background for such authors as J. T. Farrell, whose 'Studs Lonigan' trilogy continued to focus on the Irish, and Nelson Algren, himself a Jew, whose world was that of ex-peasants from the 'old countries' of Central Europe bundled derisively together as 'hunkies'. And if Hans and Mr Dooley used slang, and thus helped spread it among their readers, or at least reflect the language that they already used, the main point was their accent. Slang was merely one aspect thereof.

As for the Jews, there was the comedy team of Weber and Fields, the heavily dialectal sketches of Joe Hayman whose 'Cohen on the Telephone' (1913) sold one million transcripts, and such dialect-infused characters as 'Potash and Perlmutter', a pair of rag-trade businessmen, created by Montague Glass for a Broadway play (and subsequently a silent movie) in 1913 and novelized in 1914. And although dialect humour has never truly died, it reached its climax in the hands of a quartet (though more usually a trio) of Jews: the Marx Brothers. In their original form, prior to the movies and still touring in vaudeville, the Brothers represented well-known stereotypes: a Jew (Groucho) who was all words (in *Fun in Hi Skule*, 1910, he had been a German), an Irishman (a still-scripted Harpo, complete with stereotype red wig) named Patsy Brannigan, and an Italian (Chico) who was all bombast. Harpo was of course silenced, and Groucho's torrent of words transcended any racial origin; Chico, however, remained 'in character'. The fourth Brother, Zeppo, doomed to carry the unfunny love interest, represented, if anything, a WASP.

Dialect humour was anchored in the country. America's cities were not yet as populous as those of Europe, but at least one was developing fast: New York. Even if in 1850 the city population was nowhere near that of London, it had topped 600,000, a substantial number of citizens.

In Dickens's *Martin Chuzzlewit* the young hero pays a visit to the offices of the *New York Rowdy Journal*. In the accompanying illustration by 'Phiz' one may see lying on a cupboard a volume marked 'Slang Dictionary'. Presumably this was Dickens's nod to what he saw as the trashy standards of the contemporary New York press ('Here's this morning's New York Sewer! [...] Here's this morning's New York Stabber! Here's the New York Family Spy! Here's the New York Private Listener! Here's the New York Peeper! Here's the New York Plunderer! Here's the New York Keyhole Reporter!'[10]), but if there was a slang dictionary in use, then it must have been 'Egan's Grose' or 'Jon Bee'. America would not have one for a further fifteen years.

Newspapers, at least those of the popular sort of which the *Rowdy Journal* is an exemplar, were a vital source for the slang collector. Maximilian Schele de Vere's *Americanisms: the English of the New World* appeared in 1872. His impetus was to make up for the fact that the most recent edition of the standard work, John Bartlett's *Dictionary of Americanisms*, was more than a decade out of date and since then 'many millions of immigrants have been added to our population, and new territories and new States to our union [and] a civil war of gigantic proportions has shaken the political edifice to its foundations and altered every aspect of society. Language [...] has been proportionately enriched and modified.'[11] More of a narrative than a plain dictionary, he dealt with The Indian, Immigrants from Abroad (Dutch, French, Spanish, German, Negro and 'John Chinaman'), The Great West, The Church, Politics, Trades of All Kinds, Afloat, On the Rail, Natural History, Old Friends with New Faces, and New Words and Nicknames. He also devoted a substantial chapter to Cant and Slang.

Schele de Vere lays out a number of American slang's sources. There are terms imported from Britain (and 'America has sent a fair supply of cant terms to the home-country, and they have been welcomed and readily adopted'[12]); there is the West (which cares 'as little for the canons of verbal criticism as for the dictates of European lawgivers. Its speech is impregnated with the racy flavor of the backwoods and the prairie'[13]). There is pure sound ('rumbumptious, slantindicular, splendiferous, rumbustious, and ferricadouzer').[14]

Above all, 'the most fertile source of cant and slang, however, is, beyond doubt, the low-toned newspaper, written for the masses, which, instead, of being a monitor and an instrument of improvement in the hands of great men, has become a flatterer of the populace, and a panderer to their lowest vices. [...] Thanks to this influence, any sudden excitement, political event, or popular literary production, originates and sets a-going a number of slang words, vulgar at first, and rejected by the few who are careful of the people's English, but soon adopted as semi-respectable.'[15]

The popular press, as Dickens's fictitious list and Schele de Vere's condemnation suggests, was far from staid. It was partisan, populist, and, with its emphasis on reporting crime, well supplied with current cant and slang. Like its Australian equivalents, its regular court reports ensured a steady flow of language that came straight off the street. However, to see the print use of slang at its most dense it is necessary to look at a pair of journals, both of a 'sporting' nature: the *Spirit of the Times* and the *National Police Gazette*.

The *Spirit of the Times*, subtitled 'A Chronicle of the Turf, Agriculture, Field Sports, Literature, and the Stage', was founded to play a similar role to its London contemporary *Bell's Life in London* and to Bell's successor the *Sporting Times*. Launched in 1831 by the ex-printer William T. Porter, it was soon established as the leading chronicler of American sport, which meant horse-racing and after that prize-fighting. But Porter's use of amateur correspondents – since the modern sporting writer had yet to emerge – many of whom lived far from New York, meant that the *Spirit* became a repository for a wide range of non-standard usages, especially those of the South and West. As Barbara Lynette McClung has written, 'for some correspondents, the sports contest eventually served as a mere background for the unfolding of an obviously tall tale, embellished with the slang and colloquialisms of the day'. Porter had no desire to rein them in and his openness ensured that his magazine became 'an almost unequalled source for the study of Americanisms'.[16]

Among the terms that the *Spirit* coined was the *bear story*, otherwise known as a tall tale. And many of these words were first used by what has been termed the 'Big Bear' school of humorists. These included such backwoods anecdotalists as W. C. Hall (author of various tales of 'Mike Hooter', usually found tussling with a 'Bar' although equally ready to deal with a panther), George Washington Harris (author among much else of 'The Knob Dance— a Tennessee Frolic' and an 'Epistle from Tennessee'), perhaps the most talented of the team, and one who would leave the *Spirit* to pursue his own backwoods character 'Sut Lovingood', and J. B. Lamar ('Polly Peasblossom's Wedding', which in 1861 was used as the title for a full-scale anthology). Not all the contributors were Southerners: Francis A. Durivage and George P. Burnham, who co-wrote *Stray Subjects Arrested and Bound Over* (1846), were Yankees. Anthologies of *Spirit* sketches came out regularly, the first *A Quarter Race in Kentucky* in 1846, shortly followed by a successor *The Big Bear of Arkansas*.

The writers themselves may have been relatively well off, but their back-country homes were far from the sophisticated east. The stars of their stories, whose real-life equivalents they would have known, were what Porter's biographer Norris Yates has termed 'one-gallus whites'.[17] White trash in embryo, they enjoyed hard liquor, practical joking, hunting and rough-housing, with a good deal of bawdy, if unspecified, sex on the side. *Half-horse, half-alligator* or a *ring-tailed roarer* as he termed himself, the hero slaughters anything that moves, downs another jug or two, beats up anyone within reach (usually with much eye-gouging, lip-tearing and knife-work) and calls for more. Their aggressive racism, whether towards Indians or 'niggers', is a given. And it was all, at least as presented in the *Spirit*, one big laugh.

In 1856, for no discernible reason (perhaps ill-health – he would die in 1858 – or perhaps a lack of enthusiasm for his original creation), Porter abandoned the *Spirit* and launched a new magazine: *Porter's Spirit of the Times*. For this he took on a partner, George Wilkes (1817–85). Wilkes was a controversial figure. He had been editor of two examples of the 'flash press' – the *Flash* and the *Whip* – and worked on the politically radical *Subterranean*. A muckraking writer of lurid exposés, he had been shot at twice and arrested six times. In 1844, he was jailed in New York's Tombs, serving thirty days for libel; he came out with a pamphlet railing against the wretched conditions of the jail. He stayed with Porter's new paper through the Civil War, taking it away from its founder's pro-southern position to his own anti-slavery stance.

Wilkes was still in the Tombs when he was approached by a lawyer, Edwin C. Camp, who suggested that they found a new paper, focusing on police-related matters and taking for its pattern various equivalents in the UK. The new paper, the *National Police Gazette*, was launched in September 1845. It offered 'Lives of the Felons' – culled from police archives – but its primary purpose was investigative. That this would stir up the underworld was inevitable, and armed gangs regularly attacked the offices, sometimes leaving corpses on both sides. However the circulation soon hit 15,000 and the paper put on pages. As well as villains, Wilkes savaged the police department, under its boss George Washington Matsell. Yet in 1866, it was to Matsell that Wilkes sold the *Gazette*.

If Wilkes devoted the *Gazette* to muckraking, Matsell concentrated on interests that, while still controversial for some, delighted just as many. It was not available at most reputable newsstands, but it was to be found regularly in those all-male refuges, the bar-room and barber shop. The *Gazette* – printed on pink stock just as would be its London cousin the *Sporting Times* – became the 'barber shop bible'. Matsell offered the readers a weekly extravaganza of leg shows and larceny, a 'lad mag' before its time. Its cover invariably offered a scene from a 'den of iniquity', and thus an opportunity to display the den's semi-draped female inhabitants. Weekly features included 'Vice's Varieties: An Assorted Lot of Evil Deeds of Evil Doers' and 'Glimpses of Gotham' by 'Paul Prowler'. Its ads were 'of the most disreputable kind', its stories naturally covered crime, then added sex scandals, hangings, 'news' stories that promoted the bizarre above the topical ('An Eggciting Eggsploit' revealed the eater of fifty raw eggs in fifty minutes), along with pictures of burlesque queens in tights, and much more besides.

Racing was temporarily in decline but prize-fighting began taking a central position by 1880. Matsell left the paper in 1874, and it was taken over by an Irish journalist, Richard K. Fox. Nothing changed, except there was even more of the same. Especially as regarded sex. Fox took everything but the circulation, which peaked at 150,000 a week, even further down-market.

Given its preoccupations, the magazine was inevitably a great repository of slang. As a slang-gatherer Matsell would have appreciated the text, but Wilkes was still in charge when the *Gazette* made a major contribution to the knowledge of criminal terminology: *Leaves from the Diary of a Celebrated Thief and Pickpocket*, which the paper serialized in 1863–4 and then published in book form – some 178 double- columned pages, in the tiny print that was typical of the era. *Leaves* is more a detailed memoir than a diary as such, and its breathless subtitle, 'Incidents, Hairsbreadth Escapes and Remarkable Adventures', was presumably a sub-editor's embellishment.

Leaves is quite as fascinating and as dense in criminal language as anything ever published. It seems, unlike some of the modern 'hard man' memoirists who hymn their years of criminality in terms that one might feel owe more to the film script they hope to sell than to their actual speech patterns, absolutely without artifice. The use of contemporary cant appears unselfconscious – or as unselfconscious as it can be when every single instance is bookended with a pair of apostrophes. But the quote-marks soon vanish into the background: this, surely, is how our Burglar spoke. As for the 'incidents and adventures', they are undoubtedly there, albeit a little repetitive, as are the 'escapes', even if the Burglar and 'Joe', his main confederate, do serve a few months in jail. What matters, at least to the lexicographer, is of course the vocabulary.

The equivalent of the popular press can be found in a range of sensational literature, both fiction and 'fact', that appeared between 1830 and 1870. The essence of all this was that the city was of itself sensational and could be exploited as such. There were Asa Green's *A Glance at New York* (1837), G. G. Foster's *New York in Slices* (1849) and *New York by Gas-Light* (1856); James D. McCabe's *New York by Sunlight and Gaslight* (1862), *The Secrets of the Great City* (1868) and *Lights and Shadows of New York Life* (1872). Edward Z. Judson introduced *The G'hals of New York* in 1850 and the 'Members of the New York Press' added *The Night Side of New York* in 1866. All these were on the traditional titillation-cum-morality pattern, and larded themselves with 'authentic' slang to make sure their readers appreciated their insider expertise. Less worried about morality were the authors of sensationalist fiction whose yellow-backed works – the long-form version of the equally ribald penny papers – poured from the new Hoe cylinder presses, introduced in 1832.

Rowdy journals aside, America offered plenty of other printed popular entertainment. America's equivalent to the British penny dreadful or shilling shocker was the dime novel. The first, *Maleaska, the Indian Wife of the White Hunter*, by Ann S. Stephens, appeared in 1860. Its publisher, Beadle and Adams, used it to launch a new genre of publication: Beadle's Dime Novel. The dimes gave you approximately 100 pages, measured 6.5 by 4.25 inches (17 by 10.8 cm), though sizes would vary, and cost, as one would expect, ten cents (a dime). Though costs varied too: Beadle, for instance, issued Half-Dime Novels. At the then equivalent of one English shilling they were more expensive than the British dreadfuls, but instead of a long-running serial, one received an entire story. They thrived in the US, and were translated into a dozen European languages. The dime became a staple of US boyhood, with characters such as Nick Carter, Frank Merriwell, and heavily fictionalized 'biographies' of such as Buffalo Bill entering the youthful consciousness. They provided easy, if disapproved reading for soldiers on both sides in the US Civil War. In 1865 a chaplain from the US Christian Commission reported his confiscation of '2 "Dick Turpin"; 2 "Pirates Son", 4 "Flying Artillerist",' and one copy each of '"Red Rover", "Iron Cross", "Red King" and "Jacob Faithful".'[18]

The dimes lasted for over fifty years but like other forms of mass amusement failed to survive World War I. After that a new form of popular print emerged, harder-edged in both content and language and aimed at an older audience. Among its primary creators were one of Beadle and Adams's main competitors, Street and Smith, who were among the most successful publishers of this new style: the pulps.

The dimes could use slang but, with their strange mixture of propriety and sensation, they were never over-slangy. The Old Sleuth, for instance, in *Dock Rats of the New York* (1908) uses fifty-odd terms but many are almost 'respectable': *I'll be blowed*, *drop to* (recognize), *chicken-hearted*, *come something over*, *have dead*, *do over*, *chap*, *by ginger!*, *hot spot*, *inside track*, *in for it*, *open-and-shut*, *pipe* (to survey), *smart-alec*, *take the starch out of*, and *just the ticket*. He offers the first use of *shake*, to avoid a pursuer, and *program*, an established routine. But there are no obscenities, nothing louche, not even a double-entendre.

Of the 1,000-plus writers who contributed to the dimes – among them such un-copyrighted stars as Charles Dickens, though most were effectively anonymous and are lost to literary history – the most celebrated is Edward Zane Carroll Judson, better known by his pseudonym of 'Ned Buntline'. It was he who wrote 'The Black Anger of the Spanish Main', immortalized by its having been read by Mark Twain's Tom Sawyer. That his 1952 biography, by Jay Monaghan, is entitled *The Great Rascal* perhaps says a sufficiency. He was variously a political rabble-rouser, who advocated 'reform'; (for which read aggressive nativist hostility to immigration), street thug, con-man, journalist, playwright and all-purpose hack (his bibliography runs to at least 150 full-length books, plus many contributions to journals and other publications). His best-known single work was *Mysteries and Miseries of New York* (five volumes, 1848–9). Taking his inspiration from Eugene Sue's novel *Les Mystères de Paris* (serialized 1842–3), Judson set out in the traditional manner to plunge into the lower depths of gambling, prostitution, crime and violence and set it out in exposé form for titillated middle-class eyes. And like his predecessors in the form, he appreciated the power of slang to convey 'truth' to his tale. Of the near-400 slang terms he used, in dimes and elsewhere, just over one-third are cant (and 40% of those are to be found in Matsell).

If London could boast its rumbustious Cockney costers, and Sydney its larrikins, New York had the Bowery B'hoy. The B'hoy, whose spelling suggests his origins among the Irish immigrant population, might be a butcher, a manual labourer or a club bouncer; most often he was also a 'fire laddie', running to put out blazes with one of the city's fire companies, fiercely antagonistic groups whose scuffles over the nearest fire hydrant might well persist longer than the fire itself. Naturally, he had a uniform: 'The Bowery Boy promenaded his favorite thoroughfare with his head crowned by a high beaver hat with the nap divided and brushed different ways, while his stalwart figure was encased in an elegant frock coat, and about his throat was knotted a gaudy kerchief. His pantaloons, cut almost as full as the modern Oxford bags, were turned up over his heavy boots. The hair on the back of his head was clipped close and his neck and chin were shaven, while his temple locks were daintily curled and heavily anointed with bear's grease or some other powerful, evil-smelling unguent.' [19] He often sported a bright red shirt, indicating his connection with the fire companies, who were similarly attired. He had a rolling walk, a surly manner, puffed regularly on a 'long nine' cigar tipped up at 45 degrees into the air and, of course, came out with a good line in slang.

The B'hoy was easily recognizable, and his gang was one of those who were exploited in the sectarian rivalries of contemporary politics. But it would take the stage to render him omnipresent. The first night of Benjamin A. Baker's play *A Glance at New York in 1848* opened at the Olympic Theatre on 15 February 1848. It starred the actor Frank S. Chanfrau as 'Mose', the Bowery B'hoy and member of the city fire department. Chanfrau was Bowery-born and had been a member of a fire company; and Mose had a real-life origin, one Moses Humphreys, who was a printer on the New York *Sun* and a runner with the fire brigade's Lady Washington engine company No. 40; he was also well-known as a tough fighter. Allegedly the only man who beat him was Chanfrau's elder brother, Harvey, whereupon Humphreys quit New York for the Sandwich islands. Like Egan's *Life in London*, and the play based on his book, it was more *tour d'horizon* than sequential, plotted narrative, but unlike the Corinthian and his cousin, the cast experienced only those scenes already well-known to working-class New Yorkers. Though such plot as it did have – streetwise New Yorker Mose shepherding the naïve Yankee George (rather than the usual Jonathan) through the snares and delusions of the metropolis – was slightly reminiscent of Tom's education of Jerry.

It was a first night to remember. Chanfrau, so authentically dressed that as he waited to go onstage the theatre manager was about to throw him out as a loafer, stepped from the wings: 'He stood there in his red shirt, with his fire coat thrown over his arm, the stovepipe hat – better known as a "plug" – drawn down over one eye, his trousers tucked into his boots, a stump of a cigar pointing up from his lips to his eye, the soap locks plastered flat on his temples, and his jaw protruded into a half-beastly, half-human expression of contemptuous ferocity. For a moment the audience eyed him in silence; not a hand or foot gave him welcome. Taking the cigar stump from his mouth and turning half-way round to spit, he said: "I ain't a goin' to run wid dat mercheen no more!" Instantly there arose such a yell of recognition as had never been heard in the little house before.'[20]

Like Tom and Jerry, Mose moved beyond mere on-stage stardom. Like an urban reincarnation of America's earlier superhero Paul Bunyan, and the 'half-alligator half-horse' backwoodsmen of *The Spirit of the Times*, Mose was credited with powers beyond any human. Whether the New York fireman was 'world renowned' might be debated, but that, as the posters also proclaimed, he was 'far-famed' was in no doubt.[21] Other entertainment media – the circus, the ballet – offered alternative versions of the hero; there were posters, lithographs, humorous booklets and illustrated sets of his adventures, song-sheets. His catchphrases were heard across the nation: 'Sykesey, take the butt' (a reference both to the end of the fire hose and to that of Mose's cigar) and 'Get off dem hose or I'll hit yer wid a spanner.' His language entered the greater one: ' "Blow your horn," he says to his g'hal Lizey, requesting a song, and after its completion compliments her with, "Well I'm blowd if that ain't slap up. Lize, you can sing a few." "Gallus" was a favorite adjective of emphasis; "de butt" signified the hose, and "der merchine" the fire-engine; to "make a muss" was to start a row; "foo-foos" represented outsiders "wot can't come de big figure," i.e., three cents for a glass of grog and a night's lodgings.'[22] And there are always picturesque and popular backdrops (and trips abroad as play followed play), much knockabout humour, the defeat of evil in the form of sharpers and con-men, and the rousing finale as the fire laddies do their job, rescuing babies, ladies or both.

Mose was quite literally fantastic but Mose, even if he had a real-life avatar, was fiction. New York's slums were not. The Fourth and Sixth Wards, the notorious Five Points, what would be known as the Lower East Side, had attracted tides of immigrants, starting with Irish and

Germans and followed by Jews and Italians. There had been blacks too, but they had been driven ever further up-town by the hostility of impoverished native Americans and of Irish immigrants, whose own place at the bottom of the social ladder was only made tolerable by forcing blacks one rung lower.

By the late nineteenth century the slums were enjoying something of a celebrity. In 1891 the social commentator Jacob Riis had informed the comfortable world of *How the Other Half Lives*, and after reading him and others, the well-brought-up middle classes trooped downtown to see just that. Slumming parties were organized and sallied forth, even if they tended to stay shuddering behind the carriage door. Like London America had its slum literature, which mixed pious sanctimony with literary slumming. The former professed horror at the slum-dweller's experience of the usual demons – drink, women, tobacco – and besought him most earnestly to overcome them; praising him if he did and condemning him as lost if he failed and plunged even deeper into the pit. 'Slumming' came in such works as Edgar Fawcett's *The Evil That Men Do* (1889), Kate Douglas Wiggin's *Timothy's Quest* (1890), H. H. Boyeson's *Social Strugglers* (1893) and James W. Sullivan's *Tenement Tales of New York* (1895), which was seen as a homegrown version of H. W. Nevison's recent *Neigbours of Ours* (1895), issued in the US as *Slum Tales of London*. Realism, as pioneered in France by Zola, arrived with Stephen Crane's *Maggie, a Girl of the Streets* (1893), where slang plays an important role in delineating many characters, but there were no equivalents of the more humorous Cockney novelists such as Edwin Pugh or William Pett Ridge. Edward Townsend's 'Chimmie Fadden' (*Chimmie Fadden*, 1895, and several sequels) part-depends on laughs, but the author –whose *A Daughter of the Tenements* (1895) was built on the established plan – took his slangy youngster out of the slums within a chapter, and although his adventures occupied multiple volumes, Chimmie remained within Townshend's version of a bourgeois if at times bohemian world. Like Townshend, Sewell Ford featured a bright slum kid, heavy on the 'dese-dem-and-dose', in his stories of *Shorty McCabe* (1906) and *Shorty McCabe on the Job* (1912). He also operated uptown.

For a lighter take on life, one had to follow Chimmie or Shorty away from the slums. To the work of, among others, George Ade, 'Hugh

McHugh' (properly known as George V. Hobart), Helen Green and Clarence L. Cullen. These, and others, stayed within the middle class but veered towards its more rackety denizens.

Ade, the mid-Westerner, had no commitment to New York but often worked with such urban types as salesmen, while sending his yokels townwards with predictably unfortunate results (though not invariably for the hick). A century on Ade is quasi-forgotten, but he was a huge hit, whose credo was 'Give the People what they Think they want' and whose first best-seller, *Fables in Slang*, sold 69,000 in its launch year of 1899. There were nine further collections plus Broadway hits, novels, essays and the rest. For the twenty years of his peak success every week brought him $1,000 from newspaper syndication and $5,000 more from stage royalties. The masses loved him; so too did the contemporary critics. William D. Howells saw him as that ever-awaited messiah, the great American novelist, Mark Twain, no mean exploiter of slang, added his tenpenn'orth of adulation, H. L. Mencken fêted a genuinely original literary craftsman. A town in Indiana, a football stadium (at Purdue University) and a World War II Liberty ship were all named for him. He had a 400-acre estate where he gave dinners for hundreds and parties for thousands. President-to-be Taft launched his campaign at one of them.

Perhaps his success stemmed from his universality: fables have no geography, only a moral, which in Ade's case was invariably laced with irony. Or his mid-Western background that comforted those who believed – then as now – that New York was Satan's city. For many this made him even more important; an echt-American: as one critic noted, the mud of Indiana had stuck to him long enough to charm him against 'foreign' influences.

It is not so much whether the wit stands up. For some it still works, at least the early Fables do, with their plethora of Germanic capitalisation and their wordy, insinuating titles: 'The Fable of the Good Fairy with the Lorgnette, and Why She Got It Good'; 'The Fable of the New York Person Who Gave the Stage Fright to Fostoria, Ohio', or 'The Fable of the Brash Drummer and the Peach Who Learned that There Were Others'. Or equally early stories such as *Artie* (an office boy) or *Pink Marsh* (a black shoe-shine). For the lexicographer what matters are the near 1,600 slang terms that Ade incorporates in his works.

Ade was not alone. Late-nineteenth- to early-twentieth-century America offered a number of writers who depended on slang for effect. The journalist Helen Green (later writing under her married name Helen Green van Campen), wrote of a Broadway theatrical hotel ('The Maison de Shine') and, offering not a speck of moralizing, the con-men, morphine addicts and vaudeville acts who frequented it. George Vere Hobart published twenty-three books as 'Hugh McHugh', celebrating his character 'John Henry' and mocking his critics in prefaces that paraded his latest phenomenal sales figures. Whether P. G. Wodehouse, who was visiting New York at the time, read 'John Henry' is unknown, but his character 'Bingo Little' has undeniable similarities. Hobart also wrote plays and dialect humour, featuring both German immigrants – in *D. Dinkelspiel: his Gonversationings* (1900) – and Jews – *Ikey's Letters to His Father* (1907) – although in this there is slang rather than dialect, and Ikey's long-suffering father, recipient of the posts, speaks standard American. Among the many others were Clarence L. Cullen, who wrote two volumes of *Tales of the Ex-Tanks* (i.e. ex-alcoholics), W. J. Kountz with *Billy Baxter's Letters* (1899), 'Billy Burgundy''s *Toothsome Tales Told in Slang* (1902) and Roy McCardell's *Conversations of a Chorus Girl* (1903 and seemingly a predecessor of Anita Loos's *Gentlemen Prefer Blondes*, 1925). O. Henry occupies a category of his own, but his urban tales such as *The Four Million* (1906) and *The Voice of the City* (1908) are studded with the language of the street.

There was also a new source of amusement: newspaper comics and cartoons.

There were many, often appearing in a special section of the newspapers. Perhaps best known, and slangiest, were the cartoonist T. A. Dorgan, known as TAD and to whom slang coinages are (mis-)attributed just as one-liners are to Wilde or Dorothy Parker, and Bud Fisher's *A Mutt*, created in the form of a racing tip cartoon in 1907 and who in 1908 would gain a long-term partner called Jeff.

Alongside the public, the newspapers and the publishers, the chief beneficiaries of this outflowing of US humour were the lexicographers, notably John Russell Bartlett and Maximilian Schele de Vere (noted above). Like standard lexicographers of the period they were solo artistes, learned amateurs, but they could see that American English was rapidly moving away from its British parent, and were determined to chart that journey.

John Pickering, the first such, produced A *Vocabulary: or, Collection of words and phrases, which have been supposed to be peculiar to the United States of America* in 1816. He mentions vulgarity in his introduction, and notes that his aim is to create 'a *glossary of provincialisms*'[23] (London still being seen as the linguistically authoritative metropolis), but there is little slang on show, the nearest example being his entry for *slangwhanger*, despite appearances still a standard English term and which is defined as a 'noisy *talker*, who makes of that sort of political or other cant, which amuses the rabble, and is called by the vulgar name of *slang*'.[24]

In 1816 Pickering had still been able to regret that 'in this country we can hardly be said to have any authors by profession'.[25] By the time his successor John Russell Bartlett began the work that would appear in three editions and over 30 years,[26] American letters, both literary and even more importantly for the collection of 'Americanisms', popular, had changed. Bartlett began work as a collector of Americanisms in the mid-1840s. His initial idea had been 'to publish a supplement to Pickering's *Vocabulary*, but I soon found that I had already collected sufficient to make a volume much larger than that of Pickering. I then came to the conclusion that I would prepare and print a work on an entire different plan, viz. that of a "Dictionary". I now set vigorously to work; ran over the numerous books which contained the familiar and the vulgar or slang language of the country and thus greatly increased my vocabulary of new words with examples of their use.'[27]

The *Dictionary of Americanisms: A Glossary of Words and Phrases, Colloquially used in the United States* – in a first edition of 750 copies – appeared in 1848. It included, as far as his researches allowed, 'all the words, whatever be their origin, which are used in familiar conversation, and but seldom employed in composition—all the perversions of language and abuses of words into which people, in certain sections of the country, have fallen, and some of those remarkable and ludicrous forms of speech which have been adopted in the Western States.'[28] It offers around 200 terms that qualify as slang.

He had used all available dictionaries for research, but these were not words he could find there. For the slang he drew on newspapers, such as the *New York Evening Star*, the *New York Evening Post*, the *New York Advocate* and *The Spirit of the Times*, which he saw as the ideal repositories of colloquialism, and on the contemporary humorists: T. C. Haliburton, Seba Smith, C. A. Davis (who had produced a rival 'Major Downing'), W. T. Thomspon (*Major Jones's Courtship* and *Chronicles of Pineville*), A. B. Longstreet (*Georgia Scenes*), the autobiographical writings of Davy Crockett, Asa Greene (*A Glance at New York*), J. C. Neal (*Brother Jonathan* and *Charcoal Sketches*), 'Jonathan Slick' (*High Life in New York*), and many others.

A second edition, 'Greatly Improved and Enlarged', appeared in 1859. There were substantial cuts – around 30% of the original headwords – but Bartlett added many more than he removed and made good the oversights in his initial research. A reprint, termed the third edition, appeared in 1860 and the 'real' third, further expanded and revised, in 1877. He noted that 'To the Indian, the Dutch, the German, the French, and the Spanish elements, there have been but few contributions. From the arts, from new inventions, from new settlements, particularly those in mining districts, from commerce, many new words have been adopted; while the late civil war has also furnished its share. But, perhaps, the larger share of the additions is from the vocabulary of slang.'[29]

Bartlett remains the most important early collector of Americanisms. His work set in motion an on-going tradition, seen at its best in R. H. Thornton's *American Glossary* (1912), Sir William Craigie's *Dictionary of American English* (1936), and Craigie's former collaborator Mitford M. Mathew's *Dictionary of Americanisms* (1951). More recently the multi-volume *Dictionary of American Regional English* (1985 et seq.), based on a wide-ranging and highly detailed questionnaire, has developed Bartlett to an unprecedented extent.

Before the first dedicated slang dictionary was published in 1859, one slightly anomalous glossary appeared in 1848. This was carried in *The Ladies' Repository*, published by the Methodist church in Cincinnati and edited by a succession of preachers. The intention of the magazine was to provide women with something other than the usual diet of romantic stories and fashion tips, and replace it with moral earnestness, a selection of poetry and useful information on history and science. It wished, said its editor, to entertain as well as instruct. It was to that end, perhaps, that from 1853 it also carried a section headed 'Apothegm, Wit, Repartee, and Anecdote'. The article on slang was headed 'The Flash Language' and appeared as part of a feature 'Pencilings from Pittsburgh', based on conversations between its compiler, the Revd B. F. Tefft and a convict he encountered in the Pennsylvania penitentiary. There are 190 terms, all of which are, as would be expected, cant.

The *Vocabulum: or, the Rogue's Lexicon, Compiled from the Most Authentic Sources*, by New York City police chief George Washington Matsell, was published in 1859, contemporaneously with the first edition of John Camden Hotten's *Modern Slang, Cant, and Vulgar Words*. It was the first such volume to appear in the United States, and would remain pretty much unique for some time to come. (The next such dictionary, Alfred Trumble's 1881 *Slang Dictionary of New York, London and Paris* was a word-for-word plagiarism of Matsell). Aside from the glossaries included by Mount and Tufts, and that offered by the *Ladies' Repository*, the only possible predecessor is a short glossary appended by Edward Z. Judson to *The Mysteries and Miseries of New York*.

Matsell would not have been able to see Hotten's work, but he presumably had a copy of 'Egan's Grose', since much of that word-list is included in the *Vocabulum*. This is not to belittle Matsell: American cant still appears to have been apeing its English origins. So is the style of the work. Matsell terms himself a lexicographer, albeit much to his own surprise. 'To become a lexicographer, certainly never entered into my calculation, or even found a place in the castle-building of my younger days; and if a kind friend had suggested [it] to me ... I would have simply regarded him as a fit subject for the care of the authorities.'[30] Now Matsell was working primarily to educate his own employees. 'Experience has taught me that any man engaged in police business cannot excel without understanding the rogues' language',[31] and he intended to remedy that want.

Matsell seems to have got it right. If one accepts the late-nineteenth-century report of the writer William Cumming Wilde, both criminals and policemen backed up the *Vocabulum's* lexis. Wilde cited the book both to 'one of the most desperate characters that our city has produced' and to 'one of the best as well as oldest detectives in our country [...] a man who has followed his profession for fully half a century'. Both supported the accuracy of Matsell's lists. And 'subsequent interviews with some of the best officers on our police force fully confirmed this'.[32]

Certainly Matsell was far from wholly dependent on other lexicographers. To look only at the letter 'B' – for which *Vocabulum* lists some 127 headwords –one finds the following thirty-nine terms (nearly one-third) that for which, to date, his is the first recorded use: *badger* (a thief who rifles the pockets of a man who is currently engaged with his accomplice, a prostitute), *badger-crib* (a brothel wherein one is robbed), *barney* (a fake fight, arranged by criminals to distract a potential victim's attention), *beat* (to rob), *beaters* (boots), *bet one's eyes* (to watch a game but not get involved in the betting), *big thing* (a large amount of plunder), *bingo-boy* (a drunkard), *bit* (arrested), *blarney* (a picklock), *take a blinder* (to die), *blink* (to go to sleep), *bludget* (a female thief), *boarding house* (a prison), *boat* (to transport a convict), *boat with* (to become partners with), *boated* (sentenced to a long term in prison), *body cover* (an overcoat), *boke / boko* (the nose), *booby-hatch* (a police station), *boshing* (a whipping), *bots* (boots), *bracket-mug* (an ugly face), *break o'day drum* (all-night tavern), *break a leg* (to seduce), *broad-pitching* ('three-card monte'), *brother (of the) bolus* (a doctor), *brother of the surplice* (a priest), *brush* (to 'soften up' a victim), *buck* (an unlicensed cab-driver), *bugger* (a pickpocket), *bully* (a cosh), *bummer* (a scavenger), *bumy-juice* (beer), *burned out* (exhausted), *burner* (a card-sharp), *burst* (a spree), *burster* (a burglar), *butteker* and *butter-ken* (a shop), *buttered* (whipped), and *button* (to act as a confidence trickster's accomplice).

Matsell was undoubtedly the most colourful of such policemen-turned-lexicographers. When he edited his glossary he had recently retired after a dozen years as New York City's first ever Chief of Police. He would return in 1874 under a new title, Commissioner, but it would be a brief tenure. A former Tammany Hall politician, Matsell was a notorious character. As a politician he had been a keen supporter of a properly organized police force, replacing the random collection of municipal functionaries who had hitherto struggled to maintain law and order in the ever-expanding metropolis. When in 1845 such a body, the New York Police Department, was established, Matsell got the job. It was a generally popular appointment, although one critic apostrophized the gargantuan Chief, who weighed more than 300lb (around 22 stone), as 'a

Beastly Bloated Booby'.[33] Matsell proved nothing if not accommodating in his enforcement of the city statutes. His was a very passive regime, bending cheerfully to the current political wind. In outward show, however, Matsell was exemplary. He put the police into uniforms, on the lines of their British contemporaries, and instituted proper training. He established a rudimentary system of communication between his office and the various precincts.

But in the end Matsell was perceived to be at least as sinful as those whom his men pursued. His enforcement of the Fugitive Slave Law of 1850 had him branded a 'slave catcher' by Horace Greeley's *Tribune*; his financial affairs were seen as dubious at best; he skimmed the profits of the city's gambling dens; his dealings with the restoration of stolen property echoed those of London's Jonathan Wild, the eighteenth-century 'thief-taker' who personally fenced the stolen goods he had confiscated from the original robbers; he ran a lucrative 'referral' trade, passing on arrested people to a coterie of lawyers who paid him a kickback for every new client. It was even claimed that he extorted money from clients of the well-known, and much vilified, abortionist and specialist in contraception Madame Restell, also known as Ann Lohmann – actually an Englishwoman born Caroline Ann Trow. It was further suggested that Matsell worked as her partner. The Chief responded to all such attacks with an outraged innocence, but his tenure does seem to have brought him many material rewards. His basic salary can hardly have funded the twenty-room house in Viola, Iowa, where he and his family spent their summers. It boasted a 3,000-acre estate and a brimming wine cellar. Their parties were legendary.

What brought Matsell down, ironically in a town where the police have long been associated affectionately with the Irish community (thus such slang terms as *shamus*, *shamrock* and *muldoon* for policeman), was the accusation that he allowed too many Irish immigrants to enter the force. Matsell claimed that their representation echoed that of the population at large (some 28% of the citizens, 27% of the force), but his accusers had found a lever to topple him, and they used it. In 1857, when the NYPD was reorganized as the Metropolitan Police Department, he lost his job. He turned his attentions to the *National Police Gazette*, 'the only authentic record of Crime and Criminal Jurisprudence in the

United States'. Matsell returned, amid much controversy, as one of New York's Police Commissioners, in 1874. This time, however, he lasted but two years.

Aside from Trumble's plagiarism, America did produce one more nineteenth-century slang dictionary: the *American Slang Dictionary* (1891) by the Chicago journalist James Maitland. His aim, as stated, was 'to include what may be termed the slang of the Anglo-Saxon, whether he dwell in London or New York, in Chicago or Sydney'.[34] He claimed himself superior to all predecessors (although accepting his 'great obligations' to many of them). The sole exception was Hotten, whom he assumed to be an American and from whom, as Julie Coleman has itemized, he took many entries.[35] He is dismissive of much of the lexis. 'In [Hotten's] otherwise valuable work far too much space is devoted to the Cant of the Gipsies, to the thieves patter of St. Giles's clerks, and to obsolete matters generally [...] The Elizabethan dramatists bristle with the slang of a by-gone age, but it has been forgotten both in England and in this country. Much of the Gipsy cant is unintelligible and obsolete. The rubbishing back slang of the London school boy is not worth mention [...] The rhyming slang which speaks of rain as "Mary Jane" or "alecampane" indifferently is of no possible interest [...] For the omission of the indecent phrases which disfigure so many books upon slang no apology is needed.'[36] What remains has not been much admired. A contemporary reviewer suggested that while Maitland's work 'has no reason to show for its existence, [it] furnishes a good many reasons to suggest the desirability of its non-existence.'[37] Prof. Coleman believes that the book is not 'considerably worse than others in circulation at the time' but that its author's 'misfortune [...] was to publish at a time when reviewers, and perhaps the reading public at large, were beginning to hope for something better'.[38]

One figure who definitely hoped for something better and who might stand as America's great lexicographer *manqué* was the poet Walt Whitman.[39] While he remains best known for *Leaves of Grass* (1855), there exist a number of papers, both published and unpublished, that reveal Whitman's interest in philology, his desire to see a new dictionary of the English language that would go far beyond any predecessor, and his over-riding interest in slang. He published only two pieces on language, both magazine articles: 'America's Mightiest Inheritance', in *Life Illustrated* for 12 April 1856, and 'Slang in America', in the *North American Review* of November 1885. It has also been suggested that the book *Rambles Among Words* (1859) by William Swinton was at least partially ghost-written by the poet-philologer. It is clear from a series of notebooks, entitled simply 'Words', and the wide range of notes and clippings on language in general and slang in particular that Whitman assembled that this was an important part of his life. As he told his friend Horace Traubel in 1888, 'As to the slang itself—you know I was an industrious collector; slang was one of my specialties.'[40]

'Slang in America' does not, however, display Whitman's learning especially well. It was, as Michael Dressman has described it, 'a rather rambling and general set of observations on the nature of "slang" and some of its manifestations in the United States'.[41]

Whitman gives due credit to slang's role as a counter-language: it is 'the lawless germinal element, below all words and sentences, and behind all poetry, and proves a certain perennial rankness and protestantism [i.e. the condition of protesting] in speech'. It is, to draw a parallel with Shakespeare, a clown at the royal court of some 'mighty potentate'. It is 'an attempt of common humanity to escape from bald literalism, and express itself illimitably, which in highest walks produces poets and poems, and doubtless in pre-historic times gave the start to, and perfected, the whole immense tangle of the old mythologies. [...] Slang, too, is the wholesome fermentation or eructation of those processes eternally active in language, by which froth and specks are thrown up, mostly to pass away; though occasionally to settle and permanently chrystallize [sic].' And its essence is that it comes from the bottom up. 'Language, be it remember'd, is not an abstract construction of the learn'd, or of dictionary-makers, but is something arising out of the work, needs, ties, joys, affections, tastes, of long generations of humanity, and has its bases broad and low, close to the ground. Its final decisions are made by the masses, people nearest the concrete, having most to do with actual land and sea.' And he concludes, 'Language is more like some vast living body, or perennial body of bodies. And slang not only brings the first feeders of it, but is afterward the start of fancy, imagination and humor, breathing into its nostrils the breath of life.'[42]

As the century turned, Whitman's slang – and America's slang – was still very much in embryo. Today it dominates the slang lexis. And while the slang of the nineteenth century, at least as used and recorded, was almost universally seen as white, this new slang, the slang of the twentieth century and beyond, would come from a group who would play a vast role in other important areas of US popular culture: its black community.

12 Keeping Score: Nineteenth-century Slang Lexicography

If, with a relatively limited selection of alternative sources, one has had to look at lexicographers such as B. E. or Francis Grose to see what was developing in the slang lexis, this has changed by the nineteenth century. Rather than representing a vocabulary, the collectors and codifiers are taking on a much more modern role: riding herd on its boisterous expansion. They are, one might say, keeping score. One might have dared feel, especially prior to Grose, that what was assembled between covers was a pretty fair summation of what was on offer. This was no longer so. Those who would follow would do their best, but one has the sense that there could be more out there. Slang was developing and expanding and its sources becoming more available. In turn slang dictionaries responded by becoming more sophisticated, moving beyond the simple A [word] = B [definition] with the occasional C [etymology]. Full-scale 'historical principles' lexicography might not be achieved, but it was attempted and by the end of the century a multi-volume work would appear that, in its own sphere, could be said to echo the *New English Dictionary* that was in preparation in Oxford. The mid- to late-nineteenth-century dictionaries were far less 'personalized' than had been Grose and his predecessors. Working as a professional rather than a scholarly dilettante, the lexicographer attempted to efface himself from the text. There would be no more dictionaries like that of 'Jon Bee', which at times seemed as much a personal crusade (against Pierce Egan) as a disinterested lexicon.

Nonetheless, slang lexicographers remained, as they do today, outside the academy. Slang dictionaries were created by individuals, working as freelances, often plagued by financial problems and forced into additional 'day jobs'. The second half of the century saw three major dictionaries (one regularly expanded and then kept in print long after its author's death), written by one individual and a pair of teams: John Camden Hotten, Albert Barrère and C. G. Leland, and James S. Farmer and W. E. Henley.

It is Hotten whose dictionary, published in revised editions between 1859 and 1873, and the first ever to use the word 'slang' in its title, indicates how far slang had come since 1785. While the lexis would undoubtedly go further, the greatest importance of the two multi-volume slang dictionaries that succeeded him in the century's final decade is as much in their form – notably the inclusion of citations – as in their content.

Hotten, christened John William Hotten, was born in St John's Square, Clerkenwell, on 12 September 1832. At the age of fourteen he was apprenticed to a Chancery Lane bookseller, in whose employ he gained a precocious interest in rare and curious books. It was during his apprenticeship that Hotten was supposedly thumped with a large quarto edition by the historian Thomas Babington Macaulay, irritated by the young man's failure to make change sufficiently speedily. In 1848 he and his brother sailed for America, a trip that, according to Mark Twain, was necessitated by Hotten's having been caught out selling his master's stock for his own profit. First stop was 'the West India Islands, which was to be the field for a Robinson Crusoe scheme of adventure', with the Hottens narrowly avoiding shipwreck and landing with 'two chests of books, and two chests of tools and fire-locks—the latter we thought necessary to build and protect there a wooden house or castle we decided upon building'.[1] The castaway life lasted six weeks before the brothers moved on to America, where they separated. Hotten, who apparently worked as a miner as well as a freelance writer, remained in America until in 1856 he re-emerged in London.

Here he capitalized on his teenage interests to open a small bookshop at 151b Piccadilly. This was replaced, once Hotten had established his firm, by larger premises at 74–75 Piccadilly. Hotten seems to have been considered somewhat 'fast' and definitely modern by his contemporaries. Today he would be termed a workaholic. Writing to the *Bookseller* shortly after his death, a correspondent, 'R. H. S.' (Hotten's friend the bibliographer Richard Herne Shepherd), laid out a day that lasted, with the briefest of lunch breaks, from ten in the morning to nine at night. And after that work, or even an aspirant author, would be taken home for further consideration. There was, he suggested, 'something heroic in all this, even if of a degenerate modern kind'. Hotten, in the writer's eyes, was 'essentially "a man of the time" [who] felt he must keep pace with the railroad speed of the age, or leave others to outstrip him in the race'.[2]

While in America he had made himself into something of an expert in American literature and among his earliest publishing ventures were editions of such contemporary Americans as Bret Harte, Oliver Wendell Holmes, James Russell Lowell and Artemus Ward. Other publications included C. G. Leland's celebrated (and slangy) poem 'Hans Breitmann's Party'; in 1889 Leland himself would help compile a slang dictionary in his turn. Hotten also wrote biographies of William Thackeray, whose fictional heroine Becky Sharp was seen as epitomizing a new age when, in the novel *Vanity Fair*, she tossed aside a recently presented copy of Johnson's *Dictionary*, and of Charles Dickens. His business, somewhat slow at the start, took off between 1865 and his death in 1873, and he published 446 titles, printing nearly 1.5 million books.

Hotten was a 'near-scholar'[3] whose fame was balanced by his notoriety. Alongside his own writing, his skilfully targeted general publishing, which R. H. S. praises as 'gauging the public taste, and supplying it with exactly the sort of literary pabulum it required'[4] and his slang lexicography, his success, or at least a good deal of his income, rested on his exploitation of what Partridge called 'the by-ways'[5] of Victorian life. One by-way that he explored enthusiastically was that of pornography. Compared with less savoury publishers, whose shops clustered along the notorious Holywell Street, Hotten was a relatively admirable figure. Henry Spencer Ashbee, the bibliographer of pornography, praised him as 'industrious, clever but not always reliable'.[6] Hotten had a special affection for this side of the business, calling it his 'flower garden', in which bloomed such titles as *The History of the Rod*, the illustrator Thomas Rowlandson's *Pretty Little Games* (a series of ten erotic plates), *Lady Bumtickler's Revels* and *The Romance of Chastisement*. Ashbee noted that 'he was almost the only respectable English publisher of tabooed literature, and in this he took great delight. His private library of erotic literature was extensive, and was, at his death, purchased *en bloc* by a London amateur.'[7]

Hotten died on 14 June 1873, at his house on Haverstock Hill near Hampstead; his business was sold to form the basis of another publisher, Chatto & Windus. Cause of death was either 'brain fever' or, as some claimed, a surfeit of pork chops. Swinburne, less than grateful, noted that, 'When I heard that [Hotten] had died of a surfeit of porkchops, I observed that this was a serious argument against my friend Richard Burton's views on cannibalism as a wholesome and natural method of diet.'[8] An anecdote, featuring either the poet-sociologist George R. Sims or the American Ambrose Bierce (later author of *The Devil's Dictionary*), tells how a writer appeared at the bookshop brandishing a cheque that had bounced. He commenced shouting only to discover that those present thought he was an undertaker, and informed him that the publisher had just died. It was definitely Sims who is credited with the last word: 'Hotten: rotten, forgotten.'[9]

Rotten or otherwise, Hotten is not forgotten. The other 'by-way' along which he travelled was that of slang and for that alone he remains pertinent. His *Dictionary of Modern Slang, Cant and Vulgar Words* appeared in 1859, the work, said the title-page, of 'a London Antiquary'. It sold out quickly, was rapidly reprinted and ran to several editions. (Those published after 1864 were retitled *The Slang Dictionary*). It remained the authoritative work for nearly forty years and still holds an important place in slang lexicography. Aside from the word-list itself, which expanded from the 4,500-odd entries of the first edition to around 6,000 by the final version published in 1873, Hotten made substantial advances in every aspect of his task. For the first time ever, a slang dictionary offered an overview of its subject. Hotten prefaced his work with a 'History of Cant, or the Secret Language of Vagabonds' and a 'Short History of Slang, or the Vulgar Language of Fast Life'. B. E. and Grose both made the distinction between cant and slang, but neither had specified exactly what the distinction was. Hotten explains it in some detail, although he notes in his Preface that 'although in the

Introduction I have divided Cant from Slang, and treated the subjects separately, yet in the Dictionary I have only, in a few instances, pointed out which are Slang, and which are Cant terms'. As he says, 'Many words which were once Cant are Slang now' and gives *prig* and *cove* as typical examples. His histories of both speech varieties are extensive, if not always conclusive. A glance at the running heads gives a flavour: 'Vulgar Words from the Gypsy', 'The Inventor of Canting Not Hanged', 'Swift and Arbuthnot Fond of Slang', 'The Poor Foreigners Perplexity'. He includes, as a bonus, the entire cant glossary included in Thomas Harman's *Caveat* (1566). He sees the influence of Romani on cant as substantial but adds, after a long discussion, that 'words have been drawn into the thieves' vocabulary from every conceivable source'.[10] To that end he notes sources in foreign languages, in Celtic and Gaelic and from *lingua franca*, the Italianate pidgin that would move from merchants to sailors and beyond that into the theatre and finally the camp gay world, where it was rechristened as Polari.

As for slang, he offers what still stands as one of its best definitions: 'Slang is the language of street humour, of fast, high, and low life. Cant, as was stated in the chapter upon that subject, is the vulgar language of secrecy. It must be admitted, however, that within the past few years they have become almost indivisible. They are both universal and ancient, and appear to have been, with certain exceptions, the offspring of gay, vulgar, or worthless persons in every part of the world at every period of time. Indeed, if we are to believe implicitly the saying of the wise man, that "there is nothing new under the sun," the "bloods" of buried Nineveh, with their knotty and door-matty-looking beards, may have cracked Slang jokes on the steps of Sennacherib's palace; while the stocks and stones of ancient Egypt, and the bricks of venerable and used-up Babylon, may be covered with Slang hieroglyphs [...]. Slang is almost as old as speech, and must date from the congregating together of people in cities. It is the result of crowding, and excitement, and artificial life. [...] It is often full of the most pungent satire, and is always to the point. Without point Slang has no raison d'etre.'[11]

He has lists of rhyming slang and of back-slang, both prefaced by a brief history and discussion. There is, again for the first time ever, a Bibliography of Slang and Cant, listing some 120 titles, plus his own critical comments on each. Hotten stresses that above all this is a dictionary of '*modern* Slang – a list of colloquial words and phrases in *present* use – whether of ancient or modern formation'.[12] Thus he has omitted obsolete terms. He has also, unlike Grose, opted to exclude 'filthy and obscene words'[13] although he acknowledges their prevalence in street-talk and deals at length with oaths. He touches on jargon, without describing it as such, and thus deals, both in his Introduction and in the *Dictionary*,with the terminology of the *beau monde*, politics, the army and navy, both high and low church, the law, literature, the universities and the theatre. He has a list of slang terms for money, one of oaths, one for drunkenness and deals with the language of shopkeepers and workmen. It is, for a relatively condensed work, a little over 300 pages in all, a great achievement.

In Hotten one sees the bridge between Grose, who for all his own advances was still using only the most basic of lexicographical disciplines, and Farmer and Henley's historically based lexicography, including citations, numbered homonyms, and an attempt to include all the available vocabulary. In many ways Hotten's most important contribution is that for the first time ever one finds an effort, by no means consistent, nor invariably accurate, to trace the etymology of the slang vocabulary. Nonetheless, as he makes clear, 'Slang derivations are generally indirect, turning upon metaphor and fanciful allusions, and other than direct etymological connexion. Such allusions and fancies are essentially temporary or local; they rapidly pass out of the public mind; the word remains, while the key to its origin is lost.'[14] That problem continues to assail slang lexicographers; the underlying ephemerality of an essentially spoken language will always hinder attempts to chase down the origins of slang. Hotten did his best and manages some form of etymology for about 50 per cent of the entries.

The best-selling *Slang Dictionary* remains Hotten's only personal foray into lexicography. In the endpapers of the 1867 edition he announced 'A Dictionary of Colloquial English': it did not materialize. He did, however, publish two translations: an 1860 edition of the 1528 edition of the *Liber Vagatorum* (with its forward by Martin Luther) and that entitled *Argot Parisien* (1872), of the French lexicographer Lorédan Larchey's *Eccentricités de la langue* (1862).

If John Camden Hotten had established his work as *the* slang dictionary of the mid-nineteenth century, he was overtaken before its end. Two slang collections appeared in the 1880s. Henrich Baumann's *Londonismen (Slang und Cant)* appeared in Berlin in 1887. Baumann (*c.* 1846–1912) was born in Prussia and worked in various teaching posts in London. It expanded Hotten's word-list and effectively replaced him, but as a German publication never really impinged on the English-speaking market. Among its idiosyncrasies was the use of a tiny gallows symbol to denote the cant, rather than general slang vocabulary. He offered a substantial and wide-ranging introduction, covering all aspects of slang – and including military terms, school slang, Romani, Americanisms and so on, as well as notes on the pronunciation, syntax and grammar of Cockney – but it remained off-limits other than for those who read German. That he essayed pronunciation at all was impressive – it is rarely if ever attempted by slang lexicographers – but even here he opted for difficulty, using his publishers' in-house Toussaint-Langenscheidt method, dauntingly complex even for German speakers, rather than the new and more widely accessible IPA system, which would be instituted in 1888.

The second such work, that of Albert Barrère and C. G. Leland, which appeared in the booksellers under the title *A Dictionary of Slang, Jargon and Cant* in 1889–90 (there had already been a slightly earlier, privately circulated edition), has always suffered by comparison with that of their successors, Farmer and Henley. Their work was smaller, two volumes to their successors' magisterial seven, and they were unfortunate in having barely twelve months' pause between their first volume and the appearance of the new collection. And while they are far from devoid of merit they lack their successors' scholarship.

Barrère (*c.* 1845–1921) was a one-time teacher of French to the cadets of Sandhurst, author of a book on French grammar and idioms and co-writer of a history of French literature. His dictionary of French argot, *Argot and Slang: A New French and English Dictionary of the Cant Words, Quaint Expressions, Slang Terms and Flash Phrases used in the High and Low Life of Old and New Paris*, was published in 1887. The celebrity of his American collaborator, the prolific Charles Godfrey Leland (1824–93), lay in his creation 'Hans Breitmann' (see Chapter 11) and in his mastery of Romani culture and language. Independently wealthy, he was able to play the gentleman-scholar.

The compilers enlisted the aid of a variety of experts. As Barrère boasted in his preface, 'The present is the first Slang Dictionary ever written which has the benefit of contributors who thoroughly understood Celtic dialects, Dutch, German and French slang ... [and] Pidgin-English, Gypsy and Shelta.' Their dictionary is the first to include American slang and 'the rich and racy slang of the fifth continent – the mighty Australian commonwealth'.[15] Among the consultants are Sir Patrick Colquhoun (1815–91), a diplomat, author and oarsman, whose extensive attainments included speaking 'most of the tongues and many of the dialects of Europe';[16] Major Arthur Griffiths (1838–1908), a former inspector of prisons (and deputy-governor of both Millbank and Wormwood Scrubs jails) who turned his experiences into such non-fiction best-sellers as *Secrets of the Prison House* (1893) and *The Brand of the Broad Arrow* (1900); the Bohemian, journalist and theatrical manager John Hollingshead (1827–1904), who campaigned to permit theatrical performances before 5 p.m., thus instituting the matinée; the pro-temperance, anti-gambling campaigner the Revd J. W. Horsley (1845–1921), and Charles Mackay (1814–89) the poet and journalist, who mixed such posts as that of the *Times*'s special correspondent during the American Civil War with the writing of song lyrics and of a wide variety of books, many on London or the English countryside. Mackay's own contribution to lexicography was twofold: *A Dictionary of Lowland Scotch* (1888) and a study of *Extraordinary Popular Delusions and the Madness of Crowds* (1841). Its second volume focuses on 'Popular Follies in Great Cities'. Here he deals with catchphrases, which are 'repeated with delight, and received with laughter, by men with hard hands and dirty faces—by saucy butcher lads and errand-boys – by loose women – by hackney coachmen, cabriolet drivers, and idle fellows who loiter at the corners of streets'. As examples he offers *bad hat, quoz, (hookey) walker!, there he goes with his eye out, flare up*, and *who are you?*

Leland's introduction was 'A Brief History of English Slang'. Partridge[17] is especially condemnatory of this, describing one of its broader generalizations as 'childish', but in his attribution of much early cant to gypsy origins, his acknowledgement of the role of Celtic words in slang etymologies, especially as regards Shelta (the tinkers' jargon), as well as that of such European inputs as those from Dutch and Italian, Leland seems not so far from the opinions offered by Partridge himself. He also notes the late eighteenth-century arrival of Yiddish, the importing by veterans of the Indian army of the Anglo-Indian pidgin known from the title of the dictionary of such language that had appeared three years earlier as 'Hobson-Jobson' and 'the last and not least important element … Americanisms'.[18] None of which should have led Partridge, usually so generous, to so curt a dismissal. But he was *parti pris*: his own work would be based on Farmer and Henley. Understandably, if not wholly fairly, he seems to have stuck with the home team.

He was not alone, judging by a review of volume 1 by the soldier-scholar Col. W. F. Prideaux in *Notes and Queries*. 'The book is beautiful to look at […] but I am sorry to say I cannot speak so favourably of its contents. To those who have been looking forward with the hope of at last possessing a real dictionary of slang […] the book is decidedly disappointing. To those who have based their expectations of a dictionary upon the *opus magnum* of Dr. Murray it is not a dictionary at all, but simply a collection of memoranda *pour servir*.'[19] Backing his criticisms with his own knowledgeable comments, he is unimpressed by their sources (*Punch* but no *N&Q*, too much *Pink 'Un*, not enough ballads) and by their definitions, both of independent terms and of the fundamental concepts: slang and cant. Stationed at Jaipur, he knows British India and challenges the authors' decision to include terms from the recently appeared *Hobson-Jobson* (1886), Sir Henry Yule and A. C. Burnell's dictionary of Anglo-Indian pidgin, the lexis of which, he points out, is not in fact slang: 'The Hindustani words with which Anglo-Indians interlard their discourse are no more slang than the numerous French words which are employed in English conversation. No one calls *penchant, ennui, corset*, &c., slang, and there is no reason for considering a word as slang which expresses a Hindustani idea for which there is no exact English equivalent.' As for slang proper, 'Anglo-Indians are not an inventive race, and amongst ourselves we prefer to borrow than to originate […] when we do diverge from our usual correctness of language, we employ the floral exuberances of the Gaiety [Theatre] or the *Pink 'Un*, and do not babble Hindustani.'[20]

He is right. *Slang, Jargon and Cant* is by no means perfect: if nothing else, as indicated by its size, it lacks a number of the words that Farmer and Henley chose to include, and in their decision to allow what would elsewhere be excluded as 'jargon', Barrère and Leland extend the definition of what is properly 'slang'. The foreword promises much, as Prideaux notes, but the entries do not deliver. Their illustrative citations, while plentiful, are undated, which seems to defeat the point of their being included in the first place; their differentiation of senses, and the general arrangement of entries, is distinctly inferior to their rivals – the material, while often copious and accurately defined, is too jumbled for easy access; they are often overly discursive and not a little moralistic.

Col. Prideaux does not seem to have commented on the next multi-volume slang dictionary of the period, but it is likely that he would have appreciated it. In 1890, just as what was still known as the *New English Dictionary* was getting properly into its stride in Oxford, there was published the first of the seven volumes of what could reasonably be called its slang equivalent: *Slang and Its Analogues*, by John S. Farmer and (from volume II) his unlikely co-author, the jingoistic poet W. E. Henley. They were to Grose and Hotten as Murray and his team were to Johnson, and their work displays a similar degree of scholarship, replete with quotations from slang's equivalent of the 'classics', sometimes lengthy etymologies and synonyms from various European languages.

Farmer had produced a book of *Americanisms* (1889), which updated that produced around mid-century by John Bartlett. He edited *Musa Pedestris* (1896), a collection of canting songs and allied verses, and, like some of the Oxford lexicographers, had edited reprints of a number of long-unprinted works, in his case drawn from Tudor sources. His *Tudor Facsimile Texts* appeared in 1907. As 'Dr Farmer' he was to be found as a regular contributor to *Notes and Queries*. Farmer was also a devotee of spiritualism. His book *A New Basis of Belief in Immortality* appeared in 1881. It is a thoroughly sympathetic treatment of a quasi-religious movement which, as he admitted, still faced 'vehement opposition [from] a large section of the cultivated classes'. (Spiritualism, for whatever reasons, seems to have appealed to the lexicographers. The etymologist Hensleigh Wedgwood, an important influence on the *OED*, was a devotee and wrote regularly for the spiritualist periodical

Light. C. G. Leland, while no spiritualist, was a fan of both witchcraft and hypnosis.)

Beyond his publications, Farmer remains elusive. The American scholar Gershon Legman, who wrote an introduction to a reprint of the revised (1909) Volume I of the slang dictionary (A–B), admitted himself defeated. Farmer was 'very peculiar, believed in the occult, never had any money, and lived with a woman to whom he was not married'.[21] Dr Damian Atkinson, whose edition of *The Correspondence of John Stephen Farmer and W. E. Henley on Their Slang Dictionary* appeared in 2004, was unable to find out much more. The fact that Henley destroyed all Farmer's letters does not help. He seems to have been beset by lifelong financial problems and by a complex marital life which included a bigamous relationship. With his constant difficulties Farmer is a figure who might have stepped from the pages of Gissing's *New Grub Street.*

One suggestion that Legman did make (in his study of erotic folklore *The Horn Book,* 1963) is to attribute to Farmer certain involvements in contemporary pornography. Titles that he attributes to Farmer include *Forbidden Fruit: A Luscious and Exciting Story and More Forbidden Fruit or Master Percy's Progress* (1905), *The Horn Book: Modern Studies in the Science of Stroking* (1898), and *Love and Safety: or Love and Lasciviousness with Safety and Secrecy. A lecture, delivered with practical illustrations by the Empress of Austria (The Modern Sapho); assisted by her favorite Lizette. Written expressly for and Dedicated to Ladies of all Ages and All Countries* (1896). He also claims that 'An Old Bibliophile', author of the pornographer Charles Carrington's catalogue *Forbidden Books: Notes and Gossip on Tabooed Literature, etc.* might have been the slang lexicographer. Farmer was at times desperate for money; it is possible that like many others before and after he picked up some easy income from porn. Legman backs up his attributions with the suggestion that 'only one person writing in English in 1899 or thereabouts is known to have interested himself in English sexual slang – and particularly in sexual synonymies – and to have contacts with erotica printed abroad, and that was John Stephen Farmer'.[22] There is no hard evidence: this side of his life, if it existed, remains as unproven as all the rest. There is only one possible pointer: the compilation in 1896 of the *Vocabula Amatoria,* a French-English dictionary of erotic slang, based on citations from the French. First published anonymously, it was not openly attributed to Farmer until a New York reprint of 1966.

Farmer's co-author, William Ernest Henley (1849–1903), 'the most belligerent Tory man of letters of [his] generation',[23] who joined him on the dictionary at volume II, presents a far more substantial figure. He had his blind spots too, notably a benightedly xenophobic patriotism, but one cannot imagine him giving much truck to spectral messengers and wafting ectoplasm. Like Albert Barrère, who had enlisted C. G. Leland to help with his labours, Farmer must have felt it necessary to take on a proven literary figure and Henley was a star of late Victorian letters, even if his ultra-patriotic versifying has long since been considered a subject fitter for humour than for the homage it was paid at the time.

It was presumably in his role of organizer of the series of 'Tudor Translations' – each adorned with an introductory essay by a leading scholar of the day – that Henley met Farmer, who was also working on the resuscitation of sixteenth-century literature. Quite what Henley's involvement in the dictionary represented, other than the weight of his name in literary circles, is ambiguous. His name appears on the title page of every volume from II onwards, but Farmer seems to have done the majority of the work. As Julie Coleman has noted, it ensured that Farmer's work was known in more influential circles, and Henley's money helped with the purchase of research material as well as providing the impoverished Farmer with occasional loans. He also helped with proofing, offering suggestions and corrections.[24] Partridge leaves it there, and, presumably overlooking the potential for double-entendre, called *Slang and its Analogues* 'one of the three or four most remarkable one-handed achievements in the whole record of dictionary-making'.[25]

Whatever the balance of labour, their joint work laid down new standards for slang lexicography and, if one remembers that Partridge himself was actually handed Farmer and Henley's seven volumes as the basis on which to assemble his own efforts, remains the source of much that followed in the twentieth century. Nor had Farmer any illusions as to the importance of what he (Henley had yet to be recruited) had done. Writing in his 'Prefatory Note' to volume I he begins by citing Samuel Johnson, noting that the Great Lexicographer's problems had been his too, and then quotes his contemporary James Murray as regards the difficulties inherent in attempting to quarantine one variety of language, in this case slang, from all the others. He explains how he has made his own decision as to the borderline, basing it on the standards of literary and non-literary English laid out in Annandale's edition of Ogilvie's *Imperial English Dictionary* (which took as its source Webster, rather than Johnson). That done, Farmer set off into what he terms the '"Dark Continent" of the World of Words'.[26]

Farmer takes slang lexicography into a new dimension. Quite simply he has adopted the same historical method that the *NED*, not to mention its European peers, had done. All but a few headwords come with a number of citations, set out just as in a standard English dictionary, to illustrate usage and nuance. These quotes take in 'the whole period of English literature from the earliest down to the present time'[27] and are arranged as far as possible from 'first use' to current use. The entire work offers around 100,000 of these citations, mainly harvested by Farmer himself, although 12,000 came from G. L. Apperson, who also contributed 11,000 quotations to the *NED*, for which he sub-edited portions of the letters *B* and *C*, and whose own major work is *English Proverbs* (1929). As well as citations, Farmer included wherever possible foreign synonyms for his slang terminology. These were predominantly French (Albert Barrère is credited as a major source) and German, although the occasional foray further afield can be found. Finally, as well as listing and defining the individual terms, Farmer offers substantial lists of synonyms – that for the *monosyllable* (the vagina), for instance, runs to thirteen columns, while *greens* (sexual intercourse) runs to seven. Other substantial synonymies can be found at *barrack-hack* (prostitutes), *lush-crib*, *lushington* and *screwed* (drunk), *creamstick* and *prick* (the penis), *ride* (sexual intercourse again), *bury a Quaker* (to defecate), *mutton-monger* (pimp) and *bum* (the buttocks). No other slang dictionary, until Richard Spears's *Slang and Euphemism* (1981), would offer similar lists.

There are errors, typically in the citations, where dates and even the quotes themselves may have fallen foul of the sheer volume of the undertaking, but the overall achievement far outweighs such slips.

For all its scholarship, and despite the fact that by its conclusion, in 1904, the UK had long since moved on from the high water mark of Victorian moralism, it is impossible to assess whether *Slang and Its Analogues* received the acclaim it deserved.

The first volume, published in early 1890, did receive some reviews. They were good. The most substantial was in *Notes and Queries*, which noted that while there had been earlier treatments of slang, '[r]ecent works have, however, been catchpennies, Mr. Farmer is the first to treat the subject of slang in a manner commensurate with its importance'. And concluded, 'His book commends itself warmly to our readers, and its progress cannot be otherwise than interesting. It is artistically got up, and its type and paper are all that can be desired. As it is issued in a limited edition it can scarcely fail of becoming a prized possession.'[28] The *Scots Observer*, then edited by Henley, noted that, 'on the whole the work is so well done that it promises to be the best of its kind in modern English',[29] while the *Pall Mall Gazette* was assured that Farmer's work 'makes a beginning of what will prove to be a great and valuable work'.[30] Three years later, *Notes and Queries* noticed volumes II and III and congratulated Farmer on the resumption of his labours after 'difficulties and complications of all kinds'. They also noted that he had 'secured a brilliant and admirably efficient ally in Mr. Henley'.[31]

The *OED* used around 350 of its citations – Farmer corresponded with Murray throughout the writing and the *OED*'s historian Peter Gilliver has suggested that Murray saw 'The Slang Dictionary' as a parallel project to the standard one[32] – but it still dealt with too much that was taboo, and made no attempt to disguise the fact. *Notes and Queries* had noted that at least in volume I while '[n]ot a few of [the words] are coarse in the acceptance of to-day [...] none of the English words can be resented as infamous'.[33] This presumably would not have been said of that which followed. His printers refused to work on volume II, which, as Farmer wrote to Murray, contained 'the vernacular words for the *penis*, the female *pudendum* and the verb', i.e. *cock, cunt* and *fuck*. (This is surely incorrect, since vol. II ends with *fizzle* and therefore would not have reached *fuck*.) Farmer rejected such excisions, pointing out that 'the whole *raison d'etre* of [the] book is its Completeness'.[34] Murray, who saw, even if he did not seem to have commented on, all Farmer's proofs from volume II, agreed; the printers did not. Farmer sued them for breach of promise and lost. After that he was forced to move out of London for a printer, taking the pornographers' well-trodden path to Amsterdam. And like pornography the book would be published in a limited edition 'for subscribers'. It did not reach the open market. Nor did such sales as there were appear to improve Farmer's eternally parlous finances.

Yet in 1909 it was considered worth putting out a revised and expanded edition of volume I (A–B, originally published in 1890). No others, however, followed. A single-volume abridged (and bowdlerized, cite-free) version, *A Dictionary of Slang and Colloquial English*, appeared in 1905, published by George Routledge, who had secured the rights. In 1909 J. Redding Ware's *Passing English of the Victorian Era* was billed as 'a companion volume' and 'in the same series' as Farmer's work. Farmer and Henley's dictionary would be reprinted in full in 1966, but it was by then a period piece.

Its real legacy lay in a new direction. In 1933 Routledge published *Slang To-day and Yesterday*, a study of slang by the ex-soldier, former teacher and recently bankrupted publisher Eric Partridge. It impressed them sufficiently to offer him a new commission: the revision and expansion of Farmer and Henley. The book that followed, *A Dictionary of Slang and Unconventional English* (1936 et seq.) made Partridge the most influential slang lexicographer of the remainder of the twentieth century.

13 Gayspeak:
The Lavender Lexicon

They chirp, they chatter, they exaggerate, they flourish and
twitter, they cackle and calumnize ... all this in a sweet voice,
mincingly, with a ridiculously high timbre.
> Julien Chevallier, *Aberrations de l'instinct sexuel au point*
> *de vue ethnographique, historique et sociale* (1905)

The world of homosexuality is the perfect environment for slang.
Statutorily illegal for centuries (and continuing to be so in many
countries), it rendered gay men and women criminals. Forced into
secrecy, pushed out to the social margins, it demanded a secretive,
marginal language. A code as exclusive as that of any other criminals.
There is relatively little evidence of this prior to the twentieth century,
but one may assume that it was there, even if before that to the mass
public gaze homosexuals appeared as objects rather than subjects.
However, gay slang offers another aspect that the rest of the 'straight'
slang vocabulary has by-passed. Homosexuality has been imbued with
sexual politics since the birth of gay liberation in the Sixties. Its language,
unsurprisingly, has followed suit.

For the historian of slang things are simpler. At least as regards a
narrative. The appearance of the homosexual — around 310 terms for
male homosexuals, 130 for lesbians —within the dictionary is that of
an object: the object of others' disdain or fear (and perhaps lust, though
well disguised). Only in the gay lexicon itself – some 1,400 terms –
is this standpoint rejected. Otherwise the words are those used *about*
alternative sexuality. Typically in the eighteenth-century phrase 'bestial

back-sliding', a synonym for homosexuality that combines physical distaste with pulpit admonition. First noted in the sixteenth century, this negative attitude and the linguistic practice it underpins lasts well into modernity. Not until the twentieth century does one start to see the words used *by* homosexuals. A variety of glossaries are assembled, and at the same time gay language starts to be used in fiction. The advent of activist Gay Liberation in the late 1960s changed both the nature of the language, and of the way in which it was discussed. This intensified around 1980, since when a wide-ranging discussion, mainly within in the academic/activist world, has dominated the subject.

Slang by its nature does not make, or does not set out to make, a political statement. That it subscribes to every politically incorrect -ism available may give the lie to this, but this is politics by accretion, an assessment offered by slang's analysts rather than its speakers; for the users it suggests more of a sociological statement – quite possibly an unconscious one – than an ideological standpoint. Politics, at least intellectually, doesn't count. In the case of the language of gay and lesbian people, this is not the case. In his review of such language in 2000, the scholar Don Kulick[1] admitted himself at a loss, admitting that even the naming of these 'nonheteronormative' communities was problematic, but that given the importance of naming as a fundamental of existence, it had to be considered. The word *gay*, once apparently suitable, had been discarded; the term *queer*, recaptured from those who used it derogatively, was still too offensive for many. The current acronyms of choice, e.g. *LGBTTSQ*: Lesbian, Gay, Bisexual, Transgendered, Two-Spirit, Queer, or Questioning, seemed too cumbersome and even they might not cover the entirety of the non-heterosexual waterfront. In the end, he fell back on standard English: *gay* and *lesbian*.

The same thing went for the language itself. As its lexis is used within a closed group it might be seen as a jargon: but how closed is the group, is there even a single group, and to what extent does it overlap with 'straight' language? Alternatively is it a slang: given the oppositional status – voluntary or otherwise – of its speakers to the supposedly 'standard', i.e. heterosexual world, it could qualify as a prime example of a literal counter-language. Is there such a thing as 'gayspeak' (a term coined in 1981 in J. W. Chesebro's study *Gayspeak: Gay Male and Lesbian*

Communication) with a vocabulary and speech community to match, or is one talking about something far more fluid and indefinable, a style? Such questions, and many and far more nuanced others form the fundamentals of modern discussion of the topic. It is beyond the scope of this history to discuss them. It is important, however, to acknowledge that they exist and over the last thirty years have promoted an on-going and intense scholarly and political discussion. And that they remain unresolved.

Slang's earliest take on homosexuals – i.e. those terms recorded between the sixteenth and eighteenth centuries – falls into four primary groups: classical allusions, direct or lexical references to 'abroad' (though not for a change to France, compounds based on that example of Britain's traditional enemies being generally reserved for venereal disease; the link to fellatio, both hetero- and homosexual, emerges later), the physical aspects of man-on-man sex and, perhaps predominantly, the use of female names to characterize men who, to steal from Victorian euphemism, 'are not as other men'.

Latin provided two primary terms, both recorded around 1600. The first is *sellary*, which came from *sellarius*, a man who sits upon a *sella*, a couch, which couch is taken as being in a brothel; the term meant first a male homosexual prostitute and by extension any gay man. Alternatively there was *spintry*, which has been linked to *spinter*, a bracelet and thus those men who wear them. Beyond that lay the image of male homosexual sex as having bodies joined together like the links of a bracelet (and thus a precursor of the modern sexual *daisy-chain*).

Foreign mainly meant Italian. *Italian tricks* were synonymous with the *Italian sin*, and made disdain for man-to-man sex an aspect of contemporary anti-Catholicism. As Aphra Behn put it in *The Town-Fop* (1676): 'Art Italianiz'd, and lovest thy own Sex?' The London chronicler Ned Ward abandoned euphemism, noting 'A Crowd of Bumfirking-Italians' in his *London Spy* (1699). (*Firk* is not a mis-spelling: it meant to move briskly or to beat and in slang meant to have sex.) Anti-papism further underpinned *Jesuit*, while Cleland, in *Memoirs of a Woman of Pleasure*, apostrophized the male buttocks as 'the mount pleasants of Rome'. The near contemporary *boretto-man* was synonymous, literally a 'little borer'; it combined *bore*, a form of tool, with the Italian diminutive suffix *-etto*. (*Tool* as penis already existed and the pun may have been intentional.) Alternatively there was Spain, another country seen as prostrate beneath Rome's rampant clergy. Thomas Urquhart used *buggeranto*, combining standard English with a Spanish suffix, in his translation of *Gargantua and Pantagruel* (1653). So did Lord Rochester in a poem, although paradoxically his play *Sodom*, devoted to polymorphous perversity, uses no terms for a homosexual. (The standard English *sodomite* itself was of course long-established.) There was also *bardash*, from the Greek *bardas*, a synonym for *kinaidos*, a passive partner in homosexual coupling and which had been transmuted through the French *bardache*, an effeminate male homosexual, the partner of the 'masculine' *bougre* (a bugger). It may also be linked to Arabic, as in *bardaj* (a slave). *Bardash* is noted by John Florio in his Italian-English dictionary *The Worlde of Wordes* (1598), where he translates *cinédo* as 'a bardarsh buggring boy, a wanton boy, an ingle'. (Standard English *ingle* meant to fondle.) Other wanton boys were a *Ganymede* (mythological cup-bearer to the gods), a *trug*, equally common as a female whore, and a *pullet*, which foreshadows the modern *chicken* for an underage boy.

The physical aspects of sodomy are reflected in a variety of eighteenth-century terms sniggeringly punning on 'back'. There is the *back-door man* (whose modern incarnation is of a heterosexual adulterer), the *backdoor gentleman* or *backdoor merchant*; the *gentleman of the back door* and the *usher of the back door*. As well as these Francis Grose's *Classical Dictionary of the Vulgar Tongue* (1785 et seq.) offers the *backgammon player* and the sophomoric *navigator of the windward passage*. Grose also lists *bagpiping*, 'a lascivious practice too indecent for explanation', which is in fact intercourse beneath the armpit, a supposedly 'typical' variety of gay sex.

The remainder of the period's terms are based on proper names. Of these the most important is *molly*, first recorded in 1693 in 'Jenny Cromwells Complaint against Sodomy' which refers to one who 'skulks about the Alleys / And is content with Bettys, Nans and Mollys'. As the citation indicates, the word is based on the female name (thus too the synonyms *Nan* and *Betty*), but there may be a link both to the earlier *moll* (a woman; often a prostitute) and to the French *molle* (the female form of *mou*, soft). Latin had used *mollis delicatus* for the passive partner, and French borrowed this as *une molle*. Early modern French is profligate in such names but while Cotgrave includes *gai* (gay) as 'merrie, frolicke, blithe, jollie ... lustie', and suggestions have been made as to the term being identified with homosexual men, the modern use goes directly back to the English slang use of 'gay' to mean immoral, and as such was initially used of whores.

Molly offers a number of extensions, notably the synonymous *Miss Molly* and *Tom Molly*, the adjective *mollyish*, the *moll-cull* (a catamite), and the *molly-house*, defined by the historian Rictor Norton as 'a disorderly house where homosexual men socialized and found entertainment'.[2] After molly, *Margery*, and *madge*, from Margaret, giving the compounds *madge-cull* (a male homosexual) and *madge-coves*, excoriated by the lexicographer John Badcock in his slang dictionary of 1823 as 'infamy itself — men who enact the parts of women'. Another female name is *Sukey*, most probably no more than a diminutive of Susan, but possibly bearing a whiff of Welsh Gypsy *sukar*, to whisper. Its immediate root would have been the appearance of the maid 'Sukey' in the contemporary nursery rhyme 'Polly put the kettle on'. *Miss Nancy* is noted in 1828 but *nancy* is late nineteenth century and *nancy boy* was first recorded *c.* 1910, although *nancy* already meant the buttocks in Vaux (1812) and in 1828 Badcock's *Living Picture of London* noted that 'a soldier [...] whose nickname Nancy Cooper designated his character [...] was hanged at Newgate-door for accusing a certain gentleman, in the Strand of a beastly offence, said to have been committed in St. James's Park'.[3]

Finally, prior to the twentieth century, lesbians. If Queen Victoria notoriously refused to acknowledge their existence, her predecessors were scarcely more accommodating. Again one finds classical references, most obviously the use of *Sappho*, adopted directly from the name Sappho (*c.* 600 BC), the poetess of the island of Lesbos. There is the *she-centaur*, a development of the mythical creature 'with the head, trunk, and arms of a man, joined to the body and legs of a horse' (*OED*). In this context it is a pun, spelt out in *Erotopolis* (1684) by Charles Cotton, who talks of 'She-Centaurs shall they be [...] for in these places it is, the young Shepherdesses first learn the Art of Horsemanship and Horse-play, first riding one another.'[4] Logically the only other term reverses male practice and adopts a male name, *Tommy*, for all-girl use, and circuitously suggests in 'A Sapphic Epistle' (1781) that 'Miss Sappho [...] was the first Tommy the world has upon record.'

There was no attempt to corral such terms in a single list, any more than there might have been for Jews or fools. They were simply part of the greater slang lexis. They might appear, sparingly, in the rash of eighteenth-century trials that prosecuted gay men for sodomy, in the racy reporting of such as 'The London Spy', Ned Ward or in a variety of plays. They would doubtless be used, unrecorded, in daily speech.

The first attempt at any such list came (as so far discovered) in 1910. Writing in the *Jahrbuch für sexuelle Zwischenstufen* (Yearbook for Sexual Intermediates) No. 11, I. L. (Leo) Pavia published a six-part article entitled 'Male Homosexuality in England with Special Consideration of London'.[5] Pavia, who seems to have been well acquainted with the contemporary homosexual world, cites the slang terms *aunt* (one who is 'old and somewhat effeminate in his behaviour'), to *camp* (to 'behave effeminately') and *Mary Ann*, *Oscar* and *so*, all meaning a homosexual. Some of these might be used by heterosexuals too, but *aunt*, *camp* and the euphemistic *so* (often used in the question 'Is he so?') all seem to have been part of what may well have been a much larger gay vocabulary.[6]

The link between mental health journals and gay slang glossaries persisted. In the sixth (1927) and seventh (1938) editions of his textbook *A Manual of Psychiatry*, Aaron J. Rosanoff offered a short glossary of twenty-one terms; J. F. Oliven includes two pages of 'Excerpts from the Argot' in his *Sexual Hygiene and Pathology* (1955), and J. M. Reinhardt devoted a chapter to the lexis in *Perversions and Sex Crimes* (1957). None of these were extensive, although Rosanoff is seen as the best available guide to the gay world in 1920s America. A side line on that pre-war world can be found in Allen Walker Read's *Lexical Evidence from Folk Epigraphy in Western North America: A Glossarial Study of the Low Element in the English Vocabulary* (1935). Even with this convoluted title Read's short work – based on his study of the obscene graffiti on public lavatory walls – was unpublishable in the US; it appeared in Paris, traditional home of 'filth' in Anglo-Saxon eyes, in a limited edition of seventy-five copies which still needed the label 'Circulation restricted to students of linguistics, folk-lore, abnormal psychology, and allied branches of social science'. There is no stated focus on homosexuality, but at least some of the lavatories must have been used as *tearooms* (venues for male homosexual sexual encounters) and among much else Read recorded instances of *cocksucker* and *motherfucker* and the comments 'When will you meet me and suck my prick. I suck them every day,' and 'I suck cocks for fun.'

Although the material did not surface for mass consumption until the publication in 1988 of Lawrence R. Harvey's monograph *Perverts by Official Order: The Campaign against Homosexuals by the United States Navy*, an interesting body of gay slang was noted down in 1919. This was amassed in evidence given to the Foster Enquiry, designed (by way of entrapment of its witnesses) to amass testimonies from naval personnel about their involvement with homosexuality. The transcripts offered evidence of the sailors' taste for make-up, cross-dressing, drugs, drink and homosexual orgies. They also revealed their relatively wide range of gay slang. Among the terms extracted are *auntie, back-door* (the anus), *brown* (to sodomize), *cocksucker, drag* (i.e. a drag ball), *faggot, fairy, French* (fellatio), *blow someone's pipe, get down* and *suck off* (to fellate), *jerk, pull* or *yank someone off* (to masturbate a male partner), *have a dash of lavender*, *lily* (the penis), *load* (a portion of ejaculated semen), *peter* (the penis), *piece of tail* (a sexual partner, in this case male), *pogue* (the passive partner in anal intercourse), *queen, get some* (to have sex), *straight* (heterosexual), *trade* and *wife* (the 'female' partner of a gay couple). Though these, as ever, show a degree of crossover with heterosexual slang, it reveals an extensive sex-related vocabulary within the group.

In 1941 there appeared another academic study: G. W. Henry's *Sex Variants: A Study of Homosexual Patterns*. In it, as appendix VII, came the best yet study of gay slang, *The Language of Homosexuality* by the then twenty-four-year-old folklorist Gershon Legman. In his brief introduction, which devoted more space to explaining the relative absence of lesbian terms than to analysing the gay ones, he stated, 'The following slang glossary includes only words and phrases current in American slang, argot, and colloquial speech since the First World War, and particularly during the period between 1930 and 1940. The entire sexual vocabulary of the homosexual is not recorded in this glossary, except in the sphere of sexual practice, where every effort has been made to supply a complete and exhaustive record.' There are 329 entries, of which 139 were seen as exclusively homosexual. Whether the homosexual world, and with it its vocabulary, had expanded in the past two decades is debatable; it is possible that Legman's predecessors simply failed to research far enough. And it is interesting to see that some sixty-eight other terms included by Legman and mainly linked to homosexual use are predated by A. J. Pollock's collection of criminal cant *The Underworld Speaks* (1935).

Soon after World War II there appeared a pair of less scholarly efforts: *Gaedicker's Sodom-on-Hudson* ('Everything from the Plaza to the Pissoirs') and *The Gay Girl's Guide* ('A Primer for Novices. A Review for Roués'), both published in 1949. This pair of pamphlets aimed to introduce the neophyte – or at least out-of-town – gay man to the big cities. The first dealt with New York, the second with the country at large and included a twelve-page 'Gayese-English Dictionary'. Readers were requested to pass back their own information – a telephone number was included – and further editions would appear. A second *Gay Girl's Guide* was published in 1950. A worldwide edition, *The Gay Girl's Guide to the US and the Western World*, mainly focused on places where US troops might be stationed, appeared in 'summer 1950' and a successor is dated 'mid-Fifties'. This offered sections on gayspeak in French and German, plus a few pick-up lines with the Russian spelt out phonetically and which included 'I'd like to suck your cock' and 'I sure like your cock and balls but you need a bath.' They could be used either in the 'the case of total victory' or 'if you become a P.O.W.'.

That the pamphlets were mimeographed and distributed in plain envelopes 'with a sender's identification designed to dull almost anybody's curiosity' merely accentuated their underground status. 'Be careful who you show it to,' warned the editor. 'A wrong decision would have unfortunate results not only for you but for a few million others.' The author of both was one 'Swasarnt Nerf' 'of the American Fellatelic Society'. He was assisted for *Sodom-on-Hudson* by 'Mona Moosedike of the Canadian Clitoral Committee' and for the *Guide* by 'Peter Asti Cruising Editor of the Queen's Gazette' and 'Daphne Dilldock, Professor of Cliterology, Gomorrah U'. The author has never been revealed, but Hugh Hagius, who reprinted the pamphlets in 2004, has suggested that 'Nerf' was in fact one Edgar Leoni who, under another, more penetrable pseudonym – Noel I. Garde – published a study of *The Homosexual in Literature*, and *From Jonathan to Gide*, a guide to 'Who's Gay in History'. It was, as Hagius notes, Leoni's real telephone number that was offered to readers.

Further glossaries appeared through the 1950s. 'Donald Cory' (actually Edward Sagarin) included a ten-page treatment of gay language in his book *The Homosexual in America: A Subjective Approach* (1951) and returned to the subject in *The Homosexual and His Society: A View from Within*, written with J. P. Leroy in 1963. Two years after that the Guild Press, a small publishing house specializing in gay erotica, brought out *The Guild Dictionary of Homosexual Terms*. This fifty-one-page book offered some of what had appeared before, but included a great deal of standard content such as 'oral-genital', 'oral intercourse' and 'orgasm'. In 1964 *The Lavender Lexicon: Dictionary of Gay Words and Phrases* offered a brief quasi-scholarly introduction plus fourteen pages of slang and one page of technical terms, e.g. 'pederasty'; and 'gerontophilia'. The lexis was unexceptional, though the introduction underlined the centrality of the term gay, 'which must be defined as that element of a society, predominantly homosexually orientated, who make up a "night life" of a society of some continuity based on common acceptance of each other's sexual expressions'.[7] In 1968, just ahead of the de-criminalization of homosexuality in the UK, Richard Hauser published *The Homosexual Society*, which offered a small vocabulary, the majority of which dealt with the camp lexis, Polari.

What is still acknowledged as the outstanding dictionary of gay slang appeared in 1972: *The Queen's Vernacular* by Bruce Rodgers. It remains, as Don Kulik put it, 'the magnificent, still unsurpassed Mother of all gay glossaries, [...] making all previous attempts to document gay slang look like shopping lists scribbled on the back of a paper bag'.[8] It offers 12,000 entries, and Rodgers claimed to have conducted many interviews and taken many years to assemble his lists. It is unlikely that every homosexual would have vouchsafed the use of every word, and there is a perhaps undue emphasis on San Francisco localisms, and a number of terms may have come from nonce-uses, but nothing that has followed, in print or pixels, has really replaced Rodgers's dictionary.

It remains a monument, even if Gary Simes suggests, sensibly, that 'it must be used with caution'.[9]

The flow of 'dictionaries of gay slang' continues. Aside from glossaries of various lengths and purposes attached to academic papers, and several articles by Leonard R. N. Ashley in *Maledicta: the Journal of Verbal Aggression*, the most recent successors are Paul Baker's *Fantabulosa: Dictionary of Polari and Gay Slang* (2002) and Ken Cage's *Gayle: the Language of Kinks and Queens* (2003), which focuses on South Africa. Among the on-line dictionaries is Robert Owen Scott's *Gay Slang Dictionary* (which draws heavily on Rodgers), most recently updated in 2007. A number of gay websites feature some form of glossary, but in many cases these are not only plagiaristic, often of Scott (and thus Rodgers), and deal not simply with slang, but also list standard terms which happen to be used in a homosexual context, e.g. 'abstinence, not taking part in sexual acts'.

For the *Queen's Vernacular* Rodgers wrote a brief introduction. It sets the lexicon very much in its time: standing at the junction between the linguistic verbosity of the world of queens (for whom the book is of course named) and the new austerity of gay liberation, whose activists equated the use of traditional gay slang with volunteering to accept oppression. Rodgers looked back and forward. On the one hand he lauds the lexis he had collected, which far from representing acquiescence, flaunts its own rebellion. It 'was invented, coined, dished and shrieked by the gay stereotypes. The flaming faggot, men who look like women, flagrant wrist-benders, the women who don't shave their legs, all those who find it difficult to be accepted for what they feel they are even within the pariah gay subculture. And they stereotype others because they themselves have been labeled offensively ... They jeer because they have been mocked; they retaliate with a barrage of their own words which ridicule women, male virility, the sanctity of marriage, everything in life from which they are divorced.' Such words 'enrich ... our language immensely' as well as serving as the queen's form of protest. Nonetheless he accepts that slang is a product of the ghetto and 'those who struggle to leave the ghetto shake off its language first and then decry its message'. He acknowledged that 'many gay militants are avidly opposed to this contrived lingo with which the oppressed faggot makes himself understood, and then only to a "sister." They consider the jargon yet another link in the chain which holds the homosexual enslaved.'[10]

It is this dichotomy that has dominated the status of 'gay slang' since the 1970s and even more so since the 1980s. It has led to paper and counter-paper and glosses on both, and after that new papers to augment or replace those. It has little bearing on lexicography, nor on the nature of the vocabulary itself; it is more about whether, to reduce it to bare bones, a) gay slang is 'good' or 'bad', and b) what, in any case, actually is gay slang. This can give much to the faculty, who show no signs of reaching an end of their debates; as regards the dictionary, which deals with what is rather than what should be, it can be fascinating, but ultimately and in every sense of the word, academic.

Although one can trace slang that was used *of* homosexuals several centuries back, the finding of recorded slang as used *by* homosexuals – and which is thus, one might argue, a lifestyle-specific jargon rather than a general slang – is a relatively recent phenomenon. Glossarial information still dominates. Two works of late-nineteenth-century gay pornography have been recorded, but one at least was relatively 'literary' and while sexually descriptive neither put any exclusively gay slang into their characters' mouths. These were *The Sins of the Cities of the Plain; or, The Recollections of a Mary-Ann, with Short Essays on Sodomy and Tribadism* (1881) by one 'Jack Saul', in real life the name of a popular rent boy; the actual authors were probably the pornographer James Campbell Reddie and the artist Simeon Solomon, and *Teleny, or, The Reverse of the Medal* (1893), probably at least co-written by Wilde. The latter, as might be expected from its alleged author, is more 'aesthetic' than slangy; as for 'Jack Saul', he offers a small slang vocabulary – *arse* and *arsehole*, *balls* and *stones*, *bubby* (as in 'false bubbies'), *old buck*, *bumhole*, *charms* (the male genitals), *cunt* (in Chapter XIV's title, 'Same Old Story: Arses Preferred to Cunts'), *frig* and *frigging*, *bottom-fucking*, *jewel*, *member*, *thing*, *tool*, and *tosser* (the penis), *mary ann*, *muff*, *stand*, *tongue* (to fellate) and *well-hung* – but other than its emphasis on the male side of things, uses no terms that would have been out of place amongst the heterosexual couplings of *My Secret Life* (see Chapter 10). Perhaps the most interesting is his offering the first recorded use of *tit* to mean not a breast but a fool.

There does not seem to be any recorded mass-market gay pornography – a possible home for an otherwise underground vocabulary – on the lines of its contemporary heterosexual equivalent before the twentieth century; nor do bawdy ballads – another repository of otherwise hidden sexuality, especially via double-entendres – appear to celebrate homosexual dalliance. And while gay men might write, however circumspectly, about gay life, the language of their texts remained standard. Beerbohm and Wilde might have spoken privately of *renters*, i.e. rent-boys; they did not use such terms in their plays or prose. Nor would the most flamboyantly gay character be given the language of his sexual orientation. As late as 1945 Waugh's Anthony Blanche was *as camp as a row of tents*, but he resisted what would become known as *gayspeak*. Homosexuality was both outlawed and disdained; other than in an underground context one did not flaunt it by parading its purpose-built language.

Julia Penelope, then writing as Julia P. Stanley, suggested in 1970 in a paper on 'Homosexual Slang'[11] that US gay slang worked on two levels: a core vocabulary known to nearly all the 'community' (and often found in the general slang dictionaries of the period), and a variety of fringe vocabularies that differed as to geography and to one's own immersion in gay culture. In addition to these there were those terms, primarily sexual, which overlapped with the 'straight' slang vocabulary. This may be so, although a number of her core terms were dependent on the camp 'queen' vocabulary and have vanished other than as examples of ironic anachronism. In addition what she selected as examples of the fringe seem to have become more widely known with time. In linguistic terms she saw a number of compounds, especially those in *-queen*, a small number of rhyming terms (though not rhyming slang as such), exclamations (which as noted seem to have faded), blends and truncations. She also noted the role of sardonic humour and an over-riding pleasure in wordplay, typically double-entendre. Much of this is not true merely of gay slang, but of all slang. And as she acknowledges, much of so-called 'gay slang' comes from a wider slang-using community, especially its outlaw groups. 'If we are to speak of homosexual slang at all, in terms of a homogeneous speech community, we must speak of a core vocabulary that consists of terms borrowed from the theater and from the slang of prostitutes and the criminal underworld, as well as several stock phrases common to the slang of adolescents and of homosexuals.'[12] Even within the core vocabulary, in which she includes a number of negative terms such as *queen* and *queer* as well as *gay* itself, the terms have been appropriated or at least developed from pre-existing 'straight' uses, with which there is always some degree of semantic link. This of course parallels general slang, which to a vast extent uses standard English, albeit 'tweaked' to greater or lesser extent. The coinage of pure neologisms is far more limited.

In common again with 'heterosexual' or rather general slang, the gay lexis offers a set of long-running themes. Old and young men; parts of the body, notably the penis and its dimensions; sexual intercourse (in this case anal); man-to-man fellatio; sexual preferences (especially as appended to the all-purpose suffix *-queen*). The 'out-group', in general slang often a naïve or gullible countryman, is represented by heterosexuals. The construction of many terms also shows the regular use of female names for men (but without the prejudicial sense that is part of the 'straight' use of such terms to describe gay men) and the 'feminization' of male sexual terms, often simply reversing the gender use of words that, for instance, might be used for the vagina and for man-to-woman cunnilingus and applying them to the penis and homosexual fellatio.

What might be termed 'out' gay fiction begins in the 1920s. *Miss Knight* (c. 1925), by the Paris-based US author and publisher Robert McAlmon (1895–1956), offers *drag* (female dress as worn by a gay man), *blind* (uncircumcised), *bitch* and *sister* (both of a man), *cruising, piece* (the penis), *rough trade*, and *Mary*, used as a term of man-to-man address. In *The Scarlet Pansy* (1932) by the pseudonymous 'Robert Scully', the reader follows Fay Étrange (from Kuntsville 'in the lower Pennsylvania hills'), Henry Voyeur and Perci Chichi as they make their way around gay America. Within the text one finds *auntie, butch, bull* and *bull-dyker, fairy, femme, fruit, gay, go down* (fellate), *mantee* (a lesbian), *Miss* (used in combination as a nickname for a gay man), *queen, queer, sissy* and *tearoom* (a public lavatory popular for casual sex and assignations, the US equivalent of the UK *cottage*). Nearly all are extant.

All of these and more are found in John Rechy's *City of Night* (1963), another odyssey through homosexual America, this time by a quasi-autobiographical rent-boy. In addition are *boy-girl, cocksucker, daddy, dish* (to gossip maliciously), *eat* (to fellate), *faggot, hustler, leather bar, meat rack, mother* (as in the substitution of the personal pronoun 'I' by the deliberately camp and self-feminizing 'Your mother . . .'), *punk* (a young gay man), *stud, trade, trick* (a paid for or merely casual sexual partner) and *wolf* (a predatory older man). Rechy was something of a pioneer, but since then gay authors, including the prolific Rechy, regularly pepper their work with the language of their world. Larry Kramer's *Faggots* (1977) is typical, with several hundred discrete usages. Some terms may be arcane in the 'straight' world, but their use is unlikely to promote comment.

Although the word *gay* itself is no longer slang, but has become an accepted standard English synonym for homosexual, its origins undoubtedly were. It is semantically linked to a group of uses that begin with the fifteenth-century definition of 'wanton, lewd, lascivious' and the late-sixteenth's meaning of 'dissolute, promiscuous', still occasionally found in the mid-twentieth. These derogatory uses were not slang, but the later eighteenth-century definition: a euphemism used of a woman living by prostitution, was. Col. Prideaux, writing in *Notes and Queries* a century later, sees this use still as wholly unacceptable: 'The adjective gay has acquired a similarly restricted meaning [to French *fille*, properly a girl, en-slanged as a whore] amongst ourselves when applied to females, and no gentleman would think of calling a lady of his acquaintance, however hilarious she might be in disposition, a gay woman. This adjective when applied to women has, therefore, become slang and in course of time this restricted use may so enlarge itself as to apply to men of dissolute character, and the word will thenceforward be banished from serious writing.'[13] His reference is not obviously to homosexuals, rather to heterosexual debauchees, but one can appreciate the prescience, however fortuitous.

Gay meaning homosexual is, as so far recorded, a coinage of the 1920s. The first citations are dated 1922. Gertrude Stein, in the story 'Miss Furr and Miss Skeene', explains how 'Georgine Skeene liked travelling. Helen Furr did not care about travelling, she liked to stay in one place and be gay there. They were together then and travelled to another place and stayed there and were gay there [...] She told many then the way of being gay, she taught very many then little ways they could use in being gay.'[14] This, written in 1911 though unpublished until 1922, seems aimed directly at initiates. Fred Fisher's lyrics for the song 'Chicago' seem only marginally more obvious: 'Unless they change the laws, they'll never keep it from being gay. / I had the time, the time of my life, / I found a guy who had another guy for his wife. / Well, where else, but in Chicago.' The next appearance comes a decade later, in *The Scarlet Pansy*, where 'There were Fay and Whitey and Linberg and four or five more gay young things that fluttered as they walked along.'[15] By 1957 *Mad* magazine had picked it up, but gay does not fully emerge from the closet until late 1960s, with the emergence of the Gay Liberation Front. The publicity this received made things clear, whether or not one wished to accept the term. Since then the use has become widely accepted and as such replaced the much more offensive *queer* (now mainly used as a deliberate act of 'reclamation' by gay activists). Slang has reclaimed its own: gay is no longer a direct sexual pejorative; it is now a popular schoolyard negative, found as such since the late 1970s. The theory is that the use, deriding individuals, objects or actions, is gender-neutral. The reality is otherwise.

*

> Nantee dinarly, the omee of the carsey
> Says due bionc peroney, manjaree on the cross.
> We'll all have to scarper the letty in the morning,
> Before the bonee omee of the carsey shakes his doss.[16]
> > A Popular Busker Song, 'in 6/8 time
> > to a guitar accompaniment'

No overview can ignore an important sub-set of the homosexual lexis: Polari, originally *lingua franca*. 'Lingua Franca', in the original Italian, means literally 'the language of the Franks', i.e. French, and was born as a form of hybrid tongue, based on Occitan and Italian and used in the Mediterranean for trading and military purposes. From there it spread, and it is possibly this 'French tongue' (also known as 'Pedlar's French') that Chaucer has in mind when he teases the Prioress for speaking the 'French' of 'Stratforde-atte-Bow'. (That said, the reference may be to the generally 'provincial' character of the French spoken in England – heavily influenced by the Norman dialect.) Today's use of 'Lingua Franca' tends to sustain this image of a trader's pidgin, referring inter alia to Tok Pisin in Papua New Guinea or Krio in Sierra Leone, but in seventeenth-century Britain it began to gain an alternative role: a synonym for the language, properly a jargon or 'professional slang', used (among other vocabularies) by tramps, sailors, show people and (somewhat later) homosexuals. In this role it gained a new name, variously spelt parlyaree, palarie and, for the purposes of this discussion, Polari (suggested by some to be a strictly gay use of the term, but in fact one more spelling of a term that originated in the standard Italian *parlare*, to speak).

Quite how a trade pidgin came to form the basis of a language last heard by most Britons via the ostentatiously 'camp' cross-talk of 'Julian' and 'Sandy' (Hugh Paddick and Kenneth Williams), an unashamedly queeny duo – 'great bulging thews and wopping great lallies' – created for BBC Radio's *Round the Horne* and *Beyond Our Ken*, staples of the 1960s airwaves, needs some explanation. As far as show business is concerned, the link, as generally accepted, is that of the sea. It would seem that sailors, who naturally picked up 'Lingua Franca' on their trips abroad, brought it home and thence to their on-shore jobs: typically working as pedlars, and joining travelling fairs and circuses. The link between sailors and the stage was certainly established by the nineteenth century, and can still be seen in a variety of backstage terminology; sailors, with their skills at climbing to precarious heights, were much in demand. Such terms as 'rigging' and 'flying' were common to both professions.

The link to homosexual use, which emerges a good deal later than that with show business, forces one into the realm of stereotyping. The automatic union of the stage and homosexuality, and likewise of sailors ('rum, sodomy and the lash') and the gay world is clichéd, far from politically correct, but unavoidable. Where the two groups overlap is an opaque area – seaboard privations are the obvious point – and Kellow Chesney, in his *Victorian Underworld* (1970, and itself largely a distillation of Henry Mayhew's *London Labour and the London Poor*, 1851) suggests that the great centres of male prostitution were the nation's ports. But above all it would seem that the pre-Gay Liberation male homosexual world, like any 'secret' sub-group of society, both required and desired some form of 'secret' language, working simultaneously to affirm the secret unity of the outcast, and by 'speaking in tongues' to hide from the larger, hostile world. Polari, whether picked up from seafaring pals, or adopted from the world of the theatre, fitted the bill. Gay slang existed, but, drawn on languages other than standard English, Polari was even less accessible. It was not generated by the gay world, but came top-down as it were, a ready-made 'lingo', to use a suitably Polari term.

Despite the relative cohesion that the verse quoted above suggests, Polari has never been a 'proper' language. Unlike such constructs, it had no grammar or syntax of its own, and relied without difficulty on recognized English forms. It was not a 'foreign' language in any sense. Instead, as the American academic Ian Hancock has noted, Polari was, even at its peak, at best a lexicon, a vocabulary list of individual words (and a few phrases). Quite how many there were is unknown, but current lists, gathered irrespective of context (i.e. circus, theatre or homosexual), count barely more than one hundred in all. But its individual words and phrases could be used with ease to formulate sentences, paragraphs and, in this case, rhymes. In that it resembles slang, or more so cant, from which an early collector such as Thomas Harman could similarly construct passages – supposedly chats between sixteenth-century villains – top-heavy with the closed vocabulary of the professional malefactor.

That the show-business end of Polari has gradually declined is probably no surprise. The show business that spawned, or at least popularized it, has declined too. The vocabulary of TV and movies is harder-edged, more overtly technical. The provincial rep tour may still struggle on, but few thesps would imagine calling their landlord a 'bona omee of the carsey' (and the Londoners would wonder quite where the lavatory, another definition of carsey and sharing an etymology, fitted in). The decline in gay circles relates to general changes in gay speech. Polari was never the sole repository of gay conversation. Standard English aside, there were the camp enunciations (flourishing from the 1940s to 1960s) of what can be seen as a 'queen culture', where 'Your mother' meant 'I', 'Lily' was an all-purpose prefix, e.g. 'Lily Law': the police, and 'queen' itself appeared in a myriad of combinations, e.g. *dinge queen* (one who liked black lovers), *pine-apple queen* (an aficionado of Hawaiians), and *kaka queen* (a coprophile). They were often plucked wholesale from America, where 'Mary', as a term of address, was especially popular. They had been classified as girls, and 'girls' they would be, in spades.

The emergence of Gay Liberation in the late 1960s put paid to that. Queen culture was too self-effacing, too meek, too hole-in-the-corner for the new self-assertiveness. 'Clone culture', which replaced it in the 1970s, with its exaggerated macho imagery (both epitomized and parodied in the four stereotyped 'real men' of the group Village People), rejected Polari wholesale. There would no longer be a place for this artificial narrative, as concocted for *Gay News*: 'As feely homies ['young men'], when we launched ourselves on the gay scene, Polari was all the rage. We would zhoosh ['fix'] our riahs ['hair'], powder our eeks ['faces'], climb into our bona ['nice'] new drag ['clothes'], don our batts ['shoes'] and troll off ['cruise'] to some bona bijou ['nice, small'] bar. In the bar, we would stand around parlyaring ['chatting'] with our sisters ['gay acquaintances'], varda ['look at'] the bona cartes ['nice genitals'] on the butch homie ['masculine male'] ajax ['nearby'] who, if we fluttered our ogleriahs ['eyelashes'], might just troll over ['wander over'] to offer a light.'[17]

What counted in the new 'out' world were *buns* and *pecs*, not *riahs* and *lallies* ('legs'). Such talk was no more than kow-towing to 'the value-system of a racist patriarchal culture ... [its users] engaging in self-oppression'.[18] Using any form of camp language, however useful it might have been to a sub-culture which accepted, even if reluctantly, the oppression it faced, was simply affirming the justice of that oppression. It was another facet of the closet, and it had to go.

For a while, given the use of the once outlawed 'queer' to turn the (ironic) tables on the homophobes, it was suggested that Polari could stage an equally ironic revival. But Polari, if not dead, is in its final throes. A few terms like *fab* (from 'fabulosa'), *charva* (to fuck) and *camp* itself have survived as refugees in the mainstream. The rest have gone, longterm prisoners in the slang dictionaries, labelled 'obs.' for obsolete.

14 American Century: The Slang Capital of the World

If it is possible to follow a relatively continuous narrative for slang's development prior to the twentieth century, such hopes must be abandoned once one begins moving through that period. Certain mainstream slang lexicography continues, and moves on into the twenty-first century, but in parallel there develop a range of specialist studies, highlighting the slang of the young, the student, the drug user, and many other groups. One factor, however, does serve to unify the fissiparous rest. If the century can be seen as increasingly American in terms of global power, then American popular culture, and the slang that it both generated and spread, is the dominating force. If British slang prior to World War II was still maintaining a presence for the language of the white working class and its criminal cousins, then by the end of that war the situation had changed. What had been gradually happening since World War I had now become a given. That the slang in question was largely black is considered elsewhere. The fact remains that in the counter-language, as in many other ways, America had taken over.

The reality of American-coined slang's progress through the twentieth century and beyond is that it is virtually impossible to avoid. Certainly when one deals with the many forms that make up modern popular culture. The density of exposure obviously differs, but to some extent it is always there. One cannot list every example. Jack Kerouac used it in *On the Road*, but so too did James Joyce in *Ulysses*. Movies have always had some, television too, now the internet gives it an extra home. All that the historian can do is attempt to assess and tease out some of the primary strands and the genres and individuals who helped popularize them.

One of these is the pure orality of much of popular culture. If the word remained on the page – and it left it via vaudeville, the theatre, the movies, the radio and in time TV – it was still far more declaratory, more abrupt when found in popular writing. People said, as it were, what they meant. The subtle codes that underpin Jane Austen or Henry James were abandoned. The mass had neither the time nor the inclination for such cryptanalysis. Slang was urgent, immediate, 'in yer face'. The best-selling work of a Ring Lardner or a Damon Runyon had little if anything to do with plot: it was all about direct speech. It was not what they did – the baseball that Jack Keefe played, the beatings or killings that Harry the Horse or Little Isadore doled out were merely wallpaper – but what they said, and even more so, how they said it. Slang said in two words what 'literary' writers might say in ten, and if that excluded any helpful 'characterization' from the omnipotent author, then that same slang had the task of delineating character. Slang-filled writing is heavy on dialogue. A crime writer like George V. Higgins kept descriptions to a minimum, the players explained themselves. They were elliptical and might seem wilfully obscure – the reader had to put in work too – but they got the job done. Alternatively, for such as Raymond Chandler, the author uses the protagonist's monologue: one extended first-person speech.

Twentieth-century America was also experiencing a relatively new phenomenon: the great industrial city. Britain for once had been ahead. Slang expanded, as did the metropolis. Like the city, slang worked to a beat unfettered by nature's lethargic, predictable rhythms. Slang had played a role in the previous century's popular fiction, but, typically in the historically based dime novel, it was archaic. Not until the end of the century had it begun to reflect its own environment. If popular story-telling – crime fiction, pulp magazines, the movies – were using the city's language to tell its story, the urgency of the tales was intensified by Prohibition, a purpose-built playground that fostered corruption both criminal and civic, and which inevitably brought forward the glamour of the forbidden. W. R. Burnett's *Little Caesar* (1929) fictionalized the rise and fall of a gangland boss; his *Asphalt Jungle* (1949) gave the whole imbroglio a name. Both became films. Like the slang with which he was equipped, the 'hard-boiled dick' could not have existed outside the modern city. At the same time American crime writers persisted in a variety of sub-Sherlock Holmes inventions, dandyish dilettantes solving melodramatic whodunits, but these were clones of the British original. Holmes needed no slang; neither did they. The working classes, as in much Victorian fiction, played walk-on roles. Even the Baker Street irregulars, Holmes's band of street arabs, seem to speak in standard English; slang only appeared when, late in the canon, it was spoken through American lips.

The problem for the historian is that slang can no longer be corralled. Playing its new roles as conveyor of realism, authenticity, manifestor of the city and its peoples, voice of the dispossessed, the angry and the revolutionary, meanwhile continuing to play its traditional one as voice of the criminal – it defies easy filing. The literary novel absorbs it, not as enthusiastically as the crime one, but it is there. Among those who have embraced it are John Dos Passos, James T. Farrell, Nelson Algren, Budd Schulberg, John Steinbeck, Saul Bellow, Hubert Selby Jr, James Baldwin, Terry Southern, Norman Mailer, John O'Hara, Robert Stone, Richard Price, Stephen King, Carl Hiaasen, Jonathan Lethem and Barry Gifford. Not all slang's published employers are stars: checking the frequency of slang by author, among the most cited is the late Seth Morgan. Some have focused on the underside of life, but by no means all. Slang is everywhere and is barely remarked upon. On the contrary, for the writer who desires accuracy, slang is often a given.

Meanwhile there are the autobiographers (some criminals, others not) and the journalists. Among the former are Jack Callahan, Jack Black, Willie Sutton, Rocky Graziano, Iceberg Slim, 'Toney Betts', Piri Thomas, Ernesto Torres, and Edward Bunker. The latter include Jack Lait, Meyer Levin, Jimmy Breslin, Tom Wolfe and David Simon. But in every category one might list scores of others.

Slang has a walk-on role in another sub-set of fiction: the proletarian novel that flourished between the wars. These politicized fictions, invariably from the left, needed slang to establish their credentials. But unlike the tales of hardboiled dicks or the vignettes of big city life, they focused on the working class as often idealized and invariably suffering proletarians, and not detectives, criminals and the like. If they were slangy, that came with the territory, but it did not delineate it. The proletarian novel – whether written by long-forgotten hacks fitting their narrative to the Party line, or by such as John Steinbeck, Henry Roth, Edward Dahlberg or Richard Wright – was first and foremost propaganda. It was a novel that dealt with poverty and its struggles, whether of urban prole or the rural farmer. Consciously or not, it held a sub-text: the struggle of the left-wing intellectual, as Leslie Fiedler put it: 'to identify himself with the oppressed elements in society and with the movement which claimed to represent them'.[1]

The city predominated – it was slang's natural home – but it did not have things all its own way. The cowboy had featured in the dime novels and the pulps, and had been adopted into the movies and TV. What was the hard-boiled private eye but a cowboy riding an urban range. His Olds might be a horse, but his language was equally, and perhaps less artificially picturesque. The singing cowboy might be a folksy, even sentimental figure, but real-life cowboy songs were harder edged. The vocabulary of Guy Logsden's 1989 collection *'The Whorehouse Bells Were Ringing' and Other Songs Cowboys Sing* makes the point. Western staples such as *buckaroo*, *honky-tonk* and *ornery* are there, but they jostle for space alongside *cunt*, *motherfucker* and *the shits*. Fictional cowboys have been more restrained, but a good helping of slang establishes authenticity. Clarence Mulford (creator of Hopalong Cassidy, a rather more hard-boiled figure on the page than on screen), Max Brand (real name Frederick Schiller Faust), Zane Gray and Andy Adams were among the many who brought the 'Wild' West into town. On the whole they flourished before World War II, but Elmore Leonard, better known today for his explorations of small-time criminals, began his career out on the range.

In January 1934 W. J. Funk, of the dictionary publisher Funk and Wagnall's, offered his list of the 'ten modern Americans who have done most to keep American jargon alive'. They were Sime Silverman, editor of the 'show business bible' *Variety*, the cartoonist 'TAD' (Theodore) Dorgan, the Ziegfeld songwriter Gene Buck, Damon Runyon of 'Guys and Dolls' celebrity, Broadway columnist Walter Winchell, mid-West humorist George Ade of 'Fables in Slang', short-story writer Ring Lardner, Gelett Burgess, coiner of 'bromide' and 'blurb', columnist Arthur 'Bugs' Baer and the iconoclastic journalist, critic and lexicographer H. L. Mencken.

Lists are debatable and *Time* magazine was unimpressed. It noted, on 15 January, that Funk had failed to define his term and that '[i]f he meant the ten men who had coined the greatest number of slang words, his list would have been hard to defend. Astute commentators doubted whether any of the ten had ever coined any slang at all.'

> The late Sime Silverman, founder-publisher of Variety, helped popularize such technical theatre talk as 'wow,' 'panic,' and 'flop' but it never got far from Broadway. H. L. Mencken coined expressions like 'Bible Belt,' 'booboisie,' 'Yahwah,' which became part of the language of his imitative admirers but not slang. Cartoonist T. A. Dorgan ('Tad') put a little dog in his pictures who barked 'balogna'; the term was not, like some of Tad's, his own. 'Blessed event,' 'phttf' and 'middle-aisle' by Winchell are too conscious to be slang; 'whoopee,' old when he first used it, is already obsolete. 'Bugs' Baer's small Hearst column contains wisecracks like 'ears like handles on a loving cup' which are the opposite of slang. Ring Lardner [...] was usually careful to avoid inventions of his own, stuck close to the jargon of baseball. Columnist Damon Runyon mixes authentic underworld talk with invented freaks. Gelett Burgess' The Goops contributed a less valuable word than Sinclair Lewis's Babbitt. George Ade's Fables in Slang were funnier than real slang. Gene Buck, who, Mr. Funk said last week, had once told him he 'was responsible for 100 words that are now current in the language' was guilty of a songwriter's exaggeration.[2]

Time was debatable too, and while its criticisms hold water, the list remained a touchstone. Writing the fourth edition of his *American Language* (1938), Mencken noted the names and added some extras: among them Jack Conway, another *Variety* man, cartoonist Milt Gross, the eccentric playwright-cum-boxing manager Wilson Mizner and another songwriter, Johnny Lyman.

Mencken dropped the names in 1948, when the book was expanded into three volumes, but its premises remained. He was unimpressed by

Broadway slang – 'many of its brighter words and sayings may be readily reduced to "Oh, you son-of-a-bitch"' – but accepted that 'Nevertheless it is from this quarter [i.e. Broadway] that most American slang comes, a large part of it invented by gag-writers, newspaper columnists, and press agents, and the rest borrowed from the vocabularies of criminals, prostitutes and the lower orders of show folk. There was a time when it was chiefly propagated by vaudeville performers, but now that vaudeville is in eclipse the torch has been taken over by the harlequins of movie and radio.'[3]

It was a relationship that worked: Broadway, William R. Taylor has written, was 'the place that words built'.[4] Winchell, in his 'Primer of Broadway Slang', written for *Vanity Fair* in 1927, called it 'the slang capital of the world … it is difficult to imagine any other spot on the globe where the citizenry take so readily to slang'. But it was not for everyone: 'little of it is comprehensive [*sic*] west of the Hudson and north of Harlem'. But who else mattered. Those whom *Variety* termed *hix* and Mencken dismissed as the *booboisie* would have to gawp from outside. Broadway, which meant Times Square and the streets and avenues around it, held the nation's most important journalists and the newspapers and magazines that employed them, plus the places where they socialized and drank. As well as the *Times*, there were the *Mirror* and the *Daily News*, plus the *New Yorker*, *Vanity Fair* and Mencken's own *Smart Set*. There were places for the trade weeklies *Variety* and *Billboard*. There were a good number of the city's theatres and the offices that held those involved in theatrical life; there were those who ran and performed in vaudeville and the home base for America's touring carnivals; there was the music business and its periphery; there was also Madison Square Garden, with its emphasis on boxing and which attracted fighters, managers and promoters, and which also drew in the gamblers, on boxing, horseracing and a variety of other sports; to feed and water them all there was a thicket of cabarets and speakeasies, restaurants and bars. Where there was so much money to be made there was also the underworld. Everything, in other words, that slang could possibly need to thrive.

Mencken used the word 'invented', and the implication is that for Broadway the creation of new slang was a conscious, artificial act.

William Taylor suggests that the journalists were as much capitalizing on the material they found as they were setting out to embellish the linguistic stock. It was, one might say, lying in the streets; all the astute writer needed do was pick it up.

Mencken's 'invention' was epitomized by *Variety* and by the superstar chronicler of New York nightlife, Walter Winchell. The latter may have positioned Broadway slang as being beyond the mass – a linguistic precursor of Saul Steinberg's 1976 *New Yorker* cover 'View of the World From 9th Avenue' – but for all that *Variety's* more inward-looking showbiz jargon was reserved for those who needed it, many terms moved out to general use: *cliffhanger, soap opera, boffo, payoff, freeloader, bimbo, platter, tie-in, hoofer, smash, scram, wowed, hick, pushover, gams, disc-jockey, brush-off, chiseler, corny, screwy, nix, click, whodunit, payola, baloney, palooka, nuts,* and *emcee. Variety* may not have coined them all, what mattered is that it popularized them and most of that list remain current. And then there were the headlines. Cecil Beaton, visiting in the mid-Thirties, delighted in such as 'London Quencheries Free Pix; Exhibs Squawk; Brewery Adamant' and 'Chi Thankful for Turkey Day Hypo', and for his British readers translated the trademark 'Sticks Nix Hick Pix': 'Inhabitants of [...] small provincial towns do not like seeing movie pictures about the rough country such as forests, deserts or other rural regions of adventures.' 'Only initiates,' he added, 'can understand.'[5]

Jack Conway was an exemplar of such, and for the magazine's 21st Anniversary issue explained 'Why I Write Slang'. 'As one apt critic put it, "Without slang he would be dumb" and he might have added, hungry. Slang, in addition to providing me with seven flops weekly and three scoffs daily, has saved me from night school and made it possible for me to get the pennies without making weight for the erudite word slingers who are big leaguers in the three-syllable racket. I had sense enough to know that with my 50-word vocabulary, I'd be a busher in that company ...'[6]

Walter Winchell, who started off as half of a vaudeville song-and-dance double act (Winchell and Green) lived by his coinages. It might seem odd that they had any bearing on his seemingly infinite power over the destinies of New York society, but they were part of making the image that wielded that power. As Winchell's biographer Neal

Gabler has suggested, Winchell signified the era's turning on its head of traditional cultural norms. He was 'the barbarian at the gates', moving the culture that mattered from the high to the low. Slang represented democracy, and whatever one thought of Walter's Winchellisms, his linguistic acrobatics helped shift the dominant cultural mode. Winchell was populist, so was his language, and whether its subjects liked the column or not, those he addressed on the radio as 'Mr and Mrs America' treated his texts in a populist way. 'People began to read Winchell for his new coinages the way fans read the sports section for the latest scores.'[7]

That few Winchellisms survived is unsurprising. Their identification with their creator was simply too intimate. It was fine for his ellipsis-laden column to offer such synonyms for marriage as *welded*, *merged*, *middle-aisled*, and *Lohengrined*. And for divorcing pairs to be *telling it to a judge*, or *straining at the handcuffs*. It hardly worked in someone else's mouth. And *Time* was right: for all Funk's and Mencken's praise, the majority of Winchell's terminology was less slang than word-play. The advent of a baby, in Winchellese, was not merely birth but *getting storked* and *infanticipating*. Lovers were *that way*, *uh-huh*, and *cupiding*. Then there were the one-offs: *debutramp* (debutante), *Chicagorilla* (gangster), *Joosh* (Jewish), *sextress*, *fooff* (a pest), *moom pictures* (the movies) and *Wildeman* (a homosexual). When Winchell dipped into mainstream slang – *pash* (passion), *shafts* (legs), *giggle-water* (hard liquor) – he was on safer ground, but his own coinages lacked staying power. When he fell from grace, so did they. Seventy years after Winchell's peak, it is as hard to admire his linguistic reputation as it is to tremble at his journalistic one. Yet no Winchell, no modern 'celebrity culture', and as Gabler has written, 'Without Walter Winchell historians will be unable to explain the 20th century.'[8]

What neither Mencken nor Funk had added, nor indeed had Walter Winchell who had offered his own list of slang creators within his 'Primer' of 1927, was the importance of sportswriters. The role of slang in sports journalism was a good century old; pioneered by Pierce Egan and his successors. If anything it had intensified. Writing in *American Speech* in 1927, Harold E. Rockwell explained the sportswriters' trade, and its links to slang. '[T]he sporting writer – Facts to him are incidental.

[…] He is a freebooter. He goes into the street for his slang; he invents words when the dictionary fails him; he writes what is in his head, how and as he wishes. […] The sporting writer serves a clientele which is not so much concerned with facts as with good, rollicking tales of the diamond, the mat, the gridiron, and the boxing ring. His readers want color, they demand color, and usually they get color. To retell the thrilling moments of a boxing match in a manner appropriate for an account of a Rotarian convention would be folly. The misguided sporting writer would lose both his readers and his job. Of all the sporting writers, he who pictures the stirring battles of the ring is the breeziest. He knows no restraint. Slang, he uses in full measure, and his readers like it; they adore it and the slangier he is, the higher is he held in their esteem.'[9] And of all sports, boxing seemed to be the most slang-creative and like it or not, '[i]t cannot be denied, then, that to the sporting writer some credit must go for his aid in nourishing American speech with a picturesque, if rather coarse, food'.[10]

Ring Lardner (1885–1933) had been a sportswriter, so had Runyon; both specialized in baseball, though Runyon also covered boxing and he was a heavy gambler at the track. TAD's earliest cartoons, like those of the unmentioned but influential Bud Fisher (of *A. Mutt* and later *Mutt and Jeff*) had worked for the sports pages. Dorgan for instance replaced the sports editorial with his baseball strip 'Bonehead Barry', one of the first to celebrate the game. Fisher's Mutt – at least at the outset – provided racing tips.

Fisher used slang prolifically but he was rarely put forward as one of its coiners. Dorgan was. Among the terms that were put down to his invention were *apple-sauce* (nonsense), *benny* (overcoat), *cake-eater* and *drug-store cowboy* (a womanizer), *cat's meow* and *cat's pajamas*, *cheaters* (eye-glasses), *chin music* (talk), *dogs* (shoes), *dumb Dora* (a stupid girl), *dumbell* (a stupid person), *nickel nurser* (miser), *nobody home* (a fool), and *skimmer* (a hat). There were also phrases, notably *for crying out loud!*, *twenty-three, skiddoo* (go away) and *yes, we have no bananas*. The reality was less impressive. TAD's proven coinages were *apple-sauce*, *drugstore cowboy*, *cat's meow* but seemingly not 'pyjamas', *chin goods*, but not 'music', *dogs* as feet, *nickel nurser*, *nobody home*, and *twenty-three* (though no 'skidoo').

But did the coinage matter, other than for the etymologists, who often seemed to enjoy the argument far more than its proposed solution, and in time the obituarists? The reality was that there was an outburst of slang coinage and slang popularism in America as the century advanced. On the whole there were few attributions, and as to first recorded use, much of that was down to chance. The work of Helen Green, 'Hugh McHugh' and Clarence L. Cullen has been noted. Alongside Dorgan and Fisher, there was another sportswriter, Charles E. Van Loan, who turned his hand to fictional tales of boxing, golf and baseball even before Ring Lardner made that arena his own with his tales of his creation Jack Keeffe – as self-aggrandizing as he is self-deluding – in the series of baseball columns brought together as *You Know Me Al* (1916). Slang wasn't mandatory in sports journalism – by the time of A. J. Liebling, W. C. Heinz and Jimmy Cannon, all starting out in the 1930s, its presence was much reduced, even if the style remained vernacular – but for a while the sports beat played a major part in the general boom in slang's proliferation.

Damon Runyon (1880–1946), who arrived in New York in 1910, and was a successful journalist when Winchell was still a less than socko hoofer, came at the low life from a very different angle. Winchell had played groupie to the FBI's megalomaniac J. Edgar Hoover, seeking to act as a proxy Feeb. Runyon seemed to sympathize with the bad guys. He was a big gambler and moved regularly in those less than legitimate circles. His best friend was Dutch Schultz's accountant, Otto 'Abbadabba' Berman, who died in 1935 in the same burst of machine-gun bullets as did his boss. Runyon put him into his stories as 'Regret, the horse player'.

The first story of what would be known as the 'Guys and Dolls' of Broadway appeared in 1929. The tale runs that Runyon, with his knowledge of gangland, was told to write about the assassination that year of 'Mr Big' Arnold Rothstein. He dried, but turned for rescue to a fictional take, writing: 'Only a rank sucker will think of taking two peeks at Dave the Dude's doll, because while Dave may stand for the first peek, figuring it is a mistake, it is a sure thing he will get sored up at the second peek, and Dave the Dude is certainly not a man to have sored up at you.' Hearst bought the story for $800. The hapless naïve at whom the Dude was sore was one Waldo Winchester, Runyon's thinly disguised version of Winchell.

There would be eighty more and they would be published in what were known as the 'slicks', high-selling and high-paying magazines like *Cosmopolitan*, *Collier's* and the *Saturday Evening Post*. Runyon's characters may have walked out of the hard-boiled section of the pulp magazines, but they would never be bracketed with even the best of them. Apart from the sheer quality of the writing, Runyon's robbers and good-time girls were paradoxically soft-boiled. Their creator claimed that his basic plot was that of the fairy-tale Cinderella. And although there is a good deal of violence and not a few murders, the stories do have a fairy-tale element. They are perhaps fables, although the reader has to work out the moral for themselves. The good may not always win, but the bad invariably get their deserts. There is sentiment in Runyon's Broadway as well as sensation. The middle classes wouldn't read *Black Mask*, even when Hammett or Chandler were on the cover; they did take *Cosmopolitan* and the *SEP*.

Readers did not turn to Runyon for his plots, even if several of them became movies and one the regularly revived musical *Guys and Dolls*. Runyon was about language and *Time* was wrong: the bulk of that language was well established, whether within the underworld or elsewhere. His works can be mined for over 1,000 terms, and while there are occasions on which he tinkers, typically by adding suffixes (*-eroo*, *-aroo*, *-ola*, and *-us*), or tweaking an established slang term with a variant synonym (e.g. *Francesca* for *fanny*), Runyon's slang – often dismissed as complete fabrication – is sound. Terms such as *bim*, *collar*, *cut up old touches*, *duke*, *ear-ie*, *flogger*, *keister*, *moxie*, *potatoes*, *roscoe*, *scratch* and *yard* were all part of the speech-worlds in which he moved. A recent critic, Adam Gopnik, has compared Runyon's use of language to that of P. G. Wodehouse, who also revelled when pertinent in the slang of American low-life: 'Like Wodehouse, [...] Runyon inherited a comedy of morals and turned it into a comedy of sounds, language playing for its own sake.'[11]

Slang was simply too omnipresent for any contemporary journalist to sidestep it. Oliver Odd McMcIntyre (1884–1938) was not among those noticed by Funk, but his column 'New York Day by Day' went to more than 375 papers, and for many out-of-towners, McIntyre was their main route to Broadway. Around 3,000 of them sent him letters every week. A mid-Westerner, he began – like Runyon, though not as a sportswriter – on local papers before moving to New York in time to cover the *Titanic* disaster of 1912 as city editor of the *New York Evening Mail*. By the 1920s he was writing sketches about the big city from the perspective of a small-town boy, and the syndicated column ran from the 1920s through to his death. He also wrote a monthly piece for *Cosmopolitan*. McIntyre played the rube (though a rube with a Park Avenue address and a chauffeur), but slang came with his territory, and his columns were generous in its use. Not as idiosyncratic as Winchell (nor ever as deliberately provocative), and far from Runyon's underworld, he still found slang a necessity. Few columns appeared without a few examples. McIntyre was no coiner, but one of many who popularized the lexis.

Runyon celebrated the underworld, but his mobsters were strictly for those who bought the slicks. Middle-class voyeurs who found his stories as near real-life villainy as they wished to go. Down-market and down a couple of classes lay villainy's other fictional world: that of the pulps.

Pulp magazines, so-called from the ultra-cheap woodpulp paper on which they were printed, were born in the Twenties, reached their peak in the Thirties and Forties, and fell victim, like much else in US popular culture, to the new juggernaut of the Fifties: TV. They covered a wide range of topics: there were military pulps, sci-fi pulps, mystery pulps, adventure pulps, sports pulps, western pulps, spicy (i.e. softcore sexy) pulps and crime and detective pulps. And it was these last, ranging from *Black Mask* (the first and best) to such as *Double-Action Detective*, *Detective Fiction Weekly*, and, inevitably *Spicy Detective*, with dozens more on the newsies' racks, that remain the most celebrated of the genre. Runyon would not be tempted – there simply wasn't the money to be made – but at their best pulps could attract the likes of Dashiell Hammett and Raymond Chandler, whose careers were launched behind their hyperactive covers, and while authors such as Robert Leslie Bellem and Joe Archibald may have lasted less well, they once sold their millions too.

Between them they created a new school of fiction: the world of the hard-boiled dick. The *eye*. The *shamus*. The *private operator*. Superstars such as Hammett's Continental Op and Chandler's Philip Marlowe, and journeymen such as Bellem's Dan Turner, 'Hollywood Detective' and Archibald's Willie Klump, the bumbling 'president of the Hawkeye Detective Agency'. The big boys made it into novels, the small fry kept their hard-working authors alive. They all delighted a seemingly insatiable public.

The reasons for that delight were mixed, but what it came down to was voyeurism. The same fascination that had audiences flocking to see stars like James Cagney or Edward G. Robinson slugging it out on screen – whether as baddies or good guys – in movies like *Public Enemy, White Heat, Scarface* and the rest, usually products of the Warner Brothers lot. Guns, girls, glamour and what the mob, at least on pulp paper, would call *geetus* (money). The underworld, as ever, looked a lot sexier than the daily grind. One pulp title unashamedly billed itself as *Racket and Gangster Stories*. The penny-a-liners just had to remember to toss in a moral ending.

Language was central to the pulps' appeal. Especially the detective variety. Slang's first recorded glossaries came from 'civilians' trying to make sense of what criminals were saying and criminal slang has been central to the vocabulary for half a millennium. The pulps exploited that vocabulary, but also set about creating it. Readers didn't expect standard English, they wanted rough, tough, and vivid. A tough guy used tough terminology. Sometimes it got a little absurd: the nearest some of the words came to the real-life street was sitting on a newsstand between lurid covers, but no matter. It was all part of the atmosphere. No *private dick* worth his oft-suspended *buzzer* would have it any other way.

Bellem took it to the limit. Slang in excelsis. Synonyms like a thesaurus. His 'Dan Turner' wasn't an investigator but a *private dick, pry, skulk* or *snoop*. He met women, had women (none of Chandler's 'erotic as a stallion' for Dan: no limp-wristed *gazooks, jessies* or *she-males* invited to his spartan *shebang*). And called them *cookies, cupcakes, muffins, patooties, twists, wrens, frails, tails* and *quails*. He worked for money, which was *cabbage, greenery, salad, iron men, spondulicks, moola* and *ducats*. Guns were *cannons, gats, rodneys, peashooters, roscoes* and *equalizers*. Guns that didn't shoot, but *burned, cracked, whopped, coughed* and *yapped*. And didn't kill but *biffed, blipped, bopped, belted, browned, bumped* and *butched* and that's just the Bs. Then the *flatheads*, *gendarmes*, *harness bulls* and *slewfoots* came in and if you'd left the *ginzos*, *grifters*, *bimbos*, *slugs* and *jibones* alive, took them off to the *bastille*, the *slammer* or the *big house*. Later, when they got the *juice*, they'd *cook* in the *smokehouse*.

S. J. Perelman, who penned scripts for the Marx Brothers and called his journalism *feuilletons*, wrote up Turner for the *New Yorker*. Bellem's star was 'the apotheosis of all private detectives'. He also mentioned 'the steely automatic and the frilly pantie', which was more like it, even if he prefaced them by another three-dollar tongue-twister: 'juxtaposed'. Either way he mentioned that they paid. Bellem kept on typing.

The pulp died, as noted, with the advent of television. Yet the style survived; the phrase 'dime novel', last used in the nineteenth century, was revived, this time much more attuned to the hard-boiled heroes of the pulps. However, if the new dime novelists were just as keen on slang as their pulp predecessors (though none as much as Bellem), their heroes' occupation had changed. Still loners, they were no longer private operators but solitaries, alienated figures following a tortuous and tortured path through Fifties America. Authors included Ben Appel, Harry Whittington, Peter Rabe and Gil Brewer. The city and its authorities remained corrupt, the language as hard-edged as ever, but there was no expectation that the hero would win through. Often he did well merely to survive. Never more so than in the nihilistic, almost hallucinatory work of the type's exemplar, Jim Thompson.

Their publishers, such as Ace Books (who also had Wodehouse on their back list) or Fawcett Gold Medal, had a parallel world to exploit; that of the *JD*, the teenage juvenile delinquent. Teens had never appeared in the pulps – the demographic had yet to be spotlighted before the mid-1940s – but the world of the JD gangs, with their switchblades and leather jackets, their jailbait and gangbangs, their drugs and of course their slang, proved very popular. Authors included Harlan Ellison, usually writing as 'Hal Ellson'; Wenzell Brown, Edward de Roo and 'Vin Packer' (actually Maryjane Meaker). Ace Books also gave readers one Bill Lee, a.k.a. William Burroughs, debuting with *Junkie* in 1953, but as the title makes clear, this was a story not of juvenile delinquence but of narcotic use.

Given the dependence of all subsequent examples of youth slang (beatniks, hippies, punks and so on) on black antecedents, the slang found in JD fiction is surprisingly pallid. Perhaps it was the need to feature white gangs – usually Italian – but there is relatively little black slang. Of the near 450 terms used by genre leader 'Hal Ellson' in six novels written between 1949 and 1956 a mere twenty-seven terms are black in origin. Of the 200 terms used in three contemporary novels by Harlan Ellison, there are just five. It was anomalous, and it would not last.

With or without the pulps and their spinoffs, crime remains slang's showcase. Pulps and Fifties dimes aside, no crime novel of worth – and more important presumed authenticity – can succeed without a heavy larding of slang. Whatever the subset of the genre, whether they deal in the hard-boiled dick or focus on the criminal, authors need slang. George V. Higgins, William P. McGivern, Mickey Spillane, Walter Mosley, George Pelecanos, Andrew Vachss, Daniel Woodrell, Joe Lansdale, John Ridley, Nick Tosches and Eddie Little are merely a sample, albeit of the best. It is hardly surprising that Pelecanos, Richard Price and Denis Lehaine were recruited by creator David Simon to write regularly for *The Wire* (2002–8), a TV show so rich in slang that some viewers opted to use subtitles. Simon is responsible for bringing much slang to notice. As well as his scripts for *The Wire*, his 1997 story of the real-life Baltimore crack trade, *The Corner*, written with Ed Burns who would join him on *The Wire*, is just as dense.

The American century has passed, but American slang remains dominant. Faced with itemizing contemporary examples, one sees that it has become inescapable, almost transparent. If the taboos against what were once unspeakable obscenities have largely disappeared, then slang itself, once rigorously excluded from 'polite' or 'proper' speech, is no longer a pariah. If its role in fiction, in whatever medium, is to authenticate, then this is inevitable: this is how we speak. Nor is there any fudging of the definition: we do not hear of the 'slang of poets' or of politicians' as attacked by nineteenth-century purists. Slang is recognized as itself: the unmediated language of the street, and the street is no longer something other.

15 African-American Slang:
The Flesh Made Word

The street, at least as mediated through contemporary slang, is black. American popular culture, once segregated, is heard around the world via the sound of rap music, and perhaps no medium other than pulp fiction has ever been so imbued with the counter-language. It is the mass-produced voice of the oppressed – ironies of blinged-out superstars notwithstanding – and it can be heard, often in local variations, across the world. It is not a new story, though it may seem so. The spread and growing influence of black slang is nearly a century old. Its origins are somewhat older and like slang in Australia, it is rooted in enforced migration.

The first Africans to make the involuntary journey to North America arrived in Virginia, a British colony of what would become the United States, in 1619.[1] They were sold as indentured servants. Slavery as such is not recorded until 1661, and the institution was enshrined in law under the Slave Codes of 1705. By then the transatlantic slave trade was flourishing, and by the time it ended some 645,000 involuntary travellers had suffered the 'Middle Passage'; at the outbreak of the Civil War in 1861 the US slave population had increased to 4 million. The 2010 US census claims some 40 million citizens of African-American descent, 12.3% of the population and as such the country's second largest ethnic group.

It was necessary that the slaves should communicate: to each other and to their masters. Unlike the prisoners sent out to Australia there was no communal language. Some African languages – notably Wolof – seem to have survived amongst homogenous groups of slaves, but different tribes were unintelligible to each other and slavers were careful to split up tribal groups so as to ensure against rebellious collaboration. None would have been understood by their white masters. What developed was a form of *pidgin* English. It was this pidgin, an Afro-English blend (or in a French colony such as Lousiana Afro-French), that would have been passed on to the slave's children. At this point, in linguistic terms, it becomes a *creole*, that is a pidgin that has native-born speakers and as such moves from a mongrel status (pidgins are traditionally seen as trade languages used between local sellers and visiting buyers) to being one of the 'proper' languages of the country.

Where this language came from remains problematic. The prevailing opinion of early dialecticians was summarized in 1924 by G. F. Krapp: 'From the very beginning the white overlords addressed themselves in English to their black vassals. [...] It would be a very much simplified English – the kind of English some people employ when they talk to babies. It would probably have no uses of the verb, no distinction as of case in nouns or pronouns, no marks of singular or plural. Difficult sounds would be eliminated. Its vocabulary would be reduced to the lowest possible elements.' In his opinion it was 'reasonably safe to say that not a single detail of Negro pronunciation or Negro syntax can be proved to have any other than an English origin'.[2] The language changed, he added, moving in the nineteenth century from 'a grotesque mutilation of the English language' to becoming 'one of the colloquial forms of our many visaged mother tongue',[3] but despite referencing Gullah, a language spoken by blacks in the coastal areas of Georgia and South Carolina, and acknowledged as having links to the Krio speech of Sierra Leone, he still refused to acknowledge any vestige of African roots.

Mencken, whose *American Mercury* published the piece, believed this, as did a number of contemporary scholars. Since then the idea, implicitly racist, has been exploded. But the basis of the language remains debatable: was it, as Afrocentric scholars prefer, based on a mélange of African languages and their grammatical forms or, as Eurocentric dialecticians claim, a form of English picked up from local poor whites, who in turn had imported their dialects from the UK. The near-hysteria aroused by the Ebonics controversy of 1997 – when the educational authorities of Oakland California determined that Ebonics, literally 'ebony phonics',[4] i.e. Black English, should be considered a separate language and taught as such in schools alongside standard English – proved that a resolution remains problematic. There is simply too much weight beyond the linguistic.

None of which undermines the important fact: Black English, whether one names it African-American English (AAE), African-American Vernacular English (AAVE), Black English Vernacular (BEV), Vernacular Black English (VBE), or Ebonics, exists: it is the language spoken at least some of the time by America's black population. Its use is class-based – the poorer the speaker the more it is used, often to the virtual exclusion of standard American English – but all classes have the option of code-switching when necessary. In this it resembles slang – and the more vitriolic of Ebonics' opponents dismissed it as no more than slang and as such worthless – in that it is seen as a language of the street, another bottom-up linguistic creation. If slang is not a language – lacking the necessary linguistic rules – then AAVE is, since it has been accepted that whatever its origins – African or European – there is a discernible grammar. It is not simply a lexis of underclass illiteracies, the linguistic version of an impoverished ghetto. But even if it is not 'just slang', like any language it includes a slang lexis.

As in the world of homosexuality, the first instances of slang that relates to blacks are terms used *about* rather than used *by*. (The original standard term used of slaves was *black*, followed by *African*; others, not limited to slaves, included *Africo-American*, *free man of color* and, during the Civil War, *contraband*, coined after General Benjamin F. Butler issued a proclamation declaring slaves owned by Confederates to be 'contraband of war'). The quintessential example being, of course, *nigger*, ultimately based on Latin *niger* (black) and developed either through the early Modern English *neger*, or via Spanish *negro*. (The earlier *kaffir*, from Arabic *kefir*, an infidel, meant an African and was used of slaves, but not those sent to America.) The playwright Thomas Dekker used it ('the Blacke King of Neagers') in 1613 and a few years later it is found alongside the first slaves: on 20 August 1619 John Rolfe, husband to Pocahontas, recorded in his journal the first shipment of Africans to

Virginia: 'there came in a Dutch man-of-warre that sold us 20 negars.' The term was widely established by the end of the seventeenth century. It has yet to disappear. Blacks used it too, records of that start in the mid-nineteenth century, but while they could echo the derogatory white use, the neutral or even affectionate use, often noted in modern rap, was also available. (Records are patchy, but in 1912 an observer noted that 'among this [lower] class of coloured men the word 'nigger' was freely used in about the same sense as the word 'fellow,' and sometimes as a term of almost endearment'.[5])

Piccaninny, imported from the West Indies, is found *c.* 1650; it was adopted from the Spanish or Portuguese *pequeño*, small, or Portuguese *pequenino*, tiny. Used of children it was relatively neutral, but the patronizing aspect developed. It is one of those words noted by Grose in 1785 as a 'negroe term'. Grose also offers 'Chimney chops, an abusive appellation for a negro' and 'snowball', thus instituting a tradition of heavy-handed 'jokes' at the expense of black skin. Some terms, e.g. *Hottentot*, remained in Europe, but others reached America. *Blackee* or *blackie* is recorded in 1732, although its use in America is postponed for a century; before that references are to slaves in the West Indies or to black servants in London. The first record of *darkey / darkie* comes in 1775 in F. Moore's *Songs and Ballads of the American Revolution*. *Cuff* or *Cuffy* (from Twi *kofi*, a 'day-name' for the boy born on Friday) was used generically from the eighteenth century, as were *Quashi* (Twi *kwasi*, a boy born on a Sunday), *Mungo* (from Mandingo) and *Congo*. *Pompey*, again generic, emerged in the nineteenth century when the naming of slaves for classical heroes was fashionable, as did *Rastus*, from Erastus and giving, inter alia, Kerry Mills's song of 1896, 'Rastus on Parade' as well as a once-popular series of racist jokes featuring 'Rastus and Mandy' (or Liza).

The most notorious of such names, *Sambo*, was among the earliest, recorded in Barbados *c.* 1650 and from 1704 in America, where the *Boston News-Letter* of 2 October stated that 'There is a Negro man taken up supposed to be Runaway from his Master [...] calls himself Sambo.' The etymology of the earlier Caribbean use is in Spanish *zambo*, used to describe those of mixed black and Indian or European blood (the word also describes a breed of yellow monkey). The US use, which emerged during the era of slavery, may have a different root; the Foulah *sambo* (uncle) or Hausa *sambo* (second son, or name of the spirit). Sambo began as a neutral term, but as slavery fell into increasing disrepute, so did its terminology. The word was widely popularized by Helen Bannerman's best-selling children's book *The Story of Little Black Sambo* (1923), but the term, and that book (although in no way actively racist), have long since been considered unacceptable.

The nineteenth century added the equally derisive *coon*, even if the stereotyped animal, the raccoon, was seen as cunning rather than stupid. In that context the term had already meant a Whig, a native American, and a sly rustic before the first recorded use for 'black' in 1848. The imagery was older. In the 1767 play *Disappointment* by 'Andrew Barton' one finds this: 'RACOON [negro]: I must go dis instant and settle de place of meeting. PLACKET: Can you leave me so soon, my dear Cooney?' The term was certainly well established by the 1890s when the black lyricist Ernest Hogan offered the song, 'All Coons Look Alike to Me'. He professed to be surprised by the hostility it aroused and claimed that as a black man he could hardly be a racist. The word turned up again in 'Every Race Has a Flag But the Coon' (1899), in 'Coon, Coon, Coon' (1900), and even 'The Phrenologist Coon' (1901); all these were written by whites.

The century set in place most of the tropes of white-to-black racism. The obvious were based on colour (*blackberry, brownskin, dinge, smoked Yankee, sooty, tarbrush*). Others included lack of intelligence (*ape*), consistency of hair (*kinkyhead*), and aggressive sexuality (*buck*). The twentieth century merely developed them, taking the total of around fifty terms in use by 1899 to an end-of-the-century total of nearly 300.

Derogatory terms for American (and indeed all) blacks are easily found, surpassing in number even those coined for slang's second least favoured group, the Jews. Slang as coined and used by black Americans is more elusive, at least prior to the twentieth century. There is little evidence of black slang prior to the Civil War. Perhaps the earliest term was *backra* (a white man), first recorded in Aphra Behn's play *Oroonoko* (1688). Early uses were Caribbean but the term is used by Thomas Haliburton ('Sam Slick') in the 1830s and listed by Bartlett as an 'Americanism' in 1848. The word came from the Surinam black patois where it meant master, and it has been suggested ultimately from Efik (the language of the Calabar coast) *mba* (all), and *kara* (to encompass, to get round, to master [a subject]); thus *mbakara, makara*, a white man, a European, which offered a parallel meaning of a demon or a powerful and superior being. In 1725 the *New Canting Dictionary* lists *yam* (to eat), taken from such West African words as Swahili *nyama* (meat) and Fulah *nyama* (to eat), although at that date it probably reflected the Caribbean rather than America.

Francis Grose's 'negroe' words would also have come from the Caribbean. As well as *piccaninny*, there is *bumbo* ('the private parts of a woman'), and *dingey Christian* ('a mulato, or any who has, as the West Indian term is, a lick of the tar brush, that is, some negroe blood in them'); the term incorporates *dinge* (black), which survived into the twentieth century, and the presumption is that a 'real' Christian is white. To illustrate *scavey*, i.e. *savvy*, defined as 'sense, knowledge', he offers the phrase 'Massa, me no scavey', 'master, I don't know' and identifies it as 'negro language'. As seen, Grose also lists *lick of the tarbrush*, defined as 'One of the blue squadron; any one having a cross of the black breed'. George Matsell, whose *Vocabulum* of 1859 is the first lexicon of American slang, has no reference to black talk; in the same year John Camden Hotten's dictionary defines *cut-throat* as a tough, aggressive or frightening black man.

Grose also offers *kickerapoo* or *kickeraboo* (dead; presumed to be a black pronunciation of the phrase 'kick the bucket'). Around the same time his contemporary the ballad-maker and playwright Charles Dibdin the Younger used the term as the title of some verses that are both hedonistic and remarkably egalitarian. They begin:

> Your negro say one ting you no take offence,
> Black and white be one colours hundred year hence,
> For when massa death kick him into the grave,
> He no spare negro, buckra, nor massa, nor slave.
>
> [...]
>
> One massa, one slave, high and low all degrees,
> Can be happy, dance, sing, make all pleasure him please
> One slave be one massa, he good, honest brave,
> One massa bad, wicked, be worse than one slave[6]

Pierce Egan cited the first verse on the first page of his *Book of Sports* (1832), as part of his celebration of a 'swell dragsman' (i.e. an aristocratic driver of a coach and horses). In *Life in London* he also recounts Tom and Jerry's East End encounter with Black Sal, seen in the Cruikshank illustration of revels at the gin-shop All Max. *Black Sal* seems to have been another generic, noted as such in 1813 in the *Publications of the Colonial Society of Massachusetts*, which suggests, 'Let's tell horrible tales of black Sall, / And of babies curl'd headed and yellow,'[7] and adds a note to explain that 'Though not recognized in the dictionaries, "Sall" appears to be a generic name for a negress, as Sambo is for a negro.' Black Sal also lies behind *Aunt Sally*, a black-faced doll, popular in early-nineteenth-century London; its face also served as the shop-sign for a second-hand clothier's. In *The Season Ticket* (1860), Haliburton has a human Aunt Sally 'who was a nigger as black as the ace of spades or the devil's hind leg'.[8] Egan again, in *The Finish to the Adventures of Tom & Jerry* (1830), has the black Hannah saying, 'It's all the same in the dark, massa Jack, an't it? Me as good as silk lady?'[9]; *silk* being metonymic for the clothing of rich white women and thus their persons. The term persisted in black use well into the twentieth century.

The record of actual black terms is thin. There is *this child*, meaning oneself and first recorded in the *New York Herald* of 16 January 1837: 'When committed by the magistrate, Mary [a black woman] [...] threw herself on the floor, and screamed, "There now, carry me if you want me, but as to walking, this child don't do that!"' Another court report, in the *New York Transcript* of 15 February 1836, refers to a young black woman who responded to her sentence of two years and six months by saying that 'that she did not care a d—n if they had sent her up for *forty-eleven* years'. *Old Sam* was the devil while *Old Ned,* used generally across the South, was salt pork or bacon.

A number of black terms logically focused on whites, often the less well off. The classic term *white trash* (literally 'white rubbish') has been recorded since 1822, when the *Bangor Register* of 1 August wrote of 'Nancy Swann, a lady of color whose mighty powers of witchcraft have made "de black niggers, and de poor white trash" tremble'. In 1837 the British philanthropist Harriet Martineau noted that 'There are a few, called by the slaves *mean whites*, signifying whites who work with the hands'. White trash were also *crackers*, originally limited to Georgia, and the adjective *triflin'* was used to describe 'low-down people'. *Low-downer* itself referred to the same class in North Carolina. *No account*, used to mean worthless, insignificant, undependable, untrustworthy or criminal, seems to have been used by both blacks and whites. The term *white nigger*, used of a poor white, can be found in 1836 in Haliburton's *Clockmaker*, but Ned Ward's *London Spy*, writing of transported criminals in 1700, had already explained that '[The Irishman is] a Valuable Slave in our Western-Plantations, where they are distinguish'd by the Ignominious Epithet of White-Negroes'. As regards the plantation aristocracy, *massa*, i.e. master, is one of the first terms to be recorded, though the generics *Mr Charlie*, *Miss Ann* and *Miss Mary*, referring to the plantation's white owners, and thence to any white men and women, while surely used are not recorded until the 1920s.

The early evidence of black speech was primarily representational of a style of speech rather than of a separate vocabulary. Black characters began appearing in white American literary creations by the end of the eighteenth century, typically cast as porters, servants or labourers. They spoke in a mix of pidgin and creole, and might incorporate white slang. Thus in Samuel Low's *The Politician Outwitted* (1789), Cuffy, a porter, speaks thus: 'Tankee, massa buckaraw; you gi [give] me lilly [little] lif [lift] me bery glad dissa ting damma heby. (Puts down the trunk). —'An de deblis [devilish?] crooka [crooked] tone [stone] in a treat [street] more worsa naw [now] than a pricka [prickly] pear for poor son a bitch foot; an' de cole pinch um so too.'[10] In Hugh Henry Brackenridge's novel *Modern Chivalry* (1792–1815), Cuff, a slave, delivers a speech to a Philosophical Society: 'Massa shentiman; I be cash crab in de Wye rive; found ting in de mud; tone, big a man's foot; hole like to he; fetch Massa: Massa say, it be Indian Mocasson. —Oh! fat de call it all tone. He say, you be filasafa, Cuff! I say, O no, Massa you be filasafa. Well, two or tree monts afta … Getta ready; and go dis city, and make grate peech for shentima filasafa.'[11]

There was no dearth of examples; as well as plays and novels they came from newspapers, almanacs and magazines. Or they might be found in advertisements. In Samuel Woodworth's *The Forest Rose* (1826), a play which focused on the gullible New Englander 'Jonathan

Ploughboy', the high point for many audiences was the hero's being tricked into kissing the black maid, Rose. In one of those audiences was George W. Arnold's dialect-ridden lottery tout 'Joe Strickland', who noted, in a letter of 'Jennywerry 24' that everyone had 'laft az if heven un airth was kumin together'. That same year one of Arnold's rivals, Van Beuren & Co., created a pair of black correspondents in the hope of mimicking Arnold's successful advertising. Under the title 'De Dreem of Niggur Hannibal', the author wrote in a grotesque cod-black: 'I byd a tikket ob massa Arnuld for wun dollur-blanck – I byd annudder, and annudder – blanck – blanck – damnn, all blanck. Den I reememmbardd at de wite debbel, in Congo, sed goa too Massa Van Bore'em & Koze – niggur hadd ownlle won dollur lefft inn de wourld, wich hee gabe too Massa Van Bore'em & Koze, for aa tikket, annd by jingo, nex da hee gabe niggur Congo fiv hundrud dolleers. How niggur laff'd and grinnd, annd dancd.'[12]

By then, however, a new form of representation had appeared, one that, at least in mass consumption, would subsume all the others, turning the nuances and complexities of actual black life and speech into a simple format: popular entertainment. The on-stage portrayal of blacks who, as 'Nigger X (his mark) Hannerbal' put it, 'laff'd and grinnd, annd dancd'. And the 'blacks' who provided it would be, almost without exception, white. (One famous exception was William Henry Lane (1825–52), who performed – his own black skin blacked up – as 'Juba' and was seen and written up enthusiastically by a visiting Charles Dickens.)

Blackface minstrelsy, or as it was known in the UK where it was embraced as enthusiastically as in America, simply as 'niggers', was not merely the most popular mass entertainment form of the nineteenth century, but was also responsible for creating a fantasy world, seemingly credible to its white audiences, that made plantation slavery 'fun', with happy, chuckling darkies, plucking their banjoes, dancing like children all the live-long day and loving their white massas and their families. As Hollywood has shown, it was a comforting fantasy that persisted well into the twentieth century.

Minstrelsy's mass-market birth came in the 1820s. The former circus performer George Washington Dixon (1801–61) is credited with being first to put on the make-up when in 1827 he performed 'The Coal Black

Rose' and 'My Long Tail Blue' (a swallow-tailed coat much beloved of Northern black dandies or what slang termed 'zip coons') in Albany before bringing the show in to New York in 1828. Later that year he turned 'Coal Black Rose' (the tale of Cuffy and Sambo's rivalry for Rose) into a play, *Love in a Cloud*, and between songs and stage propelled himself to stardom. In 1834 he added a new hit, and subsequently his trademark song, 'Zip Coon' ('Old Zip Coon is a very larned scholar / He plays on the Banjo / Cooney in de hollar').

The adoption of blackface by actor Thomas Dartmouth 'Daddy' Rice (1808–60) offers minstrelsy a far more tangible creation myth. Rice, a Northerner born in Manhattan, was aware of and admired black singing and decided to use it for his own ends. On tour in a play in 1829 he supposedly persuaded a black porter, the inevitable Cuff, to accompany him to the theatre in which he was working, borrowed Cuff's ragged clothes, blackened his own face, and delivered a song in what passed for 'negro' dialect. As the writer Robert R. Nevin told readers of the *Atlantic Monthly*, 'the extraordinary apparition produced an instant effect'. That a near-naked Cuff was supposedly crouched behind a stage flat, vainly begging Rice to return his clothes so he could get back to much needed work, both embellishes the story and underpins the image of white counterfeiting of black culture. There are variations on the myth but as Eric Lott has written, the story, recounted in great and as regards Cuff condescending detail by Nivens, 'is probably the least trustworthy and most accurate account of American minstrelsy's appropriation of black culture. Indeed it reads something like a master text of the racial economy encoded in blackface performance.'[13]

The final piece of the jigsaw was the word *minstrel* itself. Dixon and Rice simply performed; the umbrella term awaited the appearance in 1843 at New York's Bowery Amphitheatre of 'the novel, grotesque, original and surpassingly melodious Band entitled THE VIRGINIA MINSTRELS'. Thereafter blackface equalled minstrels, the classical example being the Christy Minstrels, founded in 1844. Perhaps the last example was BBC television's *Black and White Minstrel Show*, which survived from 1958 to 1978.

The black activist Frederick Douglass might denounce minstrels as 'the filthy scum of white society, who have stolen from us a complexion denied to them by nature, in which to make money, and pander to the corrupt taste of their white fellow citizens',[14] and white critic Margaret Fuller, noting that even the echt-patriotic song 'Yankee Doodle' had British roots, admit that 'All symptoms of [American] invention[are] confined to the African race',[15] but in popular culture popularity was the key word. The audiences flocked to minstrel shows, with their half-circle of blacked-up singers, musicians and comedians, Bones to one side, Tambo to the other, Mr Interlocutor in the middle, revelling in ever more elaborate variations on the original theme. If the early shows were a mix of a plantation pastorale and the mockery of what were portrayed as the affectations of Northern black dandies, then by 1880, the United Mastadon Minstrels ('40 – Count 'Em – 40!'), featured a 'magnificent scene representing a Turkish Barbaric Palace in Silver and Gold' that included Turkish soldiers marching, a Sultan's palace, and 'Base-ball'.[16]

Yet for all its popularity, and purported representation of black speech, minstrelsy leaves the lexicographer frustrated. Where jazz, blues, and more recently rap have brought with them a rich slang vocabulary to be appropriated, like the musical forms, by the white listener, minstrelsy did not. And if, as has been suggested, the stage delivery of blackface performers can be stripped of its de facto racism, and equated to the dialect humour that was so popular in nineteenth-century America, it still sidestepped such black usage as may have existed. Lyrics popularized such terms as 'zip coon' and 'long-tail blue' but like the stereotypes that were portrayed, there was no attempt to dig deeper. If black slang did exist, it was no concern of the minstrels, even if, as several claimed, they went on field trips to see how those they mimicked really talked.

Minstrelsy's one undeniably slang term was *Jim Crow*. In 'Long Tail Blue', Dixon sang 'Jim Crow is courting a white gall, / And yaller folks call her Sue / I guess she back'd a nigger out, / And swung my long tail blue.' Setting aside what might well be the sexual double-entendre of the dandy's more alluring 'long tail blue' over his rival labourer's rags, Jim Crow became the staple name for a plantation black. Rice used the term in his song 'Jump Jim Crow' ('Turn about and wheel about, / And do just so– / Turn about and wheel about, / And jump, Jim Crow'), which may have been that performed in Cuffy's borrowed rags. Rice toured the UK (and married there) and was equally successful. Charles

Mackay's *Memoirs of Extraordinary Popular Delusions* (1841) recalled how 'an American actor introduced a vile song called "Jim Crow." The singer sang his verses in appropriate costume, with grotesque gesticulations, and a sudden whirl of his body at the close of each verse. It took the taste of the town immediately, and for months the ears of orderly people were stunned by the senseless chorus.'[17]

Perhaps all would have agreed with Charles Townsend, who *c.* 1891 provided a guide for minstrel performers. As well as advising on topics such as make-up – 'You can prepare the burnt cork yourself by obtaining a quantity of corks, placing them in a metal dish, pouring alcohol over them and burning them to a crisp' – he directed: '*End Men* should carefully avoid anything approaching vulgarity and no offensive personalities should be introduced. Avoid slang.'[18]

Neither Black English nor slang played a noticeable role in nineteenth-century lexicography. The first attempt came in 1884, the work of the white writer James Harrison, and was published in the German philological journal *Anglia* in 1884. His essay 'Negro English' offered a brief introduction followed by an attempt to lay out the grammar and linguistic usage of those 6–7 million black Americans by now living below the Mason-Dixon line. And while the paper notes the relation of 'Negro English' to Africa, Harrison was also an early subscriber to the 'baby-talk' theory of black speech: 'The humor and naiveté of the Negro are features which must not be overlooked in gauging his intellectual caliber and timbre; much of his talk is baby-talk, of an exceedingly attractive sort to those to the manner born; be deals in hyperbole, in rhythm, in picture-words, like the poet; the slang which is an ingrained part of his being as deep-dyed as his skin, is, with him, not mere word-distortion; it is his verbal breath of life caught from his surroundings and wrought up by him into the wonderful figure-speech specimens of which will be given later under the head of Negroisms.'[19]

Harrison offers just over 800 such 'negroisms', plus examples of black forms of interjection, address, and so on. But despite his claims there is little that qualifies as slang, and even less that represents a black-only lexis. 'It must be confessed, to the shame of the white population of the South, that they perpetuate many of these pronunciations in common with their Negro dependents; and that, in many places, if one happened to be talking to a native with one's eyes shut, it would be impossible to say whether a Negro or a white person were responding.'[20] Setting aside the undisguised racism, it seems that Harrison's own eyes were also shut: much of the list is no more than black pronunciations of either standard English or of white colloquialisms, e.g. 'to keep er good holt on de tongue = to restrain the tongue', 'to plank down de money = to put down &c.,' 'to kick one inter de middle er nex' week = to kick severely' and hundreds more. A number of terms overlap with the vocabulary Mark Twain uses in *Huckleberry Finn*, published the same year, and Harrison appears to have drawn on Joel Chandler Harris's *Uncle Remus* stories, published in 1881.

As long as the Negro, as the term then was, remained primarily in the country, i.e. the mainly agrarian South, there would not be any real change in Black English, and thus, since slang emanates from the city, in what might be termed black slang. That change can be dated to the movement 'down North' and the gradual involvement of the city in black life. And alongside this, the birth and development of jazz, and the *jazz* or *jive talk* that came with it. As is all slang, the language of jazz was seen as consciously oppositional. It owned to a mongrel lexis, typified by Mencken in 1948 as 'an amalgam of Negro-slang from Harlem and the argots of drug addicts and the pettier sort of criminals, with occasional additions from the Broadway gossip columns and the high school campus'.[21] The jazz lexicographer Robert Gold sees 'a people in rebellion against a dominant majority, but forced to rebel secretly, to sublimate, as the psychologist would put it – to express themselves culturally through the medium of jazz, and linguistically through a code, a jargon.'[22] It is the classic formulation of a counter-language.

The word *jazz* is so far first recorded in 1913, though there have been a variety of supposedly prior sightings, all of them ultimately illusory. Like the term *Big Apple*, the nickname for New York, jazz continues to fascinate and divide the etymologists. The current position links the term to mid-nineteenth-century *jism*, meaning spirit or energy; and although the music came first from New Orleans the word's first use has been traced to players on the 1913 San Francisco Seals baseball club, as reported by one 'Scoop' Gleason in the *San Francisco Bulletin*. The progress from baseball to music is uncharted, but examples of the latter usage appear almost contemporaneously. Jazz as music has never been slang, but its slang definitions include sexual intercourse, energy, nonsense, time-wasting, a catch-all term for anything unspecified, heroin, semen, a social gathering and verbal harassment. *Jive*, which was used from the early 1920s to delineate the talk of jazz musicians and their growing number of followers, and by extension of many in the black and finally white communities, is consistently slang, meaning variously sexual intercourse, nonsense, rubbish, insincere, deceitful or pretentious talk, any unspecified thing, 'stuff', goings-on, a situation, a variety of recreational drugs and one's personality or material possessions. Both Dan Burley in his *Original Handbook of Harlem Jive* (1944) and 'Mezz' Mezzrow in *Really the Blues* (1946) trace it to standard English *jibe* or *jibber* and thence *jibberish*. Mezzrow, quoting black journalist Earl Conrad, adds that 'Jive talk may have been originally a kind of "pig Latin" that the slaves talked with each other, a code – when they were in the presence of whites.'[23] The possibility of such a code is feasible, but evidence of its nineteenth-century use remains unrecorded.

For Conrad, and others, it was as much what jive did as what it said, the ideas and energy that it helped release: 'Jive ... supplies the answer to the hunger for the unusual, the exotic and the picturesque in speech. It is a medium of escape, a safety valve for people pressed against the wall for centuries, deprived of the advantages of complete social, economic, moral and intellectual freedom. It is an inarticulate protest ... a defense mechanism, a method of deriving pleasure from something the uninitiated cannot understand. It is the same means of escape that brought into being the spirituals as sung by American slaves; the blues songs of protest that bubble in the breasts of black men and women.'[24]

Jive talk, like the music and society it reflected, fascinated the lexicographers, academics and its own users. But what they listed was not uniquely black, nor, as long as musicians and listeners were solely black, did the academics acknowledge its speech. Only when a substantial white audience started turning to jazz, and to an even greater extent to the swing music of the Thirties and Forties – played equally by blacks and whites – did the list-makers turn in its direction. Some of the language was certainly used, and indeed originated by black musicians, but it was not their sole property.

The first look at the topic appears to have been in *American Speech* in 1932. James Hart wrote on 'Jazz Jargon' but the title is a misnomer: the burden of the piece is not black or white jazz or its slang but the lyrics of Tin Pan Alley hits. Assuming a creator worries more about money than language, he suggests that the songwriter is forced to allow the vernacular to slip into his compositions since '[t]he use of correct language in jazz will stamp a writer's songs as unnecessarily highbrow and hence hinder his sales'.[25] He notes 'new connotations' for such words as *mama* (' "mammy" generally means mother and tear jerks, whereas "mamma" means hot stuff and sexy connotations'[26]), *papa* and *baby* and notes that '"Heat" came in with a vengeance and assumed a new meaning which might previously have been considered nothing short of downright shocking',[27] and continues on to 'hot', including the jazz style. Scat makes its appearance ('those staccato sounds composed solely for meter but employed just as much to produce hot noises'[28]). He deals at length with the etymology of *jazz* but from a modern view the etymologies he presents represent no more than a selection of red herrings.

The first 'real' glossary was published in 1935 by Carl Cons, editor of the music magazine *Down Beat*: 'The Slanguage of Swing: Terms the "Cats" Use'. (It was expanded for *Down Beat's Yearbook of Swing* in 1939). It was broken down into 'swing phrases,' 'musicians, etc.,' and 'musical instruments.' Terms included *lick*, *break* and *jam* – all of which have survived – and the possibly journalese and definitely ephemeral terms for instruments: *dog house* (upright bass), *moth box* (piano), *grunt-horn* (tuba), *rock crusher* (accordion), *syringe* (trombone), *woodpile* (xylophone) and *squeak box* (violin). Classical musicians were *long-hairs* while mainstream popular music was *schmaltz*, *corn*, *ricky-tick*, *Mickey Mouse*, *rooty-toot*, and *schmooey*. (The Yiddish terms reflected the presence of Jewish musicians in the bands.) The fans were noted as *cats* and *alligators*, while those outside the group were *ickies*. The definitions themselves were written in jazz slang: the lexicographical rule whereby one does not define one word term by using another was rigorously broken. Thus 'Break it down!' means 'Get hot! Go to town! Swing it! etc.' If you had to ask, to paraphrase Fats Waller, you didn't get it.

Down Beat also provides colour for H. Brook Webb's 'The Slang of Jazz',[29] some eighty-three words and phrases and sorted into nine categories (e.g. 'nicknames', 'the style in which the band as a whole is playing' or 'phrases expressive of reaction to the music'); his sections are interspersed with headlines from the magazine. In 1935 *Vanity Fair* offered 'Hot Jazz Jargon' and put their findings into the mouth of a supposed swing band musician:

> That's the third date we've grooved half a dozen schmaltzy tunes for that wand-waver with never a swing item in the list. He's not making a salon-man of me: let him date the long-haired boys for his commercials. He puts a solid man like Joe on the suitcase and hires three other gutbucket boys; then his idea of good get-off is to waste sure rough tone on those corny licks he likes to wax. We'll never catch a wire in a decent nitery without pressing some barrel-house to make the cats swing. There ought to be a hot coupling on every platter; but none of these plates will be senders. He never takes the brass out of the hats so the boys can really ride a couple.[30]

American Speech took the lexis up again with Russell B. Nye's 'Musician's Word List'.[31] This mainly offered insider jargon, with such terms as *sign-painter* ('a leader who has little musical knowledge and is used as director mainly for his stage presence'). But there were more general terms: *gutbucket*, *barrelhouse* and *platter* (a recording), and while citing a term hardly unique to swing musicians, Nye chose to include *bulldike* ('a female sexual pervert').

The last of the Thirties' publications was the first supposedly black one: *Cab Calloway's Hepsters Dictionary* (1938 with six further editions by 1944). The dictionary was actually compiled by Calloway's press agent, Ned Williams, a reality that perhaps fitted its ostensible writer, since Calloway (1907–94), for all that his band had featured such stars as Dizzy Gillespie and Ben Webster, was an equivocal figure among more serious black jazzmen.

Looking at Calloway's list, the accent is definitely on jive talk, which, as he put it, 'is now an everyday part of the English language. Its usage is now accepted in the movies, on the stage, and in the song products of Tin Pan Alley.'[32] And whatever the extent of his authorship, and whether or not it was read by white swing fans rather than black jazzmen, the *Dictionary* focuses for the first time on black terminology. Among the 200-plus headwords were many musical terms, but Calloway offered much more. M, for instance, has *mellow* (all right, fine), *melted out* (broke), *mess* (something good), *mitt pounding* (applause), *moo juice* (milk), *mouse* (pocket) and *murder* (something excellent or terrific). S offers *sad* (very bad), *salty* (angry, ill-tempered), *send* (to arouse the emotions), *set of seven brights* (one week), *signify* (to declare yourself, to brag), *sky piece* (hat) and *slave* (to work, whether arduous labor or not). These were not 'jazz jargon', they were black slang.

The *Hepcats Jive Talk Dictionary* by journalist Lou Shelly appeared in 1945, with a section devoted to the world war's 'G.I. Jive'; in 1947 the academic Marcus Boulware published *Jive and Slang*, and in 1962 the black writer William Melvin Kelley put out *If You're Woke You Dig It*. However the era's major repository of black material came in *Dan Burley's Original Handbook of Harlem Jive*, by the editor of the black newspaper the *New York Amsterdam News*; it was published in 1944. The *Handbook* includes a lengthy glossary, *The Jiver's Bible*, which offers around 860 terms, and a number of jive parodies of such canonical literary productions as *Othello*. Like Calloway, but even more extensively so, Burley (1907–62) lists contemporary black vocabulary alongside a sprinkling of strictly music-related language. A good deal was destined to last, but some seems to have been very much of the Harlem of its day.

Burley included a lengthy introduction, The Technique of Jive. There he covered 'the Purpose of Jive', the 'Origin and Development of Jive', the 'Backgrounds of Jive', the A. B. C. of Basic Jive', plus various grammatical and phonological attributes. He also provided samples: '"If you're a hipped stud, you'll latch on; but if you're a homey, you ain't nowhere, ole man, understand? Like the bear, nowhere. And, ole man, why can't you dig this hard mess I'm laying down when the whole town's copping the mellow jive? Are you going to be a square all you days? Ain't you gonna click your gimmers, latch onto this fine pulp I'm dropping on you and really knock yourself out as you scoff, ace-deuce around the chiming Ben? You dig, ole man, that, from early bright to late black, the cats and the chippies are laying down some fine, heavy jive; most of it like the tree, all root; like the letter all wrote; like the country road, all rut; like the apple, all rot; like the cheese, all rat! Understand, ole man?" That, dear reader, is pure jive.'[33]

Not all examples appeared in glossaries. The influential black writer Zora Neale Hurston (1891–1960), celebrated for her stories of the black South, where she had studied folklore before turning to novel-writing, produced 'Story in Harlem Slang', published in the *American Mercury* in July 1942. Originally called 'Now You Cookin' with Gas' the story was censored by the *Mercury*, which removed some explicit sexual language. For those who couldn't understand, Hurston appended a substantial 'Glossary of Harlem Slang' which includes such terms as *dusty butt* (a cheap whore), *what's on the rail for the lizard?* (a challenge offered a passing girl), *knock the pad* (to have intercourse), *percolate* (to go looking for sexual conquests), and *jelly* (male sexual prowess). The piece features a pair of Harlem hipsters, Jelly and Sweet Back, hitting on the passing women in the hope of a meal or, better still, sex. Both men, Hurston writes, 'went into the pose and put on the look'. But the young woman on whom they focus, pitting rival verbal skills to see who can win her, is smarter than both. And just as slangy. 'It'll never happen, brother. You barking up the wrong tree. I wouldn't give you air if you was stopped up in a jug. I'm not putting out a thing. I'm just like the cemetery – I'm not putting out, I'm taking in. Dig!'[34] The *Mercury* also censored the sense of racial tension that ran through the original manuscript. Such as Sweet Back's reminiscence of an encounter with a white policeman in Georgia: 'I shot him lightly and he died politely.'[35]

About as far away from Hurston as imaginable was the comic Richard Buckley (1906–60), who had made his way up through the tent shows and speakeasies of the Depression-era West before taking on a new identity: 'his royal hipness' Lord Buckley. As Albert Goldman, later biographer of another black-loving comic, Lenny Bruce, put it, 'Eventually he opened his own club in Sin City [Chicago] and hired every famous Negro jazzman of the day. Digging the whole black scene, the jazz, the jive talk [...] this hearty, handsome son of the pioneers became that terrible thing, "a *nigger-lover*".[36] Buckley picked up on what he heard backstage, and put it into his act. It was not some latterday minstrelsy, but homage. 'Standing before his audience in a tuxedo and pith helmet, with his lobster eyes and imperious waxed mustache giving him the look of an apoplectic English lord, he would open his thin waspy lips and out would pour the thickest, blackest, funkiest stream of slum ghetto jive talk ever heard on an American stage.'[37]

Buckley was *sui generis*. Hurston, though exceptionally talented in her own right, is bracketed by literary historians in what at its birth was known as the 'new Negro movement' and has subsequently become known as the Harlem Renaissance. This flowering of black culture and racial self-awareness, that ran from the 1920s to the 1930s, had no direct links to the use of slang, but there were some writers who found it a place: Hurston aside, Langston Hughes (in poems and plays) and Claude McKay (in his novels *Home to Harlem* and *Banana Bottom*) used it for their work, as did white 'fellow-travellers' such as Carl van Vechten (in *Nigger Heaven*.) Traditionalist black critics were unimpressed, seeing such work as portraying the 'wrong' image of black life, but the young writers saw what they did, slang included, as that life's very essence.

Hollywood, of course, picked up the new lexis. Criminal slang in particular was already available on screen, but jive gained its greatest showcase in Howard Hawks's 1941 rom-com *Ball of Fire*, starring Gary Cooper as Bertram Potts, the junior member of an eccentric team of ageing academics who have just reached 'Slang' in their encyclopedia, and are seeking to research this new language. Their source is a nightclub singer, one Sugarpuss O'Shea (Barbara Stanwyck), who is in turn fleeing her gangster boyfriend, 'Duke Pastrami'. The 'rom' tended to outweigh the 'com', but thanks to a Billy Wilder script Sugarpuss comes good, explaining her lexis to the implausibly naïve Potts.

Black slang covers as many areas as does its white counterpart. And the two inevitably and increasingly overlapped. Even in the subset of jazz it is not always simple to separate one source from another. There is no doubt, however, that one strand deals with illegal drugs and lists reflect the omnipresence of recreational drugs – marijuana and narcotics such as opium and later heroin and cocaine – in music, whether jazz, rock or rap. Marijuana smokers were *vipers*, *tea hounds* and *weed hounds* and what they smoked, as hymned in Louis Armstrong's 1928 recording, was *muggles*. (Armstrong himself added a short jazz jargon glossary to his 1936 autobiography, *Swing That Music*.) Cab Calloway had used *kick the gong around* (to smoke opium), in 'Minnie the Moocher' (1930). The song also used the early use of *cokey*, latterly a cocaine user, as an opium smoker. (The image was presumably that of the smoke.)

Song titles and lyrics reveal a treatment of drugs that was unrivalled in its openness. Narcotics had been outlawed since 1914 and cannabis, which in America meant marijuana, from 1937. It made no difference, if anything accentuating the illicit thrill and cock-a-snook attitude that lay behind the musical display.

Cab Calloway was especially unrestrained. Aside from 'Minnie the Moocher', his songs included 'The Man From Harlem' (1932): 'Come on, sisters, light up on these weeds and get high and forget about everything' and 'Old Man of the Mountain' (1933), 'You have to bang the gong if you want to get along.' He was hardly unique, nor was he first. The opium celebration 'Pipe Dream Blues' came out in 1924, and Victoria Spivey's 'Dope Head Blues' in 1927 ('Just give me one more sniffle / Another sniffle of that dope'). In 1938 Trixie Smith sang 'Jack, I'm Mellow', offering an early use of what would become a favoured hippie adjective although the lyrics seem more energetic ('Just smoked some gage, / I'm a rampage [...] / I'm gonna strut like a Suzy-Q 'cause I'm on a bender!') and Chuck Webb recorded 'Wacky Dust' ('They call it wacky dust / It's from a hot cornet, / It gives your feet a feeling so breezy / And oh, it's so easy to get'). That year also saw one of the best-known dope songs of all, 'If You're a Viper' by Bob Howard and His Boys: 'Then you'll know your body's sent / You won't care if you don't pay rent / The sky is high, and so am I / If you're a viper.'

In his *Dictionary* Cab Calloway had included *mezz* which meant 'the best'. The word marijuana was unstated, but such was the original meaning, first stated in Clarence Cooper's *Here's to Crime* (1936), and it was drawn from the drug-dealing activities of Milton 'Mezz' Mezzrow (1899–1972), a white jazzman who was perhaps the ultimate example of the extent to which a white musician would embrace the black culture in which he worked. Married to Johnnie Mae, a black woman, he lived in

Harlem and declared himself a 'voluntary Negro'. In 1940, busted with forty joints at the New York World's Fair, he was jailed but managed to persuade the prison warden that he was black (citing his crinkly Jewish curls) and to be assigned to the all-black block. He spent the last twenty years of his life in Paris. Mezzrow's autobiography, *Really the Blues* (1946), charts his career, and includes four pages of contrived jive dialogue between Mezz and his street-corner marijuana buyers plus a substantial slang glossary.

For Mezzrow the slang of the Northern cities was also something quite apart from the older language of the plantation, 'the tongue of a *beaten* people'. The migration north was emotional as well as geographical. 'They brought their New Orleans music with them, and [...] their talk got more explosive too, more animated, filled with a little hope and spirit. That's when jive as we know it today really got going. [...] It was the first furious babbling of a people who suddenly woke up to find that their death-sentence had been revoked, or at least postponed, and they were stunned and dazzled at first, hardly able to believe it.' The language of Southern Negroes had been defensive, a way of hiding from Mr Charlie. Jive was something else, another code that whites couldn't understand but a code not of subjugation but of resentment, of anger, and of future attack. An assertion of self and the antithesis of the derogatory stereotypes of minstrelsy: 'Once and for all, these smart Northern kids meant to show that they're not the ounce-brained tongue-tied stuttering Sambos of the blackface vaudeville routines [...] the hipster's lingo reverses the whole Uncle Tom attitude of the beaten-down Southern Negro.'[38]

The blues, defined by the *OED* as 'A melody of a mournful and haunting character, originating among the African Americans of the southern U.S.', is first recorded as a term in 1912, in the title of W. C. Handy's 'Memphis Blues'. It was an extended use of the slang term *blue* (depressed), which had been used since the late seventeenth century. Initially merchandised as 'race records', the music was performed by and sold to the black audience. The blues offered a different take on life to the black music of the nineteenth century, which, in the form of spirituals, focused on religion or its tropes. The singers, the best-known of whom, at least in early decades, were women such as Ma Rainey and Bessie Smith, were talking about life in the here and now. As its etymology indicated, that life was hard and painful, its unhappiness often engendered by failed relationships; fantasies of the hereafter, with its delayed rewards, did not enter the picture. As for punishments, they were already available on earth. The blues had no problem in including slang.

As Stephen Calt writes in his dictionary of blues language *Barrelhouse Words*, 'Blues songs were not written compositions in the customary Tin Pan Alley manner, involving literary or poetic diction on at least a rudimentary level. As declaimed by the singer-guitarists and singer-pianists [...] the blues lyric was a snippet of vernacular speech set to song [...] Recorded blues of the period are so saturated in slang and assorted colloquialisms as to create a peculiar dialect that is only half-intelligible to present-day listeners ...'[39] Blues singers used the language of the barrelhouse, the low-down black nightspots where one could drink, gamble and hire prostitutes. The word meant the place and what one did there and it was a world that inspired W. C. Handy's 'Mr Crump Blues' (1912), in which he declared, 'Mister Crump won't 'low no easy riders here. / I don't care what he don't 'low, / I'm going barrelhouse anyhow.'

The early blues were raw, both in emotion and vocabulary. Handy, looking for a wider commercialization, complained of 'a flock of lowdown dirty blues'[40] but he was unable to stem the flow. Audiences seemed to relish the sexual references, and the singers were happy to provide them. They could be unmediated, but often they resorted to double-entendre.

Such thinly disguised smut might be discerned in minstrelsy – 'Long Tail Blue' and 'Coal Black Rose', where Sambo alludes to being ''tiff as a poker' and Rose replies, 'Cum in Sambo, don't tand dare shakin,/ De fire is a burnin, and de hoe cake a bakin'' – but the blues singers took it to another level. Nor need the entendre be remotely double. Louise Bogan (born Bessie Jackson and perhaps coincidentally taking the name of a contemporary white poet) left absolutely nothing to the imagination in 'Shave 'Em Dry' (1920s):

Now your nuts hang down like a damn bell clapper,
And your dick stands up like a steeple,
Your goddam ass-hole stands open like a church door,
And the crabs walks in like people.

Bo Carter (Armenter 'Bo' Chatmon, 1892–1964) preferred a degree of disguise, however thin. Song titles included 'Pin In Your Cushion' (1931), 'The Ins and Outs of My Girl' and 'Let Me Roll Your Lemon' (1935). In 'Banana in Your Fruit Basket' (1931) he sang:

Now, I got the washboard, my baby got the tub,
we gonna put 'em together, gonna rub, rub, rub
And I'm tellin' you baby, I sure ain't gonna deny,
let me put my banana in your fruit basket, then I'll be satisfied.

The 'occupational' lyrics of his 'All Around Man' could have been included in D'Urfey's *Pills*:

Now I ain't no butcher, no butcher's son,
I can do your cuttin' 'til the butcher man comes
'Cause I'm a all-around man, oh I'm a all-around man,
I'm a all-around man, I can do most anything that comes my
    hand.

Subsequent verses play on the miller ('grindin''), the milkman ('pull your titties'), the plumber ('screwin''), the spring-man ('bounce your springs'), and the auger man ('blow your hole').

The blues might deal with travelling (specific towns were often named), violence, partying, work and prison (some singers included the names of real-life prison wardens and guards in their songs). But many were about sex, and specifically sexual intercourse. For the last one finds *action*, to *jam*, to *ring someone's bell*, to *ball the jack* (which is also used to mean move fast), to *grind* and thus *coffee grinder*, a lover, to *jazz*, to *rock* (*and roll*), and to *squeeze someone's lemon*, immortalized in Robert Johnson's 'Travelling Riverside Blues' (1937). The penis was a *biscuit*, thus the female lover is a *biscuit roller*, the *stick of candy*, the *hambone* (which doubled as a vagina);

semen is *jelly*, *baking powder*, *medicine* and *sugar*. The vagina the *coal bin*, the *jelly* and most popularly *jelly-roll*, the *sweet potato* and the *potato field*; *cock*, in the Southern sense of vagina, is found. Adultery was a regular theme: the lover was a *back-door* or *outside man* (or *woman*) or a *triflin'* man; to cheat was to *dog* or *mess around* (which could also mean dance).

Prison has always been a repository of non-standard language,[41] and if it is, as often suggested, a college for crime, then it shares certain linguistic aspects of academic college life as well. It is literally a closed community. It has the same mix of general slang and local jargon. Some language is imported alongside the prisoner, and mixes cant and general street slang. Some, a good deal, pertains to the institution itself – the buildings, the food, the staff, the accommodation, the characteristics of certain of one's fellows, even if the traditional college does not offer the wide selection of terms for solitary confinement or of course execution. The US prison system throws up well over one thousand 'in-house' terms, and the UK equivalent another 230. Much of this will stay behind the walls and every prison, like every college, evolves its own vocabulary. The difference is that unlike the academic college, the 'students' of the criminal one are disproportionately African-American and Hispanic.

Language thus flourishes behind bars, but its use does not in general create a new folk form (although certain terms from California's prisons undoubtedly fed into the lyrics of early 1990s gangsta rap). In the case of the American prisons of the 1930s to 1960s this was changed. What emerged was the *toast*, defined as a spoken-word, quasi-poetical story as told primarily by black men in the absence of women. Like that of jazz, its etymology remains debatable. The earliest scholars of the form, Roger D. Abrahams (1964), Bruce Jackson (1974) and the team led by Dennis Wepman (1976), have rejected the simple answer: the standard term toast as used in drinking. A later assessment, by David Evans (1977), is convinced of the link to drinking, and suggests that his predecessors, because of the artificial situations (typically inside prisons or drug rehabilitation centres) in which they collected their material, overlooked the fact that such narrative poems would very often be delivered in an atmosphere enlivened and stimulated by alcohol. The *OED* admits to a possible link to the drinking term (itself a figurative use of the earliest definition: 'A slice or piece of bread browned at the fire: often put in wine, water, or other beverage') but lists it under its own homonym.

Dating toasts is almost impossible, given their origins. So too is establishing an 'authorized version'. Many of the most famous may have half a dozen variant forms. The toasting heyday appears to have run from the 1930s to 1970s, and all scholars (collecting at the end of the this period) note that the men from whom they gathered the material tended to be at least middle-aged. The majority of them also seemed to be in prison, where the toast was a regular form of entertainment. Although some toasts adapt 'straight' poetry or older cowboy or hobo ballads, the bulk of them – and very much those that have been collected and analysed – relate to 'the Life', the world of the black urban hustler. The hustler may appear as an aggressive, violent 'bad man' ('Stagolee', 'Dolomite', 'Badman Dan and Two-Gun Green'), or a trickster (most famously celebrated in 'The Signifying Monkey'). He may be a pimp ('Konky Mohair', 'Long-Shoe Sam'), who can combine elements of both. He operates alongside, and often in opposition to, a cast of fellow-pimps, whores (such as 'Duriella du Fontaine' or 'Sweet-Lovin' Nell', with whom he may have epic sexual battles), dealers and junkies (whose tales do not end well), bar-tenders and the clientele of bar-rooms, police and, often, the judges that terminate his career even if, in character, he gets off one last good line. Whites rarely appear other than as nay-saying authorities, but one of the most celebrated and probably oldest toasts – 'The *Titanic*' – sees a black man win for once: Shine, the stoker, escapes the sinking ship and is offered a range of inducements by the Captain, his wife and daughter, all of whom are begging for help; he responds to each one with the simple advice: 'Get your ass in the water and swim like me.' They refuse and go down with the ship. Shine, lowest of the low, survives.

Blues and toasts both suggest a degree of 'autobiography', but while the former tend to the general – journeys, jails, the perennial broken heart – the toast claims to recount a specific anecdote, even if its players are far larger and their actions more far-fetched than any real life. They are also set against the city rather than the country that informs many blues. And while the blues, as one would expect, bemoan life's problems, the toasts almost always come in the form of boasts: even stories that end in failure involve a good deal of self-aggrandizement. Some, of course, offer a degree of moralizing, but not until the narrator has shown us that to fall so far he has first been up so high. In language terms, as opposed to the female-dominated blues songs of the 1920s and 1930s, where slang commonly appears in the form of double-entendres, the male-delivered and created toast is always direct. Often grossly so. Toasts employ a wide range of slang, perhaps 50% labelled 'black', and there is no attempt to sidestep those terms considered highly obscene.

In slang terms toasts differ from the blues in one important way: they were a wholly black creation and have remained so. Toasts, even if they use a good deal of 'white' slang, rarely moved into the white world. Some white convicts may have picked them up during their stay in prison, but they did not create them and if they recited them, it was in mimicry of the black creators.

The toast is adult in every sense of the word. But there was also what one might see as its linguistic apprenticeship: rhyming verses, sometimes just couplets and sometimes not even rhymes, the province of teenagers and their younger siblings, which played a central role in accustoming young people to the often antagonistic world of the street. And unlike toasts, which are no longer created (or certainly no longer researched), this is a living form. These are 'the Dozens' and as these lines, from 'The Signifying Monkey' make clear, here is another style of black-to-black communication that, while not dependent on slang, undoubtedly emphasizes it.

> He got your whole family in the dozens and your sister on
>   the shelf,
> And the way he talks about your mama I wouldn't do myself.
> And one thing he said about your mama I said I wasn't going to
>   tell:
> He said your mama got a pussy deep as a well.[42]

'The Dozens', otherwise known as *sounding, signifying, joaning,* the *mama's game* and most recently and in an abbreviated form *snaps,* is a form of ritualized insult, practised by young and teenage African-Americans. A variety of theories as to its origins have been suggested; the most likely is that it was brought from West Africa with the slaves; such games are still played there, whereas, despite scholarly theorizing, the ritual has not been found in Europe or in white America other than amongst those who have a knowledge of black culture. Its essence, ritual insult, is paralleled by the seventeenth century's *flyting*, but while that was the carefully contrived product of poets (it is in William Dunbar's 'Flyting of Dunbar & Kennedy' of 1508 that one finds the first recorded use of the verb 'fuck'), the dozens are spontaneous and the product of street-level confrontations, either as a substitute for or a prelude to a fight. Flyting also makes no particular target of the mother, central to the dozens.

The etymology of the term remains unresolved. Roger Abrahams, in a 1962 article, quotes the etymologist Peter Tamony who 'suggests the derivation of the name may come from "DOZEN," v., to stun, stupefy, daze, which can be used both transitively and intransitively (OED)'.[43] Abrahams notes that 'If this were true, its etymology would concur with many other Negro words which come eminently from English parlance of the eighteenth century,' and adds that, 'This would attach an English name to a phenomenon possibly brought from Africa.'[44] The *OED* itself places the word within the headword *dozen* (twelve), and thus appears to subscribe to the theory, again unproven, that the original game properly went through twelve rounds of insult and counter-insult.

The dozens themselves are not especially sophisticated, though they are seen as the formative steps towards gaining the greater verbal facility that comes with street life. They are, or were divided into 'clean' and 'dirty' dozens, depending on the volume of obscenity used. It is in the latter that one is more likely to encounter slang:

> She's a good old soul.
> She's got a ten-ton pussy
> And a rubber asshole.
> She got hair on her pussy
> That sweep the floor.
> She got knobs on her titties
> That open the door.

The slang may not be inventive, but the terms are if nothing else consistent.

Slang runs in tandem with the scofflaw, and no one fits that description as well as that trope of black life: the 'bad man'. Slang, one might suggest, is language's own metaphorical equivalent. The bad man – defying the white enemy, making life miserable for respectable blacks who were his supposed peers – had existed in ballads and in the near-cartoonish excesses of the toasts. Most of the pre-World War I black writers had other topics: the problems of the mulatto, the establishment of a black bourgeoisie; the working class, especially as represented by this wilfully criminal, violent subset, were sidestepped. Even those who did look at the characters who would come to typify the violence of the ghetto, and would in time enter fiction unmediated, deliberately downplayed the truth. Thus John Carrothers, while he focused on the razor-wielding members of his *Black Cat Club* (1902), managed to defuse reality, even managing to render his poem 'A Carving', in which two men slash each other to death, more amusing than openly horrific. The Harlem Renaissance writers had modified the bad man, filtering him through their own middle-class perspective, and subsumed his unrestrained life into their primary aim: a general celebration of 'the folk' and the traditional black culture that their own parents, who had made the emigration north, had, like first-generation emigrants of any background who look forward to a better future, preferred to forget. Rudolph Fisher (1897–1934) is typical: his short stories, and two novels, *The Walls of Jericho* (1928) and *The Conjure-Man Dies* (1932), deal explicitly with 'bad men' but change their destinies: redemption is possible even for 'the hardest boogy in Harlem'.[45] In a scene from *Conjure-Man* two rivals are sent into a basement to fight out their rivalries, but rather than cut each other to ribbons (the topic of an earlier Fisher short story) they come out drunk and murmuring affectionately 'Ain' nuthin' to fight about [...] you my boy.'[46]

The movement to the Northern cities, with its gradual creation of black ghettoes, created a new sub-genre of black writing, featuring the bad man and his world. White culture was effectively invisible; only life on the ghetto street was portrayed. The creation was not immediate: Richard

Wright's Bigger Thomas in *Native Son* (1940), and Ralph Ellison's *Invisible Man* (1953), played the bad man role, but these books and those that imitated them were played out against the hero's struggle against white racism. A new generation of writers, published in the 1960s and 1970s, never left the ghetto and their books can be seen as the toast made book-length prose. As Jerry H. Bryant has put it, 'A cohort of black novelists seems to have deliberately set out to write the "toast" into a new form of fiction. It was a genre not destined for either mainstream popularity or critical acclaim. But it took on the world of the street player with gusto.'[47]

Just before them, forming a link between the 'race' novels and the new genre and overlapping with both, were the later works of Chester Himes (1909–84): the 'Harlem domestic' novels (although they were essentially police procedurals of the most heightened sort, Himes included enough 'local colour' to make him opt for that description), featuring his harder-than-nails black detectives Gravedigger Jones and Coffin Ed Johnson. Himes had been in college, but embraced the underworld and, so he would claim, led a double life as a gambler, pimp, bootlegger and thief; this real-life, if half-hearted example of the bad man met the bad man's usual fate: seven and a half years in jail for a bungled armed robbery. His first novel, *If He Hollers Let Him Go*, was published in 1945; like its successor *Lonely Crusade* (1947) it was very much of the Richard Wright school. *Cast the First Stone* (1952) was based on his prison experiences. Sickened by racism – general but also personal: a brief spell as a Hollywood scriptwriter ended when producer Jack Warner announced, 'I don't want no godamned niggers on this lot'[48] – Himes moved to Paris, where critics had already written admiringly of his work, in the mid-1950s. In 1957 his translator Marc Duhamel, who in 1954 had started the *Série noire* ('Black Series') of detective novels – both French and foreign[49] – suggested that Himes change tack and offer something on those lines. The nine-book series of 'Harlem domestics' were born, starting that year with *For the Love of Imabelle*, renamed as *Cotton Comes to Harlem*.

If Himes, who had read and enjoyed *Black Mask* as a young man, was black crime fiction's Dashiell Hammett, then Donald Goines (1936–74) was its Robert L. Bellem. And if Coffin Ed and Gravedigger were bad men with badges, then the Goines hero-thug (usually a gangster, pimp or combination) – in books such as *Dope Fiend* (1971), *Whoreson* (1972), *Street Players* (1973), *Daddy Cool* (1974) and *Inner City Hoodlum* (1975) – was the phenomenon unalloyed. And like Bellem, whose detective Dan Turner verged on, and even passed into parody, Goines's players embraced every stereotype of the bad man: amoral, super-sexual, ultra-violent, and until the final shootout or overdose, invariably successful. Like Himes, perhaps even more so, Goines wrote of what he claimed to know. (And in 1973 tipped his hat to his predecessor with a character named 'Chester Hines' in *White Man's Justice, Black Man's Grief*, set like Himes's *Cast the First Stone* in a prison). There is relatively little of the colour that makes Himes's portrait of Harlem so unforgettable, but the bad men came from experience. Goines had done time (seven jail terms totalling six and a half years), run in the streets, and for many years was a junkie. He gave it all up after he had found success with the white-run publisher Holloway House, a specialist in populist ghetto fiction. His sixteen novels appeared in the last five years of his life.

But while Goines attempted to exchange the streets for the bourgeoisie, the streets had not forgotten. He died in 1974, shot down alongside his wife by a pair of white killers in circumstances that have never been explained.

That ghetto novels should showcase slang is inevitable. Himes and Goines displayed a substantial lexis, adding to the authenticity of at least the linguistic aspect of their work. Himes' 'domestics' provide around 850 slang terms, of which *c.* 40% can be categorized as 'black', Goines just over 800, with 50% of them black. (The authors share 200 words, 100 of which are black-coined). The same thing went for Clarence Cooper, Jr, Hubert Simmons, Nathan Heard and others, and Goines's fellow Holloway House authors such as Odie Hawkins, Joseph Nazel, James Howard Readus, Laurie Miles and Jerome Dyson Wright. The imprint also offered the works of the former pimp Robert Beck (1918–1992), writing as 'Iceberg Slim' and a major influence on the younger Goines, not to mention lending his name to such rappers as Ice T and his legend to rap culture in general. His slang contribution is over 1,100 words, with 40% black. But if, as Jerry H. Bryant has suggested, Beck infused his reminiscences and the fictions that accompanied them, with a degree of ironic detachment, Goines and Co. rejected such modification. Theirs are two-dimensional works, keen to portray ghetto life in its most lurid, uncompromising colours. That all saw the utility of slang, was wholly to be expected. It was, after all, the language of the street.

All of which leads in one direction: hip-hop and then rap. Rap's unequal omnipresence, its crossover triumph that takes in not merely the blacks who pioneered it and are its main creators, but also whites of every class, and extends into non-anglophone countries, all suggest that it is both of 'black slang' and has come to transcend it. To that end, it is worth moving backwards in time. To the development of the teenager, and the separate, slangy language that he and she chose.

16 Campus and Counter-Culture: Teenage Skills

Slang is a product of the young, who create more and speak more than any group other than criminals. For many observers it is seen as youth's property and co-terminous with adolescence; something that one 'grows out of' with maturity. At a time when 'youth' is far extended beyond its traditional limits, this is nothing if not debatable, but if it is true, then the phenomenon is relatively recent. It is a twentieth-century development, properly limited to the era that has followed World War II. The young – or certainly the working-class young – undoubtedly used slang in the nineteenth century and earlier, but just as they were dressed in miniature versions of adult clothing, they also spoke the language of their parents, standard and oppositional. There was no attempt nor any need to record such usage in the context of youth. One area belied this norm: that of the university and college. These institutions had their internal vocabularies, which acted as do all such jargons, to reinforce the group and wall it off from outsiders. Some was naturally limited to local references, but some was not, and the cross-fertilization of the campus and the 'real world' which is now accepted, was already developing. It was such language that provided the first lists of what can be called 'youth slang'.

University, campus, is a closed world. Far more than is the official gap year that many students take between school and entering tertiary education, university or college education itself, whether three or four years long, represents an extended 'gap year' set between teenage, which all modern young people traverse, and the first steps into adulthood's 'real life'. Some of the slang the student encounters is therefore a matter of names (often nicknames), reflecting local geography and local culture. That slang, properly jargon, will not continue outside the university or college, other than at reunions or in brief indulgences in nostalgia amongst those who formerly used it as a part of daily life. The necessary adoption of such jargons is part of what is known as 'secondary socialisation'. However, student society is less hermetic than is the far more isolated world of a prison or military barracks, and while the need to learn the local terminology exists, it is not as intense as, say, that depicted in the film *If* (1968), set in a traditional UK public school where a failure to memorize the lexicon led to a caning, or as laid out in Bruce Moore's *Lexicon of Cadet Language* (1993), the vocabulary of Australia's Royal Military College, Duntroon, which runs to some 441 double-columned pages of often impenetrable terminology. No student, as happens in *If*, is punished for ignorance of the lexis, though daily life will impose a certain need-to-know.

Students are not merely academic units but also young people, and much of the slang they use exists in the outer world and is drawn from the much wider culture of their contemporaries. American researchers continue to debate what exactly makes up 'student slang'. Is it the entire lexis of the student body, which will inevitably include a good many non-campus terms, or is it to be restricted to terms that only exist in the given university? The problem with the latter is that (unlike Duntroon, where it is intended that the youthful cadets should be conscious of their difference from civilians and language is used – as it is throughout the military – to underpin this mentality), this gives a very short list, and most of it strictly defined as jargon. To counter this it has been suggested that while students should be quizzed on the entirety of their non-standard speech, they should be asked to state which terms they encountered outside the institution. Some researchers have included those terms as part of the overall campus slang lexis, others have not. It is also suggested that students will pick up 'external' slang from their peers, who may have brought it with them, during their university life. But even if one is not consciously creating a warrior caste, or a criminal underworld, the world in which one exists, in this case the university, is both reflected in and constructed by the words one uses. As Bruce Moore notes,[1] that means all the words, both local jargon and general slang.

Looking over two centuries of student slang compilations it seems that the earliest concentrated on the place-specific jargon, including in their headwords references to various aspects of student life both academic and social, while the more recent books and glossaries (e.g. Connie Eble's on-going lists of slang used at the University of North Carolina at Chapel Hill since 1972, Pamela Munro's UCLA-based *Slang U*, published in 1989 and gathered since 1984, or Tony Thorne's lists drawn since 1995 from King's College, London) have accepted the wider input. This may acknowledge the vast growth in 'teenage slang' over the past fifty years, much of which accompanies freshmen into the university, as well as the tapering off, especially in British colleges, of the institutional rituals that provided so much of the original jargon. It may also, again particularly in the UK, underline the diminishing image of 'us and them', known in college life as 'town and gown', which led to the reinforcing of 'us' – the community of scholars – by a wholly separate vocabulary as seen in eighteenth- and nineteenth-century Oxbridge and their imitators.

There are nineteen university-based terms in Francis Grose (despite advertising itself as including 'University Wit', the *Lexicon Balatronicum* only added two more), but the first full-scale attempt to classify student language came in 1803, when 'A Pembrochian', i.e. a member of Pembroke College, Cambridge, wrote *Gradus ad Cantabrigiam or, A Dictionary of Terms, Academical and colloquial, and Cant, which are used at the University of Cambridge*. The lexicon reflects contemporary academe, filled with citations drawn from the then mandatory undergraduate knowledge of the classical texts, verses, anecdotes, and insider references to the faculty. The overall tone is ponderously humorous and 'A Pembrochian' stresses that 'there can be no need of apology for being too much addicted to *joking*. You will perceive that I have spared no *puns* to gratify you.'[2] There is an underlying element of what Morris Marples described in his *University Slang* (1950) as 'intellectual gentlemen of leisure delighting in their own cleverness'.[3]

The 152 entries take up 139 pages, but many are Cambridge jargon. Of those more widely used, the *Gradus* offers these first recorded uses:

attic (the head), *bitch* (a tea-party host) and *bitch-party* (the tea party), *cool* (insolent), *cram* (to study hard) and *tick* (a creditor). Other slang, which could be found far from Cambridge, includes *save one's bacon*, *Barnwell ague* (VD), *bog* (lavatory), *bore* (a tedious person), *cut* (to ignore a task), *buck* (a rake), *dish* (to defeat in an argument), *fag* (to work hard), *phiz* (the face), *quiz* (an eccentric), *sir reverence* (excrement), *tick* (an unpleasant person), *tick* (to place on credit), and *varmint* (a fashionable person). Terms for drinking played an important role: *bosky, fuddled, half seas over, mellow* and *cut* for drunk (*cut in the back* for very drunk). To *buzz* (to drain a glass), *moisten the clay* (to drink), *row* (to break up a room), *cat* (to vomit from drunkenness), *daylight* or *skylight* (the space in a glass between top of the liquid in a glass and its and rim), and *no heeltaps!* (drain your glasses!).

Benjamin Homer Hall's *Collection of College Words and Customs* was published in 1851. It was drawn from research in American universities and initiated when the author was still an undergraduate. There are as many customs as words, and among the words many, like those in *Gradus*, are local usages. A dozen of the purely slang usages overlap with 'A Pembrochian'. A second edition, revised and expanded, appeared in 1856. There remain around 130 slang entries. The majority of these are still not general slang, but continue to appear in a succession of glossaries of campus language throughout the century, typically W. C. Gore's pamphlet *Student Slang*, some 800 terms written for the University of Michigan in 1896, and E. H. Babbitt's 'College Words and Phrases', published in *Dialect Notes*, vol. II (1900), which was based on a questionnaire circulated to the heads of some 400 educational institutions by the American Dialect Society. This excluded general usage, although certain terms, e.g. *peachy*, were taken up in the wider world, and others, such as *cad* (an academy or prep school student), were simply place-specific variations on general slang. It also made it clear that many college expressions were used at multiple colleges: for instance *cram* came up in sixty-three answers, *crib* in thirty-six. Hall was followed by Charles Bristed's *Five Years at an English University*, another study of Cambridge, while in 1871 L. H. Bagg's *Four Years at Yale* devoted several pages to the university's language, not all of which is jargon.

While British universities were either too restricted in overall number, or offered too small a student sample for many attempts to list their slang, American colleges were subjected to frequent analysis. In their essay 'Kansas University Slang: A New Generation' (1963), Alan Dundes and Manuel R. Schonhorn listed twenty-six studies from the first thirty years of *American Speech* alone, the first of which was an earlier study of the language of Kansas University carried out by Carl Pingry and Vance Randolph (later celebrated for his studies of 'Unprintable' Ozark Folksongs and Folklore) in 1928. Plus a further seven published by individual colleges. They cite as justification the increasing nineteenth-century research into the oral rather than the written tradition and cite E.B. Taylor, 'one of the founders of modern anthropology, [who] felt that an analysis of the evolution of slang would reveal those general laws common to the growth of all language'.[4] The problem with most of these studies, however, was that they remained isolated; local student words were listed but there was no attempt to place them in the context of general slang, to compare them with what might be found at other colleges, or to separate what Dundes and Schonhorn call the 'academic' from the 'social'.[5]

The authors concluded with a call for greater stress on analysis and regular assessments of college slang's development. 'This would serve the dual purpose of recording the development of slang at individual institutions and of providing a sound basis for comparative studies of college slang generally.' They suggested the establishment of a comprehensive questionnaire which might be 'circulated with additions at regular intervals among American colleges and universities'.[6]

The rush of *American Speech* compilations faded in the 1960s, replacing lists with articles debating rather than itemizing student use. But not all twentieth-century surveys were published in academic journals. One of the most wide-ranging was Brown University's *College Undergraduate Slang Study* of 1967–8, created by three English-language students. Designed 'as a large-scale study of U.S. college slang', the compilers noted the challenge of covering every regional variation and restricted themselves to north-east colleges 'settling for a scattering for elsewhere in the country'.[7] Based on a questionnaire, its answers submitted to the Brown computers, the material went some way towards achieving the sort of analysis that Dundes had called for. As Julie Coleman notes, 'What sets this study apart from other student slang projects is the innovative analysis of its results.'[8] There were interesting tables, for instance the co-relation of obscenity use in different colleges, and maps showing the geographical distribution of synonyms, but the conclusions drawn were not generally up to the potential of the information gathered.

Contemporary research also provided the four-year run of *Current Slang* (1966–71), published by the University of South Dakota. This was not deliberately focused on student terms, but the entries are almost all attributed to colleges. Thus the first number (Summer 1966) 'was collected entirely on the campus of the University of South Dakota'. Subsequent numbers added in the students of other institutions. Occasional special issues included such as II: 2–3 which featured the cadet slang of the Air Force Academy and V: 2 which drew on contributions from 'the seven male Black undergraduates at the University of South Dakota' while 1968's volume III: 2, at fifty-one pages the largest collection, was on 'The Slang of Watts'. Volume VI, Winter 1971, was the last. It explained that 'appearing accidentally with the rapid expansion of the drug culture and with a diversification of life styles, it recorded the expansion of the language to adapt to these changes and to allow everyone to "do his thing" linguistically'. The editor regretted that 'the burst of invention typical of the last five years is over [...] terms as old as three and four years now make up the bulk of the items submitted', and thus announced that *Current Slang* was shutting down.[9]

The one twentieth-century collection of English university slang was that of Morris Marples, published in 1950. His *Public School Slang* had appeared a decade earlier. Its headwords focus almost wholly on jargon, abstruse and obscure nonce-terms culled from a couple of hundred years of Oxbridge self-absorption, plus the gradual appearance of terms from the Universities of Durham, London, Exeter and elsewhere. Virtually none of Marples's lists attempted to escape the various aggregations of dreaming spires and self-referential coinages. This was no doubt his intent, and it would be foolish to assume that 'his' students were not as well versed in general slang uses as any of their generation. Two mid-nineteenth-century fictional Oxonians – Cuthbert Bede's mid-nineteenth-century Candide Mr Verdant Green[10] (and his equally well-named friend Mr Bouncer) and Thomas Hughes's Tom Brown (despite being as priggish and earnest at Oxford as he had been at Rugby) – both display their knowledge of non-standard language. They overlap on a dozen or so occasions, typically such 'academic' terms as *grind*, *cram*, *pony* (a translation) and *cut*, but elsewhere they go their own way and Green, unlike Brown, resists the use of 'Jew' as a pejorative.

College slang continues to draw researchers, much of it now on-line. *Da Bomb*, at Cal Poly (California State Polytechnic University), represented the state of slang at the college in 1997, while Hope College issued 'A Dictionary of New Terms' covering 1997–2004. A search on google for 'college slang' offers around 50,000 hits. Much of the material included in the *Urban Dictionary* comes from the college generation – for instance it includes, and often predates, all entries in Professor Eble's latest (Spring 2011) list – and the successive editions of Britain's *Roger's Profanisaurus*, though essentially playing for laughs, come out of the same world.

Breaking down current student slang into thematic groupings, it reflects the slang used by contemporaries in the larger world. Professor Tony Thorne, working over a decade at KCL, has assembled the following hierarchy:

1. Intoxication by drink or drugs (17.46%)
2. Terms of approbation (15.23%)
3. Romance, sex and related body parts (12.06%)
4. Insults and terms denoting misfits (11.42%)
5. Terms of disapproval/disappointment (8.25%)
6. Greetings, farewells and exclamations (5.07%)
7. Social or ethnic categorizations (4.76%)
8. Relaxation (4.44%)
9. Money (3.80%)
10. Negative or unsettling states (3.49%)
11. Anger or excited states (3.17%)
12. Food (2.53%)
13. Clothes (2.22%)

Although there are differences – no references to either clothes nor money, and the presence of 'jargon' referring to local culture – the terms amassed by Connie Eble's contributors present a similar list.

The language of the campus, perhaps due to its role as the creation of youthful elites, had been analysed for a century before the less privileged and younger sector of the population came under the microscope. In 1903, writing in the *Pedagogical Seminary*, a journal of child psychology, Edward Conradi offered a selection of data on 'Children's Interests in Words, Slang, Stories, etc.' The piece dealt with various aspects of the language enjoyed by those under eighteen, and its centre-piece was a list of some 850 slang terms, gleaned from 295 answers to a questionnaire circulated by high-school teachers. These were divided by the gender of those who offered them – 'Boys', 'Girls' and 'Sex Not Specified' – and broken down into various sub-sections: 'Rebuke to Pride', 'Negatives', 'Shock', 'Exaggerations', 'Exclamations', 'Mild oaths', and a substantial section entitled 'Unclassified' and which included the majority of nouns and verbs. 'Unclassified' themes show terms for 'boasting and loquacity, hypocrisy, […] attending to one's own business and not meddling or interfering, names for money, absurdity, neurotic effects of surprise or shock, honesty and lying, getting confused, fine appearance and dress, words for intoxication, […] for anger […] crudeness or innocent naiveté, love and sentimentality'.[11] The interviewees included their opinions on slang: '60 thought slang more emphatic' […] '90 considered slang vulgar' […] '53 considered boy's slang rougher than girl's', etc. A graph was compiled which suggested that slang use peaked between ages thirteen and sixteen.

That the bulk of terms in question were slang is undeniable; that the young people fell into the age range that would make them modern teenagers equally so. And as G. S. Hall noted in 1906, there was a degree of code-switching between classroom and elsewhere: 'Most high school and college youth of both sexes have two distinct styles, that of the classroom which is as unnatural as the etiquette of a royal drawing-room reception or a formal call, and the other, that of their own breezy, free, natural life. This informal lingua franca [is] often called "slanguage".' Hall adds that these two have no relation to or effect upon each other; only a 'very few, and these generally husky boys, boldly try to assert their own rude but vigorous vernacular in the field of school requirements'.[12]

Yet this is not 'youth' or 'teen slang'. There is no sense that the lists are designed to set the speakers apart, even if the 'husky boys' who used slang in class make them the predecessors of the gang kids of half a century ahead. Not that the slang was fresh-minted by the young people who used it. There is a certain overlap with contemporary lists of college usage (and it was noted at the time and since that college imports a certain amount of high school usage), but the words and phrases are those of the era's general slang. Few represent a first use. Most have been in place for the last decade and many for longer. Certain current linguistic fads are suggested, for instance the twenty-five variations on 'wouldn't that ...' as used to preface a phrase of shock ('... rattle your slats', '... fade the stripes on your grand dad's socks', '... jiggle your slats', etc.), but there was no generational distinction and the majority of terms are used by all age groups.

Other than probable links to the Berkshire dialect *vlapper* ('applied in joke to a girl of the bread-and-butter age'), and the Northumbrian *flap* (an unsteady young woman), the earliest use of the term *flapper* as applied to a girl is first recorded in Barrère & Leland's slang dictionary of 1889, where one finds 'Flippers, *flappers*, very young girls trained to vice, generally for the amusement of elderly men'. By the late 1910s the definition, while still that of a young girl, had softened: the flapper was now a flighty, but not actively 'immoral' girl or young woman, usually middle-class, in her late teens or very early twenties, who sported short, bobbed hair, lipstick and skimpy dresses and generally led a lifestyle as far as possible removed from that desired by her parents.

The term was already common enough in 1892 for the *Evening News* of 20 August to ponder its etymology: 'The correspondent of *Notes and Queries* has been troubling his mind about the use of the slang word "flapper" as applied to young girls. Another correspondent points out that a "flapper" is a young wild duck which is unable to fly, hence a little duck of any description, human or otherwise. The answer seems at first sight frivolous enough, but it is probably the correct solution of this interesting problem all the same.' That opinion stands, although the word may be underpinned by SE *flap*, to act in an emotional manner, supposedly typical of such young women.

Quite when the meaning shifted from vice to what was seen as frivolity, however shocking at the time, is hard to judge. Examples are ambiguous: the *Sporting Times* (11 July 1908) referred to 'the dear little flappers in the chorus' and in 1914 'Bartimeus', in *Naval Occasions*, described 'Little pigtailed girls with tight skirts enclosing immature figures, of a class known technically as the "Flapper," drifted by with lingering, precocious stares'. But by 1922 when the flapper's antithesis, Sinclair Lewis's mid-West bourgeois George F. Babbitt, 'weightily pondered flappers smoking in Zenith restaurants',[13] the change was set in stone. She entered the movies, whether played by Colleen Moore or Clara Bow, John Held Jr drew her for *Vanity Fair*, and her fictional embodiments were championed above all by F. Scott Fitzgerald, whose wife Zelda was stereotyped as the style incarnate. She crossed the Atlantic. P. G. Wodehouse hymned the fictional exploits of a number of her British sisters. She could be claimed for feminism, though her ambitions were less political than social.

The word *teenage* can be found in 1921 ('in one's teens' has been recorded in 1684), but the modern concept of the teenager as representing a segregated social group is a creation of the 1940s, if not the decade that followed; it required rock and roll for the teenager proper. The flapper cannot thus be a teenager any more than could her late-nineteenth and early-twentieth-century peers, whether at school or college. But while these predecessors certainly embraced slang, it was never date-tied; the flapper's slang, as much as her rolled stockings, her shingled hair, her cigarettes and her petting parties, underlined how much her lifestyle reflected the arrival of what would in time be called the generation gap. That slang is not all her own work – and it is interesting to wonder to what extent, and quite at odds with the usual generation of slang, this was indeed *her* own work rather than that of her beau – and the line between flapper slang and contemporary college usage is hard to define, and there are naturally overlaps into general usage, but a good proportion is different to that of the wider world. Some of it would, as youth slang does, eventually filter into that world, but a distinct line can be seen between the nature of Conradi's list and any representative lexis of flapper-talk.

Such talk, of which a glossary was compiled in 1922 and reprinted as 'The Flapper Dictionary' in a number of local newspapers, had its own themes. The flappers themselves, their boyfriends, the parties and dances they attended, the dancing and sexual activity they enjoyed (which latter appeared to stop short of intercourse, or certainly as regards slang coinages), drink, automobiles and so on. The over-thirties were barely mentioned. It is a vocabulary of ephemerality and hedonism and while some seems contrived, it flourished alongside its much publicized speakers. Many such themes had appeared in Conradi's lists, but again, these used terms that did not co-exist in general slang: *Barlow* (a flapper), *biscuit* ('a pettable flapper'), *Brooksy Boy* (a classy dresser), *cellar smeller* (a young man who always turns up where liquor is to be had without cost), *dimbox*, (a taxicab), *embalmer* (a bootlegger), and more than 120 others.

While the flappers undoubtedly used a language – however frivolous and short-lived – that marked them as distinct, it is harder to unravel youth slang of the next two decades from that of the mainstream. On the whole it was not analysed, and was usually seen through the prisms of college language or the slang attached to jazz and then swing. The language of World War II, with its wide range of military neologisms, slang and others, further crowded out the period's young civilians. The bobbysoxers who made crooner Frank Sinatra into a superstar were credited with a few terms, e.g. *able Grable* or *whistle bait* (a sexy girl), *glad lad* (an attractive boy), *jive bomber* (a good dancer), and they were duly written up in the press, but none of it lasted and like many such articles, one wonders how much was contrived: whether by the interviewee, keen to please the journalist, or the journalist, keen to amuse the readers.

The growing self-segregation of the teenager, carving out their own space in parallel to the adult norms, required a separate language. This was not always especially different: youth would continue to adopt adult slang as well as to create its own. As such much of the vocabulary was not considered worthy of comment. But certain areas generated notice, often as a side-effect of the wider moral panics – blending the inevitable mix of voyeuristic titillation and uncomprehending terror that can be found as earnestly propounded in the sixteenth century as in the twentieth – that focused on the much analysed 'juvenile delinquent', enjoying and embodying that triple threat of sex, drugs and rock 'n' roll. The 'JD' pulps (see Chapter 16), were filled with slang to maximize their authenticity (and Harlan Ellison did indeed run with a gang before his 'Hal Ellson' titles began appearing), and the whole thing was rendered suitably anodyne by the musical *West Side Story*, turning the mean streets into a reworked *Romeo and Juliet* – a play that was not without its own share of slang: notably such double-entendres as *et-caetera* and *medlar* (the vagina), *poperin pear* and *bauble* (the penis), *bird's nest* (the pubic hair), and *ladybird* or *smock* (a whore).

In 1961 the *Saturday Evening Post* commissioned pollster George Gallup to take a look at what they headlined 'Youth: The Cool Generation'.[14] Gallup discussed what he termed 'youthese – the lingo of youth' and offered a micro-dictionary. It included *Big Daddy* ('an older person'), *cube* or *square* ('a normal person'), *ankle-biter* ('a child'), *bread* ('money'), *pad* ('home'), *bitching* ('joyous term as in: "I had a bitching (or joyous) time"'), *like crazy* ('more joyous than merely cool'), and such phrases as *It's been real* ('Thank you for the pleasant evening'), *who rattled your cage?* ('who asked for your opinion?') and *I dig you the most* ('I like you').

Working-class delinquents aside, slang permeated the language of a succession of what the Sixties would christen 'youth cults' and what the Fifties had already termed 'youth culture' (first noted in 1958). Beats, then beatniks, zoot-suiters and teen gangs, and then hippies all offered a distinct subset of speech. And while slang as ever followed its predictable themes, two strands become increasingly important; the language of recreational drug users and the expanding influence of black slang on white speakers. Like everything the world's post-war young saw as imitable and alluring it began in America, but the move first to the UK and then beyond soon accelerated. The world-embracing primacy of modern rap, the slang of which has moved beyond anglophone speakers, shows the current breadth of the phenomenon.

And as with the slang of rap, the slang that moved from the black world into the white in the early 1950s and beyond was that which came with music, in this case jazz. It is not, perhaps, especially surprising that the proselytes of the language that both called 'hip' were white men, both praising the racial inventiveness that created it. For Mezz Mezzrow terms like *hip* itself, or *solid*, *righteous*, and *groovy*, were both revolutionary and aspirational; they represented 'the qualities the young cats go for, the ones they've invented new phrases to describe. Fitted together, they form a portrait of Uncle Tom – in reverse, a negative print. They add up to something mighty impressive, a real man. As their new American lingo tells you, that's what these hip kids mean to become.'[15] Had Mezzrow still been in America a decade later one might have suggested him as the inspiration for an essay, published in 1957 by the writer Norman Mailer: 'The White Negro: Superficial Reflections on the Hipster'. In Mailer's heightened, hyperactive prose, 'If marijuana was the wedding ring, the child was the language of Hip for its argot gave expression to abstract states of feeling which all could share, at least all who were Hip. And in this wedding of the white and the black it was the Negro who brought the cultural dowry.' He lauded

> the cunning of their language, the abstract ambiguous alternatives in which from the danger of their oppression they learned to speak ('Well, now, man, like I'm looking for a cat to turn me on...') [...] it is not too difficult to believe that the language of Hip which evolved was an artful language, tested and shaped by an intense experience and therefore different in kind from white slang [...] What makes Hip a special language is that it cannot really be taught – if one shares none of the experiences of elation and exhaustion which it is equipped to describe, then it seems merely arch or vulgar or irritating.[16]

In another ten years Tom Wolfe would skewer such white liberal adulation as 'radical chic' but when Mailer in particular was writing, he struck a chord, even if black writers such as Ralph Ellison and James Baldwin were less impressed with his seeming worship of what looked to them like a clichéd portrait of noble savagery embellished with a saxophone and a syringe. White swing fans had taken on some black slang, but the image of the African-American – or at least the existential, jazz-playing, junkie version – as the symbol of absolute authenticity had started with the late 1940s *beats* – Burroughs, Ginsberg, Kerouac, Ferlinghetti, Corso and Cassady. Later it moved on towards the mass-popular world of what in 1958 San Francisco journalist Herb Caen christened the *beatnik*, boosted by the success of Kerouac's *On the Road* (1957, although the original 'scroll' was typed up in 1951) and Ginsberg's epic poem 'Howl' of 1956. Kerouac summed up the fantasy that informed many of the young whites fighting against the conformism of Fifties America as he wrote of 'walking in the Denver colored section, wishing I were a Negro, feeling the best the white world had offered was not enough ecstasy for me, not enough life, joy, kicks, darkness, music […] wishing I could exchange worlds with the happy true-hearted ecstatic Negroes of America'.[17]

The reality was otherwise and the beats were not and could not be black. And those blacks who joined the party would, by the Sixties, start moving into the more radical world of Black Power, where whites, however sympathetic, were surplus to any requirements other than that of donations. Terry Southern captured this liberal cultural tourism best, with 'The Night the Bird Blew for Dr Warner' (1954). This story, which should resonate for slang lexicographers as well as musicologists, charts the academic Dr Warner's attempt to attain the absolute epitome of hipness. He understands jazz, he speaks black slang, he is cool incarnate. But there is a final step:

"'I'll have to be a hipster," Dr. Warner said […] "A very *hip* hipster," he continued genially, and withdrew himself slightly, for emphasis, "if not, indeed, something *more*." "Something *more*?" said professor Thomas, stressing his mock surprise with a sickly smile. He loathed strange jargon. "Don't tell me there's anything more, Ralph, than being a hipster!" Dr. Warner allowed his own gaze to grow sober […] "Yes," he said evenly, "you might say that a *junky* is something more than a hipster."'[18]

Perhaps, but not for Dr Warner. Seeking to score in an alleyway he meets not the super-cool black man of his dreams but a simple delinquent who sees him as just one more vulnerable square. 'An arm swung out from the darkness and laid a short segment of lead pipe across the back of the Doctor's head. As he staggered between two mountains of refuse, he was hit again, and the white light was shot through with coils and bolts of purple and gray and flooded out on a heavy wave of blood blackness.'[19]

It was safer simply to appropriate the slang.

As beatnik transmogrified into hippie, and the census of countercultural youth notched up ever higher numbers, so too did the users of what had once been exclusively black slang. Whether the love 'n' peace generation of the Sixties realized that they were spouting a language that had once belonged to junkies and jazzmen is debatable. Like the music they loved, plucked so often from black origins but all too rarely acknowledged as such, they didn't bother with the source. One need look no further than the origins of the word *hippie* itself. While by the later 1960s it had become indelibly associated with the world of beads and bells and psychedelic drugs, and all the popular marketing that went with the movement, hippie, to a cool 1950s black speaker was definitely a put-down. It was the antithesis of the desirable role of the hipster, a dismissive diminutive that meant one was in fact *not* hip, however hard they were trying.

The hippies didn't care, if they even registered the irony. If the beats and beatniks wanted to be black and in some way take on the black experience, the counter-culture's latest representatives were satisfied merely to use black language. They coined relatively little, much of it to do with drugs, notably lysergic acid diethylamide or LSD. For instance *bummer*, which came to mean a bad LSD trip and thus any unpleasant experience, had begun life as a Hells Angels term for a bad crash; *trip*, with its adjectival form *trippy*, and the various names (*Strawberry Fields, Blue Cheer, microdot*) for the drug itself. But terms such as *heavy, bag, groovy, freeby, hang-up, out of sight, far out,* and the ever-popular *cool* were no more than borrowings.

Slang would play a part in every iteration of the counter-culture. In its role as counter-language this was its natural place. To pervert, mock and undermine the status quo required one to step aside from the language of the established and the conventional. It was a conscious, rebellious subversion, delineated by Mezzrow in the context of post-war African-Americanisms. 'Deny the Negro the culture of the land? O.K. He'll brew his own culture – on the street corner. Lock him out from the seats of higher learning? He pays it no nevermind – he'll dream up his own professional doubletalk, from the professions that are open to him, the professions of musician, entertainer, maid, butler, tap-dancer, handyman, reefer-pusher, gambler, counterman, porter, chauffeur, numbers racketeer, day laborer, pimp, stevedore. These boys I ran with [...] they were the new sophisticates of the race, the jivers, the sweettalkers, the jawblockers.'[20] Mezzrow, the racial convert, has all the unrestrained enthusiasm of the type, but he is not wholly wrong. For the young whites, embracing social opposition meant embracing language that was oppositional too. It might expose them to mockery, to the role of *wigga*, Mailer's *white negro* reinterpreted cruelly for the era of rap, but they were undeterred.

Eric Partridge, publishing his first edition in 1937, could, as noted, offer nothing but English slang, and forget that of America. World War II put paid to that, and the ever accelerating Americanization of popular culture has merely accelerated the process. Purely English, purely white working-class slang has been in decline for a while, its Cockney rhyming version as much of a London tourist attraction, and as fading, as Routemaster buses and unarmed bobbies. The middle class, on the whole, don't create slang. The actual black ghetto, for all the rappers' material success, remains far more of a world apart. Slang has needed such 'alien' worlds for its finest, sustained production. The white assumption of such language may well be a form of linguistic voyeurism, but like the more traditional form, it's something the devotees can't resist.

Not everyone wanted to be a beatnik, a hippie nor yet embrace the image of the 'white negro'. But black culture fascinated, and for those who wanted rebellion by proxy there was a simpler way: the proliferation of rock 'n' roll, and the voices and language of the disc-jockeys who were playing it.

The term disc-jockey is first recorded in 1937 when H. L. Mencken noted '*disk jockey*, or *pancake-turner*, one who changes phonograph records'[21] (the abbreviation *DJ* does not seem to appear in print at least until 1959). The first was apparently Jack L. Cooper, broadcasting on the black station WSBC in 1931, but the DJ wouldn't gain his dominance until the 1940s and beyond. It was not merely the player, it was what was played and even more important for slang, was said between the records. The bottom line for a commercial jock was selling, and to sell one needed a personality. The traditional format was to create some virtual space, typically the 'Magic Ballroom', a 1930s show that could be heard on KFWB in Los Angeles and WSNEW in New York. But that was all about the metropolis and offering an invitation to the glamorous big city. This changed in the 1950s: stations focused more on local audiences, and DJs, rather than offering invitations to places the audience would never go, presented themselves as one of a community, playing the music that they, and with them their radio 'friends' enjoyed.

Jubilee, the biggest 'Negro variety show' of the Forties, was fronted by 'your emcee, that walkie-talkie butterball Ernie – the 'Q' for cute – Whitman'. Susan Douglas records some of his chat: 'Ernie Q starts off with "Much water's passed under the oil tower trestle of this fessel vessel since we made with the riffs." He then then introduces a "hepster with the hottest licorice stick in town"; little Ida James is a "chick" [while] Art Tatum "will manipulate the eighty-eights" [...] Modes of address to performers and the audience include "papa," "brother," and "cats." He signs off "Dig you later".'[22]

Then there was rock 'n' roll. It appealed to a new audience, the teenager. It was black music, or so it began until the record producer Sam Philips famously found the white boy who sounded black, Elvis Presley, and turned what were still known as 'race records' into a crossover industry. It soon dominated youthful listeners, who in turn had new and independent access to the airwaves through another new invention: the transistor. Disc-jockeys aimed straight at the young.

Most important for the era was Memphis's WDIA, the South's main black station, home of Rufus 'Bear Cat' Thomas, Maurice 'Hot Rod' Hulbert, Jocko Henderson and many other black stars. It was, suggests Susan Douglas, the station that changed the style not just of black but through that white radio. 'African American DJs of the late 1940s and early 1950s [...] brought a rhyming and rapping style to the air widely imitated by their white counterparts.'[23] Other cities' black DJs might echo it, but in a new take on minstrelsy white jocks simply stole the black style, down to the accents in which the words were delivered. Typically

Dewey Phillips, the first DJ to play Elvis, was white but broadcast to a mainly black audience on WHBQ ('WH-Bar-B-Que') in Memphis. He took the slang, the jive and even the black accented speech. He was one of many. On radio, with a teen audience, everyone wanted to sound black. Every station seemed to have its 'black' white DJ. They took nicknames – Moondog and Hound Dog, the Mad Daddy and Dr Daddy-O, Poppa Stoppa, the Rockin' Bird, Wolfman Jack and Murray the K – and perfected a patter that indulged teen fantasies of cool and hip. It was naturally filled with slang.

In a couple of cases this slang ended up between covers: Lavada Durst, 'Dr Hepcat' of KVET in Austin, Texas, put out *The Jives of Dr. Hepcat* in 1953. Hepcat's on-air intro ran 'Jumpin' Jills and jivin' cats, upstate Gates in Stetson hats, lace your boots and tighten your wig, here's some jive, can you dig? I'm Dr Hepcat on the scene, with a stack of shellac on my record machine. I'm hip to the tip and bop to the top, I'm a long time coming and I just won't stop. It's a real gone deal that I'm gonna reel, so stay tuned while I pad your skulls.' A musical generation later Hy Lit (Hyman Lit), broadcasting from various Philadelphia stations, notably WIBG, published *Hy Lit's Unbelievable Dictionary of Hip Words*. Even if, as Tom Dalzell has noted,[24] he drew heavily on Lord Buckley.

Hip-hop began in the mid-1970s in New York's City's impoverished Bronx. It was essentially party music, making its way out of disco (a term frequently mentioned in its lyrics) into a new world. As the Funky Four + 1 explained in 'Rappin and Rockin the House' (1979), 'We're here to please everybody out there / Forget about your problems, get 'em out of your hair.' Those who dismissed hip-hop as a fad could not have been more wrong, but the music that would soon be bracketed with other threats from the 'underclass' was some way off. There were a few slang terms, but the 'old school' was more likely to be requesting dancers to 'so-so-socialise', to 'throw your hands in the air' or 'rock the house', to celebrate the audience 'in the place to be', to name-check the group's MCs, offer a shout-out to the locals and a reference to a popular dance such as the 'Patty Duke'. A few performers – typically Spoonie G with his 'player' pose – added a range of sexual innuendos while Grandmaster's Flash's downbeat 'The Message' offered a darker image of the street and threw in the odd word of prison slang, but the lyrics remained essentially AAVE, or even standard English.

It is with the advent of more politicized, more consciously 'black' groups such as Run DMC, and then, on the West Coast, the creation of what became known as 'gangsta rap', with which performers such as NWA, Ice T, Snoop Dogg and Dr Dre took the lyrics out of the high-school disco and on to the streets, that the language, as required, hardened up. The nonsense lyrics of 'Rapper's Delight' gave way to the violent melodramas of '6 'N' The Mornin''. It was as if the ghetto melodramas of Donald Goines had been set to music and the bragging, hedonistic materialism, unrestrained violence and overt sexuality of the lyrics linked directly back to the 'bad man' toasts. To what extent the gangsta rappers actually spoke from experience was irrelevant (though hotly debated): they played the part (flashing gang colours and hand signals, displaying supposed bullet wounds and sloganeering tattoos) and slang, as much as anything, conferred its usual authenticity. And if the street criminality was not uniformly practised by blacks, nor was the language theirs alone. The black-to-white pattern repeated itself yet again. Running surveillance on a pair of pallid crack dealers aping the gestures, the subterfuges, the uniforms and above all the language and accents of the black originals across town, *The Wire's* black detective Carver observes bitterly: 'They steal *everything*, don't they.'[25]

The arrival of the mass use of rap slang represents the current state of the art as regards the crossover influence of African-American culture on the larger, whiter world. New coinages continue to appear but the over-riding movement of black slang to white use has been a reality for more than half a century. The difference is the speed of assimilation. The beatniks and hippies, consciously or otherwise, were talking black, but black that was already between twenty and thirty years old. The young of the twenty-first century, thanks to the vastly accelerated speed of communications, are picking up black coinages within weeks. It is not all black slang, but the pre-war domination of the counter-language by the white working class and its criminal cousins has gone for good.

The UK does boast an extra additive, or at least a small twist on the mainstream adoption of African-Americanisms: the language of the second generation of immigrants from the West Indies. (There should, too, be some degree of linguistic input from the young Asian community, but while their music, Bhangra, has made some inroads it would seem that there exists insufficient slang, at least in English, to make a real impression.) The first immigrants from the Caribbean, arriving in the 1950s and 1960s, pretty much kept their slang to themselves, and in any case it is often hard to distinguish from island patois. Such immigrant narratives as the Trinidadian Samuel Selvon's *The Lonely Londoners* (1956), which did offer the language, remained rare, and the better-known Colin MacInnes, another immigrant but white and Australian, while embracing the culture, especially in *City of Spades* (1957), gives no particular linguistic insights (although he seems to be the first to print the insult *raasclat*). Nor is MacInnes's *Absolute Beginners* (1959), focused on a much poorer, multicultural Notting Hill than today's wealthy ghetto, and reaching its climax in the race riots of 1959, especially revelatory. There is no real sense of an especially youthful, let alone black lexis.

The new generation of young black Britons is less constrained. The language of 'grime', most easily, if inaccurately, described as British hip-hop (other names include one-step and esky – referring, inevitably, to 'cool') and of UK garage (definitely pronounced 'garridge' and another US import) blends West Indian patois, Cockney, and America's rap slang to create its own subset. (American West Indians have had less of an impact, even if *baby-mother*, the woman, to whom one is not married, who bears your child – there is also *baby-father* – seems to have made the leap.)

In 2008 Britain's press and media were touting a brand new linguistic phenomenon: Jafaikan. Jafaikan, it was claimed, was a blend of 'Jamaican', 'African' and 'Asian' and represented for popular consumption what its academic discoverers termed Multicultural London English (MLE), in other words the indigenous speech of young, often but not invariably black or brown Londoners. The concept served the press, but missed the linguistic mark. The actuality of Jafaikan is that while it is indeed a blend, and one of the terms is certainly Jamaican, the other is 'fake'. Fake as in not Jamaican but wanting to pose as such. The black-on-black equivalent of rap's *wigga* or *wanksta* (any boy playing at being a gangsta). Jafaikan is most usually applied to those whose Caribbean roots lie in one of the other islands, but it can equally be applied to anyone, black or Asian, who wants to hide their middle-class trappings and come on like they stepped out of the gritty streets of Bob Marley's Trenchtown. But a subset of contemporary British slang? The language of young London? As MLE speakers have it, that's so *bait*. Or as everyone might say, 'bullshit'. Though MLE does exist. The first modern Black immigrants (Black Britons can be found in the early eighteenth century and indeed earlier) arrived in the 1950s and while they continued to speak patois (their hometown dialects and slang) among themselves, it remained essentially invisible. A decade later and things were changing as young whites started to dance to bluebeat and ska. But it was the reggae explosion of the Seventies that watered the first shoots of the future MLE. Anyone who knew Bob Marley's lyrics soon knew *Babylon*, the Rastaman term for the police in particular and the 'downpressing' Western society in general. Other terms would follow, even if they still sounded strange on white lips. The last decade, however, as the grandchildren of those first immigrants grew up, and London began producing its homegrown rivals to US rap, has seen MLE truly take off. Words such as *bait* (absurd), *bare* (lots of), *creps* (trainers), *murk* (to beat or kill) and *armshouse* (a fight with guns) are up and running hard. If as yet the Asian constituent remains relatively minimal, that may change. However, Caribbean patois remains based in English and the transfer to the streets of London is far simpler than that of Urdu or Hindi. Either way, there's plenty more to come.

17 War:
One Thing It's Good For

Pistol's cock is out and flashing fire will follow.

Shakespeare, *Henry IV* part 2

The world of the professional soldier (and sailor and to lesser extent airman and woman) is too productive of slang that has crossed over into wider use to be sidelined as mere jargon. There is jargon, a great deal of it – the naming of officers and non-coms and their ranks and occupations, the nicknaming of weaponry and its parts, friendly and otherwise, of regiments and of course of the enemy – but there is more. Wars end and the troops, at least the fortunate ones (and those less fortunate who have been severely wounded but still survive) come home. And they bring at least a sample of their language with them. It too survives, in their conversations, their memoirs and, later, in the history books, or certainly those that call on oral testimony. Hotten's introduction to his dictionary posits the sources of slang as 'the congregating together of people [...] the result of crowding, and excitement, and artificial life'.[1] He was thinking of cities, but nowhere could qualify any better for his congregation, crowding and excitement than does war, especially those protracted engagements such as World War I. If the use of cant in studies and novels of crime confers unarguable authenticity on the texts, so too does slang on those of war.

It is not simply proximity that produces fertile soil for slang's generation. The battlefield was, and largely remains, a male territory. Slang is a man-made language and projects a male point of view. Extend that combination, as in World War I, for four years, and the opportunity for extending male language seems almost limitless. Its use might be toned down on those occasions when one encountered women – World War I diarists, for instance note how language might be modified among nurses, although the Frenchwomen who ran estaminets and cafes seem to have been treated less scrupulously – but these were relatively rare occasions. The soldier's basic existence is alongside other men.

In its list of 'canters' Awdeley's *Fraternitye of Vacabondes* lists the 'Ruffeler', second in rank only to the 'Upright man', who 'goeth wyth a weapon to seeke seruice, saying he hath bene a Seruitor in the wars, and beggeth for his reliefe'. And although many such self-appointed veterans were in fact out-of-work servants, it is very possible, but as is too often the period's case undocumented, that the ex-soldiers who formed at least a proportion of the sixteenth century's canting crew brought with them the slang they had used in the ranks. Certainly the hierarchical organization that underpinned the crew seemed to owe something to the military. In his *Jovial Crew* Brome includes a soldier among those reduced to vagrancy, and perhaps some of the amputees who paraded their stumps to seek alms had been genuinely wounded in some European campaign.

Although the soldier was undoubtedly a common enough figure to generate a range of slang synonyms, prior to the American Civil War (1861–5) there was no sense of a coherent body of military slang that could be linked to a single campaign. That this conflict has been considered as the first example of 'modern' warfare is not coincidental. The Crimea, which preceded it, has left no linguistic remains other than the standard *Balaclava*, the head-encompassing woolly helmet.

The language generated by the Civil War is not wide-ranging, and records show that a good deal of common slang was used by soldiers on both sides; but there were a number of important additions to the lexis. While the North was just that, or the *Union*, the South became known as *Dixie*, a word that had not been coined for the war, but was widely popularized by it, especially through the song 'Dixie's Land', first sung by the 'minstrel' Daniel D. Emmett in April 1859. Of the various possible etymologies the preferred choice is an abbreviation of the Mason–*Dixon* line (which divided the North and South in 1763–7). 'Dixie's land' was also a common term in contemporary children's games of tag.[2] Less common was *Cousin Sally Ann* (or *Cousin Sal* or *Sally*) from the initial letters of the Confederate States of America.

The soldiers themselves were either *Yanks*, *Yankees* or *Feds* and after the war *Billy Yank* and on the Confederate side were *Confeds* or the punning *cornfeds*; from their opponents' point of view they were *Johnny Rebs*, *Rebs* and *Johnnies*; the Southerner might also be a *secesh* (from secessionist). *Black and tan* was another synonym for Southerner: a nod to the states' abuse of their slaves and a pun on *tan* (to beat). An infantry soldier was a *flatfoot*, *webfoot* or a *worm-pounder*. *Non-com*, for a non-commissioned officer, and *old head*, for a veteran, were both coined in the war. The soldiers' uniforms naturally played their part. The Northern blue gave *bluebelly*, *bluebird*, *blue coat*, *blue Johnny* and *brothers in blue*. The Southern gray gave *grayback*. A *butternut* was a Northerner who backed the Confederacy: in the early stages of the war Southerners fought in uniforms dyed brown by a mixture of copperas and walnut hulls. Such much-abused turncoats were also *copperheads*, from the venomous snake. Pro-slavery Northerners were also *doughfaces*, while vehement Unionists were *niggerheads* or *rads*, as in radicals. Colour also lay behind the enemies' respective currency. The Union dollar bill was a *greenback*, the Confederate one a *blueback*, which notes were also known as *shucks*, from standard English shucks, the shells of peas, husks of corn and similar vegetable refuse and thus implying the worthlessness of the Confederate currency.

Some Southerners supported the Union; they were known as *buffalos* (which originated in North Carolina). *Buffalo* also meant a looter, although the far more popular term was *bummer*. By extension the word was used for general abuse, which definition also covered *culls*, *yellow dogs*, *croakers* and *deadbeats*; a *coffee-cooler* was a soldier who ' blows his coffee while the brigade is going by', i.e. one who is constantly searching for a soft job. What the Vietnam war would term *REMFs* ('rear-echelon motherfuckers') were *bombproofs* (men who never faced the perils of the front lines). The war also coined *skedaddler* (a deserter), the etymology of which remains unknown. Southerners who hid out in woods and forests to avoid conscription were *mossybacks*, while those irregulars who took advantage of the situation to profit themselves by murder and marauding were *jayhawkers*, imported, according to Schele de Vere, from Australia.

A variety of terms are first recorded during the period, used in letters and memoirs of the conflict, although they had no especial military links. *Mug* (from *member mug*) (a chamberpot), *take the cake, keep someone posted, dirt* (a mean action or malicious remark), *whale* and *jim-hickey* (both an exceptional individual), *knock* (to shoot dead), *gunboats* (large heavy boots), and *sell-out* (an act of betrayal or renunciation of beliefs and principles for money or position). Perhaps the best-known phrase on either side was the jocular cry of *Here's your mule!* noted by William Pittenger in *Daring and Suffering* (1864): 'The cry of "Here's your mule," and "Where's my mule," have become national, and are generally heard when, on the one hand, no mule is about, and on the other when no one is hunting a mule. It seems not to be understood by any one.'[3]

The war also offered what remains the earliest use of *fucked up* in its sense of objects, intentions or plans that are broken, wrecked or ruined. An anonymous soldier asked, 'What the bloody Hell is wanted now? This is a fucked up company anyhow, and always has been since the guard came on shore. To Hell with such a company and all connected with such a damned concern!'[4] A fastidious Confederate private noted that phrase as well as much more in the way of rough language, writing to his wife in 1864 to deplore military life as 'one unceasing tide of blasphemy and wickedness, coarseness and obscenity'.[5]

Among the many encomia that the music-hall star Albert Chevalier received was his being 'the Kipling of the music hall, for he takes the common clay of Whitechapel, and fashions it into real works of art'.[6] Rudyard Kipling, who had arrived in London in 1890, was the current darling of the London critics, fêted by nearly all as the writer of *Plain Tales from Hills, Departmental Ditties, Barrack Room Ballads* and perhaps most important of all at that stage, the stories that made up *Soldiers Three*, his fictions of life amongst the 'other ranks' of the Indian Army. Kipling is hardly limited to tales of war, but the background of these stories, and many that would follow, was the military world, and it is generally considered that in his vocalizing of his trio of privates

Ortheris (the Cockney), Learoyd (the Yorkshireman) and Mulvaney (the Irishman) he had taken portrayal of the working classes into a new world. If, as suggested by P. J. Keating, the nineteenth-century Cockney stereotype had been successively Dickens's Sam Weller and Milliken's 'Arry, then Kipling's portrait of Tommy Atkins replaced the pair. And if he was not invariably portraying the real military world, then his stories often look to other kinds of warfare: that of the schoolboys Stalky and Co. against authority, or, in his sole foray into the slums, of goodness against the corruptions of poverty. It is with that in mind that he will be considered here.

Kipling is not at first sight a particularly 'slangy' author. In his children's tale 'How the First Letter Was Written',[7] he (as Tegumai) admonishes Taffy (his daughter Josephine) for using 'awful' to mean 'great'. 'Taffy,' said Tegumai, 'how often have I told you not to use slang? "Awful" isn't a pretty word.'' Yet when one starts dissecting the work one finds that it plays a regular role. There are hundreds of slang words and phrases in the works, as well as a wide range of job-specific jargon, typically in his sea stories. He uses it for the most basic of reasons: to confer authenticity. He is not a coiner, but a recorder, and his slang lexis is that of the contemporary world, leavened, as in the conversations of the Soldiers Three, by the specifics of a given background. He claimed himself to be implacable in his choice of terms: 'I will write what I please. I will not alter a line. If it pleases me to do so I will refer to Her Gracious majesty – bless her! – as the little fat widow of Windsor and fill the mouth of Mulvaney with filth and oaths.'[8] But there were limits. He suggests that 'Thomas [i.e. Tommy Atkins] really ought to be supplied with a new Adjective to help him express his opinions'[9] but we never read it and see only blanks. (Judging by the evidence of Frederick Manning's *Her Privates We* and other World War I memoirs of Army life one may assume it was 'fucking' – 'bloody' being claimed by Australia). He was also capable of bending to his audiences. The language of stories originally written in India, where his readers would have had a good smattering of what a newly published new dictionary of Anglo-Indian imperial pidgin termed 'Hobson-Jobson', had to be simplified for those 'at home'. Thus in 'The Post That Fitted', one of the *Departmental Ditties* (1888), the original 'eight paltry dibs' became 'eight poor rupees', and in its accompanying tale 'Municipal', 'A Commissariat *hathee, nautching* gaily down the Mall; becomes 'A Commissariat elephant careering down the Mall' (although the same poem does not alter *musth*, elephantine aggression, usually in the rutting season, or *shikared*, hunted, and one wonders whether *nautch*, which had been known to mean dance in the UK for over a century, was simply considered too suggestive). Though such changes are not mandatory and *Soldiers Three* – where it would have been foolish and anomalous to put standard English into the mouths of men who rarely speak it – is full of pidgin, e.g. *jildi, mafeesh, dekko, chee-chee, pukka, peg* and *baksheesh*.

It was Kipling's use of English that drew most comment. 'Among Mr. Kipling's discoveries of new kinds of characters,' said his fan, poet and critic Andrew Lang, 'probably the most popular is his invention of the British soldier in India.' Kipling was less grateful than Lang might have expected. A letter of 1890 states how 'the long-haired literati of the Savile Club are swearing that I "invented" my soldier talk in *Soldiers Three*. Seeing that not one of these critters has been within earshot of a barrack, I am naturally wrath.'[10] Kipling had not invented it. He had picked it up, along with the prototypes of his characters, in such oases of expatriate tedium as the barracks at Mian Mar, where as a journalist he had enjoyed relatively privileged access.

Barrack Room Ballads (1892, 1896) and *Departmental Ditties* (1896) are also permeated by slang. The first draws on the life of the other ranks with language to suit. Terms that had yet to be recorded include: *sling the bat* (to talk Hindi or Urdu; he had already introduced *bat* in *Plain Tales from the Hills*), *blind* (to swear and in its adverbial use, e.g. *go it blind*), *clobber* (as *clob*, to beat or kill), *crack on* (to boast), *Fuzzy-Wuzzy* (a Sudanese), *grouse* (to grumble), *hairy* (first-rate), *hell for leather*, *jildi* (speed, energy), *give the knock* (to knock down), *oont* (a camel), *go on the shout* (to go drinking) and *snig* (to pilfer). The *Ditties*, with their in-jokes and *poèmes a clef* stories of such as Potiphar Gubbins, C. E., Ahasuerus Jenkins and Delilah, are not based on soldiers' lives: *masher, skittles!* (nonsense!), *fanti* (eccentric) and *screw* (a salary) are more middle-class.

Whether, as P. J. Keating claims, Kipling's rendition of Tommy Atkins (a nickname he had not invented but popularized as never before) also made 'a complete break with convention and provides English fiction with a new cockney archetype'[11] is debatable. Of the Soldiers Three one is Irish, and on occasion not a little of a stage Irishman as well, one from Yorkshire, and thus dialectal, and Ortheris, the Cockney (who would presumably have called himself 'Aw'fris'), is relatively quiet, or at least as compared with the loquacious Mulvaney, on whom the burden of tale-telling rests. His vocabulary is far smaller and far more mundane than is that of the self-consciously worldly 'Arry, but his background is much poorer, while 'Arry is more lower-middle than truly working-class.

If Kipling looked hard, and as is suggested with unique perception, at the life of the working class in the cantonments of the Raj, he stepped only once into Chevalier's back yard: the East End. And then it was not into the music-hall star's sentimental stage fantasies of coster life and emotions. Kipling was appalled by London, hating its foggy weather, its dirt (both literal and metaphorical), and appalled by its human beings, whether the long-haired aesthetes or what he generalized as a drunken, violent underclass. His one essay into the existence of the latter came in the 1890 story 'The Record of Badalia Herodsfoot', included in the book *Many Inventions* (1893). This is the story of an East End slum woman who volunteers her local knowledge to augment and improve upon the church's official charitable work and who, even after being kicked almost to death by her drunken husband, still refuses to betray him with her final breath. She too, like Arthur Morrison's Dicky Perrott, is unable even *in extremis* to abandon the code of the slums. In its unyielding pessimism Kipling's tale is all Morrison and offers not a vestige of Pugh or Pett Ridge. As in India, Kipling's creation of Cockney speech patterns lie more in dropped initial h's and final g's, double negatives and eye-dialect than in slang as such. Thus 'port wine' is 'pork wine', a 'curate' a 'curick', 'diphtheria' 'diptheery', 'what', as similarly pronounced by Ortheris, is 'wot', and so on. There is slang, as there needs to be, but it is of the quotidian sort, including *slop* (policeman), *garn!*, *shut your head*, and the epithets *blooming*, *blasted*, *bleeding* and a possible use of *fucking* in 'that's a — lie!'. Like Tommy Atkins, their cousin overseas, these East Enders have a vocabulary of 'less than six hundred words, and the Adjective'.[12]

Kipling's most prolific use of slang – some 40% of the terms he uses– came in the quasi-biographical school stories that appeared in *Stalky and Co* (1899) and various subsequent collections. The context here, since the school had been established to prepare boys to take the army's entrance examinations, was also military, though 'Stalky' and 'M'Turk' are soldiers only in embryo, while 'Beetle', i.e. Kipling, is destined only for literary campaigning.

Much of the slang is in general use, but many terms are not that far from Billy Bunter, who, although he would not appear in print until 1908, had been invented by 'Frank Richards' in an unpublished story of the 1890s. They include: *ass* and *ass about* (the animal, rather than the posterior), *bags I!*, *bait* (a rage), *biznai*, *blub* (to cry), *brew* (a study feast), *bug-hunter* (an entomologist), *buzz* (to throw), *cat* (to vomit), *cave!* (look out!), *cram* (a tutor or last-minute pre-examination work), *cribber* (one who uses some form of illicit aid when taking examinations), *dicker* (a dictionary), the suffix *-croo*, *funk* (a coward), *impot* (an imposition, i.e. punishment of 'lines'), *jammy* (easy), *padre* (a chaplain), *pi-jaw* (an earnest, moralizing lecture), *ripping!*, *rot* (to talk nonsense), *scrag* (to beat up), *slack* (lazy), *sneak* (to tell tales), *swot* as noun or verb, *tip* (of a parent to pass over money) and *wigging* (a telling-off). Kipling was not a pioneer of school stories – although here, as in his soldier tales, he had a new and more realistic take on the language: such slang as Tom Brown and his chums use is almost wholly adult – but it is hard to believe that many of his successors in the field had not read *Stalky*.

The four-month Spanish-American War broke out and concluded in 1898. It ended the Spanish Empire and can be seen as the start of an American one. Some of Damon Runyon's earliest short stories were set amongst the troops fighting in the Philippines, but the great source of the campaign's slang can be found in the books of Chauncey M'Govern: *Sarjint Larry an' Frinds* (1906) and *By Bolo and Krag* (1907). M'Govern, known as 'The Kipling of the Philippines' followed up with the post-war *When the Krag Is Laid Away* (1910), which caused something of a stir with its underlying proposition: that ex-soldiers could and should set up with Filipina partners and establish a mixed-race society. The two war books are slang-heavy, and both offer readers a glossary; as well as the first recorded use of *re-up* (to re-enlist; more recently adopted for the resupply of a drug dealer's supplies).

The slang of the Boer War – where Clarence Rook's 'Young Alf', once hooligan, now hero, supposedly fell – left relatively little impact on the lexis: the conflict's primary effect on the language was the addition of a number of Dutch or Afrikaans words to mainstream English, while many of the troops brought with them the terminology of the Indian Army. Kipling wrote of the war, which he visited, but language of his stories, in *Traffics and Discoveries* (1907) reflect nothing beyond that pattern.

The conflict which followed was wholly different. It is arguable that no single event, war or otherwise, triggered so great an efflorescence of the slang lexicon as did the First World War. It was noted by all concerned not just in the war's aftermath, but for the four years through which it dragged on. As the war progressed, journals and magazines of all sides ran regular reports of the way soldiers were talking. W. J. Burke, in his bibliography *The Literature of Slang* (1939), cites some thirty glossaries produced between 1915 and 1918, with eighteen others appearing within a year of the Armistice and further lists published through the Twenties and Thirties.

Perhaps the first was the French slang lexicographer Lazare Sainéan's dictionary – *L'Argot des Tranchées* – of 1915, compiled from soldiers' letters and trench magazines, and Sainéan's short book lays down the essence of the soldiers' slang: names for the enemy, for themselves, for ways of killing, e.g. with the bayonet, for weapons and their payloads, for ranks and military specialities, for engagements, for clothing, for rations and (though not in British lexicons) for wine, for the constituent parts of trenches, and so on. What the French, of course, did not require, were the sometimes grotesque mispronunciations of their own language, used in the pidgin that underpinned all forms of inter-ally relationships, which rendered town and village names far more bizarre than the original French could ever have been. And while *brown bess* may once have signified the British musket, the Tommies resisted an equivalent to the French *Rosalie* (the bayonet).

The language had a variety of sources: regulars of the British Army, for instance, imported terms long used by those who had served in India: the Soldiers Three would have felt quite at home, although less so as civilian volunteers and then conscripts joined up. Americans brought the slang of their cities and many regionalisms; Sainéan's 1915 discussion notes how much Parisian language made its way unchanged to the front. Much was coined on the battlefield and would never leave, other than for a brief reappearance in memoirs and at reunions: just as the soldiers of the US Civil War had terms for among much else a variety of artillery missiles – *lamp posts, camp kettles, cook stoves* and *iron foundries* – so too, and in similar terms, did their successors of '14–'18. Still, talk of *coal scuttles, black marias* and *Jack Johnsons,* or *saucissons* and *marmites* had no real pertinence very far beyond the trenches. But less specific slang served as a form of lingua franca, in a world where so many men from so many varied backgrounds had been brought together. It might not unite nations – British Tommies, Australian Diggers and American Yanks or *doughboys* had their own discrete lexes, and each branch of every service had their own terminology to add – but it worked within the group.

As the war proceeded – and setting aside the on-going flow of pieces in the press – the language was recorded, incidentally, in the many trench newspapers, such as the British *Wipers Times, BEF Times,* and *New Church Times* (and after the Armistice, *The Better Times*), Australia's *Aussie, Digger* and the *Kia-Ora Cooee,* Canada's *Beaver* and *Dead Horse Gazette* and for the French *Le Poilu* or *Le Crapouillot.* The last of these, unlike most of these short-lived sheets, went on to be a successful anti-establishment journal and on the eve of the next world war, in 1939, was serializing its own illustrated dictionary of *argot* (the third and final section would not appear until 1950). The Civil War produced a number of 'soldier papers' but the US, a late-comer to this one, seems to have been satisfied with its authorized paper *The Stars and Stripes,* although stateside camps did offer some publications, e.g. *The Wadsworth Gas Attack and Rio Grande Rambler* of Camp Wadsworth, South Carolina. These however, were suspended once the troops went to France.

On all sides and in every theatre of war there were diarists. Among the terms culled from their records are these that had not been found prior to the war but survived beyond it. *Abdul* and *Johnny* (a Turk), *banger* (a sausage), *beat* (to avoid, i.e. duty), *Blighty* (a wound sufficient to take one out of France), *booby hatch* (as a hiding place), *get the breeze up* (to be frightened), *cootie* (a body louse), *corned willie* (corned beef), *dolly* (pleasant), *Fritz* and *Jerry, furphy* (a rumour), *gravy* (easy, privileged), *give someone a hurry-up*, *imshee* (to go away or to make go away), *lose one's lunch* (to vomit), *napoo* (finished, ended, no more), *nellie* (a homosexual or effeminate man), *oh boy!*, *go to the pack* (to decline either socially or economically), *posh*, *souvenir* (to steal), *squiz* (to look at), *old sweat* (a veteran), *Turkey trot* (diarrhoea), *well away* (drunk), *go west* (to die or be killed), *whacked* (exhausted), *get* or *give what-ho* (to receive or give punishment) and *get* or *put the wind up* (to be scared or to frighten).

With peace declared, the collection of slang was given over to the glossarists, the memoirists and the writers of fiction. In October 1921 the London *Times* announced that the Imperial War Museum, using the scholarly journal *Notes and Queries* as a collection point, was canvassing for contributions to a collection of war slang. 'The Secretary of the Imperial War Museum will be glad to receive any notes on the subject, giving the slang, terms used in the British Army, together with the meaning of the term, and, if possible, the derivation. It is quite understood that many of these terms are not entirely fit for polite conversation, but at the same time it is considered that they will be valuable for record purposes.' On 1 November the paper devoted a leader to the first list to appear in *Notes and Queries* (six more followed) and added some examples: *Buckshee, lash-up, all cut, lead-worker, hard skin, wangle, lit, talking wet, napoo, san-fairyann, the duration, soaked, stiff, touch-out, blighty, windy, click, cushy, win, jam on it, swinging the lead, oojar, scrounge, stunt, umteen, wash-out, go west, cold feet, strafe, work your ticket, where are you working, soft job, some lad, issue, muck in, sweating*, and the *gear.* Around two-thirds have survived.

The first post-war book-length glossaries to emerge were Australian, one published, one destined to remain in manuscript until it was made available on line in 2007. These were *Digger Dialects* (1919), by W. H. Downing (1893–1935) and the unpublished *Glossary of Slang and Peculiar Terms in Use in the A.I.F. 1921–1924* by A. G. Pretty. The latter overlaps largely with the former, and unless both glossaries drew on a common source such duplications in Pretty may be assumed to be have been extracted from Downing. The AIF Glossary was initiated as part of the early plans for some form of Australian War Museum (achieved as the Australian War Memorial), a project that was acutely conscious of the possibility of using memories of the war to create an 'official' version of a heroic national identity. The cause of its failure to appear in print has never been specified, but in her essay on the text Amanda Laughesen has suggested that the 'irreverent vernacular culture of the soldier, rather than the idealized ANZAC version of the digger, did not perhaps fit the image' [13] that the authorities sought to create. Certainly it was ordained that its vulgarity required that only a male member of staff should type up the material.

Downing, who served first in Egypt and then France, where he won the Military Medal, naturally includes a range of tried and tested Australian slang, but he is also responsible for a number of first recorded uses. Many naturally vanished after the war, but others joined the main slang lexis. These are taken from the first half of the alphabet: *put the acid on* (as meaning put a stop to or test out), *bollocks* (nonsense), *beer-up* (a riotous party), *beetle* (to wander about, used originally of flying), *bite* (an attempt obtain a loan), *box on* (to persevere), *bullsh* (nonsense), *bung* (cheese), *cane* (to treat harshly, to defeat), *cheese* (a wife or girlfriend), *doer* (a 'character'), *dressed up like a sore thumb*, *fanny adams* (i.e. fuck all), *gay and frisky* (whisky), *giggle house* (a psychiatric institution), *good oil* (the truth), *guts* (information or essence), *maggoty* (tetchy) and *mick* ('tails' in two-up). Downing was not infallible. His inclusion of two terms *carksucker* for an American soldier and *fooker* for a British one show that someone must have been having fun. He was still a student when he joined up – in a more innocent world perhaps he didn't know what they actually meant.

Two British additions had arrived by 1930: *Soldier and Sailor Words and Phrases* (1925) by Edward Fraser and John Gibbons and *Songs and Slang of the British Soldier* by John Brophy and Eric Partridge (1930). The first was commissioned by the Imperial War Museum, and is thus the fruit of their contributors' efforts. The second, which acknowledges its debt to Fraser and Gibbons, is perhaps most important as being the first attempt at slang lexicography by the man who was to stand as its leading twentieth-century exponent. Eric Partridge's fascination with slang sprang directly from his involvement in World War I, in which he fought as one of the New Zealanders who trekked across half the world to fight for the Empire of which they were still a part. It is, thus, a suitable point at which to consider the man and his work.

Eric Honeywood Partridge was born in 1894 on a farm in the Waimata Valley, near Gisborne, North Island, New Zealand. He moved with his family to Brisbane, Australia, in 1907 and there attended grammar school. His love of literature showed itself early: aged thirteen he had already written a novel (an English public school story) and a number of short stories. His translations from French poetry began appearing in 1914. He was also, thanks to a literary father, able to use dictionaries – 'those ... sources of sober, never-disillusioning entertainment'[14] – from the age of seven. He won a scholarship to the University of Queensland but, as it did for so many of his contemporaries, the First World War interrupted his studies, and in April 1915 he joined the Australian infantry. He served successively in Egypt, at Gallipoli and on the Western Front, where he fought in that sub-section of the battle of the Somme known as 'the second Pozières'. More than 15,000 ANZACs died fighting for this single ridge; Partridge was wounded but he survived.

Back in Australia he returned to university, took his BA, then departed for Oxford University, where he read for his MA in eighteenth-century English romantic poetry and for a BA in comparative literature. In 1927, after some desultory teaching experience, he launched himself on a new career: that of 'man of letters'.

To back this he founded the Scholartis Press (a blend of 'scholarly' and 'artistic'); it survived until 1931 when, like so many small businesses, it foundered in the Depression, leaving its proprietor bankrupt. There were nearly 100 titles in all. Twenty-two came from Partridge himself, either as author or editor. Most, including three novels by 'Corrie Denison' (Partridge's pseudonym), were ignored by the literary world but three of them indicated an important new interest for the editor-in-chief: *Songs and Slang of the British Soldier,* Partridge's edition of Francis Grose's *Classical Dictionary of the Vulgar Tongue* (1931) and a British edition of Godfrey Irwin's *American Tramp and Underworld Slang* (1930).

In 1932 Partridge went freelance and a year later came his first essay at lexicology: *Words, Words, Words!* This was swiftly succeeded by his first look at the topic that would dominate his professional life: slang. Commissioned by Routledge, where the publisher Cecil Franklin had noticed his language-related Scholartis publications, *Slang To-day and Yesterday* appeared in 1933: it was the first exhaustive attempt at a history and analysis of slang since Hotten's introduction to his *Modern Slang and Cant* of 1859. The book that sprung from these relatively tentative explorations into the topic, *A Dictionary of Slang and Unconventional English*, was published in 1937. It was based on, but expanded far beyond Farmer and Henley's *Slang and Its Analogues*, to which Routledge held the rights. Seven expanded and amended editions would appear in his lifetime. An eighth, posthumous edition (edited by Paul Beale) appeared in 1984. *A Dictionary of the Underworld*, dealing with English and American cant, was published in 1949; revised editions appeared in 1961 and 1968. A thoroughly revised new edition of *A Dictionary of Slang and Unconventional English,* covering the period from 1945 and notable in its admission of American slang for the first time, appeared in 2005, edited by the American slang lexicographer and lawyer Tom Dalzell and an English colleague, Terry Victor.

Assessing Partridge's slang work nearly eighty years since he began, it is hard not to see it as outdated. His refusal to include American slang might just have been feasible in 1937, but it was always a debatable decision, and one that looked foolish in the post-World War II world when American culture played an ever-increasing role in that of the UK. Nor was Partridge ever very confident with that modern world: the phenomenon of the teenager and the slang they created eluded him; to him all drug users were 'addicts' and he accepted too many secondary sources. He worked from print sources (although he does not offer citations in *A Dictionary of Slang and Unconventional English*, and although they exist in the *Dictionary of the Underworld*, there is no attempt at full-scale 'historical' sampling) and fell foul of those who prioritized fieldwork. Julie Coleman has written informatively on his clash with the American cant specialist David Maurer, played out in the pages of *American Speech*.[15]

Yet his work remains of profound importance. In the long run, as Tom Dalzell has suggested, the work itself – like all lexicography – may be flawed, but what matters is that Partridge's dedication brought it into a new century, and in so doing perpetuated slang lexicography. The author of *A Dictionary of Slang and Unconventional English* may lack, as Randolph Quirk has pointed out, 'the magisterial scholarship, meticulous authentication and consistency of presentation'[16] that make the *OED* so monumental a work, but without Partridge there could never have been the same level of modern slang lexicography. The *OED* cites him more than 770 times.

Partridge, above all, offers a human dimension. He has, in a world where wit is at a premium, a sense of humour. As Anthony Burgess put it, he was not a linguist but a philologist, quite literally a 'lover' of words.[17] And on his amorous passage he trips, he stumbles, he falls. Cheerfully refusing to admit linguistics into his lexicographical work, he always wants to make some kind of statement. The *OED*, especially when it comes to slang, is filled with the hard-nosed, factual, but ultimately frustrating admission: 'Etymology unknown'. Such an admission was wholly alien to Partridge. For him something was always better than nothing – even if that something often erred dangerously on the side of guesswork. Indeed, Partridge's refusal to acknowledge defeat could lead to terrible howlers (and he was duly pilloried by such as Gershon Legman), but he could also be inspired.

Of all the allies America appeared least immediately interested in its soldiers' slang. The war produced *Doughboy Dope from A-Z* (1918) by D. G. Rowse, but this was a light-hearted exercise, as much to amuse the troops as to inform them. A number of articles appeared in journals, notably a series written in 1929–30 by ex-Captain Elbert Colby in the magazine *Our Army*, later republished as the book *Army Talk* (1942), but there was no major coverage until in 1972 Jonathan Lighter produced for *American Speech*[18] his magisterial lexicon *The Slang of the American Expeditionary Forces in Europe 1917–1919*. This 'historical glossary', taken from his on-going researches towards what would become the sadly unfinished *Historical Dictionary of American Slang* (1994, 1997) remains the outstanding example of its kind. Lighter used secondary sources, rather than interviewing ageing veterans, and as it is doing for all lexicographers the relatively recent arrival of internet searches will inevitably change the dating of certain terms, but a twenty-three-page bibliography of 750-plus titles suggests that he left few available stones unturned.

In addition to the memoirs that began appearing even before the war was over, best-selling fiction writers and popular poets were adding their contribution. Many rejected slang – unpatriotic – but others saw it, as ever, as conferring authenticity on their military subjects. In Australia, C. J. Dennis, already well known for the slang-imbued *Sentimental Bloke* (1916) brought out *The Moods of Ginger Mick*, which takes the truculent rabbit-o from active disdain for enlistment through to a heroic death. E. J. Dyson, of *Factory 'Ands*, added his war poems: *Hello Soldier* (1919). The world of the ANZAC (never a slang term itself but productive of a number of compounds that were) also gave memoirs such as Hugh Knyvett's *Over the Top with the Australians* (1915).

For the UK there was the playwright and novelist Ian Hay (Major General John Hay Beith, 1876–1952), whose three books – *The First Hundred Thousand* (1915), *Carrying On – After The First Hundred Thousand* (1917) and *The Last Million* (1919) – offered a humorous but never negative take on a conscripts' army. Their underlying theme reflected the stiff upper lip as required: 'War is hell, and all that, but it has a good deal to recommend it. It wipes out all the small nuisances of peace-time.'[19] The army and the navy both had popular chroniclers. 'Sapper' (Herman Cyril McNeile, 1888–1937) would go on to worldwide fame as the creator of Bulldog Drummond, but as a serving officer during the war (he quit the army in 1919 as a Lieutenant-Colonel) offered a steady output of often quite sombre stories from the trenches, collected as *The Lieutenant and Others* (1916), *No Man's Land* (1917), *The Human Touch* (1918) and *Mufti* (1919). His equivalent in the senior service was 'Bartimeus' (Capt. Lewis Anselm Da Costa Ricci RN, 1885–1967). Again drawing on personal experience, he poured out short stories of navy life, generally among the midshipman and junior ranks, in titles that included *Naval Occasions* (London 1914), *The Navy Eternal* (1918) and *An Awfully Big Adventure* (1919). 'Taffrail' (H. Taprell Dorling), another pseudonymous Naval officer, produced similar works such as *Stand By!* and *The Watch Below* (1918). Both sailors were still writing in World War II, shortly after which 'Bartimeus' was appointed press attaché to King George VI.

American contributions were more literary, although the plethora of slangy War Pulps of the 1920s compensated for that, and many books relied on personal experience. In 1922 e.e. cummings (1894–1962) published *The Enormous Room*, the story of his four months' incarceration in a French prison camp for alleged 'anti-war sentiments'. Slang plays its role, as might be expected, but the appearance, at that time, of so many examples of *fuck* or *fucking*, and a good representation of the remainder of the obscene canon, must have shocked many. Cummings had arrived in France in 1917 as a volunteer in the Norton-Harjes Ambulance Corps. So too did his Harvard contemporary John Dos Passos (1896–1970). Dos Passos used the war in a number of novels: *One Man's Initiation: 1917* (1920), *Three Soldiers* (1920), and the trilogy *USA* (1938), especially in its second book *Nineteen Nineteen* (1932).

The Mint by 'Aircraftsman J.H. Ross', better known as T. E. Lawrence ('of Arabia') (1888–1935) was written in 1925. However, the book, which charts Lawrence's post-war training in the RAF, was held back on the author's instructions until after his death. When it did appear, in 1955, two editions were produced – one expurgated and the other tightly limited – and demonstrated all the slang, much of it obscene, that Lawrence had noted in his two years of training and service. A number of terms had not been recorded before the date of composition: *aerated* (angry), *axe* (to close down, to dismiss), *bind* (to bore) and *binder* (a bore), *bit of skin* (girlfriend), *blanket drill* (masturbation), *bob on* (anticipate), *bolshie* (in the non-political use of a complainer), *brama* (enjoyable, good), *cheese* (smegma), *doggy* (sex-obsessed), *eff and blind*, *erk* (any of the lowest ranks of the RAF), *gnat's piss*, *with knobs on*, *oppo* (a friend), *pack up* (to stop doing something), *have a pot on* (to be drunk), *pound-note* (pompous) and *toffee-nosed*. But obscenities were disproportionately represented: of the 150 slang terms 'Ross' used, sixty were obscene and nearly half of those hitherto unrecorded.

Ross's fellow erks were hardly unique. The reality was that the average serviceman's speech reflected neither Rupert Brooke's mawkish sentimentality nor Wilfred Owen's acerbic disdain. The American Civil War historian B. I. Wiley noted that both Johnny Reb and Billy Yank, however well brought up they may have been, took on a far more obscene vocabulary on the front lines. Brutal experiences produced brutal language irrespective of chronology. The soldiers may have been conscripts rather than old sweats, but Kipling's 'adjective' remained paramount. For those who had doubts, there was Frederick Manning's punningly titled *The Middle Parts of Fortune* (1929). Like Eric Partridge and many others, Manning had come from the Antipodes to fight in the war and like Partridge experienced the Somme and life in the trenches. He used his army number 'Private 19022' as a pseudonym and the book appeared in a limited edition of 500. As faithful to soldiers' speech as was *The Mint*, it was unavailable to the mass market until 1977, although an expurgated edition, now entitled *Her Privates We* (both titles punning on an exchange between Hamlet and the courtiers Rosencrantz and Guildenstern) was published in 1930, and in 1943 Manning was posthumously credited with the authorship.

That war, even conducted under the strictures of military discipline, loosens and lowers social standards is well-known. It has the same effect on language. 'Pistol's cock is out and flashing fire will follow' punned Shakespeare of his British soldier. The style has continued. If slang focuses on the harder areas of life, then war slang refines the process further. US Civil War soldiers were noted for their obscenity; so too those of World War I. Looking at a range of coinages of the 1939–45 period, one sees it again. Many World War II British squaddies may have been carrying a Penguin book in one of their uniform's conveniently sized pockets, but sex and drink and *bitching* still carried the conversational day. There are many genuine neologisms (and many more than remained within the bounds of military jargon), but while none of this small sample had been previously noted or used in any form of publication, it is safe to assume that in many cases the troops arrived 'ready-armed' and didn't meet their language on the battlefield.

The pattern and nature of war-generated slang continues. A certain number of neologisms arrive home and are absorbed into the language. It is these that are featured in the press and discussed in the journals. But the reality is that brutal circumstances breed, or at least popularize, brutal language. Perhaps the most celebrated term to emerge from World War II was Norman Mailer's semi-euphemistic *fug*, used in *The Naked and the Dead* (1948), which allegedly elicited Tallulah Bankhead's comment: 'So you're the young man who doesn't know how to spell "fuck".' Soldiers remain profane. Although profanity is not the whole of their vocabulary. They used the mainstream slang that they have brought with them and terms that were generated by their respective services.

Some terms would be created in-country. They adopted local language, such as those encountered in Korea or Vietnam, and brought some of it home. Each war produced its crop of veterans and the language they had absorbed lasted with them. The longer the campaign, the more productive of slang it was. World War II, long but lacking the trench warfare of its predecessor produced less soldier talk. The Falklands and the two Gulf Wars produced little; nor did Bosnia nor has the current imbroglio in Afghanistan. In an increasingly high-tech battlefield, a world of drones that do their job at the behest of controllers in rooms half a world away, there are no crowded, static trenches for language to develop. Nor is there the leavening of millions of civilian conscripts or volunteers, bringing their own terminology to the front lines and in turn making what they learn there visible to those at home. The majority of such slang that is coined remains outside the troops' home countries. The military's careful gelding of 'embedded' reporters and an ever-swelling lexis of euphemisms – *collateral damage, friendly fire, kinetic military action* – have worked against the open access to what the soldiers are actually saying. Compared to 1914–18 the river of neologisms has slowed to a trickle.

And yet it comes. It seems, even, to be bred into the soldier. Looking at Bruce Moore's *Lexicon of Cadet Language* (1993), his study of the slang used at Australia's equivalent to Sandhurst and West Point – the Royal Military College Duntroon – one sees only the well-worn themes. There is local jargon, there is imported, mainstream slang; and there is the slang of the embryo soldier. As in the US military, where screaming drill sergeants vilify the girls back home with the generic *Rosie Rottencrotch*, the cadets are taught to see women as universally bad. Dirty, whorish, devouring, stupid, the *vagina dentata* made flesh. Duntroon's neophytes can choose from *boff bag, boof bag, cum bag, dirtbag, fuck bag, horrorbag, maggot bag, root bag, slag bag, slime bag* and *troop bag*. The cadets would doubtless agree with the Austrian satirist Karl Kraus: 'A woman occasionally is quite a serviceable substitute for masturbation. Though it takes a wealth of imagination, to be sure.' Nastiest of all are *maggot*, and *grogan*, available in a variety of combinations. While the etymology of the latter is debatable, it appears to be a borrowing of the mainstream slang *grogan* (a turd). Homosexuals are similarly reviled, although all the slurs come from the mainstream, as are New Zealanders (*sheep fuckers*), and Asians (*power points*, a supposed resemblance of the Asian physiognomy to the three-pin plug). The dehumanization of the enemy is a long-established facet of military training; it would appear that such 'enemies' include the opposite sex.

18 Conclusion:
As It Was in the Beginning

As they haue begonne of late to deuyse some new termes for
certien thinges, so wyll they in tyme alter this, and deuyse as
euyll or worsse.

Thomas Harman, *Caveat for
Common Cursetours* (1566)

Slang, at least as we can see it in the form of glossaries and then
dictionaries, began with lists that were numbered in tens of examples; the
most recent print dictionary offers well over 110,000 words and phrases.
It existed prior to that – certainly in the classical languages, possibly in
others – but was never considered worthy of notice. Nor, when the
fifteenth- and sixteenth-century 'beggar-books' began appearing, were
there available that wide a range of monolingual dictionaries of any sort.
And like the beggar books, the earliest dictionaries, at least in England,
were seen as means to an end: informative and educative rather than
simply listing the vocabulary of a culture. For their makers and users the
early slang glossaries were of a part with a larger movement that aimed
to assemble the lexes of specific interests, such as those dedicated to
cooking or archery, which in time would be absorbed into larger works.
The difference was simply that they focused on crime.

The marginal nature of slang has meant that in its beginnings at
least one is forced to look at such collections. The nature of history, of
any history, is that one can only work from what is on record. We are
frustrated as regards slang because for a lengthy period it was seen as

beyond culture proper, and the records are therefore few. Gradually that changed: one sees it incorporated in popular fictions and, often in the form of criminal memoirs or biographies, in non-fiction. Because its use was considered alien to what was seen as culturally valuable, it tends to remain a thing apart. Surrounded by literal or figurative quotation marks. Not until the 20th century is it seamlessly and transparently incorporated in writing, whether on paper or on a screen. Coming from the street, the antithesis of the usual top-down progress of culture, it was problematic. As 'the people' grew to play an increasingly influential role in society, so too did their language. James Murray set slang as an equal among other subsets of English, but not everyone agreed, and for some, albeit a minority, that remains the case.

Fortunately the history of slang is not co-terminous with that of its collection, however important that has always been, especially in the earliest days of record. Like money for the very rich, for whom its accretion becomes little more than a means of 'keeping score' the assembly of slang words in a dictionary can be seen as icing rather than the actual cake. The dictionary is ultimately a parasite on the language it records: a valuable parasite, an informative and useful parasite, but ultimately a separate creation. The evolution of slang, the embellishment of the themes will continue irrespective of those who choose to catalogue it.

Slang is a language of themes. Much of this book has aimed to establish that, an over-riding theme in itself. Which is why at times it may seem, in its historical direction, to lean towards the past, laying down the fundamentals and foundations of slang's long-term obsessions. For me that is inevitable: slang represents humanity, humanity fails to change. In terms of slang new speakers, new writers and above all new words appear but they tend not to create but to embellish. Sex is always there, and violence, insults and derogations too; drugs may be a late arrival but intoxication is listed in the first of cant's glossaries. The afflicted are not comforted. Slang's role is to mock, to undermine, to showcase scepticism and doubt. It is the *roman noir* of language and when laughing, its farce.

It defeats the linguists, and while inspiring some outstanding lexico-graphers, their supposedly authoritative dictionaries remain edifices built on unavoidably shifting sands. No dictionary is ever perfect, none ever 'completed' since language continues to expand, but slang's corner of the reference shelves (now the reference websites), is especially challenging. The word's etymology is unproven, a unitary definition has yet properly to be established. What goes in a slang dictionary and what does not is often a matter of individual choice: instead of concrete rules there are theories of inclusion that base themselves on a variety of qualifications, a Boolean assessment of AND, OR, IF and NOT. Spelling is mutable, pronunciation is almost wholly unknown; finding an accurate first use is often impossible, although this last is no bad thing. No dictionary is ever 'finished' other than in meeting an arbitrary date required for publication. Research continues and research will lead to revision.

One should not, in any case, confuse the content with the form. The appearance of new technologies, the expansion through them of new sources and of new means of passing on one's findings to users, and perhaps of involving those users – when duly mediated – in the lexicographical process does not change the essential nature of slang's lexis. There are, of course, shifts in emphasis. As pointed out in the context of war, the changes in war-fighting, notably in the greater control by the principals and the increased use of highly sophisticated technology, have meant that less slang is generated and of that less is brought back for general use. And as can be seen across the last century, the lexis itself has become more fissiparous. The *omnium gatherum* of 'slang' is harder to pin down. Interest groups have their own vocabularies. One can assess these as jargons, but to what useful extent can that rule be enforced? That a slang has been used to reinforce the identity of a group has always been seen as one of the counter-language's sociolinguistic qualifications, but in a world of niche marketing, one must acknowledge the validity of niche slangs. It is perhaps over-neat, but slang began, in the form of cant, as a linguistic representative of a niche: the underworld of vagabond criminality. It would appear to be moving in the same direction, but there are now a multiplicity of niches.

What has run parallel with the history of slang is what could be termed an erosion of taboo. Not simply in the use of what were once considered 'unspeakable' and indeed 'unprintable' terms – and even there if one looked one was always able to find – but in the shifting of slang from the outer limits. Nor is this to suggest that the content of slang has changed; the themes remain the same, expressing as ever the downside of human nature. Perhaps what has happened is that as a society we have become less reticent. It remains, at heart, the language of the margins, but the margins have shifted and the boundaries are so much less obvious today. If it is true that modern western society is predominantly middle-class, then it could be argued that it is only the most aristocratic who now comprise an 'upper-class' and those, the very poorest, and condemned as an underclass, the 'lower class'. The logical extension of this being of course that to a far greater extent than hitherto everyone speaks much the same language. That does not mean that everyone speaks slang, or wishes to, but that slang is far more widely spoken or at least understood. The proof of this lies in the media, where slang, rather than was once the case, would be used simply to prove the creator's authenticity, or to underline the delineation of a given group, is now so common as to be far more transparent. There are few novels, movies or TV scripts that are wholly slang-free. This makes the lexicographer's task that much harder – there is so much to research – but paradoxically it makes it easier, since slang is so much more simple to find.

One aspect of slang, another basic qualification, that has pretty much vanished is the concept of secrecy. Or certainly of long-term separateness. Vastly accelerated speeds of communication make up the primary cause of this, but society at large has become less hostile to slang. Entrenched nay-sayers continue to decry it, but it is many years since a knowledge of slang has been considered in some way demeaning. Its use is no longer a badge of inferiority. The lexicographer sees this in the continuous expansion of sources. Even in the context of print, the twentieth century, especially its second half, saw a substantial expansion of material that needed to be assessed. Factor in the digital world and one must acknowledge that the tsunami of new sources that is flooding the internet may mean that few of slang's current dictionary-makers will live long enough to make a real dent in what is on offer; it also means that the potential for a succession of generations remains remarkable and alluring.

If, of course, there are to be successor generations. Bad language, in this case literally so, drives out good. The net is geared to multiple 'truths' and minimal attention spans; accuracy is no longer at a premium. All is relative and the assertion of authority and expertise is damned as 'elitism'. An attitude that runs antithetical to any lexicography of value. But it is better not to be pessimistic, and the old must resist the temptation to posit a golden age that never was. The urge to record and classify slang has never been a job for many; it requires only a few dedicated individuals who wish to do it justice.

If one were to forecast the future of slang, the answer seems obvious: more of the same. The specifics of its content may perhaps change – new synonyms will continue to replace their predecessors – but the thematic form is constant. Slang long since took to itself the lexis of humanity's emotional and social downside, our less admirable but absolutely unavoidable selves. The unrestrained self-gratifying id, if one takes a Freudian view. Such is humanity and such is this aspect of its linguistic expression. It has always been needed. It still is. It always will be.

Notes

Preface

1. Julie Coleman, *The Story of Slang* (Oxford, 2012).

1 Introduction

1. *Wikipedia* as of 18 January 2012.
2. S. Freud, *New Introductory Lectures on Psychoanalysis* (1933) in Penguin Freud Library, pp. 105–6.
3. A. C. Baugh and T. Cable, *History of the English Language* (London, 1993), p. 189.
4. ibid., p. 308.
5. E. Partridge, *Slang To-day and Yesterday* (London, 1933), p. 2.
6. J. C. Hotten, *Slang Dictionary* (London, 1873), p. 40.
7. ibid., p. 41.
8. J. Moore, *You English Words* (London, 1962), p. 42.
9. G. Eliot, *Middlemarch* (London, 1872), ch. XI.
10. H. Balzac, *Splendeurs et Misères des Courtisanes* (1849, trans. *A Harlot High and Low*, 1970), p. 441.
11. V. Hugo, *Le Dernier Jour d'un Condamné* (Paris, 1866), pp. 21/1.
12. V. Hugo, 'Argot', in *Les Misérables* (Paris, 1862; trans. 1976), IV, 7, pp. 1214–17.
13. 'The Rationale of Slang', *Overland Monthly*, 4, February 1870, p. 187.
14. B. Matthews, 'The Function of Slang', *Harper's*, 88, p. 304.
15. Personal communication.
16. http://www.gale.cengage.com/free_resources/glossary/glossarys.htm.
17. J. F. Genung, *Outlines of Rhetoric* (Boston, 1893), p. 32.
18. J. C. Fernald, 'The Impoverishment of the Language: Cant, Slang, Etc.', in *Progressive English* (1918), p. 238.
19. ibid., p. 253.
20. J. Lighter and B. K. Dumas, 'Is Slang a Word for Linguists?', *American Speech*, 53: 1 (1978), pp. 5–17.
21. ibid., p. 5.

22. J. Lighter, in *The Cambridge History of the English Language*, vol. VI: North America (Cambridge, 2001), p. 220.
23. Mads Holmsgaard Eriksen, 'Translating the use of slang' (Institut for Sprog og Erhvervskommunikation, Aarhus School of Business, Aarhus University, 2010), pp. 25–6.
24. ibid., p. 13.
25. M. Adams, *Slang: The People's Poetry* (New York, 2009), p. 49.
26. C. Eble, *Slang and Sociability* (Chapel Hill, NC, 1996), p. 12.
27. J. B. McMillan, 'American Lexicology 1942–1973', *American Speech*, 53, p. 146.

2 In the Beginning

1. L. R. Palmer, *The Latin Language* (Faber, 1954), p. 149.
2. J. Allen, *The Latin Sexual Vocabulary*, p. 34.
3. E. Dickey, *Latin Forms of Address* (2002), pp. 173–6.
4. Palmer, *The Latin Language*, p. 149.
5. Partridge, *Slang To-day and Yesterday*, p. 41.
6. This material has been taken from C. E. Bosworth, *The Medieval Islamic Underworld* (2 vols, Leiden, 1976).
7. F. Chandler, *Literature of Roguery* (London, 1907), 1, p. 47.
8. ibid.
9. P. Guiraud, 'Inédits', in *Marges linguistiques* (Saint-Chamas, September 2003); see this posthumous article for the author's wide-ranging etymological analyses of Coquillard jargon.
10. L. Sainéan, *Les Sources de l'argot ancien* (Paris, 1912), vol. 1, p. 111.
11. 'At Paris the great lookout point [lit. scaffold or 'Mount Joy']/Where fools are strung up and blackened [a reference to the decomposing corpse]/And by the 'angels' on the track of crime/Are rounded up and taken, five or six –/

There are crooks installed in the highest seats, / Where they're exposed to rain and upper winds.' Translation by Robert Mills, *Suspended Animation* (London, 2005), p. 36.

3   Lewd, Lousey Language

1. *ODNB* (on-line): Alexander Barclay.
2. J. Dillenberger (ed.), *Martin Luther* (New York, 1960), p. 461.
3. E. H. Zeydel (trans.), *Ship of Fools* (New York, 1944), p. 209.
4. ibid., pp. 210–11.
5. D. B. Thomas, introduction to *The Book of Vagabonds and Beggars* (*The Liber Vagatorum*) (1932), pp. 9–10.
6. Paula Pugliatti, *Beggary and Theatre in Early Modern England* (Aldershot, 2003), p. 132.
7. S. Rowlands, *Martin Mark-all* (London, 1610), G3ᵛ.
8. In A. V. Judges, *Elizabethan Underworld* (London, 1930), p. 24.
9. ibid., p. 3.
10. ibid.
11. ibid., p. 9.
12. ibid.
13. ibid., p. 13.
14. E. Viles and F. J. Furnivall, *Rogues and Vagabonds of Shakespeare's Youth* (London, 1907), p. i.
15. ibid., p. 2.
16. Judges, *Elizabethan Underworld*, pp. 53–5.
17. Viles and Furnivall, *Rogues and Vagabonds*, pp. 12-16.
18. E. Partridge, *Dictionary of the Underworld* (3rd edn, London, 1968), p. 13 / 2.
19. Viles and Furnivall, *Rogues and Vagabonds*, pp. 78, 81.
20. ibid., p. 82.
21. For a detailed analysis of Harman's lists, see J. Coleman, *A History of Cant and Slang Dictionaries*, 1 (Oxford, 2004), pp. 20–28.
22. Viles & Furnival, p. 86.
23. Partridge, *Slang To-day and Yesterday*, p. 45.
24. Viles and Furnival, *Rogues and Vagabonds*, pp. vii, ix.
25. Judges, *Elizabethan Underworld*, p. 495.
26. W. Carroll, quoted in L. Woodbridge, 'English Literary Renaissance Jest Books, the Literature of Roguery, and the Vagrant Poor in Renaissance England', *English Literary Renaissance* (May 2003).
27. L. Woodbridge, 'English Literary Renaissance Jest Books' (see note 23 above).
28. Coleman, *A History of Cant and Slang Dictionaries*, p. 27.
29. ibid.
30. J. C. Jordan, *Robert Greene* (New York, 1915), p. 5.
31. S. Greenblatt, *Will in the World* (Prince Frederick, MD, 2004), p. 204.
32. William Shakespeare, *Henry IV part 2*, II: 4.
33. Robert Greene, *Second part of Coneycatching* (London, 1592), pp. 5–10.
34. ibid.
35. ibid., p. 96.
36. Quoted in Judges, *Elizabethan Underworld*, p. 67.
37. T. Harman, *Caveat*, p. 27.
38. Greene, *Second part of Coney-catching*, p. 14.
39. *Notes and Queries*, 10th series, 4, 5, 9.
40. 'Cuthbert Conny-Catcher', *The Defence of Conny Catching* (1592, reprint 1924) p. 7.
41. ibid., p. 37.
42. A. Bayman, 'Rogues, Conycatching and the Scribbling Crew', *History Workshop Journal* (2007), 63 (1): 1–17.
43. S. Rowlands, *Greene's Ghost Haunting Cony-catchers* (London, 1602), sig. A4.

4   Crime and Punishment

1. *Catholic Encyclopedia* (New York, 1913) p. 430.
2. F. Aydelotte, *Elizabethan Rogues and Vagabonds* (Oxford, 1913), p. 82.
3. 8-9 William III, c. 27, s. 15. Against those who resisted arrest for debt in these pretended liberties.
4. T. Macaulay, *History of England from the Accession of James II* (London, 1849) p. 76.
5. E. Ward, *London Spy* (London, 1698–1700), facsimile 1924, p. 123.
6. *ODNB* [online].
7. T. Dekker, *A Rod for Run-Awayes* (London, 1625), sig. Bv.
8. 'The poore Knight her Husband is troubled with the City Gowt, lyes i'the Counter', *Match Me in London*, I: 4.

9. Quoted in Aydelotte, *Elizabethan Rogues and Vagabonds,* pp. 129–30.

10. T. Dekker, *The Bellman* (London, 1608), sig. E.

11. ibid.

12. Judges, *Elizabethan Underworld,* p. 510.

13. T. Dekker, *O Per Se O* (London, 1616), sig. L2v.

14. Aydelotte, *Elizabethan Rogues and Vagabonds,* p. 135.

15. ibid., p. 133.

16. G. Noyes, 'Development of Cant Lexicography in England, 1566-1785', *Studies in Philology,* 38:3 (1941), p. 467n.

17. Rowlands, *Greene's Ghost,* sig. A2v

18. ibid., sig. A4.

19. Rowlands, *Martin Mark-all,* p. 5.

20. P. Blank, *Broken English* (London, 1996), p. 57.

21. *DNB,* 1st edn.

22. 'This young tramping girl can spin a good yarn, and fucks well for a penny; and steals and cheats so smartly, all over the countryside.'

23. R. Head, *The English Rogue* (London, 1665), sig. Iiiiv

24. R. Head and F. Kirkman, *The English Rogue,* pt II (London, 1666), sig. A3r.

25. G. W. R. D. Moseley, 'Richard Head's "The English Rogue"', *Yearbook of English Studies I* (1971), p. 103.

26. R. Head, *The Canting Academy* (London, 1673), p. 123.

27. *Scoundrel's Dictionary* (1754), p. 3.

28. G. Parker, *Life's Painter,* pp. 136–7.

29. ibid., pp. 129, 131.

30. ibid., p. 152.

31. T. Dekker, *English Villainies* (London, 1632), Sig.J3z.

32. P. Shaw, 'Thomas Dekker in Jacobean Prison Literature,' *PMLA,* LVII: 2, p. 367.

33. J. Harington, *A briefe view of the state of the Church of England* (London, 1653), p. 192.

34. Judges, *Elizabethan Underworld,* pp. 292, 295.

35. ibid., p. 278.

36. ibid., p. 439.

37. Shaw, 'Thomas Dekker', p. 384.

38. *ODNB*: Gamaliel Ratsey.

39. G. Harvey, *Peirce's Supererogation* (London, 1600), p. 146.

40. Chandler, *Literature of Roguery,* pp. 144–5.

41. Quoted in A. B. Dawson, 'Mistris Hic & Haec', in *Studies in English Literature, 1500–1900,* 33: 2, p. 388.

42. Blank, *Broken English,* p. 59.

43. J. McMullan, 'Criminal organization in London', *Social Problems,* 29: 3, p. 319.

44. Quoted in Dawson, 'Mistris Hic & Haec', p. 394.

45. ibid.

5 Play's the Thing

1. Quoted (from Nichols Literary Anecdotes) in A. S. Borgman, *Thomas Shadwell His life and Comedies* (London, 1969), p. 214.

2. Manuscripts of His Grace the Duke of Rutland: Letters and papers, 1440–1797, vol. 3 (London, 1889), p. 119.

3. T. Shadwell, *Complete Works* (London, 1927), p. 263.

4. William Shakespeare, *A Winter's Tale,* IV: 4, line 2150.

5. T. Dekker, *Lanthorne and Candlelight* (Facsimile, London, 1905), p. 187.

6. S. Rowlands, *Martin Mark-all* (London, 1610) in J. S. Farmer, *Musa Pedestris* (London, 1896), p. 5.

7. H. Ainsworth, *Rookwood* (revised edn, London, 1837), p. xxxi.

8. T. Durfey, *Pills to Purge Melancholy* (6 vols, London, 1917), passim.

9. *ODNB*: Joseph Woodfall Ebsworth.

10. B. E., *New Dictionary of the Canting Crew* (London, *c.* 1698), title page.

11. Coleman, *The Story of Slang,* pp. 76–104 passim.

12. ibid., p. 79.

13. J. Sorenson, 'Vulgar Tongues', *Eighteenth-Century Studies,* XXXVII: 3 (Spring, 2004), p. 442.

14. Partridge, *Slang To-day and Yesterday,* p. 62.

15. *ODNB*: Alexander Smith.

16. Quoted in D. T. Starnes and G. E. Noyes, *The English Dictionary from Cawdrey to Johnson, 1604–1755* (Chapel Hill, NC, 1946), p. 222.

17. *New Canting Dictionary* (London, 1725), introduction A2v

6 The Sound of the City

1. Quoted in H. W. Troyer, *Ned Ward of Grub Street* (London, 1968), pp. 227–8.

2. Quoted in C. H. Firth, *Commentary on Macaulay's History of England* (London, 1938), pp. 90–91.

3. T. Cibber, *The Lives of the Poets* (London, 1753), vol. IV, pp. 293–4.

4. R. Porter, *Social History of London* (London, 1994), p. 184.

5. A. Pope, *Dunciad* (London, 1728), iii, 34.

6. *Spectator*, vol. VIII (1717), p. 44.

7. J. Swift, *Polite Conversation* in *Works*, vol. VI (London, 1741), introduction.

8. J. Swift, *Proposal for Correcting, Improving, and Ascertaining the English Tongue* (London, 1713), p. 13.

9. E. Partridge (ed.), *Polite Conversation* (London, 1963), pp. 17–18.

10. Swift, *Polite Conversation*, p.231.

11. ibid., p. 235.

12. ibid., p. 234.

13. ibid., p. 228.

14. ibid., p. 231.

15. Letter of 1728, quoted in *Gentleman's Magazine*, 1773, p. 464.

16. This was not Dalton's first biography: a *Genuine Narrative of all the Street Robberies committed [...] by James Dalton, and his Accomplices* was published in 1728; it included 'a key to the canting language'.

17. Quoted in A. McKenzie, 'The Real Macheath', *Huntington Library Quarterly*, 69: 4 (2006), p. 586.

18. E. Partridge (ed.), *Classical Dictionary of the Vulgar Tongue* (London, 1931), p. 381.

19. ibid., p. 382.

20. Quoted ibid., p. 384.

21. *Gentleman's Magazine*, June 1791, I: 493.

22. Sorenson, 'Vulgar Tongues', p. 447.

23. *Lexicon Balatronicum* (London, 1811), introduction, p.vii.

24. P. Egan, *Life in London* (2nd edn, London 1830), p. 84 [note].

25. ibid, p.vi.

26. 'Egan's Grose' (London, 1823), introduction, p. xxi.

7 Flash

1. In *Works* (1787), XI, p. 329.

2. H. Fielding, *Enquiry into the Cause of the Late Increase of Robbers* (London, 1751), p. 116.

3. Cited in *PMLA*, vol. 84, No. 3 (May 1969), pp. 492.

4. *A Notable and Pleasant History ...* (1652), p. 2.

5. *The Universal Songster* (London, 1825), I: 40.

6. Quoted in H. Berry, 'Rethinking Politeness in Eighteenth-Century England', *Transactions of the Royal Historical Society*, Sixth Ser., Vol. 11 (2001), p. 71.

7. G. Parker, *Life's Painter of Variegated Characters in Public and Private Life*, (London, 1789), p. 144.

8. W. T. Moncrieff, *Selections from the Dramatic Works*, vol. 3 (London, 1851), p. 12.

9. J. Coleman, *History of Cant and Slang Dictionaries*, vol. II (London, 2004), p. 259.

10. Quoted in Berry, 'Rethinking Politeness in Eighteenth-Century England', p. 75.

11. *The Life and Character of Moll King* (1747), pp. 11–12.

12. ibid., pp. 23–4.

13. ibid., p. 13.

14. N. McLachlan (ed.) *Memoirs of James Hardy Vaux*, (London, 1964), p. 240.

15. *The Letters of John Keats, 1814–1821*, edited by Hyder Edward Rollins (Cambridge, MA, 1958), II, p. 192.

16. *Poetical Works of Lord Byron* (London, 1885–6), II, p. 144.

17. ibid., p. 503.

18. T. Moore, *Tom Crib's Memorial* (London, 1819), p. ix.

19. ibid., p. 18.

20. *Blackwood's*, XXXVI: 6 (March 1820), p. 610, col. 1.

21. 'Geoffrey Crayon, gent' [i.e. Washington Irving] *Tales of a Traveller* (Paris, 1824), p. 338.

22. A. J. Liebling, *Sweet Science* (New York, 1956, 2004), pp. 7–8.

23. ibid., p. 8.

24. However, given that this volume has been ascribed to John Badcock, it may be that boxing's favourite self-description was coined not by the celebrated Egan, but by his most bitter rival.

25. J. C. Hotten, introduction to P. Egan, *Life in London* (reprint London, 1869), p. 18.

26. D. Atyeo, *Violence in Sport* (London, 1979), p. 146.

27. *DNB*: William Thomas Moncrieff.

28. P. Egan, *The Finish to the Adventures of Tom, Jerry and Logic* (London, 1830, reprint 1889), p. 7.

29. R. S. Surtees, *Mr Sponge's Sporting Tour* (London, 1853), p. 187.

30. 'Cuthbert Bede', *Adventures of Mr Verdant Green* (London, 1853, 1982), p. 118.

31. Egan, *Life in London* (2nd edn, London, 1830), p. xiii.

32. ibid., p. 293.

33. ibid., p. 295.

34. ibid., pp. 286–7.

35. G. Dart, 'Flash Style', *History Workshop Journal*, LI (Spring, 2001), p. 191.

36. ibid., p. 197.

37. Coleman, *History of Cant and Slang Dictionaries*, II, p. 161.

38. 'Egan's Grose', pp. xix–xx.

39. ibid., p. xxviii.

40. J. Bee, *Slang. A Dictionary of The Turf, The Ring, The Chase, The Pit, Of Bon-Ton and the Varieties of Life* (London, 1823), pp. 79–80.

41. ibid., p. iii.

42. ibid., p. ix [note].

43. Coleman, *History of Cant and Slang Dictionaries*, II, p. 192.

44. Coleman, ibid., pp. 131–7, analyses this dictionary in detail.

45. J. Flanders, *The Invention of Murder* (London, 2011), pp. 117–23 *passim*.

46. We were in a beer-house, playing cards, with nothing to drink and no money; in comes a sucker; he's very drunk and showing off his purse; we noticed, chatted to him about his lodgings and worked out what to do: we put pretty Sal on to him, she gave him a Mickey Finn, then ran off to his place, unlocked the door, grabbed his money from the cashbox and left.

47. W. M. Thackeray, *Vanity Fair* (London, 1843), p. 43.

48. Note to *Catherine* in *Fraser's Magazine*, May 1839, p. 617.

49. H. Ainsworth, *Rookwood* (London, 1834), pp. 210–11.

50. Quoted in S. M. Ellis, *William Harrison Ainsworth and His Friends* (London, 1911), I, p. 254.

51. K. Hollingsworth, *The Newgate Novel* (Detroit, 1963), p. 104.

52. In her essay 'The Language of Dickens', in D. Paroissien, *A Companion to Charles Dickens* (London 2008), p. 129, Patricia Ingham notes that Oliver's given name comes from the cant phrase, listed by Vaux [255], '*Oliver is in town*: a phrase signifying that the nights are moonlit and consequently unfavourable to depredation'.

53. C. Dickens, *Oliver Twist* (3rd edn, 1941), Preface, p. xxvii.

54. C. Dickens, *Pickwick Papers* (4th edn, 1838), p. viii.

55. R. Kipling, 'My Son's Wife', in *A Diversity of Creatures* (London, 1913), p. 314.

56. *ODNB*: Robert Smith Surtees.

57. J. Greenwood, *Seven Curses of London* (London, 1869), p. 1331.

58. E. Salmon, *Fortnightly Review*, 45, 1 February 1886, pp. 225–6, quoted in P. Duane, 'Penny Dreadfuls', *Victorian Studies*, 22: 2, 1979, p. 138.

59. E. S. Turner, *Boys Will Be Boys* (London, 1948, 1975), p. 64.

60. John Springhall, in *Victorian Studies*, 33: 2 (Winter, 1990), p. 236.

8 Down Under

1. J. H. Vaux, *Memoirs* (London, 1819), I, pp. 144–5.

2. R. Hughes, *The Fatal Shore* (London, 1987), pp. 425, 435.

3. Vaux, *Memoirs*, p. 152.

4. Coleman, *History of Cant and Slang Dictionaries*, p. 141.

5. andc.anu.edu.au/ozwords/Nov%20 2002/Botany%20Bay.html.

6. Vaux, *Memoirs*, II, p. 185.

7. ibid., p. 216.

8. Suggestions have been made that identify him with the manager Henry Charles O'Flaherty (?1818–54), at whose Royal Victoria Theatre the play was to be staged; these remain unproven, although O'Flaherty was patently involved.

9. Quoted in *Australian Dictionary of Biography* [on line]: Browne, Thomas Alexander.

10. ibid.

11. Quoted in E. E. Morris, *Austral English* (London, 1898), p. ix.

12. B. Moore, 'The Sydney Slang Dictionary', *Ozwords*, April 2010.
13. ibid.
14. Morris, *Austral English*, p. xi.
15. C. Crowe, *Australian Slang Dictionary* (Melbourne, 1895), introduction.
16. Figures from J. Robertson, 'Australian Lexicography 1880–1910: An Evaluation', PhD thesis.
17. Quoted in S. Lawson, *Archibald Paradox*, p. 171.
18. J. Robertson, 'Plagiarism in Australian Dictionaries', London Papers in Australian Studies, No. 9 (2004), p. 20.
19. B. Moore, *Speaking Our Language* (Melbourne, 2008), p. 86.
20. Richard Fotheringham (ed.), *Australian Plays for the Colonial Stage: 1834–1899* (Queensland, 2006), p. 83.
21. J. Rickard, 'Lovable Larrikins and Awful Ockers', in *Journal of Australian Studies* (Queensland, 1998), LVI, p. 78.
22. H. Mayhew, *London Labour and the London Poor* (London, 1861), I, p. 51/1.
23. W. T. Goodge, 'Great Australian Slanguage', *Bulletin* (Sydney), 4 June 1898.
24. For a discussion of the phenomenon, see M. Bellanta, 'Leary Kin: Australian Larrikins and the Blackface Minstrel Dandy', *Journal of Social History*, 42: 3 (Washington DC, 2009).
25. Will Whitburn, 'The Larrikins' Hop', c. 1888.
26. E. Dyson, *Fact'ry 'Ands* (Melbourne, 1906), pp. 149–51.
27. ibid., p. 163.
28. Quoted in S. Lawson, *The Archibald Paradox* (Ringwood, Victoria, 1983), p. 175.
29. ibid., p. 88.
30. S. J. Baker, *New Zealand Slang* (Melbourne, 1941), preface.
31. G. W. Turner, 'A landscape known as home', *Round Table*, 66, 1976, p. 53.
32. Quoted in Craig Munro and Robyn Sheahan-Bright, *Paper Empires: a history of the book in Australia 1946–2005* (Queensland, 2006), p. 29.
33. P. St Pierre, *A Portrait of the Artist as Australian* (Montreal, 2004), p. 50.

9 Sex in the City

1. *Kruptadia* (1888–1911), vol. IV, 394–5.
2. *The Collected Essays of Leslie Fiedler*, vol. 2 (New York, 1971), p. 386.
3. T. Urquhart (trans.), *Gargantua and Pentagruel* (London, 1635, reprint 1927), I Bk I, p. 44.
4. J. Cleland, *Memoirs of a Woman of Pleasure* (London, 1748–9), p. 73.
5. ibid., p. 99.
6. In H. Love, *Works of John Wilmot, Earl of Rochester* (London, 1999), p. 169.
7. *Wandring Whore* (London, 1660) vol. 1, p. 6.
8. See R. Darnton, *Forbidden Best-Sellers of Pre-Revolutionary France* (New York, 1996).
9. J. Peakman, *Mighty Lewd Books* (London, 2003), p. 4.
10. 'Roger Pheuquewell', *New Description of Merryland* (London, 1741), p.25.
11. ibid. p. 23.
12. ibid. p. 23.
13. ibid., p. 29.
14. ibid., p. 15.
15. ibid., p. 7.
16. Mayhew, *London Labour and the London Poor*, I, p. 41/1–2.
17. M. Mason, *The Making of Victorian Sexuality* (London, 1995), ch. 3 passim.
18. Lisa Z. Sigel, 'Name Your Pleasure', *Journal of the History of Sexuality*, IX: 4 (October 2000), pp. 395–419.
19. Mayhew, *London Labour and the London Poor*, I, p. 42/1.
20. W. M. Thackeray, *The Newcomes* (London, 1855), pp. 19–20.
21. Mason, *The Making of Victorian Sexuality*, p. 127.
22. R. D. Altick, *The English Common Reader* (London, 1957), p. 347.
23. W. M. Thackeray, 'Half a Crown's Worth of Cheap Knowledge', *Fraser's Magazine*, XVII (1838), p. 290.
24. J. C. Hotten, *Modern Slang, Cant and Vulgar Words* (London, 1859), p. 39.
25. Sigel, 'Name Your Pleasure', p. 409.
26. For the time: many of 'Walter's' prostitute partners would now be considered unacceptably young, but the age of consent was then twelve.
27. See P. Fryer, *Mrs Grundy* (London, 1963), ch. 1; the author has extracted many of

F & H's lists; the American Henry N. Carey appears to have based his *Slang of Venery* (1916) entirely on their work.

10   Cockney Sparrers

1. Although this has been attributed to Dickens, the substitution can be found at least as early as the start of the century, e.g. in a number of the ballads included in *The Universal Songster* (1825), which drew on earlier material.
2. J. Franklyn, *Rhyming Slang* (London, 1984), p. 7.
3. ibid., p. 24.
4. H. Mayhew, *London Labour and the London Poor*, (London, 1867), vol. I, p. 418/1.
5. D. Maurer, 'Australian Rhyming Argot in the American Underworld', *American Speech*, 19, 3 (1944), p. 186.
6. Mayhew, *London Labour and the London Poor*, I, Preface, p. xv.
7. *Punch*, 9 March 1850, p. 93.
8. E. P. Thompson, 'The Political Education of Henry Mayhew', *Victorian Studies*, 11 (1967), p. 42.
9. G. Himmelfarb, 'Mayhew's Poor: a Problem of Identity', *Victorian Studies*, 14: 3 (1971), pp. 307–20.
10. Mayhew, *London Labour and the London Poor*, I, Preface, p. xv.
11. Quoted in H. J. Dyos, *Exploring the Urban Past* (Cambridge, 1982), p. 243.
12. 'Slang', *Household Words*, 24 September 1853, p. 73/2; the piece is not signed and a number of sources attribute it to the journalist George Augustus Sala.
13. ibid.
14. ibid., p. 74/2.
15. ibid., p. 75/1.
16. *Punch*, vol. III (1842), p. 136.
17. ibid., p. 168.
18. ibid., vol. XIII (1847), p. 213.
19. P. J. Keating, *The Working Classes in Victorian Fiction* (London, 1971).
20. The potential for an equation with a rhyming slang use of *cunt* is very likely coincidental, although Liza's role qualifies her to illustrate several senses of that word; Morrison would surely have known it.
21. A. Morrison, *Child of the Jago* (London, 1896), pp. 13–14.
22. W. E. Henley, 'Some Novels of 1899', in *North American Review* (February 1900), pp. 253–62.
23. ibid., pp. 257-8.
24. R. Whiteing, *No. 5 John Street* (London, 1899), p. 1.
25. C. Rook, *The Hooligan Nights* (London, 1899), p. 4.
26. ibid., introduction.
27. ibid., p. 16.
28. C. Rook, *London Side-lights* (London, 1908), p. 245.
29. *ODNB*: Harry Champion.
30. F. C. Burnand, *Records and Reminiscences* (London, 1904), p. 214.
31. E. J. Milliken, *Punch's Almanac* (1880), p. 12.
32. E. J. Milliken, ''Arry on Crutches', *Punch*, 3 May 1879.
33. E. J. Milliken, letter quoted in H. M. Spielmann, *History of Punch* (New York, 1895), p. 380.
34. E. J. Milliken, ''Arry on the Sincerest Form of Flattery', *Punch*, 20 September 1890.

11   America

1. N. Webster, *Dissertations on the English Language* (Boston, 1789), i, p. 22.
2. ibid., pp. 20–23.
3. J. F. Cooper, *Notions of the Americans* (Philadelphia, 1828), p. 125.
4. D. Williams, 'Possibilities in the Rogue Narrative of Henry Tufts', *Early American Literature*, XIX, 1 (Spring, 1984), p. 14.
5. A. W. Read, 'The World of Joe Strickland', *Journal of American Folklore*, 76, 302 (1963), p. 277.
6. C. G. Leland, 'Hans Breitmann in Church' (1870).
7. C. G. Leland, 'Breitmann in Battle' (1869).
8. F. P. Dunne, *Mr Dooley in Peace and War* (Chicago, 1898), p. x.
9. Quoted in H. Kersten, 'The Creative Potential of Dialect Writing', *Nineteenth-Century Literature*, LV, 1 (June 2000), p. 103.
10. C. Dickens, *Martin Chuzzlewit* (London, 1843–4), ch. xvi.
11. M. Schele de Vere, *Americanisms* (New York, 1872), p. 4.

12. ibid., p. 275.
13. ibid., p. 274.
14. ibid., p. 276.
15. ibid., p. 275.
16. B. L. McClung, 'Horse Racing Accounts in "The Spirit of the Times"', *American Speech*, 40, 1 (1965), pp. 20–21.
17. N. W. Yates, *William T. Porter* (Baton Rouge, 1957), p. 111.
18. Quoted in B. I. Wiley, *The Life of Billy Yank* (New York, 1951), p. 156.
19. H. Asbury, *The Gangs of New York* (New York, 1928), p. 32.
20. T. A. Brown, *A History of the New York Stage* (New York, 1903), p. 284.
21. Playbill for 1856; cited in Richard M. Dorson, 'Mose the Far-Famed and World-Renowned', *American Literature*, Vol. 15, No. 3 (November 1943), p. 295.
22. ibid., p. 292.
23. J. Pickering, *Vocabulary* (Boston, 1816), p. v.
24. ibid., p. 173.
25. ibid., p. v.
26. There were technically four, but that of 1860 merely reprinted that of 1859.
27. J. R. Bartlett, *Autobiography* (Providence, RI, 2006), p. 43.
28. J. R. Bartlett, *Dictionary of Americanisms* (New York, 1848), p. iv.
29. J. R. Bartlett, *Dictionary of Americanisms* (4th edn, 1877), p. iii.
30. G. W. Matsell, *Vocabulum* (New York, 1859), p. iii.
31. ibid., p. v.
32. W. C. Wilde, 'Thief Talk', *Journal of American Folklore*, 3, 11 (October–December, 1890), p. 303.
33. Quoted in J. F. Richardson, *The New York Police* (New York, 1970), p. 56.
34. J. Maitland, *American Slang Dictionary* (1891), p. ix.
35. J. Coleman, *History of Cant and Slang Dictionaries*, vol. III (Oxford, 2009), pp. 155–60.
36. Maitland, *American Slang Dictionary*, pp. ix–x.
37. Cited in R. Chapman, *New Dictionary of American Slang* (New York 1986), p. ix.
38. J. Coleman, *History of Cant and Slang Dictionaries*, vol. III, p. 160.
39. For an extended discussion of Whitman's philological pursuits, see Michael R. Dressman, 'Walt Whitman's Plans for the Perfect Dictionary', *Studies in the American Renaissance* (1979), pp. 457–74.
40. H. Traubel, *With Walt Whitman in Camden, I: March 28–July 14, 1888* (Boston, 1906), p. 462.
41. Dressman, 'Walt Whitman's Plans', p. 458.
42. W. Whitman, 'Slang in America', reprinted in *Prose Works 1892*, (New York, 1964) vol. II, p. 573.

12 Keeping Score

1. Cited in H. S. Ashbee, *Index Librorum Prohibitorum* (London, 1877), p. 251.
2. *The Bookseller*, 2 July 1873, p. 549.
3. Partridge, *Slang To-day and Yesterday*, p. 95.
4. *The Bookseller*, 2 July 1873, p. 548.
5. Partridge, *Slang To-Day and Yesterday*.
6. Ashbee, *Index Librorum Prohibitorum*, p. xix.
7. ibid., p. 252.
8. Quoted in T. E. Welby, *A Study of Swinburne* (London, 1926), p. 26.
9. Cited in S. Eliot, 'Hotten: Rotten: Forgotten? An Apologia for a General Publisher', in *Book History*, III (2000), pp. 61–93.
10. Hotten, *Slang Dictionary* (London, 1867), p. 20.
11. ibid., p. 34.
12. ibid., p. viii.
13. ibid., p. xv.
14. ibid., p. 65.
15. A. Barrère and C. G. Leland, *Slang, Jargon and Cant* (London, 1889–90), p. vii.
16. *DNB*.
17. Partridge, *Slang To-day and Yesterday*, p. 105.
18. Barrère & Leland, *Slang, Jargon and Cant*, p. xviii.
19. *Notes and Queries*, 2 November 1889, p. 341.
20. ibid., pp. 342–3.
21. G. Legman, introduction to *Slang and Its Analogues*, Vol. I (revised edn, 1966), p. lvii.
22. G. Legman, *The Horn Book* (New York, 1964), p. 51.
23. J. Gross, *The Rise and Fall of the Man of Letters* (London, 1969).
24. Coleman, *History of Cant and Slang Dictionaries*, vol. III, pp. 81–2.

25. Partridge, *Slang To-day and Yesterday*, p. 106.
26. J. S. Farmer and W. E. Henley, *Slang and Its Analogues*, p. viii.
27. ibid., p. x.
28. *Notes and Queries*, 8 February 1890, p. 119.
29. *Scots Observer*, 15 February 1890, pp. 341–2.
30. *Pall Mall Gazette*, 17 April 1890.
31. *Notes and Queries*, 2 December 1893, p. 460.
32. P. Gilliver, 'Collaboration, Competition, Confrontation', in M. Adams (ed.), *Cunning Passages, Contrived Corridors* (Milan, 2011), p. 80 [note].
33. *Notes and Queries*, 2 December 1893, p. 460.
34. Letter to James Murray, 23 July 1890, quoted in Gilliver, 'Collaboration, Competition, Confrontation'.

13 Gayspeak

1. D. Kulick, 'Gay and Lesbian Language', *Annual Review of Anthropology*, 29 (2000), pp. 243–85.
2. R. Norton, *Mother Clap's Molly House* (2006), p. 87.
3. 'Jon Bee', *Living Picture of London* (London, 1828), p. 159.
4. D. Bruster, 'Female–Female Eroticism and the Early Modern Stage' in Mary Beth Rose (ed.) *Perspectives on Renaissance Drama* XXIV (Chicago, Il, 1995), p. 9.
5. *Die männliche Homosexualität in England mit besonderer Berücksichtigung Londons.*
6. For a detailed analysis of the material in both Pavia and Rosanoff, see Gary Simes, 'Gay Slang Lexicography', in *Dictionaries*, XXVI (2005), pp. 1–159.
7. Anonymous, *Lavender Lexicon* (San Francisco, 1964), introduction.
8. D. Kulick, 'Gay and Lesbian Language', *Annual Review of Anthropology*, XXIX (2000), p. 251.
9. Simes, 'Gay Slang Lexicography', p. 7.
10. B. Rodgers, *Queen's Vernacular* (San Francisco, 1972), pp. 11–12.
11. In *American Speech*, 45: 1/2 (1970), pp. 45–59.
12. ibid., p. 55.
13. *Notes and Queries*, 2 November 1889, p. 341.
14. G. Stein, 'Miss Furr and Miss Skeene' (New York, 1922) in J. Katz (ed.) *Gay/Lesbian Almanac* (New York, 1983), p. 406.
15. 'Robert Scully' *The Scarlet Pansy*, (New York, 1932), p. 194.
16. No money, the landlord says it's two shillings apiece and food for free; / We'll have to leave lodgings in the morning before the landlord (lit. 'good man of the house') gets out of bed.
17. Quoted in D. Cameron and D. Kulick, *Language and Sexuality Reader* (London, 2003), p. 92.
18. J. P. Stanley, 'When We Say "Out of the Closets!"', *College English*, 36, 3 (November 1974), p. 385/2.

14 American Century

1. L. Fiedler, *Love and Death in the American Novel* (New York, 1960), p. 481.
2. *Time*, vol. 43, 15 Jan. 1934, p. 46.
3. H. L. Mencken, *American Language*, Supp. 2 (New York, 1948), p. 646.
4. W. R. Taylor, *Inventing Times Square* (1993), p. 212.
5. C. Beaton, *Cecil Beaton's New York* (London, 1938), pp. 60–61.
6. Quoted in 'Argot a Go-go', on http://www.simesite.net/articles.asp?id=130.
7. N. Gabler, *Winchell* (New York, 1995), p. 71.
8. ibid., p. xiv.
9. H. Rockwell, 'Color Stuff', *American Speech*, 3, 1 (1927), pp. 28–9.
10. ibid., p. 30.
11. A. Gopnik, in *New Yorker*, 2 March 2009 [on-line edn].

15 African-American Slang

1. A small group had been imported in 1526 as part of a short-lived Spanish attempt to colonize North Carolina; when this collapsed they fled into the interior.
2. G. F. Krapp, 'English of the Negro', *American Mercury*, 193/1, 191/1.
3. ibid., p. 195/2.
4. B. I. Wiley, *Life of Billy Yank* (1952), p. 119, cites 'an Illinois soldier' of the US Civil War: 'It would make you laugh yourself blind almost if you could see a lot of 'ebonics' congregated by moonlight' [etc.].

5. J. W. Johnson, *Autobiography of an Ex-Coloured Man* (1912, edn 1927), p. 92.

6. C. Dibdin 'Kickeraboo' in *Songs of Charles Dibdin* (London, 1848), p. 113/2.

7. Reprinted in *Publications of the Colonial Society of Massachusetts* (Boston, MA, April 1907) vol. 10, p. 140.

8. T. Haliburton, *Season Ticket* (London, 1860), p. 54.

9. P. Egan, *The Finish to the Adventure of Tom and Jerry* (1830, reprinted edn 1889), p. 185.

10. Quoted in J. L. Dillard, *Perspectives on Black English* (The Hague, 1975), p. 98 [note].

11. H. H. Brackenridge, *Modern Chivalry* (1792–1815), I, p. 109.

12. Quoted in A. W. Read, 'The World of Joe Strickland' in *Jrnl of American Folklore*, vol. 76, (Oct–Dec, 1963), p. 284.

13. E. Lott, 'Love and Theft', *Representations*, No. 39 (Summer, 1992), pp. 24–5.

14. F. Douglass, in *The North Star*, 27 October 1848.

15. M. Fuller, 'Entertainments of the Past Winter', *The Dial*, July 1842, p. 52.

16. Quoted in S. Herring, 'Du Bois and the Minstrels', *MELUS*, 22, 2 (1997), p. 8.

17. C. Mackay, *Memoirs of Extraordinary Popular Delusions* (London, 1841), p. 241.

18. C. Townsend, 'Negro Minstrels', in A. Bean et al., *Inside the Minstrel Mask* (Hanover, NH, 1969), p. 122.

19. J. Harrison, 'Negro English', *Anglia* 7 (1884), p. 233.

20. ibid., p. 232.

21. H. L. Mencken, *American Language*, Supp. 2 (New York, 1962), p. 704.

22. R. Gold, 'Vernacular of the Jazz World', *American Speech*, 32, 4 (1957), p. 274.

23. M. Mezzrow, *Really the Blues* (New York, 1946), p. 221.

24. E. Conrad, *Dan Burley's Original Handbook of Harlem Jive*, Introduction, p. ii.

25. James D. Hart, 'Jazz Jargon', *American Speech*, 7, 4 (1932), p. 241.

26. ibid., p. 243.

27. ibid., p. 244.

28. ibid., p. 248.

29. *American Speech*, 12 (1937), pp. 179–84.

30. E. J. Nichols and W. L. Werner, 'Hot Jazz Jargon', *Vanity Fair* (November 1935), pp. 38, 71.

31. *American Speech*, 12, 12 (1937), pp. 45–8.

32. C. Calloway, *Cab Calloway's Hepster's Dictionary* (New York, 6 edns, 1938–44), passim.

33. D. Burley, *Dan Burley's Original Handbook of Harlem Jive* (New York, 1944, reprint Chicago, IL, 2009), p. 91

34. Z. N. Hurston, *Complete Stories* (New York, 1995), p. 133.

35. Z. N. Hurston, 'Story in Harlem Slang' in *Novels & Stories* (New York, 1995), p. 1005.

36. A. Goldman, 'The Lord Buckley Phenomenon', *Life*, 19 December 1969, p. 13/2.

37. ibid., p. 13/3.

38. Mezzrow, *Really the Blues*, pp. 220–26 *passim*.

39. S. Calt, *Barrelhouse Words* (New York, 2009), pp. xi, xiii.

40. Quoted in ibid., p. xiv.

41. For a detailed treatment of US and UK prison language, see my *Crooked Talk* (London, 2011).

42. In R. Abrahams, 'The Negro Stereotype', *Journal of American Folklore*, 83 (April–June 1970), p. 244.

43. R. Abrahams, 'Playing the Dozens', *Journal of American Folklore*, 75 (July–September 1962), p. 219 [note].

44. ibid.

45. R. Fisher, *Walls of Jericho* (New York, 1928), p. 250.

46. R. Fisher, *The Conjure-Man Dies* (New York, 1932), p. 211.

47. J. H. Bryant, *Born in a Mighty Bad Land* (Bloomington, 2003), p. 119.

48. Quoted in Mike Davies, *City of Quartz* (New York, 1980), p. 43.

49. The *Série Noire* introduced France to many top-rated American writers; however, Duhamel's first title, before he turned to stars such as Hammett, Chandler and Jim Thompson, was *This Man is Dangerous*, by the laughable English copyist Peter Cheyney.

16 Campus and Counter-Culture

1. B. Moore, *A Lexicon of Cadet Language* (Canberra, 1993), p. xviii.

2. 'A Pembrochian', *Gradus ad Cantabrigiam* (Cambridge, 1893), p. A4v

3. M. Marples, *University Slang* (London, 1950), p. 7.

4. A. Dundes and M. R. Schonhorn, 'Kansas University Slang: A New Generation', *American Speech*, 38 (1963), p. 163.

5. ibid., p. 165.

6. ibid., p. 177.

7. *College Undergraduate Slang Study* (1967–8), introduction, p. 1.

8. J. Coleman, *History of Cant and Slang Dictionaries*, Vol. IV (Oxford, 2010), p. 197.

9. *Current Slang*, VI, Introduction, n.p.

10. *The Adventures of Mr Verdant Green* by 'Cuthbert Bede' appeared 1853–7; he was not the first so eponymized: *Bell's Life in Sydney* offered a series 'Verdant Green's First Visit to the Races' in June 1850.

11. G. S. Hall, *Youth: Its Education, Regimen, and Hygiene* (New York, 1906), p. 164.

12. ibid., p. 165.

13. S. Lewis, *Babbitt* (New York, 1922; 1974), p. 258.

14. *Saturday Evening Post*, 23 December 1961.

15. Mezzrow, *Really the Blues*, p.227.

16. N. Mailer, 'The White Negro', in *Advertisements for Myself* (New York, 1959), pp. 340, 348.

17. J. Kerouac, *On the Road* (New York, 1957), pp. 179–80.

18. T. Southern, 'The Night the Bird Blew for Dr Warner', in *Red-Dirt Marijuana* (New York, 1967), p. 45.

19. ibid., p. 54.

20. Mezzrow, *Really the Blues*, pp. 225–6.

21. Mencken, *American Language*, p. 729.

22. S. Douglas, *Listening In* (Minneapolis, 2004), p. 235.

23. ibid., p. 234.

24. T. Dalzell, 'The Word of the Lord', on LordBuckley.com (1996).

25. *The Wire* (HBO TV), season 2, episode 5.

17 War

1. Hotten, *Slang Dictionary* (London, 1864), pp. 34–5.

2. Herbert Asbury, in *Sucker's Progress* (1938), suggested an alternative: 'A few years after the Louisiana Purchase one of the New Orleans banks issued ten dollar notes, on one side of which was the French word for ten, dix. To the flatboatmen one of the notes was a dix, and collectively they were dixies, while New Orleans was known as "the town of the dixies," and, later, simply as Dixie. The word does not appear to have been used to designate the entire South until after 1859, when D. D. Emmett wrote his famous song.' Schele de Vere, who opts for Mason-Dixon, adds another reference to a supposed slaveholder, one Dixey, who had allegedly treated his slaves very well, thus leading to the 'minstrel' song.

3. W. Pittenger, *Daring and Suffering* (1864), p. 82.

4. Quoted in 1863 in D. M. Sullivan, *The United States Marine Corps in the Civil War* (2000), III, p. 267.

5. O. C. Bumpass, letter 2 March 1865, quoted in B. I. Wiley, *Life of Johnny Reb* (1943), p. 50.

6. *Morning Leader*, 30 May 1893.

7. R. Kipling, *Just So Stories* (London, 1902), p. 115.

8. Quoted in Jessie B. Sherwood, 'Kipling's Women', *Fine Arts Journal*, 37, 3 (March 1919), p. 42.

9. R. Kipling, 'In The Matter of a Private', *Soldiers Three* (London, 1890), p. 77.

10. Quoted in P. J. Keating, *Working Classes in Victorian Fiction* (London, 1979), p. 148.

11. ibid., p. 139.

12. Kipling, 'In The Matter of a Private', p. 78.

13. A. Laughesen, 'Australian First World War "slanguage"', *Journal of the Australian War Memorial*, 38 (2007) (http://www.awm.gov.au/journal/j38/slanguage.asp).

14. Quoted in J. Green, *Chasing the Sun*, (London, 1996), p. 353.

15. J. Coleman, 'Historical and Social Methods in Slang Lexicography', in M. Adams (ed.), *'Cunning Passages, Contrived Corridors', Unexpected Essays in the History of Lexicography* (Monza, Italy, 2010), pp. 129–46.

16. Quoted in D. Crystal, *Eric Partridge in His Own Words* (London, 1980), p. 24.

17. Quoted in ibid., p. 26.

18. *American Speech*, 47: 1/2 (1972), pp. 5–142.

19. 'Ian Hay', *First Hundred Thousand* (London, 1915), p. 120.

Bibliography

(This bibliography lists those authors who have been quoted in the text and whose work has been footnoted. I have generally omitted authors and titles, usually fictional, whose work is explained and dated in the text, especially when listing examples of a given genre.)

'A Pembrochian', *Gradus ad Cantabrigiam* (Cambridge, 1893)

'Andrew Barton' *Disappointment* (New York, 1767)

'Argot a Go-go', on http://www.simesite.net/articles.asp?id=130

'Cuthbert Bede', *Adventures of Mr Verdant Green* (London, 1853)

'Ian Hay', *First Hundred Thousand* (London, 1915)

'Jon Bee', *Living Picture of London* (London, 1828)

'Jon Bee', *Slang. A Dictionary of The Turf, The Ring, The Chase, The Pit, Of Bon-Ton and the Varieties of Life* (London, 1823)

'Roger Pheuquewell', *New Description of Merryland* (London, 1741)

'The Rationale of Slang', *Overland Monthly*, 4, February 1870

A Notable and Pleasant History of the Famous renowned Knights of the Blade, commonly called Hectors, or, St. Nicholas Clerkes (London, 1655)

Abrahams, R. 'Playing the Dozens', *Journal of American Folklore*, 75 (July–September 1962)

Abrahams, R. 'The Negro Stereotype', *Journal of American Folklore*, 83 (April–June 1970)

Adams, M. *Slang: The People's Poetry* (New York, 2009), p. 49.

Ainsworth, H. *Rookwood* (revised edn, London, 1837)

Allen, J. *The Latin Sexual Vocabulary* (Baltimore, Johns Hopkins U. Press 1982)

Altick, R. D. *The English Common Reader* (London, 1957)

andc.anu.edu.au/ozwords/Nov%202002/Botany%20Bay.html

Anonymous, *Lavender Lexicon* (San Francisco, CA, 1964)

Asbury, H. *The Gangs of New York* (New York, 1928)

Ashbee, H. S. *Index Librorum Prohibitorum* (London, 1877)

Atyeo, D. *Violence in Sport* (London, 1979)

Australian Dictionary of Biography (on-line)

Aydelotte, F. *Elizabethan Rogues and Vagabonds* (Oxford, 1913)

Baker, S. J. *New Zealand Slang* (Melbourne, 1941)

Balzac, H. de *Splendeurs et Misères des Courtisanes* (1849, trans. *A Harlot High and Low*, 1970)

Barrère, A. & C.G. Leland *A Dictionary of Slang, Jargon and Cant* (2 vols, London, 1889–90)

Bartlett. J. *Dictionary of Americanisms: A Glossary of Words and Phrases, Colloquially used in the United States* (New York 1848, 1859, 1860, 1877)

Baugh, A. C. and T. Cable, *History of the English Language* (London, 1993)

Bayman, A. 'Rogues, Conycatching and the Scribbling Crew', *History Workshop Journal* (2007)

Beaton, C. *Cecil Beaton's New York* (London, 1938)

Bellanta, M. 'Leary Kin: Australian Larrikins and the Blackface Minstrel Dandy', *Journal of Social History*, 42: 3 (Washington DC, 2009)

Berry, H. 'Rethinking Politeness in Eighteenth-Century England', *Transactions of the Royal Historical Society*, Sixth Ser., Vol. 11 (2001)

Blackwood's, XXXVI: 6 (March 1820)

Blank, P. *Broken English* (London, 1996)

Borgman, A. S. *Thomas Shadwell His life and Comedies* (London, 1969)

Bosworth, C.E. *The Medieval Islamic Underworld* (2 vols, Leiden, 1976)

Brackenridge, H. H. *Modern Chivalry* (1792–1815)

Brown, T. A. *A History of the New York Stage* (New York, 1903)

Bryant, J. H. *Born in a Mighty Bad Land* (Bloomington, 2003)

Burley, D. *Dan Burley's Original Handbook of Harlem Jive* (New York, 1944)

Burnand, F. C. *Records and Reminiscences* (London, 1904)

Calloway, C. *Hipster's Dictionary* (New York 1944)

Calt, S. *Barrelhouse Words* (New York, 2009)

Cameron, D. and D. Kulick, *Language and Sexuality Reader* (London, 2003)

Chandler, F. *Literature of Roguery* (2 vols. London, 1907)

Chapman, R. *New Dictionary of American Slang* (New York 1986)

Cibber, T. *The Lives of the Poets* (London, 1753), vol. IV, pp. 293–4.

Cleland, J. *Memoirs of a Woman of Pleasure* (London, 1748–9)

Coleman, J. 'Historical and Social Methods in Slang Lexicography', in M. Adams (ed.), *'Cunning Passages, Contrived Corridors', Unexpected Essays in the History of Lexicography* (Monza, Italy, 2010)

Coleman, J. *A History of Cant and Slang Dictionaries* (4 vols, Oxford, 2004–11)

Coleman, J. *The Story of Slang* (Oxford, 2012).

College Undergraduate Slang Study (1967–8)

Cooper, J. F. *Notions of the Americans* (Philadelphia, 1828)

Crowe, C. *Australian Slang Dictionary* (Melbourne, 1895), introduction.

Crystal, D. (ed.) *Eric Partridge in His Own Words* (London, 19

Current Slang (1966–71)

Dalton, J. *A Genuine Narrative of all the Street Robberies committed [...] by James Dalton, and his Accomplices* (London 1728)

Dalzell, T. 'The Word of the Lord', on LordBuckley.com (1996)

Darnton, R. *Forbidden Best-Sellers of Pre-Revolutionary France* (New York, 1996)

Dart, G. 'Flash Style', *History Workshop Journal*, LI (Spring, 2001)

Davies, M. *City of Quartz* (New York, 1980)

Dawson, A.B. 'Mistris Hic & Haec', in *Studies in English Literature, 1500–1900*, 33:2

Dekker, T. *A Rod for Run-Awayes* (London, 1625)

Dekker, T. *Match Me in London* (London 1598)

Dekker, T. *O Per Se O* (London, 1616)

Dekker, T. *The Bellman* (London, 1608)

Dickens, C. 'Slang', *Household Words*, 24 September 1853

Dickens, C. *Martin Chuzzlewit* (London, 1843–4)

Dickens, C. *Oliver Twist* (3rd edn, London 1841)

Dickens, C. *Pickwick Papers* (4th edn, London, 1838)

Dickey, E. *Latin Forms of Address* (2002)

Dillard, J. L. *Perspectives on Black English* (The Hague, 1975)

Dillenberger, J. (ed.), *Martin Luther* (New York, 1960)

Dorson, R.M. 'Mose the Far-Famed and World-Renowned', *American Literature*, Vol. 15, No. 3 (November 1943)

Douglas, S. *Listening In* (Minneapolis, 2004)

Douglass, F. in *The North Star*, 27 October 1848

Downing, W. H. *Digger Dialects* (Melbourne, 1919)

Dressman, M. R. 'Walt Whitman's Plans for the Perfect Dictionary', *Studies in the American Renaissance* (1979)

Dundes, A. and M. R. Schonhorn, 'Kansas University Slang: A New Generation', *American Speech*, 38 (1963)

Dunne, F. P. *Mr Dooley in Peace and War* (Chicago, 1898)

Dyos, H. J. *Exploring the Urban Past* (Cambridge, 1982)

Dyson, E. *Fact'ry 'Ands* (Melbourne, 1906)

E. Ward, *London Spy* (London, 1698–1700), facsimile 1924

E. B. Gent., *New Dictionary of the Canting Crew* (London, *c.* 1698)

Eble, C. *Slang and Sociability* (Chapel Hill, NC, 1996), p. 12.

Egan, P. (ed.) *Grose's Classical Dictionary of the Vulgar Tongue* (London, 1823)

Egan, P. *Life in London* (London, 1821)

Egan, P. *The Finish to the Adventures of Tom, Jerry and Logic* (London, 1830)

Eliot, G. *Middlemarch* (London, 1872)

Eliot, S. 'Hotten: Rotten: Forgotten? An Apologia for a General Publisher', in *Book History*, III (2000)

Ellis, S. M. *William Harrison Ainsworth and His Friends* (London, 1911)

Eriksen, M. H. 'Translating the use of slang' (Institut for Sprog og Erhvervskommunikation, Aarhus School of Business, Aarhus University, 2010)

Farmer, J. S. and W. E. Henley, *Slang and Its Analogues* (7 vols. London 1890–1904)

Fernald, J.C. 'The Impoverishment of the Language: Cant, Slang, Etc.', in *Progressive English* (1918)

Fiedler, L. *Love and Death in the American Novel* (New York, 1960)

Fielder, L. *Collected Essays* vol. 2 (New York, 1971)

Fielding, H. *Enquiry into the Cause of the Late Increase of Robbers* (London, 1751)

Firth, C. H. *Commentary on Macaulay's History of England* (London, 1938)

Fisher, R. *The Conjure-Man Dies* (New York, 1932)

Fisher, R. *Walls of Jericho* (New York, 1928)

Flanders, J. *The Invention of Murder* (London, 2011)

Fotheringham, R. (ed.), *Australian Plays for the Colonial Stage: 1834–1899* (Queensland, 2006)

Franklyn, J. *Rhyming Slang* (London, 1984)

Fraser's Magazine, May (London, 1839)

Fryer, P. *Mrs Grundy* (London, 1963)

Fuller, M. 'Entertainments of the Past Winter', *The Dial*, July 1842

Gabler, N. *Winchell* (New York, 1995)

Gentleman's Magazine, (London 1773)

Gentleman's Magazine, (London, June 1791)

Genung, J.F. *Outlines of Rhetoric* (Boston, 1893)

Gibson I. *The Erotomaniac* (London, 2002)

Gilliver, P. 'Collaboration, Competition, Confrontation', in M. Adams (ed.), *Cunning Passages, Contrived Corridors* (Milan, 2011)

Gold, R. 'Vernacular of the Jazz World', *American Speech*, 32, 4 (1957)

Goldman, A. 'The Lord Buckley Phenomenon', *Life*, 19 December (New York 1969)

Goodge, W. T. 'Great Australian Slanguage', *Bulletin* (Sydney), 4 June 1898

Gopnik, A. in *New Yorker*, 2 March 2009 (on-line)

Greenblatt, S. *Will in the World* (Prince Frederick, MD, 2004)

Greene, R. *Second part of Coney-catching* (London, 1592)

Grose, F. *Classical Dictionary of the Vulgar Tongue* (London 1785, 1788, 1796)

Gross, J. *The Rise and Fall of the Man of Letters* (London, 1969)

Guiraud, P. 'Inédits', in *Marges linguistiques* (Saint-Chamas, September 2003)

Haliburton, T. *Season Ticket* (London, 1860)

Hall, G. S. *Youth: Its Education, Regimen, and Hygiene* (New York, 1906)

Harington, J. *A briefe view of the state of the Church of England* (London, 1653)

Harman, T. *Caveat for Common Coney-Catchers* (London 1566)

Harrison, J. 'Negro English', *Anglia* 7 (1884)

Hart, J. D. 'Jazz Jargon', *American Speech*, 7, 4 (1932)

Head, R. and F. Kirkman, *The English Rogue*, pt II (London, 1666)

Head, R. *The Canting Academy* (London, 1673)

Head, R. *The English Rogue* (London, 1665)

Herring, S. 'Du Bois and the Minstrels', *MELUS*, 22, 2 (1997)

Himmelfarb, G. 'Mayhew's Poor: a Problem of Identity', *Victorian Studies*, 14: 3 (1971)

Hollingsworth, K. *The Newgate Novel* (Detroit, 1963), p. 104.

Hotten, J. C., introduction to P. Egan, *Life in London* (reprint London, 1869)

Hotten, J. C. *Modern Slang, Cant and Vulgar Words* (London, 1859)

Hotten, J. C. *Slang Dictionary* (London, 1873)

http://www.gale.cengage.com/free_resources/glossary/glossarys.htm

Hughes, R. *The Fatal Shore* (London, 1987)

Hugo, V. 'Argot', in *Les Misérables* (Paris, 1862; trans. 1976)

Hugo, V. *Le Dernier Jour d'un Condamné* (Paris, 1866)

Hurston, Z. N. *Complete Stories* (New York, 1995)

Ingraham, P. 'The Language of Dickens', in D. Paroissien, *A Companion to Charles Dickens* (London 2008)

Johnson, J. W. *Autobiography of an Ex-Coloured Man* (1912, edn 1927)

Jordan, J. C. *Robert Greene* (New York, 1915)

Judges, A. V. *Elizabethan Underworld* (London, 1930)

Keating, P. J. *The Working Classes in Victorian Fiction* (London, 1971)

Kersten, H. 'The Creative Potential of Dialect Writing', *Nineteenth-Century Literature*, LV, 1 (June 2000)

Kipling, R. 'In The Matter of a Private', *Soldiers Three* (London, 1890)

Kipling, R. *Just So Stories* (London, 1902)

Kipling, R. 'My Son's Wife', in *A Diversity of Creatures* (London, 1913)

Krapp, G. F. 'English of the Negro', *American Mercury* (New York 1924)

Kruptadia vol. IV (London, 1888)

Kulick, D. 'Gay and Lesbian Language', *Annual Review of Anthropology*, 29 (2000)

Laughesen, A. 'Australian First World War "slanguage"', *Journal of the Australian War Memorial*, 38 (2007)

Lawson, S. *The Archibald Paradox* (Ringwood, Victoria, 1983)

Leaves from the Diary of a Celebrated Thief and Pickpocket (New York, 1865)

Legman, G. introduction to Farmer & Henley *Slang and Its Analogues*, Vol. I (revised edn, 1966)

Legman, G. *The Horn Book* (New York, 1964)

Leland, C. G. *Hans Breitmann's Ballads* (Philadelphia, PA, 1884)

Lewis, S. *Babbitt* (New York, 1922)

Lexicon Balatronicum (London, 1811)

Liebling, A. J. *The Sweet Science* (New York, 1956)

Lighter, J. *The Slang of the American Expeditionary Forces in Europe 1917–1919* in *American Speech*, 47: 1/2 (1972)

Lighter, J. and B. K. Dumas, 'Is Slang a Word for Linguists?', *American Speech*, 53: 1 (1978)

Lighter, J. in *The Cambridge History of the English Language*, vol. VI: North America (Cambridge, 2001)

Lott, E. 'Love and Theft', *Representations*, No. 39 (Summer, 1992)

Macaulay, T. *History of England from the Accession of James II* (London, 1849)

MacInnes, C. *City of Spades* (London, 1957)

MacInnes, C. *Absolute Beginners* (London, 1959)

Mackay, C. *Memoirs of Extraordinary Popular Delusions* (London, 1841)

Mailer, N. 'The White Negro', in *Advertisements for Myself* (New York, 1959)

Maitland, J. *American Slang Dictionary* (1891)

Manuscripts of His Grace the Duke of Rutland: Letters and papers, 1440–1797, vol. 3 (London, 1889)

Marples, M. *University Slang* (London 1950)

Mason, M. *The Making of Victorian Sexuality* (London, 1995)

Matsell, G. W. *Vocabulum* (New York, 1859)

Matthews, B. 'The Function of Slang', *Harper's* 88 (1893)

Maurer, D. 'Australian Rhyming Argot in the American Underworld', *American Speech*, 19, 3 (1944)

Mayhew, H. *London Labour and the London Poor* (4 vols. London, 1861)

McClung, B. L. 'Horse Racing Accounts in "The Spirit of the Times"', *American Speech*, 40, 1 (1965)

McKenzie, A. 'The Real Macheath',
    Huntington Library Quarterly, 69: 4 (2006)
McMillan, J. B. 'American Lexicology
    1942–1973', *American Speech*, 53 (1978)
McMullan, J. 'Criminal organization in
    London', *Social Problems*, 29: 3
Mencken, H. L. *American Language*, Supp. 2
    (New York, 1948)
Mencken, H. L. *American Language*, Supp. 2
    (New York, 1962)
Mezzrow, M. *Really the Blues* (New York,
    1946)
Mills, R. *Suspended Animation* (London,
    2005)
Moore, B. 'The Sydney Slang Dictionary',
    Ozwords, April 2010
Moore, B. *A Lexicon of Cadet Language*
    (Canberra, 1993)
Moore, B. *Speaking Our Language*
    (Melbourne, 2008)
Moore, J. *You English Words* (London, 1962)
Moore, T. *Tom Crib's Memorial* (London,
    1819)
Morris, E. E. *Austral English* (London,
    1898)
Morrison, A. *Child of the Jago* (London,
    1896)
Morrison, A. *Tales of the Mean Streets*
    (London, 1894)
Moseley, G. W. R. D. 'Richard Head's "The
    English Rogue"', *Yearbook of English
    Studies I* (1971)
Mount, T. *The confession, &c. of Thomas
    Mount, who was executed at Little-Rest,
    in the state of Rhode-Island, on Friday
    the 27th of May, 1791, for burglary*
    (Middletown, CT, 1791)
Munro, C. and R. Sheahan-Bright, *Paper
    Empires: a history of the book in Australia
    1946–2005* (Queensland, 2006)
My Secret Life (London 1888–94)
New Canting Dictionary (London, 1725)
Nichols, E. J. and W. L. Werner, 'Hot Jazz
    Jargon', *Vanity Fair* (November 1935)
Norton, R. *Mother Clap's Molly House*
    (London, 2006)
Notes and Queries, 10th series (passim)
Notes and Queries, 2 December 1893
Notes and Queries, 2 November 1889
Noyes, G. 'Development of Cant
    Lexicography in England, 1566-1785',
    Studies in Philology, 38:3 (1941)

Oxford Dictionary of National Biography
    (on-line)
Pall Mall Gazette, 17 April 1890
Palmer, L. R. *The Latin Language* (Faber,
    1954)
Parker, G. *View of Society in High and Low
    Life* (London, 1781)
Parker, G. *Life's Painter of Variegated
    Characters in Public and Private Life*
    (London, 1789)
Partridge, E. (ed.), *Classical Dictionary of
    the Vulgar Tongue* (London, 1931)
Partridge, E. (ed.), *Polite Conversation*
    (London, 1963)
Partridge, E. *Dictionary of the Underworld*
    (3rd edn, London, 1968)
Partridge, E. *Slang To-day and Yesterday*
    (London, 1933)
Peakman, J. *Mighty Lewd Books* (London,
    2003)
Pett Ridge, W. *Mord Em'ly* (London 1898)
Pickering, J. A *Vocabulary: or, Collection
    of words and phrases, which have been
    supposed to be peculiar to the United
    States of America* (Boston, 1816)
Pittenger, W. *Daring and Suffering* (1864)
Poetical Works of Lord Byron (London,
    1885–6)
Pope, A. *Dunciad* (London, 1728)
Porter, R. *Social History of London*
    (London, 1994)
Pretty, A. G. *Glossary of Slang and Peculiar
    Terms in Use in the A.I.F. 1921–1924*
    (unpub. ms.)
Pugliatti, P. *Beggary and Theatre in Early
    Modern England* (Aldershot, 2003)
Punch, 9 March 1850
Punch, vol. III (1842)
Punch, XIII (1847)
Read, A. W. 'The World of Joe Strickland',
    Journal of American Folklore, 76, 302
    (1963)
Richardson, J. F. *The New York Police* (New
    York, 1970)
Rickard, J. 'Lovable Larrikins and Awful
    Ockers', in *Journal of Australian Studies*
    (Queensland, 1998)
Robertson, J. 'Australian Lexicography
    1880–1910: An Evaluation', PhD thesis
Robertson, J. 'Plagiarism in Australian
    Dictionaries', London Papers in
    Australian Studies, No. 9 (2004)

Rockwell, H. 'Color Stuff', *American Speech*, 3, 1 (1927)

Rodgers, B. *Queen's Vernacular* (San Francisco, CA, 1972)

Rollins, H. E. (ed.) *The Letters of John Keats, 1814–1821* (Cambridge, MA, 1958)

Rook, C. *London Side-lights* (London, 1908)

Rook, C. *The Hooligan Nights* (London, 1899)

Rowlands, S. *Greene's Ghost Haunting Cony-catchers* (London, 1602)

Rowlands, S. *Martin Mark-all* (London 1610)

Rowlands, S. *Martin Mark-all* (London, 1610)

Sainéan, L. *Les Sources de l'argot ancien* (Paris, 1912)

Salmon, E. *Fortnightly Review*, 45, 1 February 1886, pp. 225–6, quoted in P. Duane, 'Penny Dreadfuls', *Victorian Studies*, 22: 2, 1979

Saturday Evening Post, 23 December 1961

Schele de Vere, M. *Americanisms* (New York, 1872)

Scots Observer, 15 February 1890

Scoundrel's Dictionary (London, 1754)

Shakespeare, W. *A Winter's Tale*

Shakespeare, W. *Henry IV* part 2

Shaw, P. 'Thomas Dekker in Jacobean Prison Literature,' *PMLA*, LVII: 2

Shelly, L. *Hepcats Jive Talk Dictionary* (New York 1945)

Sherwood, J. B. 'Kipling's Women', *Fine Arts Journal*, 37, 3 (March 1919)

Sigel, L. Z. 'Name Your Pleasure', *Journal of the History of Sexuality*, IX: 4 (October 2000)

Simes, G. 'Gay Slang Lexicography', in *Dictionaries*, XXVI (2005)

Sorenson, J. 'Vulgar Tongues', *Eighteenth-Century Studies*, XXXVII: 3 (Spring, 2004)

Southern, T. 'The Night the Bird Blew for Dr Warner', in *Red-Dirt Marijuana* (New York, 1967)

Spectator, vol. VIII (London, 1717)

Spielmann, H. M. *History of Punch* (New York, 1895

Springhall, J. in *Victorian Studies*, 33: 2 (Winter, 1990)

St Pierre, P. *A Portrait of the Artist as Australian* (Montreal, 2004)

Stanley, J. P. 'Homosexual Slang' in *American Speech*, 45: 1/2 (1970)

Stanley, J. P. 'When We Say "Out of the Closets!"', *College English*, 36, 3 (November 1974)

Starnes, D.T. and G. E. Noyes, *The English Dictionary from Cawdrey to Johnson, 1604–1755* (Chapel Hill, NC, 1946)

Stephens A.G. & S.J. O'Brien *Materials for a Dictionary of Australian Slang* (1900-1910, unpub.)

Sullivan, D. M. *The United States Marine Corps in the Civil War* (2000)

Surtees, R. S. *Mr Sponge's Sporting Tour* (London, 1853)

Swift, J. Proposal for Correcting, Improving, and Ascertaining the English Tongue (London, 1713)

Swift, J. *Polite Conversation* in *Works*, vol. VI (London 1741)

Taylor, W. R. *Inventing Times Square* (New York, 1993)

Thackeray, W. M. 'Half a Crown's Worth of Cheap Knowledge', *Fraser's Magazine*, XVII (1838)

Thackeray, W. M. *The Newcomes* (London, 1855)

Thackeray, W. M. *Vanity Fair* (London, 1843)

The Bookseller, 2 July (London, 1873)

The Life and Character of Moll King (1747)

The Universal Songster vol. 1 (London, 1825)

The Wire (HBO TV)

Thomas, D.B. introduction to *The Book of Vagabonds and Beggars* (*The Liber Vagatorum*) (1932)

Thompson, P. 'The Political Education of Henry Mayhew', *Victorian Studies*, 11 (1967)

Townsend, C. 'Negro Minstrels', in A. Bean et al., *Inside the Minstrel Mask* (Hanover, NH, 1969)

Traubel, H. *With Walt Whitman in Camden*, I: March 28–July 14, 1888 (Boston, 1906)

Troyer, H.W. *Ned Ward of Grub Street* (London, 1968)

Tufts, H. *Narrative of the Life, Adventures, Travels and Sufferings of Henry Tufts* (Dover, NH, 1807)

Turner, E. S. *Boys Will Be Boys* (London, 1948)

Turner, G. W. 'A landscape known as home', *Round Table*, 66 (1976)

Tyler, R. *The Contrast* (Philadelphia, PA, 1790)

Vaux, J. H. *Memoirs* (London, 1819)

Viles, E. and F. J. Furnivall, *Rogues and Vagabonds of Shakespeare's Youth* (London, 1907)

W. E. Henley, 'Some Novels of 1899', in *North American Review* (February 1900)

Webster, N. *Dissertations on the English Language* (Boston, 1789)

Whiteing, R. *No. 5 John Street* (London, 1899)

Wikipedia

Wilde, W. C. 'Thief Talk', *Journal of American Folklore*, 3, 11 (October–December, 1890)

Wiley, B. I. *Life of Johnny Reb* (1943)

Wiley, B. I. *The Life of Billy Yank* (New York, 1951)

Williams, D. 'Possibilities in the Rogue Narrative of Henry Tufts', *Early American Literature*, XIX, 1 (Spring, 1984)

Woodbridge, L. 'English Literary Renaissance Jest Books, the Literature of Roguery, and the Vagrant Poor in Renaissance England', *English Literary Renaissance* (May 2003)

Yates, N. W. *William T. Porter* (Baton Rouge, 1957)

Zeydel, E. H. (trans.), *Ship of Fools* (New York, 1944)

Acknowledgements

As with my history of lexicography, *Chasing the Sun: Dictionary-makers and the Dictionaries They Made* (1996), to which it is possible to see this work as a somewhat more focused sequel, *Sounds of the City* does not pretend to unalloyed primary source scholarship. I have looked at such material as I can, and have drawn to a substantial extent on my own researches for the vocabulary and citations in *Green's Dictionary of Slang*, and the many pieces on slang lexicography that I have written. Slang history as such is an under-researched topic, but it draws in many ancillary histories, and I have been fortune in the expertise on offer. Therefore I would be the first to thank the many scholars upon whose work I have drawn. I hope that no one feels that their insights have gone without due credit. I would like especially to single out Professor James Adams, former Senior Research Fellow of All Souls, Oxford, who generously passed on his knowledge of Latin slang and directed me to other experts in the area.

Thirty years pursuing slang have left me in the happy position of being able to draw on a number of experts who are also friends. Tom Dalzell, a notable slang lexicographer in his own right, Jesse Sheidlower, former editor-at-large of the *OED* in New York, and Peter Gilliver, associate editor of the *OED* in Oxford, Professors Charlotte Brewer of Hertford College, Oxford, and Julie Coleman of the University of Leicester have all responded generously to my questions. I have also been helped on matters Australian by Bruce Moore, until 2011 Director of the Australian National Dictionary Centre in Canberra.

My thanks, too, to the team at Atlantic Books who have shepherded the book to publication: copy-editor Annie Lee, proofreader Sarah Marcus and my editor James Nightingale, who, in the way of modern publishing's continuing evolutions, found himself responsible for my work at a somewhat later date than is usual. Such errors as remain, a declaration that may be rote but remains true, are all mine.

Above all I wish to thank Richard Milbank, who became my editor in the dying pre-publication days of the original *Cassell Dictionary of Slang*, continued through its first revision, then oversaw a number of intermediary titles and most importantly was the commissioning editor of *Green's Dictionary of Slang*. Fortunately the attrition of publishers that marred the smooth production of that book has not been the case this time, and while he has now moved on, Richard was fully involved in its creation. I am grateful to him, as ever, for his care and his skills. It is a better book for his attentions. So far, we have worked together for thirteen years. They have not been unlucky.

Index

Note on the Author

Jonathon Green is Britain's foremost lexicographer of slang. His many publications include the *Chambers Slang Dictionary*, the *Slang Thesaurus*, *Slang Down the Ages* and the multivolume *Green's Dictionary of Slang*. He has also compiled dictionaries of quotations and oral histories of modern culture. He lives in London and Paris.